THE YOUNG MAN

in American Literature

PERSPECTIVES ON AMERICAN LITERATURE

Robert H. Woodward and James J. Clark
General Editors

THE
YOUNG MAN
in American Literature
The Initiation Theme

EDITED BY

WILLIAM COYLE

Florida Atlantic University

Bobbs-Merrill Educational Publishing
Indianapolis

The Bobbs-Merrill Company, Inc.
4300 West 62nd Street
Indianapolis, Indiana 46268

First Edition
Fourth Printing—1979

Library of Congress Catalog Card Number: 68-31707
ISBN 0-672-63147-4 (pbk.)

ACKNOWLEDGMENTS

The author is grateful to the following writers, publishers, and literary
agents for permission to use the materials listed below.

American Society for Aesthetics: "What Is an Initiation Story?" by Mordecai Marcus. From *Journal of Aesthetics and Art Criticism.* Copyright
© 1960 by The American Society for Aesthetics. Reprinted by permission
of the Society and Mordecai Marcus.

Farrar, Straus & Giroux, Inc.: "The Magic Barrel" from *The Magic Barrel.*
Copyright © 1958 by Bernard Malamud. Reprinted by permission of
Farrar, Straus & Giroux, Inc.

Sigmund Freud Copyrights, Ltd.: "Some Reflections on Schoolboy Psychology." From *The Complete Psychological Works of Sigmund Freud,*
Vol. XIII. By permission of Sigmund Freud Copyrights, Ltd., The In-
stitute of Psycho-Analysis, Mrs. Alix Strachey, and The Hogarth Press,
Ltd.

Harcourt, Brace & World, Inc.: "Total Stranger" by James Gould Cozzens.
Copyright 1936 by Curtis Publishing Co., renewed 1964 by James Gould
Cozzens. Reprinted from his volume, *Children and Others* by permission
of Harcourt, Brace & World, Inc. "Blackberry Winter" by Robert Penn
Warren. From *The Circus in the Attic and Other Stories,* copyright 1947
by Robert Penn Warren. Reprinted by permission of Harcourt, Brace
& World, Inc.

Holt, Rinehart and Winston, Inc.: "The Function of Male Initiation Ceremonies" by John W. M. Whiting, Richard Kluckholm, and Albert An-
thony. From *Readings in Social Psychology,* 3rd edition, edited by E. E.
Maccoby, T. M. Newcomb, and E. L. Hartley. Copyright 1947, 1952, ©
1958 by Holt, Rinehart and Winston, Inc. Reprinted by permission of
Holt, Rinehart and Winston, Inc.

PREFACE

THIS VOLUME contains essays, autobiographical narratives, and fiction pertaining to the representation of young men in American literature. It is designed to be used either as an anthology in literature and composition classes or as a source of topics and materials for research and critical papers.

A major difficulty in assembling selections that illustrate the depiction of *young* men by American writers is to limit the controlling adjective. Since few male Americans of eighteen will admit to being young and few of thirty-eight will admit to being anything else, the word obviously cannot be defined with precision. Although chronological limits are unsatisfactory for so elusive a term, it suggests the teens and early twenties—the transitional state between the relative freedom of boyhood and the obligations of adulthood. Characters in the stories reprinted here range in age from nine to twenty-seven, but the average age is about sixteen. In each of the stories, the young hero passes from innocence to knowledge and takes at least a tentative step toward maturity.

Another difficulty in assembling a volume like this one is created by the wealth of material from which to choose. Perhaps because Americans think of themselves as a youthful nation, their literature, especially fiction, has dealt preponderantly with youth. Exceptions can readily be found, but in general American writers have treated middle age in terms of frustration and old age in terms of pathos. Although their attitudes have ranged from exuberance to despair, from nostalgia to nausea, writers have concentrated on the youthful years as the most significant portion of a man's life. From the vast amount of literature available, I have chosen pieces that are varied yet significantly representative and that have literary merit. The essays in the introductory "Perspectives" section discuss American youth from a variety of viewpoints and contain generalizations that can be applied analytically to the literary selections.

In depicting young men, American writers have expressed a wide range of themes. Most popular perhaps has been the agonizing self-consciousness caused by a variety of indignities from acne to zippers. Usually comic in a condescending way, this kind of treatment is found in popular fiction like Owen Johnson's prep school stories of the early 1900's or Booth Tarkington's *Seventeen* (1916) and today is common in the family situation comedies of television. Other, more serious themes include man's loneliness, the search for a father, sexual anxieties, the formation of personal values, the difficulty of communicating with others, the discovery of a vocation, the acceptance of personal limitations, protest against social injustice, the loss of childhood illusions, awakening to the tragic nature of human life, and rebellion against parental authority. Each of these, including the humorous portrayal of social awkwardness, is related to the passage from youth to maturity, and this "initiation" motif unifies the stories that follow.

Leslie Fiedler, in a series of articles first published in *The New Leader* and later collected in *No! In Thunder* (1960), makes some perceptive comments on the initiation theme, which he defines as the "confrontation of adult corruption and childish perceptions." Americans, Fiedler believes, are preoccupied with initiation because they aspire to "maturity" rather than to "salvation." They are fascinated by a character like Huck Finn or Holden Caulfield because they idealize "his unfallen freshness of insight, his unexpended vigor, his incorruptible naïveté" and unconsciously they reject the doctrine of original sin. Furthermore, they see the young man as an image of America itself, "crude and unruly" but potentially mature and responsible.

Another book that students might find useful is *Radical Innocence* (1961) by Ihab Hassan, especially the second chapter, "The Dialectic of Initiation in America." Hassan defines initiation as "the first existential ordeal, crisis, or encounter with experience in the life of a youth . . . a process leading through right action and consecrated knowledge to a *viable* mode of life in the world." He believes that since World War I three intellectual or esthetic trends—naturalism, primitivism, and romanticism—have affected the concept of initiation. Naturalism, which sees man as helpless in the grip of biological and social forces, portrays martyrdom more often than initiation. In Theodore Dreiser's *An American Tragedy* (1925) or James T. Farrell's *Studs Lonigan* (1935), for example, the main character is first corrupted and then destroyed by the false values of society. Instead of initiation, there is submission or defeat. Primitivism, influenced by Freud, concentrates on emotional and instinctual levels of experience deep within the individual self. Instead of initiation, there is frustration. Romanticism, with its emphasis on introspection, egoism, and rebellion, is more adaptable to the initiation theme; but because of the romantic devotion to high ideals and a tendency toward self-pity, experience often results in loneliness and disillusionment instead of meaningful initiation. Hassan believes that Hemingway and Faulkner, whose works contain elements of all three trends, have succeeded best in portraying initiation.

Hassan's discussion is a useful reminder that it is extremely easy to confuse initiation with victimization. In stories such as Henry

James's *Daisy Miller* (1878) or Herman Melville's *Billy Budd* (1891, published 1924), the central character is overly innocent and therefore unable to cope with evil. A sacrificial victim is not an initiate. I have limited the selections in this volume to pieces in which a young man achieves, however painfully, a measure of self-awareness and have not included stories in which he is totally defeated or destroyed.

Although all of the selections included here share the general theme of initiation, they differ greatly in effect and purpose. To recognize this variety and to facilitate comparative discussion of similar stories, I have grouped them in three admittedly artificial categories, emphasizing respectively the world of nature, the world of men, and—often most terrifying of all—the world of the self. I have placed each selection according to its major emphasis, but some are virtually interchangeable, and one or two might conceivably be placed in any of the sections. The pieces within each section are arranged in the order of their publication. Introductions to each section are intended to provide only a brief overview of the selections that follow and to suggest several novels and short stories with which they might be compared.

I have tried to keep editorial intrusion at a minimum. To facilitate the use of the selections in controlled research, I have used reputable and accessible texts so that a student can consult the original if he wishes. Bibliographical information for each selection appears in a footnote. The selections in the "Perspectives" section follow a "casebook" format so that the original source can be cited in a documented essay. The original pagination appears within brackets; the number before the virgule (/) indicates the end of the original page, and the number after it signals the beginning of the next page. If a page in the original ends with a divided word, the bracketed page numbers have been placed at the end of the word. Original pagination is not given for the literary selections: if a student writing a paper quotes from one of the stories, his footnotes should cite the page number in this anthology. At the end of the book are questions on each selection that are intended to provoke discussion and suggest topics for papers; they will be most useful if they start a train of thought that culminates in a student's discovering a topic for himself. The book concludes with brief notes identifying the authors.

WILLIAM COYLE

Florida Atlantic University
Boca Raton

CONTENTS

I

Perspectives

THE ESSAYS in this introductory section discuss American youth from diverse points of view—conventional psychology, Freudian psychology, sociology, anthropology, and literature. Each essay contains a number of provocative generalizations which can be related to the narratives that follow. The summary by Horrocks reminds us that each social environment has its own distinctive qualities and that each individual adolescent is unique. This diversity makes all-inclusive generalizations suspect and suggests a significant function of literature: the creative writer portrays one particular character in one particular place at one particular time, thus acknowledging the existential singularity of each human life. The ideas of Freud have transformed both the writing and the interpretation of literature. Some aspects of his most influential theory, the Oedipus complex, are summarized in simple terms in a letter he wrote at the age of fifty-nine. The tensions of father-son relationships have, of course, always existed, but Freud gave them new significance and new poignancy. At least half of the stories in this volume can be considered in terms of latent or overt hostility between a son and his father or a father-substitute. Max Lerner discusses the traumas of growing up in an affluent, class-conscious society, which expects the young men of each generation to surpass their fathers socially, intellectually, and economically. In the fourth article, anthropologists analyze the function of initiation in primitive cultures. In defining the initiation story, Mordecai Marcus comments on several of the stories reprinted in this anthology. His article, along with the other selections, should encourage and enable each student to reach his own conclusions as to the significance of the initiation theme.

English has no term equivalent to the German *Bildungsroman* or *Erziehungsroman* (education-novel) for a story of a young man's encounter with the adult world. In fact, this theme is not restricted to the novel but appears in all forms of literature, particu-

1

larly in the short story, but less often than one might expect in
poetry and drama. Such terms as *education, apprenticeship, maturation,* and *coming-of-age* are sometimes used; and if one wished
to invent a term, *threshold story* might do, since the young man
usually is poised to enter a new phase of his life. Still, *initiation,*
even though it has been borrowed from anthropology, seems the
most appropriate term because it suggests a formative change involving not only pain or loss but also the beginning of a new
stage of life. The youth undergoes an experience that reveals hitherto unrecognized or uncomprehended aspects of the human condition. Modern life and the modern imagination being as they are,
his new knowledge is more likely to be unpleasant than otherwise.
It does not seem necessary to limit the term to stories involving
some form of ritual, although ritual is an intrinsic part of the anthropological meaning of initiation.

American writers have seldom developed this theme in fiction
about young women. A few exceptions are Willa Cather, *My Anto-
nia* (1918), Booth Tarkington, *Alice Adams* (1921), Ruth Suckow,
The Odyssey of a Nice Girl (1925), and Carson McCullers, *The
Heart Is a Lonely Hunter* (1940) and *The Member of the Wedding*
(1946). Of course, more fiction is written by men than by women,
but this does not fully account for the discrepancy. Perhaps the
American girl is assumed to be born with knowledge that the
young man must acquire through experience.

Although the initiation motif can be found in such diverse British works as Shakespeare's *Henry IV* or Samuel Johnson's *Rasselas*
(1759), it assumed major importance in the Romantic Movement,
which idealized youth and emphasized the transformational possibilities of human nature. One of the masterpieces of Romanticism
is Wordsworth's *Prelude* (1805, published 1850), significantly subti-
tled *Growth of a Poet's Mind.* The theme also appears in such
diverse works as Thackeray's *Pendennis* (1849), Dickens's *Great Expectations* (1861), Kipling's *Captains Courageous* (1897), Maugham's
Of Human Bondage (1915), Joyce's *Portrait of the Artist as a Young
Man* (1916), Conrad's *The Shadow Line* (1917) and several of his
other stories. But it is in American literature that the theme of youthful initiation has found fullest expression.

The importance initiation stories ascribe to the instructive results of experience may appeal to the empirical "learn by doing"
tendency in American thought. Initiation also correlates with the
general American view of youth as a formative period that deter-
mines the course of an individual's future. The initiatory experience is basic to many of the roles in which young Americans have
traditionally found themselves: the "greenhorn" on any of the

frontiers, the newly arrived immigrant, the apprentice in a factory, the army recruit, or the bewildered freshman at a large university. Although initiation is adaptable to either an optimistic or a pessimistic view of life, the latter predominates in twentieth century writing.

A random sampling of American literary works involving the initiation theme would include such factual narratives as the first part of Benjamin Franklin's *Autobiography* (1793), Richard Henry Dana's *Two Years Before the Mast* (1840), Francis Parkman's *The Oregon Trail* (1849), E. E. Cummings's *The Enormous Room* (1922), and a wide range of novels like Charles Brockden Brown's *Edgar Huntly* (1801), Mark Twain's *Huckleberry Finn* (1884), Stephen Crane's *The Red Badge of Courage* (1895), F. Scott Fitzgerald's *The Great Gatsby* (1925), John Steinbeck's *The Grapes of Wrath* (1939), John Knowles's *A Separate Peace* (1959), all of Thomas Wolfe, and much of Herman Melville and Ernest Hemingway. Such a sampling merely skims the surface, because the initiation theme has engaged the imaginations of most major American writers of fiction. No war stories have been included in this anthology because they involve special and unnatural conditions which distort motives and behavior, but virtually all war fiction belongs to this genre. In fact, the initiation theme is so pervasive in American literature that a full bibliography is impossible.

JOHN E. HORROCKS

The Nature of Adolescence

AN ADOLESCENT is the product of the interaction of his biological heritage and the culture in which he lives. The adolescent is a product of his culture because he has spent the years of his childhood as a participant in that culture; has, figuratively speaking, sat as a child upon the knee of his culture. It is now a common assumption of cultural anthropologists, psychologists, sociologists, and others who deal with the problems of human behavior that the years of an individual's childhood are of exceeding importance in creating the kind of person he is. The only controversy involved, insofar as differences of opinion exist, is in how large terms one interprets the term "exceeding." In any event the individual may not be considered apart from the structure of the society in which he lives including every perceived element in it.

Adolescence, as it is generally used, is a descriptive term of the period during which an emotionally immature individual in his teens approaches the culmination of his physical and mental growth. Although potentially an adult, he still plays the role of an inexperienced child bound and restricted by the culture in which he lives. In its nonphysical aspects adolescence is culturally determined and represents a period of difficult adjustment if the environment is a restrictive one. In a nonrestrictive environment the adolescent's problems tend to be primarily those of gaining and applying experience.

In a culture, as in some existing primitive ones, in which early responsibility and status are accorded to youth, the period of adolescence may be attenuated or greatly simplified. In contrast, the period of adolescence in Western culture is more complex and more beset by problems. This complexity is due in part to lack of emancipation from parents, vocational dependence and extension of training, sex restrictions and taboos, and inferior status. How-

From John E. Horrocks, *The Psychology of Adolescence: Behavior and Development,* 2nd edition. Boston: Houghton Mifflin Company, 1962.

ever, it is recognized that the ease or difficulty of the transition from childhood through adolescence into adulthood is a function of the amount of facilitation the culture offers to the individual who is going through the transitional period. The greater the facilitation, the easier the transition.

In former years adolescence was alleged to be inevitably a period of great and excessive storm and stress; it was supposed to represent a complete [28/29] and sudden "rebirth" and change of personality. According to this point of view, difficulty during adolescence was held to be inevitable. The theory of storm and stress has been abandoned today. It is now believed that adolescence is culturally determined, that the amount of difficulty is a direct function of the restrictiveness of the environment, and to only a very small degree a function of biological change within the individual.

A true understanding of adolescence includes a recognition of the existence of individual differences. Surface similarities may often conceal crucial differences. It must be remembered that even if two or more adolescents are in similar physical environments, their psychological environments are not necessarily also similar. It is a mistake to generalize too broadly about adolescence from experience with it in any given environment, even within a fairly homogeneous culture. Intracultural differences do exist, such as differences caused by technological change, climate, historical period, socio-economic status, and literally thousands of other factors. Not only do adolescents differ with different environments, but an adolescent who moves from one environment to another will also display certain differences from his former self. The depression and the period of World War II are examples of historical changes that reflected upon the problems and ways of life of those who were adolescents during the 1930's and early 1940's.

An understanding of a given adolescent requires a wide and extensive knowledge of his past as well as his present physical and psychological environments. He must be viewed as an adolescent, but he must also be viewed as a human being, and his behavior as an adolescent must be interpreted with the aid of that view.

In Western culture there are five points of reference from which to view adolescent growth and development:

1. It is a time of physical development and growth.

2. It is a time when group relations become of major importance.

3. Adolescence is a time of seeking status as an individual.

4. It is a time of intellectual expansion, development, and academic experience.

5. It is a time of development and evaluation of values.

Adolescence is viewed as a period of adjustment to cultural demands; and of expectations as to commonalities of behavior and development, within which individual differences may also be expected. [29]

SIGMUND FREUD

———•••———

Some Reflections on Schoolboy Psychology

It gives you a queer feeling if, late in life, you are ordered once again to write a school essay. But you obey automatically, like the old soldier who, at the word 'Attention!,' cannot help dropping whatever he may have in his hands and who finds his little fingers pressed along the seams of his trousers. It is strange how readily you obey the orders, as though nothing in particular had happened in the last half-century. But in fact you have grown old in the interval, you are on the eve of your sixtieth birthday, and your physical feelings, as well as your mirror, show unmistakably how far your life's candle is burnt down.

As little as ten years ago, perhaps, you may have had moments at which you suddenly felt quite young again. As you walked through the streets of Vienna—already a grey-beard, and weighed down by all the cares of family life—you might come unexpectedly on some well-preserved, elderly gentleman and would greet him humbly almost, because you had recognized him as one of your former schoolmasters. But afterwards you would stop and reflect: 'Was that really he? or only someone deceptively like him? How youthful he looks! And how old you yourself have grown! How old can he be to-day? Can it be possible that the men who used to stand for us as types of adulthood were really so little older than we were?'

At such moments as these, I used to find, the present time seemed to sink into obscurity and the years between ten and eighteen would rise from the corners of my memory, with all their guesses and illusions, their painful distortions and heartening successes—my first glimpses of an extinct civilization (which in my

From *The Complete Psychological Works of Sigmund Freud,* Vol. XIII. London: The Hogarth Press, 1955.

This essay, translated from the German by James Strachey, was written by Freud in 1914 for a volume commemorating the semicentennial of the founding of a school he attended as a young man in Vienna.

case was to bring me as much consolation as anything else in the
struggles of life), my first contacts with the sciences, among which
it seemed open to me to choose to which of them I should dedi-
cate what were no doubt my inestimable services. [241/242] And I
seem to remember that through the whole of this time there ran a
premonition of a task ahead, till it found open expression in my
school-leaving essay as a wish that I might during the course of my
life contribute something to our human knowledge.

Later I became a physician—or a psychologist, rather—and was
able to create a new psychological discipline, something that is
known as 'psycho-analysis,' which is followed to-day with excited
interest, and is greeted with praise and blame, by physicians and
enquirers in neighbouring, and in distant, foreign lands—but least
of all, of course, in our own country.

As a psycho-analyst I am bound to be concerned more with
emotional than intellectual processes, with unconscious than with
conscious mental life. My emotion at meeting my old schoolmaster
warns me to make a first admission: it is hard to decide whether
what affronted us more and was of greater importance to us was
our concern with the sciences that we were taught or with the per-
sonalities of our teachers. It is true, at least, that this second concern was a perpetual undercurrent in all of us, and that in many
of us the path to the sciences led only through our teachers. Some
of us stopped half-way along that path, and for a few—why not
admit as much?—it was on that account blocked for good and all.

We courted them or turned our backs on them, we imagined
sympathies and antipathies in them which probably had no existence, we studied their characters and on theirs we formed or mis-
formed our own. They called up our fiercest opposition and forced
us to complete submission; we peered into their little weaknesses,
and took pride in their excellences, their knowledge and their justice. At bottom we felt a great affection for them if they gave us
any ground for it, though I cannot tell how many of them were
aware of this. But it cannot be denied that our position in regard
to them was a quite remarkable one and one which may well have
had its inconvenience for those concerned. We were from the very
first equally inclined to love and to hate them, to criticize and
respect them. Psycho-analysis has given the name of 'ambivalence'
to this readiness to contradictory attitudes, and it has no difficulty
in pointing to the source of ambivalent feelings of such a kind.
[242/243]

For psycho-analysis has taught us that the individual's emotional
attitudes to other people, which are of such extreme importance to
his later behaviour, are already established at an unexpectedly

early age. The nature and quality of the human child's relations to people of his own and the opposite sex have already been laid down in the first six years of his life. He may afterwards develop and transform them in certain directions, but he can no longer get rid of them. The people to whom he is in this way fixed are his parents and his brothers and sisters. All those whom he gets to know later become substitute figures for these first objects of his feelings. (We should perhaps add to his parents any other people, such as nurses, who cared for him in his infancy.) These substitute figures can be classified from his point of view according as they are derived from what we call the 'imagos' of his father, his mother, his brothers and sisters, and so on. His later acquaintances are thus obliged to take over a kind of emotional heritage; they encounter sympathies and antipathies to the production of which they themselves have contributed little. All of his later choices of friendship and love follow upon the basis of the memory-traces left behind by these first prototypes.

Of all the imagos of a childhood which, as a rule, is no longer remembered, none is more important for a youth or a man than that of his father. Organic necessity introduces into a man's relation to his father an emotional ambivalence which we have found most strikingly expressed in the Greek myth of King Oedipus. A little boy is bound to love and admire his father, who seems to him the most powerful, the kindest and wisest creature in the world. God himself is after all only an exaltation of this picture of a father as he is represented in the mind of early childhood. But soon the other side of this emotional relationship emerges. One's father is recognized as the paramount disturber of one's instinctual life; he becomes a model not only to imitate but also to get rid of, in order to take his place. Thenceforward affectionate and hostile impulses towards him persist side by side, often to the end of one's life, without either of them being able to do away with the other. It is in this existence of contrary feelings side by side that lies the essential character of what we call emotional ambivalence. [243/244]

In the second half of childhood a change sets in in the boy's relation to his father—a change whose importance cannot be exaggerated. From his nursery the boy begins to cast his eyes upon the world outside. And he cannot fail to make discoveries which undermine his original high opinion of his father and which expedite his detachment from his first ideal. He finds that his father is no longer the mightiest, wisest and richest of beings, he grows dissatisfied with him, he learns to criticize him and to estimate his place in society; and then, as a rule, he makes him pay heavily for the disappointment that has been caused by him. Everything that is hopeful, as well as everything that is unwelcome, in the new generation is determined by this detachment from the father.

It is in this phase of a youth's development that he comes into contact with his teachers. So that we can now understand our relation to our schoolmasters. These men, not all of whom were in fact fathers themselves, became our substitute fathers. That was why, even though they were still quite young, they struck us as so mature and so unattainably adult. We transferred on to them the respect and expectations attaching to the omniscient father of our childhood, and we then began to treat them as we treated our fathers at home. We confronted them with the ambivalence that we had acquired in our own families and with its help we struggled with them as we had been in the habit of struggling with our fathers in the flesh. Unless we take into account our nurseries and our family homes, our behaviour to our schoolmasters would be not only incomprehensible but inexcusable.

As schoolboys we had other and scarcely less important experiences with the successors of our brothers and sisters—our schoolfellows—but these must be described elsewhere. In a commemoration of the jubilee of our school it is on the masters that our thoughts must rest. [244]

MAX LERNER

Growing Up in America

THE GROWING UP YEARS are not easy in America because the choices
to be made are so many and the securely prescribed areas of conduct relatively few. I shall deal in this section not so much with the
biological [570/571] universals involved in growing up as with the
interplay of the biological, the emotional, and the cultural in the
American frame.

In his early years the child is mainly concerned with the discovery of his body and its functions, and with his emotional relations
to his parents and family. He "catches on" to social experience as
well, but it is largely filtered and mediated, as if by osmosis,
through the envelope of the family. As the child grows into adolescence, and the adolescent in turn into the young adult, the agencies
by which his personality and character are shaped broaden out
from family to community, from immediate kin to the whole social milieu. These are the years of the "latency period" in the
Freudian description, when little is really latent, followed by the
period of puberty and its immediate consequences. They are the
years when the young American, bursting with discoveries and
searching always for new experience, reaches outward from the
family to the peer groups of school and "camp," to street gangs,
cliques and clubs, sand-lot and water-front sports, dating and dressing, odd jobs, summer adventures, college, and military service.

The American family does not let go of him early but tries to
hold on as long as possible, recognizing his need for self-reliance
but anxious to protect him and eager to enjoy him. Unlike the
British, it does not push the boy abruptly into the "public
school," where he is away from home and wholly on his own, sub-
jected to the cruel rules and taboos of his fellows. It allows the
boy or girl to make the break away from home by easier stages—at
first in the "summer camp," whose use is growing among middle-

From Max Lerner, *America as a Civilization*, Vol. I. (New York: Simon and
Schuster. 1957).

class parents, then perhaps in a private boarding school (still confined to the upper income groups), finally (for the boys) in the Army. This blending of home and away-from-home experience is one of the things Americans are learning to do best, although one must remember the large number of still overprotective parents who cling to the child, and the equally large number of working-class parents who let him drift off into a job of his own as soon as he has passed school age or been in a trade school. There are also the middle-class parents who send him off very early to a military academy or school on the convenient theory that he will learn independence and discipline but actually to shift to someone else the burden of the decisions about his rearing.

On the formal level the qualities he is taught, both in the family and the peer groups, are those that will fit him best into the competitive race: to be resourceful, industrious, persuasive, friendly, popular, an easy mixer, strong of purpose, inventive, self-reliant. The emphasis in a mobile society built on immigration is on outdoing your parents—getting a better education, marrying into a better social stratum, making [571/572] more money, living in a better neighborhood and with higher living standards. The traits stressed are those of packaging your abilities in the best salesman's fashion, and of a constant quality of *push*. These traits, inculcated and renewed in each generation, take on a cumulative strength in the culture. They leave little room for the withdrawn and reflective personality, who may be detached from the competitive struggle. In fact, when American parents or teachers find these traits in a boy, they may regard them as signs that he is "badly adjusted" and in need of therapy.

Some American scientists, like W. H. Sheldon, see the physical constitution as shaping temperament and even character, and a number of biologists stress the "built-in" mechanisms which set the frame for all growth. Yet there is little of determinist thinking in the attitude of most Americans toward the growing-up years. The pluralism of stocks, the high living standards, and the strides in medicine, all tend to disarrange any preconceived frames of physical growth for Americans and put the stress on will. Similarly, the stress in popular thinking about personality and career is not on the limits but on the potentials of development. "Be a king in your dreams," said Andrew Carnegie to the young American. "Say to yourself, 'My place is on the top.' "

Thus the young American grows up to see life as a cornucopia spilling its plenty into the lap of those who are there to take it. Within the limits of his family's income, and sometimes beyond it, there are few things denied to the growing son and daughter.

Their attention is focused on what they can *get*, first out of their parents, then out of life. The growing girl learns to get clothes and gifts from her father and later from her husband. The boy fixes his attention on a succession of artifacts, from a toy gun and an electric train to a car, preferably a convertible. Their levels of aspiration stretch to infinity. Often the parents are blamed for this pliancy and indulgence, yet it is also true that the culture, with its sense of plenty, contains the same principle of infinite possibility. It tells the boy that if only he wants something hard enough, even the Presidency of the nation, he can achieve it. This spurs his striving but it also sets unrealizable goals, since his capacities may not equal the tasks he sets himself, or his class and status handicaps may be too crippling. Thus he misses the sense of security which one gets from the compassable. No limits are set to his goals, and often he reaches for incompatible sets of goals. Rarely does he learn the tolerance of deprivation or the recognition of limits which are a matter of course in less dynamic cultures and which exact a lesser psychic toll than the sense of infinite possibility.

Such an oceanic sense of possibility has its elements of strength [572/573] for the boy or girl in growth. The feeling of impasse that so many of the youth of Europe have, in cul-de-sac economies where the job chances are narrow and they feel they must break through doors shut against them, does not crop up often in America. It is hope and not hopelessness that runs like a repeated chord through the growing-up years. They are the years in which heroisms are dreamed, tight-lipped resolutions made, values first crudely formulated. The emotional life awakens in all its tumbling confusion, the imagination ranges far, the lights and shadows of the moral life are accented, the shapes of good and evil take on their most intense forms. Anything is possible, and everything is fraught with far-reaching meanings. There is a sense of limitless potentials, of obstacles to be overcome by a surpassing display of energy and talent. At home, as in school, the archetypal prizes held up are the big ones and the stories told are the success stories. There is a constant demand for vitality, in season and out, regardless of whether it is charged with meaning. The emotional dangers that the young American runs are not those of apathy or despair but of anxiety about success or failure. He finds it hard to keep from wondering whether he is swift and strong enough to win in so exacting a race. Even within the minority ethnic groups, with their residual sense of status restrictions, the young American feels the pressure to succeed within the standards of the minority mold, or even to break out of it, especially to break out of it. And if he fails he cannot assign the failure to his goals or society but only to himself.

Growing up with the assumption that he will "make his mark" and "knock them dead," he is rarely allowed to forget that he lives in an expanding civilization in which he must accomplish "bigger and better" things. Just as he is enveloped by the sounds of cars, trains, planes, so the symbols investing his life are those of speed and movement, violence and power—the symbols of competitive drive. They don't have to be preached to him: they come through the culture-in-action. He picks them out of the air—from how his family behaves, from what his teachers and schoolmates say and what he reads and hears, from the men and careers held up to him for emulation.

Asked for more than he feels he can fulfill, he comes in turn to ask more of his family and milieu than they can fulfill, with a resulting insecurity and bleakness of mood. He turns to his age peers to find with them the expressiveness and sense of kinship not to be found among their elders. Their families may be too distraught to pay much attention, or too protectively concerned with providing for their children's outward wants to be able to gauge their inner nature with wisdom. An adult society, with churches that seem distant and "preachy" and with [573/574] spinster-staffed schools that seem only an extension of the nursery, offers little that exacts loyalty or heroism from young people who are hungry for both. Their hunger arises from the fact that when they are torn away from the primary ties to their parents there is no corresponding growth in their confidence of their own strength. They yearn for the sense of belonging which will restore those primary ties, and they attach them now to agencies of their own peers.

Into this vacuum come the teen-age activities, some of which amuse the elders, while others worry them. Among the first are the hero worship of the gods of popular culture, the love affair with the TV screen, the calf-love obsessions that turn the teen-agers "girl crazy" or "boy crazy," the jazz or jive madness that "sends" them. Less amusing are the "hot-rod" frenzies in which they court mechanized suicide, the escapades of bored baby-sitters that break into the headlines, or the sexual antics of the high-school "non-virgin" clubs which shock parents and teachers without jolting them into an understanding of their emotional sources.

There is a passage in Thomas Wolfe's *You Can't Go Home Again* describing "the desolate emptiness of city youth—those straggling bands of boys of sixteen or eighteen that one can always see at night or on a holiday, going along a street, filling the air with raucous jargon and senseless cries, each trying to outdo the others with joyless catcalls and mirthless quips and jokes which are so feeble, so stupidly inane, that one hears them with strong mixed feelings of pity and shame." Wolfe asks "what has happened to the spontaneous gaiety of youth," and answers that these youngsters "are without innocence, born old and stale and dull and empty . . . suckled on darkness, and weaned on violence and noise." In his *Studs Lonigan* novel sequence James Farrell shows similarly the social violence and cultural emptiness which condition the emotional bleakness of a boy's life on the city streets.

Yet in his formative years the city boy, especially from the working class, learns more—bad and good—from the gang than from any other group except the family. The gang is a group on the margin between rebellion and crime, forming a clannish community in play and war against parents, elders, teachers, police, and rival gangs. Sometimes it is a harmless effort of normal youngsters in a disturbed and impressionable life phase to huddle together for human warmth, sometimes it is a desperate attempt to channel floating aggressions. The gang brings into the emotional vacuum of the boy's life a structure of authority which makes demands on loyalty, on spartanism in the face of adversity, even on honor and heroism of a sort; above all, on a sense of acting together. That is where the boy learns crudely and even brutally the [574/575] mystery of sex, the warmth of friendship, and the heady sense of prestige gained not through class position but through strength and natural leadership. It is ironic that the lack of effective codes in the larger society should leave the gang codes as the only substitutes: or perhaps these are only negative parallels of the middle-class codes from which the boys (most of them coming from the lower classes) feel themselves shut out as from an Eden; and so they turn the Eden upside down into a Hell. But even the gang codes prove tawdry and worse as the gangs move over the margin into the pathology of violence and rape and crime.

Not many young Americans follow them that far. But most of them look back to the adventures of their all-male peer groups as their time of expressiveness. It may be that the gang gatherings, on city street corners, the loitering counter at small-town drugstores, and the crossroads taverns in the rural areas where you smoke and buy cokes and play the juke boxes are for American boys the playing fields of Eton.

What is true of the gang for the urban working class is also true of college for the educated classes. It is remembered as the Golden Age of their lives. It has relatively few economic pressures and is the last phase of growing up, just before the boy breaks wholly from the tutelage of family and local community and goes off on his own. It makes its demands in terms of prowess, popularity and prestige: intellectual content in most American colleges is secondary to friendships, fraternities, "contacts," "bull sessions," sports, and the furious crossfire of campus politics and extracurricular activities. The boy can wreak some of his strongest drives on college life, including heroisms and hero cults, fierce intellectual loyalty, combativeness, the sense of honor, the straining of nerve and will for a cause which at the time seems real enough to evoke an effort beyond the human. In most college novels, as in Scott Fitzgerald's *This Side of Paradise,* there is always an Amory Blaine —a grown man who goes back nostalgically to the time at college when he caught a forward pass and wooed a beautiful girl. They may be mock battles and mock victories, a preparation for something that in the end fails to come off. But here too, as with the gangs, the later remembrance of these rivalries and loyalties reveals them as an outlet for youthful energies that the growing boys does not otherwise express.

What happens in the process of growing up in America is an emphasis on the individual that results in a feeling of separateness without [575/576] the quality of distinctiveness. The growing boy (or girl) is taught by the whole cultural environment to assert his individual self, and the way he is expected to find himself is by breaking his ties with his family and rebelling against parents, teachers, neighborhood. In the process he wrenches himself free of bonds and codes, only to find himself isolated from what had given him security. He comes to miss most the sense of belonging, or relatedness, to the "primary ties." Much of the feeling of loneliness in the growing-up years comes from this sense of loss and isolation, and the yearning to recapture the primary ties from which he has been too sharply separated.

In the families where there is close contact between parents and children, in a freewheeling, affectionate atmosphere, these ties can be recaptured adequately enough to tide the child over until he has made ends meet in his personality struggle and is on the threshold of adulthood. It is true that the old cohesive relations, which families had when they did their work together and had to stick together, have largely been lost. But with the new leisure there is a chance for families to spend vacations together, go on automobile trips together, watch and discuss the media programs together, talk and play together. This does something, if not enough, to alleviate the sense of isolation. It is in the families where this closeness of relationship does not exist that the yearning to belong is left unsatisfied. They may be families where both parents are at work, or where the father is hardly ever at home, or where alcoholism or grinding poverty or lovelessness creates a destructive vacuum. At the other extreme they may be families which, even with a high living standard and an outward show of affection, are emotionally empty. It is from the families at both these extremes that most of the cases of failure in the growing-up process come.

I must add the factor of discrepancy between class perspectives. Most commentators on American life have moved away from discussion of class experience and class conditioning. Yet much of the human material that comes to grief in American society will be found in the working class, in the case of youngsters brought up in working-class families and working-class neighborhoods but surrounded everywhere by middle-class and leisure values. That is to say, their subculture is a working-class subculture, while the larger culture is a middle-class culture. Their whole sensate world of striving and their glory dreams are middle-class strivings and middle-class dreams. Yet they find themselves shut out of the world they long for, much as Adam and Eve (as I have suggested above) were shut out of Eden after the Fall by a flaming sword. [576/577]

Thus the "opportunity line" which exists for young people in America, given its rapid class mobility, is accompanied by an insecurity line—or better, by an isolation line. There is scarcely a culture in the world where the longing to belong in the growing-up years is as intense, and where the failure to satisfy it is as destructive of the potentials of personality.

When a culture trains young people there is much that it tries to train out of them. Growing up thus becomes not only a process of *inculcation* of the socially approved virtues, but—shall we say—of *exculcation* of the socially disapproved ones as well. Thus there is a need of exculcating the primitive sense of equality with which children start. In the early years before the social norms begin to harden, as I have noted above, the children of every stock and religion play together: only later does the society teach them what is expected of them. Lillian Smith, in her novel *Strange Fruit,* pictures a beating a young Negro mother gives her small son when he has dared dispute something with a white boy: she must show him that his mortal life is in peril if he does not observe the man-made fence between him and those who hold supremacy. And from the side of the whites, Miss Smith has told how "the mother who taught me what I know of tenderness and love and compassion taught me also the bleak rituals of keeping Negroes in their places —which could be applied to other minority groups as well." The mingling of status groups becomes less frequent as the child moves through the grades into high school and college, and goes dating and dancing and week-ending. The growing-up process in America involves the loss of the social innocence with which children start.

Similarly, the growing boy is taught to develop mainly his vendible talents. "I couldn't stand Asheville now," Thomas Wolfe wrote in one of his remarkable letters to his family from college. "I couldn't stand the silly little grins on the silly little drugstore faces. I couldn't stand the silly little questions 'What're you doing now?'—and the silly little 'oh' and the silly little silence that follows when you say you are writing."

For all except the strongest-willed youngster (and Wolfe was one) the cult of the vendible means the exculcation of other talents and impulses. Neither family nor school can protect him against these tyrannies of the culture: for are they not themselves caught up in the same tyrannies? So they discourage "woolgathering" and "daydreaming," which lead nowhere, get you into mischief, don't pay off as action and business do. Rarely is a protective sheath thrown around the contemplative impulses that are as crucial in the growth of personality as the impulses to action. Rarely is there support for the brooding exploration [577/578] of the whole enriching range of emotional life in a culture as complex and paradoxical as the American. In the end the children become themselves the taboo-enforcing censors, and anyone violating their canons of orthodoxy is an outsider, a "square," a "goon."

This is reinforced on the side of the parents by the pressure to "mix well" and be "popular"—but within socially acceptable groups. The impulse toward popularity flows at once from the cult of success and the shaky self-image of its devotee. It narrows the complex realm of personal relations to the art of manipulation. Tragically, it cuts the child from his fellows just at the phase where such a severance is most destructive to him. For the tissue of human connections cannot be reduced to the manuals of popularity. Which may explain why, in the most glittering of cultures, so many Americans are scarred—as Fitzgerald's Jay Gatsby was all through his years—with the sense of having lost what they have so insistently been taught to capture.

To strive for popularity, yet to feel alone and unwanted; to hunger for use, yet to go unused; to carry the sense of comradeship like a burning city in your heart, yet to have to extinguish it in order to keep your position in the hierarchy; to replace the idle impulse and the brooding intensity by the attitudes of Faustian power, of violence, of speed and aggrandizement: for all too many youngsters this is what growing up comes to mean.

Aside from what the society tries to inculcate into him or exculcate from him the growing child has a double task of preparation: for making a living and for making a life—one, the problem of finding a career; the other, that of finding himself. In the case of the girl—except in the instances where she is in earnest about a career—the two preparations are merged into the preparation for marriage, which is viewed as both a living and a life. With the boy the pressures are to give primacy to making a living, so that he finds himself thrust into choosing the job or career for which he must train before he has gone far enough in his emotional unfolding to have much basis for choice. The result is often a gnawing conflict between what is expected of him and what he finds welling up within himself, rebelling against the plans for him.

Both processes—of finding himself and finding his vocation—involve the boy's spur-winning. He measures himself against the strength of his age peers, of his older brothers, even his father. A time comes when his father notes proudly that the son has caught up with him in stature and strength, and even towers over him. He has a "paper route," mows lawns, shovels the snow off sidewalks, does odd jobs after school; in the summer he perhaps overestimates his age to pick up some quick money [578/579] in a factory or at the shipyard. He saves his money carefully to buy some prized possession, with the calculation of a junior capitalist. He starts learning the trades, skills, tactics out of which competence and success will later come. In American society his expected growth as a person takes largely the form of the kinds of spur-winning that lead into a career and into business habits. And the way he is assessed by his elders and assesses himself is also in those terms.

The American theory is that a boy "chooses" his job or career. For many, however, the choice is narrowly restricted. Sometimes the limited choice of jobs, especially on the lower-class level, is frustrating and embittering. Sometimes, however, it may be a saving fact physically, since it does not burden the boy with the sense of inadequacy which a middle-class boy has when he finds few choices where there are supposed to be many and comes to blame himself. To avoid this self-doubt he may be more precipitous than is good for him as a person. The process John Milton described, of seeking what was to become his epical life work—"long-choosing, the beginning late"—is a luxury that most Americans deny themselves. Even at college American students (like German university students as well) are anxious to choose the courses that will lead directly into their chosen career and thus give them a start in the competitive race. Only a good deal later do some of them come to

20 THE YOUNG MAN IN AMERICAN LITERATURE

understand the cost that the personality had to pay for their career haste. But in a culture so nervously paced and so poised for the big killing, any other choice is difficult.

On some scores it is easier in the American case than in others. There is not the same need to rebel against a tyrannical father, or the same galling sense of being caught in a blind alley with no chance either to develop or show one's abilities. On other scores it is harder. The boy (or girl) comes to biological maturity a good while before either of them comes to emotional maturity. The society—permissive in so many other respects, restrictive in this—cracks down on sexual expression before marriage. In the case of the boy, the military draft has recently become an organic part of the life cycle: while the sexual taboos are relaxed for military personnel, the all-male society and the severe discipline of the Army conflict; and the need to postpone both career and marriage during the most crucial years is a chafing one.

From the parents' behavior and their responses to his own the child forms the crucial image of himself. He has a need to understand and emulate his father's job, as the girl has a need to play house, but a job at "the office" is a hard one for the boy to use as an effective model, and often the substance of the job slips out of the child's mind and all that remains with which he can identify himself is its aura of respectability or power. In an earlier society, where the struggle with nature [579/580] and the conquest of animals had meaning, the boy's spur-winning might take the form of the hunt or the fishing expedition. Americans today who read Faulkner's long story, "The Bear," or Hemingway's *The Old Man and the Sea*, find it hard to attach much meaning to the hunt for the killer bear or the apprenticeship of a boy to an old fisherman, since it has no parallel in their own experience; yet they are drawn to such stories because of this vacuum in their growing up.

Their own spur-winning experiences are likely to follow more closely the pattern of the American boyhood in *Tom Sawyer* and *Huckleberry Finn*, with the swimming hole, the fence-painting, the treasure hunt, the bloodcurdling oaths of gang secrecy, the cult of male separateness from females. One of the striking facts of this Mark Twain tradition of boyhood is its emphasis on both the "badness" and the maleness of boys. Every American boy is expected, as he grows toward his teens, to be intractable about soap and water, to look (whatever his family's means) like a ragged and tattered waif, to resist the blandishments of school and teachers, to be awkward with little girls and flee their advances, and to regard any dancing class or other frippery as a conspiracy of the Devil. This tradition of the good-bad boy is one the elders cherish as part of their recognition that the American household and school are governed by a regiment of women, and its antifeminine bias (included in the anti-"sissy" complex) is the price they pay for continuing that government. From the boy's side, however, it is part of the necessity for breaking away from this domination and of finding who he is.

In the process his reading helps him, and it is notable that he seeks out the reading about bad men (the old frontier and bandits have given way to whodunits) and science fiction. In the city life that has replaced the farm and frontier, spur-winning gives new forms to the old activities—learning how to smoke and swear, hearing about sexual exploits, showing athletic prowess, taking part in school pranks and escapades. One can view this as the impact of crowded city life on the boy, but it is better to view it as part of the quest for identity. "Who am I?" the boys asks, and his answer is first given in terms of being part of a male peer group.

Then in the teens comes the further process of awakening identity, in which he splits himself from even his earlier boys' groups. He is breaking away from the ways of a child but has not yet learned the ways of an adult. He goes to parties and dances, he needs spending money, he works and saves in order to learn his own nature: for it is his own job, his own car, his own girl, that he now wants. Even in his courtship he is perhaps less concerned with erotic aims than either Freudians or Americans generally suppose and more concerned with that [580/581] ceaseless problem of probing and parrying by which adolescents of both sexes come to discover their identity. They want their own sense of rightness, grope for their own codes. This is where they come to feel most split away from their elders, and that struggle between the generations which the parents find so intolerable an ordeal emerges most sharply. In fact, the two generations become almost subcultures, the younger one finding both its goal and its modes of expression within the new social situations more readily than the older one.

It is in the teens, unhappy as they are because of this struggle and the difficult quest for identity, that all the new wealth and excitement of social experience in America impinge on the young people. They experiment with adult modes of consumption, learn the terrifying ways of speed and travel, enter into the kingdom of the Big Media. They are able to move about the country, trying themselves in a variety of occupations. The typical American first novel, for example, is likely to be a novel of these apprentice years, and every first novelist puts on his dust jacket the calendar of his job and migratory experiences, just as he is likely to focus his story around his boyhood, with its trials and triumphs. The critics may continue to call for a novel of manners or of mission, but the kind the American first writes is either a novel of adolescent unhappiness or one of the tribulations of early life and loves, and at the end of it the hero has finally discovered who he is.

I have not meant to say earlier that America crushes every diversity and irons out the nonconformers. The adolescent finds ways of evading many of the cultural pressures and often grows adept in the process of finding his own growth pattern in spite of them. Success and power and competitiveness are not the only American growth goals, even though they are the principal ones. For they are only one aspect of the individualist ideal. The other is self-fulfillment, and the young Americans (sometimes a minority) who learn how to know themselves are on the way to learning how to become themselves.

They develop, in the process, a life style which they partly shape and which partly is shaped for them, inside the frame of their work, their class, their locale, their culture. They have first to find some models on which to mold the personality through imitation: they find them in their parents, older brothers and sisters, teachers, age peers. Out of these and out of the personality images presented to them in the culture as a whole they form an ideal image of self toward which they probe experimentally as they play one role after another, fitting each of them on for size and looks in the mirror of others as well as of themselves.

But in this copying and playing of roles a dangerous clash takes place [581/582]—the clash between what I want to call the *cultural image* of self and the *identity image* of self. The cultural image is the one borrowed and imposed from without, and inevitably it tends toward conformity. The identity image is one that emerges from the quest for a distinctive selfhood and is the product of a continual interplay between the individual's need and whatever measure of cultural elements he is able to absorb in growing up. The clash is always there because there has been no culture in history in which the individual has been able to ignore the cultural demands and pressures. But where it is too great the result is alienation on the one hand, or else an overreceptiveness to the cultural pressures in order to resolve it, or else some form of breakdown. Yet there are unmistakable evidences that the child growing up in America is learning to make the resolution tolerably well. When he does, there is a richness of the final personality style which is itself both the index and product of the difficulties encountered in the process of growing up. [582]

JOHN W. M. WHITING
RICHARD KLUCKHOLM
ALBERT ANTHONY

———◆◆———

The Function of Male Initiation
Ceremonies

OUR SOCIETY gives little formal recognition of the physiological and social changes a boy undergoes at puberty. He may be teased a little when his voice changes or when he shaves for the first time. Changes in his social status from childhood to adulthood are marked by a number of minor events rather than by any single dramatic ceremonial observance. Graduation from grammar school and subsequently from high school are steps to adulthood, but neither can be considered as a *rite de passage*. Nor may the accomplishment of having obtained a driver's license, which for many boys is the most important indication of having grown up, be classed as one. Legally the twenty-first birthday is the time at which a boy becomes a man; but, except for a somewhat more elaborate birthday party this occasion is not ceremonially marked and, therefore, cannot be thought of as a *rite de passage*. Neither physiologically, socially, nor legally is there a clear demarcation between boyhood and manhood in our society.

Such a gradual transition from boyhood to manhood is by no means universal. [359/360] Among the Thonga, a tribe in South Africa, every boy must go through a very elaborate ceremony in order to become a man.[1] When a boy is somewhere between ten

From *Readings in Social Psychology*, 3rd edition, edited by E. E. Maccoby, T. M. Newcomb, and E. L. Hartley. New York: Holt, Rinehart and Winston, 1958.

[1] The following account is taken from Henri A. Junod, *The Life of a South African Tribe* (London: Macmillan & Co., Ltd., 1927), pp. 74–95.

and sixteen years of age, he is sent by his parents to a "circumcision school" which is held every four or five years. Here in company with his age-mates he undergoes severe hazing by the adult males of the society. The initiation begins when each boy runs the gauntlet between two rows of men who beat him with clubs. At the end of this experience he is stripped of his clothes and his hair is cut. He is next met by a man covered with lion manes and is seated upon a stone facing this "lion man." Someone then strikes him from behind and when he turns his head to see who has struck him, his foreskin is seized and in two movements cut off by the "lion man." Afterwards he is secluded for three months in the "yards of mysteries," where he can be seen only by the initiated. It is especially taboo for a woman to approach these boys during their seclusion, and if a woman should glance at the leaves with which the circumcised covers his wound and which form his only clothing, she must be killed.

During the course of his initiation, the boy undergoes six major trials: beatings, exposure to cold, thirst, eating of unsavory foods, punishment, and the threat of death. On the slightest pretext he may be severely beaten by one of the newly initiated men who is assigned to the task by the older men of the tribe. He sleeps without covering and suffers bitterly from the winter cold. He is forbidden to drink a drop of water during the whole three months. Meals are often made nauseating by the half-digested grass from the stomach of an antelope which is poured over his food. If he is caught breaking any important rule governing the ceremony, he is severely punished. For example, in one of these punishments, sticks are placed between the fingers of the offender, then a strong man closes his hand around that of the novice practically crushing his fingers. He is frightened into submission by being told that in former times boys who had tried to escape or who revealed the secrets to women or the uninitiated were hanged and their bodies burnt to ashes.

Although the Thonga are extreme in the severity of this sort of initiation, many other societies have rites which have one or more of the main features of the Thonga ceremony. [360] . . .

An illustration of cultural conditions which should intensify the dependency of a boy on his mother and rivalry with his father is found in the following case.

Kwoma Dependency. The Kwoma,[2] a tribe living about 200

---

[2] For a description of the Kwoma child-rearing reported here see J. W. M. Whiting, *Becoming a Kwoma* (New Haven: Yale University Press, 1941), pp. 24–64.

miles up the Sepik River in New Guinea, have initiation rites similar to those of the Thonga. Examination of the differences in the relationship of a mother to her infant during the first years of his life reveals some strong contrasts between the Kwoma and our own society. While in our society an infant sleeps in his own crib and the mother shares her bed with the father, the Kwoma infant sleeps cuddled in his mother's arms until he is old enough to be weaned, which is generally when he is two or three years old. The father, in the meantime, sleeps apart on his own bark slab bed. Furthermore during this period, the Kwoma mother abstains from sexual intercourse with her husband in order to avoid having to care for two dependent children at the same time. Since the Kwoma are polygynous and discreet extramarital philandering is permitted, this taboo is not too hard on the husband. In addition, it is possible that the mother obtains some substitute sexual gratification from nursing and caring for her infant.[3] If this be the case, it is not unlikely that she should show more warmth and affection toward her infant than if she were obtaining sexual gratification from her husband. Whether or not the custom can be attributed to this sex taboo, the Kwoma mother, while her co-wife does the housework, not only sleeps with her infant all night but holds it in her lap all day without apparent frustration. Such a close relationship between a mother and child in our society would seem not only unbearably difficult to the mother, but also somewhat improper.

When the Kwoma child is weaned, a number of drastic things happen all at once. He is suddenly moved from his mother's bed to one of his own. His father resumes sexual relations with his mother. Although the couple wait until their children are asleep, the intercourse takes place in the same room. Thus, the child may truly become aware of his replacement. He is now told that he can no longer have his mother's milk because some supernatural being needs it. This is vividly communicated to him by his mother when she puts a slug on her breasts and daubs the blood-colored sap of the breadfruit tree over her nipples. Finally he is no longer permitted to sit on his mother's lap. She resumes her work and goes to the garden to

[3] This is, of course, difficult to determine and is a presumption based upon the following factors: (1) Kwoma informants reported that mothers had no desire for sexual intercourse as long as they were nursing the infant and (2) clinical evidence from women in our own society suggests that nursing is sexually gratifying to some women at least. See Therese Benedek, "Mother-child, the Primary Psychomatic Unit," *Am. J. Ortho-Psychiatry*, 1949, XIX; Helene Deutsch, *The Psychology of Women* (New York: Grune & Stratton, Inc., 1944–45), Vols. I and II; Sears, Maccoby, and Levin, *op. cit.*

weed or to the swamp to gather sago flour leaving him behind for the first time in his life. That these events are traumatic to the child is not surprising. He varies between sadness and anger, weeping and violent temper tantrums.

It is our hypothesis that it is this series of events that makes it necessary, when the boy reaches adolescence, for the society to have an initiation rite of the type we have already described. It is necessary to put a final stop to (1) his wish to return to his mother's arms and lap, (2) to prevent an open revolt against his father who has displaced him from his mother's bed, and (3) to ensure identification with the adult males of the society. [362/363]

In other words, Kwoma infancy so magnifies the conditions which should produce Oedipus rivalry that the special cultural adjustment of ceremonial hazing, isolation from women, and symbolic castration, etc., must be made to resolve it. [363] . . .

THE SOCIOPSYCHOLOGICAL IMPLICATIONS

We are not concerned with the bizarre rites of the Thonga or the peculiar life of a Kwoma infant, for their own sakes, but rather in discovering some general truths about human nature. We, therefore, wish to state what we believe to be the underlying processes that are involved. These are processes that we have not directly observed and which must be accepted or rejected on the grounds of their plausibility or, more important, on the basis of further research implied by our theory.

We believe that six sociopsychological assumptions are supported by our findings:

1. The more exclusive the relationship between a son and his mother during the first years of his life, the greater will be his emotional dependence upon her.

2. The more intensely a mother nurtures (loves) an infant during the early years of his life, the more emotionally dependent he will be upon her.

3. The greater the emotional dependence of a child upon a mother, the more hostile and envious he will be toward anyone whom he perceives as replacing him in her affection.[4]

4. If a child develops a strong emotional dependence upon his mother during infancy, and hostility toward and envy of his father

---

[4] If, however, the mother herself is perceived by the child as the one responsible for terminating the early intense relationship, this should lead the boy to both envy her and identify with her. This should produce conflict with respect to his sex role identity, which initiation rites would serve to resolve.

in early childhood at the time of weaning and the onset of independence [369/370] training, these feelings (although latent during
childhood) will manifest themselves when he reaches physiological
maturity in (a) open rivalry with his father and (b) incestuous approaches to his mother, unless measures are taken to prevent such
manifestations.

5. Painful hazing, enforced isolation from women, trials of endurance or manliness, genital operations, and change of residence are
effective means for preventing the dangerous manifestation of rivalry and incest.

6. Even a moderate or weak amount of emotional dependence
upon the mother and rivalry with the father will be dangerous at
adolescence if the father has no right to (or does not in fact) exercise
authority over his son during childhood.

If these sociopsychological hypotheses are true, they have some interesting implications for individual diferences in our own society.[5]
It has long been known that there is an association between certain
types of juvenile delinquency and broken homes.[6] We would predict
that the probability of a boy becoming delinquent in such instances
would be highest where the separation of the mother and father occurred during the early infancy of the boy and where she remarried
when he was two or three years old.

We would further predict that insofar as there has been an increase in juvenile deliquency in our society, it probably has been
accompanied by an increase in the exclusiveness of mother-child relationships and/or a decrease in the authority of the father. It is not
unreasonable that industrialization and urbanization have done just
this, but, of course, this matter should be investigated before such
an interpretation is accepted.

Finally, if further research shows that juvenile delinquency in our
society is in part a function of the early childhood factors that have
been described in this paper, then it can be countered either by de-
creasing the exclusiveness of the early mother-child relationship, increasing the authority of the father during childhood, or instituting

[5] In a study of infant training William Sewell reports that "the children who
slept with their mothers during infancy made significantly poorer showings on
the self-adjustment, personal freedom, and family relations components of the
California Test of Personality and suffered more sleep disturbances than did
those who slept alone." W. H. Sewell, "Infant Training and the Personality of
the Child," *Am. J. Sociol.*, (1953), LVIII, 157.

[6] *Cf.* for example, E. Glueck and S. Glueck, *Unravelling Juvenile Delinquency*
(New York: Commonwealth Fund, 1950); W. W. Waltenberg and J. J. Balistrieri,
"Gang Membership and Juvenile Misconduct," *Am. Sociol. Rev.*, (December,
1950), XV, 744–752.

a formal means of coping with adolescent boys functionally equivalent to those described in this paper. Change of residence would seem more compatible with the values of our society than an initiation ceremony. The Civilian Conservation Corps camps of the 1930's were an experiment which should provide useful data in this regard. The present institution of selective service would perhaps serve this purpose were the boys to be drafted at an earlier age and exposed to the authority of responsible adult males. [370]

MORDECAI MARCUS

What Is an Initiation Story?

MUCH RECENT CRITICISM, apparently beginning with Brooks and Warren's comments on Hemingway's "The Killers" and Anderson's "I Want to Know Why" in *Understanding Fiction*[1], has used the term "initiation" to describe a theme and a type of story. Ray B. West's history of *The Short Story in America, 1900–1950*[2] uses the term for one of two major types of short story. Several short story textbooks and textbook manuals employ the term, and other criticism applies it to novels.

The prevalence of inadequate criticism employing the concept of initiation suggests that the term requires clarification. I propose to examine the origins and definitions of this concept, to test it through application to a variety of stories, and to suggest its usefulness and its limitations. For the sake of convenience, I will—with the exception of a few short novels—confine my discussion to short stories.

The name and analytic concept of the initiation story derive basically from anthropology. The most important rites of most primitive cultures center around the passage from childhood or adolescence to maturity and full membership in adult society. Anthropologists call these rites initiation or puberty ceremonies. These ceremonies involve physical torture, cutting of various parts of the body, abstension from and ritualistic use of food, isolation, and indoctrination in secret tribal beliefs. According to most anthropologists the purpose of these rites is to test the endurance of the novice, to assure his loyalty to the tribe, and to maintain the power of the adult community. But a few anthropologists, believe that they stem from a psychological compulsion to propitiate the adult community or supernatural powers.

Certain "literary anthropologists" propose a concept of initiation

From *Journal of Aesthetics and Art Criticism,* Vol. XIX, (Winter, 1960).
[1] New York, 1943.
[2] Chicago, 1952.

apparently based on the idea of propitiating the adult or supernatural world. For example, Joseph Campbell's *The Hero with a Thousand Faces* (1949) describes initiation as a stage in all human life. He derives his description of initiation from the experience of the typical mythical hero as he seeks adjustment and union with the forces of existence, such as the tempting woman and the threatening father. Other writers have analyzed similar initiation rituals in medieval literature.

A brief description of the ways in which fiction can embody ritual will help to show the relationship between these anthropological ideas and the initiation story, and will also be helpful in analyzing certain initiation stories. Ritual is difficult to define and to apprehend because most human behavior follows prescribed patterns unreflectively. Everyday patterns of behavior are recognized as ritualistic only when they are so exaggerated or deliberate as to appear out of the ordinary. Therefore, the formalized behavior of so-called civilized people will appear ritualistic in fiction chiefly under two circumstances: when it involves a response to an unusually trying situation in which a person falls back on socially formalized behavior, or when an individual pattern of behavior results from powerful psychological compulsion. Ritual may appear [221/222] in fiction in two more guises: through the portrayal of the formalized behavior of primitives or folkpeople and through symbols which suggest mythological parallels in people or action. Certain psychologists and anthropologists, particularly the disciples of Jung, tend to see a basic unity in all these manifestations of ritual, but it is safe to ignore without refuting this questionable doctrine, for it would not seriously alter most of my analysis.

The anthropologist's ideas about initiation would suggest that an initiation story shows adult society deliberately testing and indoctrinating the young, or shows the young compelled in a relatively universal manner to enact certain experiences in order to achieve maturity. But only a very small proportion of works called initiation stories, or meeting the definitions for them, show adults testing or teaching the young. Ritual does occur in some initiation stories, but it is more often of individual than of social origin. Education is always important in an initiation story, but it is usually a direct result of experience rather than of indoctrination. One concludes that the initiation story has only a tangential relationship to the anthropologist's ideas of initiation.

The various critical definitions of the initiation story fall into two groups. The first group describes initiation as a passage of the young from ignorance about the external world to some vital knowledge. The second describes initiation as an important self-discovery and a resulting adjustment to life or society. But definitions within these two categories vary considerably.

According to Adrian H. Jaffe and Virgil Scott initiation occurs when "a character, in the course of the story, learns something that he did not know before, and . . . what he learns is already known to, and shared by, the larger group of the world."[3] Several critics, including Brooks and Warren (p. 344), and West (p. 75), explicitly define initiation as a discovery of evil. Brooks and Warren also state that the protagonist seeks to come to terms with his discovery, and West suggests that in learning to live with his knowledge the protagonist begins to achieve self-understanding.

The remarks of Brooks and Warren, and West, about achieving adjustment and self-understanding give their theories continuity with those which make self-understanding central to the initiation story. Curiously balanced between the two classes of definition is Leslie Fiedler's belief that "An initiation is a fall through knowledge to maturity; behind it there persists the myth of the Garden of Eden, the assumption that to know good and evil is to be done with the joy of innocence and to take on the burdens of work and childbearing and death."[4] Less ambiguous concepts of initiation as self-discovery are presented in two discussions of stories by Conrad. Carl Benson believes that *The Shadow Line* presents initiation as "the passage from egocentric youth to human solidarity."[5] Albert J. Guerard finds initiation in *Heart of Darkness* and "The Secret Sharer" to be "progress through temporary reversion and achieved self-knowledge, the theme of man's exploratory descent into the primitive sources of being," but Guerard believes that this knowledge of evil makes us capable of good.[6]

Three of the critics cited insist or imply that initiation stories contain ritual but they offer no distinctions between kinds of ritual. Jaffe and Scott compare initiation plots to fraternity initiation ceremonies. West suggests that Hemingway is always ritualistic (p. 93), and refers to the "ritual of initiation" in "The Killers" and in Faulkner's "That Evening Sun" (p. 99). (The Faulkner story, I believe, does not present initiation.) Guerard's insistence on psychological compulsion and on the appropriateness of bloodshed in "a true initiation story" suggests that he may consider ritual vital to the form.[7]

[3] *Studies in the Short Story* (New York, 1949), p. 155.
[4] "From Redemption to Initiation," *New Leader*, XLI (May 26, 1958), 22.
[5] "Conrad's Two Stories of Initiation," *PMLA*, LXIX (March, 1954), 49–50.
[6] "Introduction," *Heart of Darkness* (New York: Signet Books, 1950), p. 14.
[7] *Conrad the Novelist* (Cambridge, Mass., 1958), p. 40n.

A synthesis of these ideas will provide a working definition. An initiation story may be said to show its young protagonist experiencing a significant change of knowledge about the world or himself, or a change of character, or of both, and this change must point or lead him towards an adult world. It may or may not contain some form of ritual, but it should give some evidence that the change is at least likely to have permanent effects.

Initiation stories obviously center on a [222/223] variety of experiences and the initiations vary in effect. It will be useful, therefore, to divide initiations into types according to their power and effect. First, some initiations lead only to the threshold of maturity and understanding but do not definitely cross it. Such stories emphasize the shocking effect of experience, and their protagonists tend to be distinctly young. Second, some initiations take their protagonists across a threshold of maturity and understanding but leave them enmeshed in a struggle for certainty. These initiations sometimes involve self-discovery. Third, the most decisive initiations carry their protagonists firmly into maturity and understanding, or at least show them decisively embarked toward maturity. These initiations usually center on self-discovery. For convenience, I will call these types tentative, uncompleted, and decisive initiations.

Stories of tentative initiation typically show shocking experiences which leave their protagonists distraught. Since such experiences do not always lead towards maturity, one may demand evidence of permanent effect on the protagonist before ascribing initiation to a story. Stories of very young children offer the greatest problem here. In Chekov's "A Trifle from Life," Katherine Mansfield's "Sun and Moon," and Katherine Anne Porter's "The Circus," young children experience disillusionment in the trustworthiness of an adult, in the permanence of a delightful and picturesque event, and in the joyfulness and sincerity of a circus performance. In each story, a child is violently distressed, while the surrounding adults remain uncomprehending or unsympathetic. Only Miss Porter's story suggests that the disillusioning experience will have long-range effects, and its implication that they will be damaging suggests the possibility of yet another type of initiation.

Despite one's hesitation to find initiation in these three stories, they are not far removed in theme and structure from many works which critics have called typical initiation stories—for example, several much discussed stories by Hemingway. Among these stories is "Indian Camp," in which Nick Adams watches his father perform a Caesarian operation on an Indian woman and then sees that the woman's husband has killed himself to avoid witnessing her suffering. The story emphasizes Nick's discovery of death, but its conclusion asserts that Nick could not believe he would ever die. If Nick's discovery is to have permanent effects, one must assume that the story's conclusion describes a protective rationalization which cannot last. If this is true, then the story shows an approach to and a temporary withdrawal from mature realization.

Other stories by Hemingway show longer-lasting struggles at thresholds of maturity. "My Old Man" shows its protagonist learning that his father was a cheat despised by various people, and he is left struggling for an adjustment to this bitter knowledge. Hemingway's two stories of adolescent discovery of violence, "The Killers" and "The Battler," are perhaps more problematic than "Indian Camp" and "My Old Man." In "The Killers" Nick Adams is confronted with brutal and somewhat impersonal violence in the actions of the gangsters, and with despairing passivity in the behavior of the prizefighter Andreson. Various details suggest that Nick has never before witnessed such behavior. The end of the story shows Nick struggling for adjustment to his new knowledge, and contrasts his sensitivity to evil and despair with the insensitivity of Sam and George.

This story marks a tentative initiation into maturity, but analysis of its initiation theme has led to irresponsible interpretations. Brooks and Warren propose that Nick experiences "the discovery of evil" (p. 322), but this phrase makes Nick's experience uniquely symbolic of evil in general, which is more weight than the story can carry. Jaffe and Scott, probably building on Brooks and Warren's interpretation, find the story showing "a person who suddenly discovers the basic nature of existence," and claim that it is "about the meaning of life and man's place in the universe" (pp. 209–210). These interpretations are a far cry from the rather elementary experience of Nick Adams in "The Killers."

Quite possibly the idea that an initiation must be profound and universal has misled these critics. Jaffe and Scott's insistence that initiation is always "into the larger [223/224] group of the world" may also mislead them, for Hemingway's heroes are always initiated into a select group. Hemingway's "The Battler" records comparable encounters by Nick Adams, but this time he discovers treachery and uncertainty as well as violence. If the experience in "The Killers" is to be called *the* initiation into the meaning of existence, one might as well propose the same interpretation for "The Battler"; but again the idea appears irresponsible. Ray West's idea that "The Killers" is an initiation ritual finds little support in the story, for its only ritual element appears to be the operation of the narrow social codes of the gangsters and the prizefighter.

Disillusion, uncertainty, and violence also create the tentative initiation of Jody Tiflin in Steinbeck's three-part story "The Red Pony," yet the emphasis in this story is markedly different from that in Hemingway's two stories. Jody's farm life bristles with evidence of the uncertainty of life and the dependence of life on death, but only a series of incidents which involve him deeply begin to bring these truths home to Jody. Steinbeck does not show Jody's final realization, but Jody's feelings after he has seen Billy Buck's struggle to bring the colt to birth suggest that Jody will remember his initiating experiences. "The Red Pony" contains occasional suggestions of ritual (chiefly through parallels to primitive rites) in its emphasis on the slaughter of farm animals, and (in the form of individual compulsion) in Jody's constant attention to his pony and to the pregnant mare. In this story Steinbeck's view of the cycle of life is somewhat sacramental. Faulkner's view of nature in "The Old People" is distinctly sacramental. In this story, Ike McCaslin is ritualistically initiated into a communion with nature by Sam Fathers, the old Indian-Negro (the rites derive from a primitive culture), after which Ike sees a vision of the buck he has slain. Sam's instructions and Ike's own vision teach him to respect the sacredness of nature. Faulkner's story places less emphasis than does Steinbeck's on the pervasiveness of death, but it does stress the interdependence of life and death. Both of these stories present tentative initiations, for they give only slight evidence that their protagonists are achieving maturity.

Although stories involving some self-discovery usually move beyond tentative and towards uncompleted initiation, self-discovery may be slight enough or sufficiently compounded with other feelings, so that it does not lead beyond the tentative. For example, the protagonist of Joyce's "Araby" is disillusioned about the bazaar he longed to visit, and at the same time gains an insight into his own vanity. Perhaps because we see in him little struggle for adjustment, the shame which Joyce's protagonist suffers may seem less of a step towards maturity than the shock which Nick Adams experiences in "The Killers" and "The Battler." Another story which combines some self-discovery with tentative initiation is Dorothy Canfield Fisher's "Sunset at Sixteen," a story about a young girl whose first romantic yearnings and disappointments make her realize that she must experience years of struggle and pain to win through to the final peace of maturity.

The dividing line between tentative and uncompleted initiation is, of course, impossible to establish precisely. Initiation into knowledge of sex and into sexual desire might easily fit all three categories of initiation stories, but in two well known stories such experience illustrates uncompleted initiation. In Anderson's "I Want to Know

Why" a boy recognizes moral complexity in the lives of two men whose sexual behavior contrasts with their other actions and reveals a combination of good and evil. Although Anderson's protagonist remains profoundly puzzled, the depth of his concern makes it likely that he will continue to strive for understanding. More complex is the uncompleted initiation in Alberto Moravia's short novel *Agostino,* which portrays a boy of thirteen first learning about the nature of sexual relations, then tortured by his relationship to his young and beautiful widowed mother, and finally unable to gain admittance to a brothel, where he had hoped to destroy his oedipal vision of his mother. Agostino's desperation and seething conflicts perhaps give more assurance that he will struggle towards maturity than does the dilemma of Anderson's protagonist. [224/225]

Another harsh self-discovery accompanying a discovery about human life occurs in Lionel Trilling's "The Other Margaret." As this highly complex story concludes, a thirteen year old girl is forced to recognize that another person, and presumably all men, are responsible for their moral lives no matter what extenuating circumstances exist. From this insight she immediately moves to recognition of her own responsibility. Although the story ends with the girl weeping uncontrollably, the force with which she makes her discovery, its profoundly personal nature, as well as the girl's intelligence and sensitivity, strongly suggest that her discovery will have permanent effects. The smashing of the clay lamb, which object the protagonist's father identifies with her, is certainly symbolic and may introduce a ritualistc element through association with primitive rites, but ritual, I believe, is not essential to the story.

Self-discovery may be a more gentle correlate of discoveries about human life, as in stories of uncompleted initiation by Jessamyn West and Katherine Mansfield. Miss West's "Sixteen" (the final story in *Cress Delahanty*) portrays a self-centered girl who reluctantly goes home from college to be present at her aged grandfather's death. Details throughout the story suggest that Cress is scornful of the sensibilities of the old, of other people in general, and proud of the rare flowering of her own sensibilities. As her dying grandfather speaks to her of his love for the flower she wears and compares her to his dead wife, Cress realizes that his humanity is like hers, and so she discovers that she has been falsely separating herself from others. The story ends on a note of communion between the dying man and the girl, suggesting that she will change.

A parallel but more complex initiation occurs in Miss Mansfield's "The Garden Party," in which the adolescent protagonist, Laura, is intensely concerned with her relationships to everyone she deals with. Her self-centeredness, unlike Cress Delahanty's, is patronizing and she is concerned to do what appears right. As the story concludes, Laura discovers the reality and the mystery of death, which discovery seems to ease the burden of living and yet demand that life be understood. Although her problems are not solved, the conclusion suggests that she is in a better position to find life's realities. Laura's almost compulsive concern with the dead man is perhaps psychologically ritualistic, and—as Daniel A. Weiss has observed[8]—her descent to the cottage of the dead man parallels Proserpine's descent to the dead. But these ritual elements are slight.

A somewhat comparable theme is presented in Katherine Anne Porter's "A Grave." This story at first portrays a girl of nine who confronts the mystery of birth and death as she bends over the open body of a pregnant dead rabbit. But it is twenty years later that the meaning of this experience crystallizes for her. Rather than portraying an actual initiation, this story shows a mature person remembering from her years of immaturity a symbol for more recent knowledge. But its revelation that growth has occurred strongly parallels the initiation theme. Robert Penn Warren's "Blackberry Winter," which Ray B. West analyzes intensively as an initiation story (pp. 77–80), slightly resembles "A Grave." Warren presents a series of potentially disillusioning experiences which a nine year old boy experiences on one day. At the story's end, flashing ahead thirty-five years to the present, the first-person protagonist implies that the experiences of that day prefigured all of his subsequent life. Unlike Miss Porter's story, however, Warren's gives no indication of how or when the early experience was recognized as a prototype of the later, and the result is a feeling of melodramatic cheating in the conclusion. West's detailed analysis of the story mistakenly insists that the nine year old boy understands the meaning of his experience.

Although these stories by Miss Porter and by Warren make a special use of the initiation theme, they stand at the borderline between stories of uncompleted and decisive initiation. As one might expect, some stories of sexual initiation are likely to stand at a similar crossroads, for initial sexual intercourse is in one sense always decisive but also points toward character development. Hemingway's somewhat cynical story "Up in Michigan" portrays the simple disillusionment of a girl who is half-willingly [225/226] raped by a man whom she has admired from a distance, but the story stops rather abruptly after her sexual initiation. Far more complex is Colette's short novel *Le Blé en Herbe* (translated as *The Ripening*). In this story, sixteen year old Phillipe spends an idyllic and yet often bitter

[8] "Crashing the Garden Party," *Modern Fiction Studies*, IV (Winter, 1958–1959), 363–364.

summer at the sea-shore in the company of a fifteen year old girl, Vinca. Both children are pained by the uncertainties of growing up, but before the summer is over Phillipe has had an extended sexual initiation with a sensual woman of thirty, and then one brief and somewhat unsatisfactory intercourse with Vinca. Although Phillipe develops no sense of sexual guilt from his major experience, its unde-cided effect on his future, and his great passivity and uncertainty, leave him still bitter and unhappy. Two symbolic details help com-municate these feelings and add touches of ritual to the story through association with myth or primitive rite. When Phillipe's lover first invites him into her house, she presses on him a glass of very cold orangeade, and Phillipe repeatedly thinks of the bitterness of the drink as he struggles with his feelings about the woman. When Phillipe returns to the woman's house he tosses a bunch of thistle-flowers into her garden and accidentally wounds her face. Summoning him into the garden, she presses a drop of blood onto his hand. The next time Phillipe returns, their sexual affair begins. Both ritualistic details symbolize his partially disillusioning experi-ence.

Moravia's short novel *Luca,* which portrays a more profound and decisive initiation than Colette's, employs a sexual initiation to cre-ate its denouement. *Luca* is pervasively ritualistic, often combining psychological compulsion and mythical parallels. The story traces out the struggles of a fifteen year old boy who feels progressively alienated from his mother and father, his school, and his once pre-cious pursuits. He compulsively rejects all contacts because of their hypocrisy and impurity, and proceeds to cut himself off from life. Ritualistically he gives away his most valued possessions, rejects ges-tures of friendship, and imagines himself passively dead. In a ritual-istic game of hide and seek in the dark (an exaggerated version of the cultural ritual of the beckoning but elusive woman), he grows interested in a woman, but she dies before he can keep an appoint-ment with her. Finally, after long illness and delirium, he is ini-tiated into sex by a much older woman, whom he perceives as an earth goddess; and feeling at last in vital contact with all of life, he moves decisively towards mature acceptance.

A fusion of psychological accuracy and familiar archetypes is less certain in Conrad's "The Secret Sharer." Albert J. Guerard finds in this story the archetype of the mythical night journey, which repre-sents a descent into the unconscious.[9] "The Secret Sharer" unques-tionably shows psychological ritual: its protagonist must exert him-self to an extreme to conceal his double, and he acts in a trance-like

[9] *Conrad the Novelist,* p. 26.

manner. Most striking is his compulsion to drive his ship as close to the land as possible, presumably so that he may show Leggatt his gratitude for the experience of self-discovery. How far he has gone beyond the discovery of courage and endurance amidst loneliness remains problematic, but the final sentences of the story reveal that he has achieved a decisive initiation. The exploratory night journey is well established as an initiatory myth.

Clearly formalized primitive ritual occurs in two well known stories which portray decisive initiations: Steinbeck's "Flight" and Faulkner's "The Bear." Pepé, the Mexican boy in "Flight," is suddenly projected into manhood when he must bear the consequences of having killed a man over a point of honor. From the story's opening Pepé's behavior shows rituals of his culture: he practices knife throwing, yearns for manhood, dons his father's garments. Perhaps more ritualistic is his flight from the avenging pursuers. The act itself, with foreknowledge that he is probably doomed, is ritualistic, as are his preparations, his course through the mountains, and his final deliberate confrontation of death after his case is hopeless.

The primitivistic ritual in Faulkner's "The Bear" is identical with the ritual in "The Old People," of which story it is a sequel. Sam Fathers marks the forehead of Ike McCaslin with the blood of his first slain [226/227] deer, thereby bringing Ike into communion with the wilderness and nature. This incident is less detailed in "The Bear" than in "The Old People," but its meanings are much more deeply explored in additional incidents. Other ritualistic details in the story include Ike's abandonment of his watch, gun, and compass before he can get his first glimpse of the bear, Old Ben, and Sam Fathers' patient training of the dog Lion, who is to bring down Old Ben. Both incidents combine psychological compulsion and the sense of a half-intuited myth, the feeling that nature demands a certain rite. More distinctly psychological are the ritualistic intensity with which Ike pores over his grandfather's ledgers in pursuit of evidence of iniquity, and Ike's decision to renounce the land he has inherited from that grandfather and to adopt the Christ-like trade of a carpenter. All of these rituals are part of a decisive initiation: Ike's establishing a correct understanding of what it means to own the land and of how men may redeem their right to own the land. Faulkner's primitive and psychological rituals in this story are always convincing.

Ritualistic elements lend much coherence and power to these stories of decisive initiation, but ritual is not necessary in such a story. F. Scott Fitzgerald's "The Freshest Boy" describes a decisive point in the life of Basil Lee, which turns him away from egoism and snobbery towards self-discovery and social acceptance. Unfortunately, the turning point in the story—Basil's observation of a major frustration in the life of a football hero—is sentimental, as are some of the accompanying details. Fitzgerald's inability to create a vivid event to change his protagonist makes the story unlike most initiation stories, but Basil's final and decisive turn toward maturity is convincing.

The greater prevalence of ritual in stories of decisive rather than tentative or uncompleted initiation is striking, but it is not too difficult to explain. The full initiations which these stories present usually grow out of strong desires for self-discovery rather than from accidents. Use of psychological compulsion and struggle makes it easy for the writer to incorporate primitive or mythological ritual material when it is available. Primitivistic ritual is perhaps too rare in fiction to be generalized about, but it seems chiefly to accompany decisive initiation. Ritual elements are absent from or unimportant in most stories of tentative and uncompleted initiation, and they are not a definite requirement for decisive initiation.

If such stories as several by Hemingway, Anderson, Trilling, and Miss Porter are to remain in the canon of initiation stories—where they have been placed by various critics—a comprehensive definition like the one I have suggested must be adopted. This definition has the virtues of separating stages of initiation and of avoiding insistence on universal and profound meanings. Furthermore, not only should the critic show caution in ascribing ritual to a story, but he should analyze its type and its precise manifestation. These virtues, in turn, may assist careful analysis of meaning and construction. This definition, of course, has the defect of being so broad that almost any story of developing awareness or character can fit it. However, it is possible to exclude stories of simple recognitions about people and perhaps most stories about adults.

The alternative to my broad three-part definition is the close restriction of initiation to what I have called decisive initiation. Such a definition would insist on a clear-cut entrance into the adult world. Ritual would not be a central requirement for the form, but it would be a distinct likelihood. (Some critics, of course, might wish to limit initiation to stories containing ritual.) This definition might reduce the possibility of over-interpretation of stories such as "The Killers" and "Blackberry Winter," but sensibility will always remain more important than critical terms.

We see, then, that a certain anarchy has unnecessarily prevailed in the idea of the initiation story. Its relationships to anthropological ideas, even those of the "literary" anthropologist, are somewhat tenuous, and its use of archetypes and rituals is exaggerated. As is the case with many literary ideas, its central danger lies in its insistence on phenomena where they simply do not exist—in relying on a concept as a matter of faith. If one believes that initiation stories [227/228] must present ritual, he may find ritual in "Indian Camp" or "The Circus," where they do not exist (except in the manner in which all human behavior is ritualistic). Leslie Fiedler's insistence that initiation is basically a discovery of guilt is an equally mistaken matter of faith. Many of the initiation stories I have discussed lack ritual and guilt.

Clearly defined and applied with sensibility and without fanaticism, the concept of the initiation story may assist thorough understanding of many works of fiction. But without these virtues, it may well serve only as another tool for reductive or misleading interpretation. [228]

2

Blood Rites

EACH OF THE STORIES in this section involves contact with nature and such elemental matters as birth, struggle, and death, and in each the main character attains a degree of maturity from this contact. To the men who tamed the American wilderness, nature was an adversary, pitiless and cruel; but writers in an industrialized urban culture, looking back to a simpler age, frequently soften the image of nature to something like Rousseau's idealization of the primitive. Even when it is most destructive, nature seems preferable to the assembly line or the slum, and it imbues its initiates with confidence, courage, and wisdom. Initiation stories developing this theme are usually anti-civilization, as they extol simple and natural, even primitive virtues. They also tend to be didactic, at least by implication, as the young man learns a lesson from his initiation into the world of nature.

Jody Tiflin in *The Red Pony,* as is true in many initiation stories, is a partially autobiographical character. In other segments of the story, his new pony dies of pneumonia and buzzards swoop down to eat its flesh, and Jody talks with an old man who has returned to die in the mountains where he lived as a youth. In a story published separately, "The Leader of the People," Jody senses the pathos of his grandfather's monologues about the Western migration. All of the episodes in these interrelated stories suggest Jody's gradual awakening to the suffering and loss in human life.

"Open Winter" does not involve a ritualistic death, but it resembles "The Promise" in depicting the world of nature and in portraying a young man's maturation under the guidance of a wise old veteran. This kind of relationship is particularly common in stories of the Frontier. It is not the major theme in *The Way West* (1949) by A. B. Guthrie but is effectively integrated with other aspects of an emigrant party's trek to Oregon. Under the tutelage of an experienced mountain man, young Brownie Evans comes of age and outgrows his dependence on his parents. *Honey in the Horn* (1935) by H. L. Davis similarly portrays the maturing of Clay Calvert, "a

41

drip-nosed youth of about sixteen," in Oregon just after the turn of the century.

This type of initiation story often involves hunting or fishing and a boy's attainment of the skill and patience necessary for success. *Home from the Hill* (1957) by William Humphrey contains a succinct description of the significance of the hunt:

> For he knew, had always known, that it was not just being able to line up the front sight in the rear one, not just the meat you brought home for the table. It was to learn to be a man, the only kind of man, to learn it in and from the woods themselves and from the woodsmen, the hunters, who had learned it as boys from their fathers there—and so back through the generations, making you a link in the long strong chain of men of courage and endurance, of cunning and fairness, of humility as well as becoming pride.

The young man becomes part of the timeless continuum of wilderness lore, the art of the hunt, and traditional virtues. Humphrey correlates father-son rivalry with this theme as the boy strives to surpass his father's hunting exploits. According to Leslie Fiedler, stories that deal with boys' hunting or fishing have a deeper significance:

> In the United States it is through murder rather than sex, death rather than love that the child enters the fallen world. He is not asked, to be sure, to kill a fellow human, only an animal, deer or bear, or even fish, some woodland totem, in slaying whom (sometimes he is even smeared with the blood of his victim) he enters into a communion of guilt with the natural world in which hitherto he has led the privileged existence of an outsider.

In contemporary America, where the natural landscape is rapidly being transformed into factories and housing developments or is being obscured by billboards, it is understandable that relatively few stories portray primitive initiation rites like those described in the fourth essay of the "Perspectives" section, in which a youth is required to undergo an ordeal or perform a prescribed feat to demonstrate his endurance, bravery, and general worthiness. If he succeeds, his adult status is commemorated in what anthropologists call a rite of passage. He is regarded as a child one day and as a man the next. Such a conclusive recognition of adulthood is possible only in a simple culture with fixed, absolute values. Certainly in our culture the assumption of adult status is never a single definitive act. In an open society with its complex network of options and obligations, maturity is achieved, if at all, not by opening a door but by traversing a corridor. It is a prolonged and complicated process.

Perhaps it is partly the simplification of experience in stories re-creating primitive initiation rites that gives them their appeal. Two of the best examples of such stories are "The Old People" (1940) and "The Bear" (1942) by William Faulkner. In the first, Sam Fathers, an old man part-Indian and part-Negro, trains young Isaac McCaslin and counsels him to be patient: "You wait. You'll be a hunter. You'll be a man." When Isaac kills his first deer and Sam ritualistically baptizes him with its blood, he senses that "in less than a second he had ceased forever to be the child he was yesterday." In "The Bear," a more complex story that involves the same characters and setting, Isaac McCaslin's initiation is consummated. The annual hunt is described as a "pageant-rite," and Isaac is said to be serving an "apprenticeship," a "novitiate," under the tutelage of Sam Fathers. Old Ben, a huge bear that the hunters pursue each year, symbolizes the savage but doomed wilderness. Isaac cannot see Old Ben until he goes into the forest alone, leaving behind his watch, gun, and compass—symbols of civilization. The bear is killed, and the wilderness is destroyed for its timber. Isaac, who has learned humility and renunciation from Sam Fathers, refuses to accept his inheritance because it originated in the injustice and evil of slavery. He becomes a carpenter, lives simply, and makes an annual pilgrimage to the diminishing wilderness with a band of younger hunters.

The mentor-neophyte relationship between an older man wise in the ways of nature and an inexperienced young man is a recurring situation in such stories. Often, as in the Faulkner stories, the older man belongs to another culture or way of life. Similar examples are Ishmael and Queequeg in *Moby Dick* (1851), Huck and Jim in *Huckleberry Finn* (1884), and Manolin and Santiago in Hemingway's *The Old Man and the Sea* (1952). And in other novels of the Leatherstocking saga, Natty Bumppo becomes a Nestor-like advisor to several young men.

JAMES FENIMORE COOPER

The Deerslayer

DAY HAD FAIRLY DAWNED before the young man, whom we have
left in the situation described in the last chapter, again opened his
eyes. This was no sooner done, than he started up, and looked
about him with the eagerness of one who suddenly felt the importance of accurately ascertaining his precise position. His rest had
been deep and undisturbed; and when he awoke, it was with a
clearness of intellect and a readiness of resources that were very
much needed at that particular moment. The sun had not risen, it
is true, but the vault of heaven was rich with the winning softness
that "brings and shuts the day," while the whole air was filled with
the carols of birds, the hymns of the feathered tribe. These sounds
first told Deerslayer the risks he ran. The air, for wind it could
scarce be called, was still light, it is true, but it had increased a
little in the course of the night, and as the canoes were mere feathers
on the water, they had drifted twice the expected distance; and,
what was still more dangerous, had approached so near the base of
the mountain that here rose precipitously from the eastern shore,
as to render the carols of the birds plainly audible. This was not
the worst. The third canoe had taken the same direction, and was
slowly drifting towards a point where it must inevitably touch,
unless turned aside by a shift of wind, or human hands. In other

From James F. Cooper, *The Deerslayer; or, The First War-Path* (Leather-stock-
ing Edition). New York: G. P. Putnam's Sons, 1841, (pp. 105–121). The five novels
in the Leatherstocking saga cover the life-span of Natty Bumppo, a legendary
frontier scout. Although it was the fourth to be published (1841), *The Deerslayer* treats the earliest phase of his life. In the episode reprinted here,
Bumppo has come to Ostego Lake with "Hurry Harry" to visit Tom Hutter,
who lives with his two daughters in a "castle" in the middle of the lake. He
also expects to meet Chingachgook, a young Delaware chief and close friend.
Harry and Hutter are captured by hostile Iroquois, and while Natty is patrolling
the shore to prevent the Iroquois from acquiring canoes and attacking the
castle, he is called upon to kill his first Indian.

respects, nothing presented itself to attract attention, or to awaken alarm. The castle stood on its shoal, nearly abreast of the canoes, for the drift had amounted to miles in the course of the night, and the ark lay fastened to its piles, as both had been left so many hours before.

As a matter of course, Deerslayer's attention was first given the canoe ahead. It was already quite near the point, and a very few strokes of the paddle sufficed to tell him that it must touch before he could possibly overtake it. Just at this moment, too, the wind inopportunely freshened, rendering the drift of the light craft much more rapid than certain. Feeling the impossibility of preventing a contact with the land, the young man wisely determined not to heat himself with unnecessary exertions; but first looking to the priming of his piece, he proceeded slowly and warily towards the point, taking care to make a little circuit, that he might be exposed on only one side, as he approached.

The canoe adrift being directed by no such intelligence, pursued its proper way, and grounded on a small sunken rock, at the distance of three or four yards from the shore. Just at that moment, Deerslayer had got abreast of the point, and turned the bows of his own boat to the land; first casting loose his tow, that his movements might be unencumbered. The canoe hung an instant on the rock; then it rose a hair's-breadth on an almost imperceptible swell of the water, swung round, floated clear, and reached the strand. All this the young man noted, but it neither quickened his pulses, nor hastened his hand. If any one had been lying in wait for the arrival of the waif, he must be seen, and the utmost caution in approaching the shore became indispensable; if no one was in ambush, hurry was unnecessary. The point being nearly diagonally opposite to the Indian encampment, he hoped the last, though the former was not only possible, but probable; for the savages were prompt in adopting all the expedients of their particular modes of warfare, and quite likely had many scouts searching the shores for craft to carry them off to the castle. As a glance at the lake from any height or projection would expose the smallest object on its surface, there was little hope that either of the canoes would pass unseen; and Indian sagacity needed no instruction to tell which way a boat or a log would drift, when the direction of the wind was known. As Deerslayer drew nearer and nearer to the land, the stroke of his paddle grew slower, his eye became more watchful, and his ears and nostrils almost dilated with the effort to detect any lurking danger. 'Twas a trying moment for a novice, nor was there the encouragement which even the timid sometimes feel, when conscious of being observed and commended. He was entirely alone, thrown on his own re-

sources, and was cheered by no friendly eye, emboldened by no en-
couraging voice. Notwithstanding all these circumstances, the most
experienced veteran in forest warfare could not have behaved better.
Equally free from recklessness and hesitation, his advance was
marked by a sort of philosophical prudence, that appeared to render
him superior to all motives but those which were best calculated to
effect his purpose. Such was the commencement of a career in forest
exploits, that afterwards rendered this man, in his way, and under
the limits of his habits and opportunities, as renowned as many a
hero whose name has adorned the pages of works more celebrated
than legends simple as ours can ever become.

When about a hundred yards from the shore, Deerslayer rose in
the canoe, gave three or four vigorous strokes with the paddle, sufficient of themselves to impel the bark to land, and then quickly laying aside the instrument of labor, he seized that of war. He was in
the very act of raising the rifle, when a sharp report was followed by
the buzz of a bullet that passed so near his body as to cause him involuntarily to start. The next instant Deerslayer staggered, and fell
his whole length in the bottom of the canoe. A yell—it came from a
single voice—followed, and an Indian leaped from the bushes upon
the open area of the point, bounding towards the canoe. This was
the moment the young man desired. He rose on the instant, and lev-
elled his own rifle at his uncovered foe; but his finger hesitated
about pulling the trigger on one whom he held at such a disadvantage. This little delay, probably, saved the life of the Indian, who
bounded back into the cover as swiftly as he had broken out of it. In
the meantime Deerslayer had been swiftly approaching the land,
and his own canoe reached the point just as his enemy disappeared.
As its movements had not been directed, it touched the shore a few
yards from the other boat; and though the rifle of his foe had to be
loaded, there was not time to secure his prize, and carry it beyond
danger, before he would be exposed to another shot. Under the circumstances, therefore, he did not pause an instant, but dashed into
the woods and sought a cover.

On the immediate point there was a small open area, partly in native grass, and partly beach, but a dense fringe of bushes lined its
upper side. This narrow belt of dwarf vegetation passed, one issued
immediately into the high and gloomy vaults of the forest. The land
was tolerably level for a few hundred feet, and then it rose precipitously in a mountain-side. The trees were tall, large, and so free
from underbrush, that they resembled vast columns, irregularly scattered, upholding a dome of leaves. Although they stood tolerably
close together, for their ages and size, the eye could penetrate to con-

siderable distances; and bodies of men, even, might have engaged beneath their cover, with concert and intelligence.

Deerslayer knew that his adversary must be employed in re-loading, unless he had fled. The former proved to be the case, for the young man had no sooner placed himself behind a tree, than he caught a glimpse of the arm of the Indian, his body being concealed by an oak, in the very act of forcing the leathered bullet home. Nothing would have been easier than to spring forward, and decide the affair by a close assult on his unprepared foe; but every feeling of Deerslayer revolted at such a step, although his own life had just been attempted from a cover. He was yet unpracticed in the ruthless expedients of savage warfare, of which he knew nothing except by tradition and theory, and it struck him as an unfair advantage to assail an unarmed foe. His color had heightened, his eyes frowned, his lips were compressed, and all his energies were collected and ready; but, instead of advancing to fire, he dropped his rifle to the usual position of a sportsman in readiness to catch his aim, and muttered to himself, unconscious that he was speaking—

"No, no—that may be redskin warfare, but it's not a Christian's gifts. Let the miscreant charge, and then we'll take it out like men; for the canoe he *must* not, and *shall* not have. No, no; let him have time to load, and God will take care of the right!"

All this time the Indian had been so intent on his own movements, that he was even ignorant that his enemy was in the woods. His only apprehension was, that the canoe would be recovered and carried away before he might be in readiness to prevent it. He had sought the cover from habit, but was within a few feet of the fringe of bushes, and could be at the margin of the forest in readiness to fire in a moment. The distance between him and his enemy was about fifty yards, and the trees were so arranged by nature that the line of sight was not interrupted, except by the particular trees behind which each party stood.

His rifle was no sooner loaded, than the savage glanced around him, and advanced incautiously as regarded the real, but stealthily as respected the fancied position of his enemy, until he was fairly exposed. Then Deerslayer stepped from behind his own cover, and hailed him.

"This a way, redskin; this a way, if you're looking for me," he called out. "I'm young in war, but not so young as to stand on an open beach to be shot down like an owl, by daylight. It rests on yourself whether it's peace or war atween us; for my gifts are white gifts, and I'm not one of them that thinks it valiant to slay human mortals, singly, in the woods."

The savage was a good deal startled by this sudden discovery of the danger he ran. He had a little knowledge of English, however, and caught the drift of the other's meaning. He was also too well schooled to betray alarm, but, dropping the butt of his rifle to the earth, with an air of confidence, he made a gesture of lofty courtesy. All this was done with the ease and self-possession of one accustomed to consider no man his superior. In the midst of this consummate acting, however, the volcano that raged within caused his eyes to glare, and his nostrils to dilate, like those of some wild beast that is suddenly prevented from taking the fatal leap.

"Two canoes," he said, in the deep guttural tones of his race, holding up the number of fingers he mentioned, by way of prevening mistakes; "one for you—one for me."

"No, no, Mingo, that will never do. You own neither; and neither shall you have, as long as I can prevent it. I know it's war atween your people and mine, but that's no reason why human mortals should slay each other, like savage creatur's that meet in the woods; go your way, then, and leave me to go mine. The world is large enough for us both; and when we meet fairly in battle, why, the Lord will order the fate of each of us."

"Good!" exclaimed the Indian; "my brother missionary—great talk; all about Manitou."

"Not so—not so, warrior. I'm not good enough for the Moravians, and am too good for most of the other vagabonds that preach about in the woods. No, no; I'm only a hunter, as yet, though afore the peace is made, 't is like enough there'll be occasion to strike a blow at some of your people. Still, I wish it to be done in fair fight, and not in a quarrel about the ownership of a miserable canoe."

"Good! My brother very young—but he is very wise. Little warrior —great talker. Chief, sometimes, in council."

"I don't know this, nor do I say it, Injin," returned Deerslayer, coloring a little at the ill-concealed sarcasm of the other's manner; "I look forward to a life in the woods, and I only hope it may be a peaceable one. All young men must go on the war-path, when there's occasion, but war isn't needfully massacre. I've seen enough of the last, this very night, to know that Providence frowns on it; and I now invite you to go your own way, while I go mine; and hope that we may part fri'nds."

"Good! My brother has two scalp—gray hair under t'other. Old wisdom—young tongue."

Here the savage advanced with confidence, his hand extended, his face smiling, and his whole bearing denoting amity and respect. Deerslayer met his offered friendship in a proper spirit, and they shook hands cordially, each endeavoring to assure the other of his sincerity and desire to be at peace.

"All have his own," said the Indian; "my canoe, mine; your canoe, your'n. Go look; if your'n, you keep; if mine, I keep."

"That's just, redskin; though you must be wrong in thinking the canoe your property. However, seein' is believin', and we'll go down to the shore, where you may look with your own eyes; for it's likely you'll object to trustin' altogether to mine."

The Indian uttered his favorite exclamation of "Good!" and then they walked side by side, towards the shore. There was no apparent distrust in the manner of either, the Indian moving in advance, as if he wished to show his companion that he did not fear turning his back to him. As they reached the open ground, the former pointed towards Deerslayer's boat, and said emphatically—

"No mine—pale-face canoe. *This* redman's. No want other man's canoe—want his own."

"You're wrong, redskin, you're altogether wrong. This canoe was left in old Hutter's keeping, and is his'n according to law, red or white, till its owner comes to claim it. Here's the seats and the stitching of the bark to speak for themselves. No man ever know'd an Injin to turn off such work."

"Good! My brother little old—big wisdom. Injin no make him. White man's work."

"I'm glad you think so, for holding out the contrary might have made ill blood atween us, every one having a right to take possession of his own. I'll just shove the canoe out of reach of dispute at once, as the quickest way of settling difficulties."

While Deerslayer was speaking, he put a foot against the end of the light boat, and giving a vigorous shove, he sent it out into the lake a hundred feet or more, where, taking the true current, it would necessarily float past the point, and be in no further danger of coming ashore. The savage started at this ready and decided expedient, and his companion saw that he cast a hurried fierce glance at his own canoe, or that which contained the paddles. The change of manner, however, was but momentary, and then the Iroquois resumed his air of friendliness, and a smile of satisfaction.

"Good!" he repeated, with stronger emphasis than ever. "Young head, old mind. Know how to settle quarrel. Farewell, brother. He go to house in water—muskrat house—Injin go to camp; tell chiefs no find canoe."

Deerslayer was not sorry to hear this proposal, for he felt anxious to join the females, and he took the offered hand of the Indian very willingly. The parting words were friendly, and while the redman

walked calmly towards the wood, with the rifle in the hollow of his
arm, without once looking back in uneasiness or distrust, the white
man moved towards the remaining canoe, carrying his piece in the
same pacific manner, it is true, but keeping his eye fastened on the
movements of the other. This distrust, however, seemed to be altogether uncalled for, and as if ashamed to have entertained it, the
young man averted his look, and stepped carelessly up to his boat.
Here he began to push the canoe from the shore, and to make his
other preparations for departing. He might have been thus employed a minute, when, happening to turn his face towards the land,
his quick and certain eye told him, at a glance, the imminent jeop-
ardy in which his life was placed. The black, ferocious eyes of the
savage were glancing on him, like those of the crouching tiger,
through a small opening in the bushes, and the muzzle of his rifle
seemed already to be opening in a line with his own body.

Then, indeed, the long practice of Deerslayer, as a hunter, did
him good service. Accustomed to fire with the deer on the bound,
and often when the precise position of the animal's body had in a
manner to be guessed at, he used the same expedients here. To cock
and poise his rifle were the acts of a single moment and a single motion; then aiming almost without sighting, he fired into the bushes
where he knew a body ought to be, in order to sustain the appalling
countenance which alone was visible. There was not time to raise
the piece any higher, or to take a more deliberate aim. So rapid were
his movements that both parties discharged their pieces at the same
instant, the concussions mingling in one report. The mountains, indeed, gave back but a single echo. Deerslayer dropped his piece, and
stood with head erect, steady as one of the pines in the calm of a
June morning, watching the result; while the savage gave the yell
that has become historical for its appalling influence, leaped
through the bushes, and came bounding across the open ground,
flourishing a tomahawk. Still Deerslayer moved not, but stood with
his unloaded rifle fallen against his shoulders, while, with a hunter's
habits, his hands were mechanically feeling for the powder-horn and
charger. When about forty feet from his enemy, the savage hurled
his keen weapon; but it was with an eye so vacant, and a hand so
unsteady and feeble, that the young man caught it by the handle as
it was flying past him. At that instant the Indian staggered and fell
his whole length on the ground.

"I know'd it—I know'd it!" exclaimed Deerslayer, who was already
preparing to force a fresh bullet into his rifle; "I know'd it must
come to this, as soon as I had got the range from the creatur's eyes.
A man sights suddenly, and fires quick when his own life's in danger;
yes, I know'd it would come to this. I was about the hundredth part

of a second too quick for him, or it may have been bad for me. The riptyle's bullet has just grazed my side—but say what you will for or ag'in 'em, a redskin is by no means as sartain with powder and ball as a white man. Their gifts don't seem to lie that a way. Even Chingachgook, great as he is in other matters, isn't downright deadly with the rifle."

By this time the piece was reloaded, and Deerslayer, after tossing the tomahawk into the canoe, advanced to his victim, and stood over him, leaning on his rifle, in melancholy attention. It was the first instance in which he had seen a man fall in battle—it was the first fellow creature against whom he had ever seriously raised his own hand. The sensations were novel; and regret, with the freshness of our better feelings, mingled with his triumph. The Indian was not dead, though shot directly through the body. He lay on his back motionless, but his eyes, now full of consciousness, watched each action of his victor—as the fallen bird regards the fowler—jealous of every movement. The man probably expected the fatal blow which was to precede the loss of his scalp; or perhaps he anticipated that this latter act of cruelty would precede his death. Deerslayer read his thoughts; and he found a melancholy satisfaction in relieving the apprehensions of the helpless savage.

"No, no, redskin," he said; "you've nothing more to fear from me. I am of a Christian stock, and scalping is not of my gifts. I'll just make sartain of your rifle, and then come back and do you what sarvice I can. Though here I can't stay much longer, as the crack of three rifles will be apt to bring some of your devils down upon me."

The close of this was said in a sort of soliloquy, as the young man went in quest of the fallen rifle. The piece was found where its owner had dropped it, and was immediately put into the canoe. Laying his own rifle at its side, Deerslayer then returned and stood over the Indian again.

"All inmity atween you and me's at an ind, redskin," he said; "and you may set your heart at rest on the score of the scalp, or any further injury. My gifts are white, as I've told you; and I hope my conduct will be white also!"

Could looks have conveyed all they meant, it is probable Deerslayer's innocent vanity on the subject of color would have been rebuked a little; but he comprehended the gratitude that was expressed in the eyes of the dying savage, without in the least detecting the bitter sarcasm that struggled with the better feeling.

"Water!" ejaculated the thirsty and unfortunate creature; "give poor Injin water."

"Ay, water you shall have, if you drink the lake dry. I'll just carry you down to it, that you may take your fill. This is the way, they tell me, with all wounded people—water is their greatest comfort and delight."

So saying, Deerslayer raised the Indian in his arms, and carried him to the lake. Here he first helped him to take an attitude in which he could appease his burning thirst; after which he seated himself on a stone, and took the head of his wounded adversary in his own lap, and endeavored to soothe his anguish in the best manner he could.

"It would be sinful in me to tell you your time hadn't come, warrior," he commenced, "and therefore I'll not say it. You've passed the middle age already, and, considerin' the sort of lives ye lead, your days have been pretty well filled. The principal thing now, is to look forward to what comes next. Neither redskin nor pale-face, on the whole, calculates much on sleepin' forever; but both expect to live in another world. Each has his gifts, and will be judged by 'em, and I suppose you've thought these matters over enough not to stand in need of sarmons when the trial comes. You'll find your happy hunting-grounds, if you've been a just Injin; if an onjust, you'll meet your desarts in another way. I've my own idees about these things; but you're too old and exper'enced to need any explanations from one as young as I."

"Good!" ejaculated the Indian, whose voice retained its depth even as life ebbed away; "young head—old wisdom!"

"It's sometimes a consolation, when the ind comes, to know that them we've harmed, or *tried* to harm, forgive us. I suppose natur' seeks this relief, by way of getting a pardon on 'arth; as we never can know whether He pardons, who is all in all, till judgment itself comes. It's soothing to know that *any* pardon at such times; and that, I conclude, is the secret. Now, as for myself, I overlook altogether your designs ag'in my life; first because no harm came of 'em; next, because it's your gifts, and natur' and trainin', and I ought not to have trusted you at all; and, finally and chiefly, because I can bear no ill-will to a dying man, whether heathen or Christian. So put your heart at ease, so far as I'm consarned; you know best what other matters ought to trouble you, or what ought to give you satisfaction in so trying a moment."

It is probable that the Indian had some of the fearful glimpses of the unknown state of being which God, in mercy, seems at times to afford to all the human race; but they were necessarily in conformity with his habits and prejudices. Like most of his people, and like too many of our own, he thought more of dying in a way to gain applause among those he left than to secure a better state of existence hereafter. While Deerslayer was speaking, his mind was a little bewildered, though he felt that the intention was good; and when he had done, a regret passed over his spirit that none of his own tribe were present to witness his stoicism, under extreme bodily suffering, and the firmness with which he met his end. With the high innate courtesy that so often distinguishes the Indian warrior before he becomes corrupted by too much intercourse with the worst class of the white men, he endeavored to express his thankfulness for the other's good intentions, and to let him understand that they were appreciated.

"Good!" he repeated, for this was an English word much used by the savages, "good! young head; young *heart*, too. *Old* heart tough; no shed tear. Hear Indian when he die, and no want to lie—what he call him?"

"Deerslayer is the name I bear now, though the Delawares have said that when I get back from this war-path, I shall have a more manly title, provided I can 'arn one."

"That good name for boy—poor name for warrior. He get better quick. No fear *there*,"—the savage had strength sufficient, under the strong excitement he felt, to raise a hand and tap the young man on his breast,—"eye sartain—finger lightning—aim, death—great warrior soon. No Deerslayer—Hawkeye—Hawkeye—Hawkeye. Shake hand."

Deerslayer—or Hawkeye, as the youth was then first named, for in after years he bore the appellation throughout all that region—Deerslayer took the hand of the savage whose last breath was drawn in that attitude, gazing in admiration at the countenance of a stranger, who had shown so much readiness, skill, and firmness, in a scene that was equally trying and novel. When the reader remembers it is the highest gratification an Indian can receive to see his enemy betray weakness, he will be better able to appreciate the conduct which had extorted so great a concession at such a moment.

"His spirit has fled!" said Deerslayer, in a suppressed, melancholy voice. "Ah's me! Well, to this we must all come, sooner or later; and he is happiest, let his skin be what color it may, who is best fitted to meet it. Here lies the body of no doubt a brave warrior, and the soul is already flying towards its heaven or hell, whether that be a happy hunting-ground, a place scant of game, regions of glory, according to Moravian doctorine, or flames of fire! So it happens, too, as regards other matters! Here have old Hutter and Hurry Harry got themselves into difficulty, if they haven't got themselves into torment and death, and all for a bounty that luck offers to me in what many would think a lawful and suitable manner. But not a farthing of such money shall cross my hand. White I was born, and white will I die; clinging to color to the last, even though the King's majesty, his governors, and all his councils, both at home and in the colonies, forget from what they come, and where they hope to go, and all for a little advantage in warfare. No, no, warrior, hand of mine shall never molest your scalp, and so your soul may rest in peace on the p'int of making a decent appearance when the body comes to join it, in your own land of spirits."

Deerslayer arose as soon as he had spoken. Then he placed the body of the dead man in a sitting posture, with its back against the little rock, taking the necessary care to prevent it from falling or in any way settling into an attitude that might be thought unseemly by the sensitive, though wild notions of a savage. When this duty was performed, the young man stood gazing at the grim countenance of his fallen foe, in a sort of melancholy abstraction. As was his practice, however, a habit gained by living so much alone in the forest, he then began again to give utterance to his thoughts and feelings aloud.

"I didn't wish your life, redskin," he said, "but you left me no choice atween killing or being killed. Each party acted according to his gifts, I suppose, and blame can light on neither. You were treacherous, according to your natur' in war, and I was a little over-sightful, as I'm apt to be in trusting others. Well, this is my first battle with a human mortal, though it's not likely to be the last. I have fou't most of the creatur's of the forest, such as bears, wolves, painters, and catamounts, but this is the beginning with the redskins. If I was Injin born, now, I might tell of this, or carry in the scalp, and boast of the expl'ite afore the whole tribe; or, if my inimy had only been even a bear, 't would have been nat'ral and proper to let everybody know what had happened; but I don't well see how I'm to let even Chingachgook into this secret, so long as it can be done only by boasting with a white tongue. And why should I wish to boast of it a'ter all? It's slaying a human, although he was a savage; and how do I know that he was a just Injin; and that he has not been taken away suddenly to anything but happy hunting-grounds. When it's onsartain whether good or evil has been done, the wisest way is not be boastful—still, I *should* like Chingachgook to know that I haven't discredited the Delawares, or my training!"

Part of this was uttered aloud, while part was merely muttered between the speaker's teeth; his more confident opinions enjoying the first advantage, while his doubts were expressed in the latter mode. Soliloquy and reflection received a startling interruption, however, by the sudden appearance of a second Indian on the lake shore, a few hundred yards from the point. This man, evidently another scout, who had probably been drawn to the place by the reports of the rifles, broke out of the forest with so little caution that Deerslayer caught a view of his person before he was himself discovered. When the latter event did occur, as was the case a moment later, the savage gave a loud yell, which was answered by a dozen voices from different parts of the mountain-side. There was no longer any time for delay; in another minute the boat was quitting the shore under long and steady sweeps of the paddle.

As soon as Deerslayer believed himself to be at a safe distance, he ceased his efforts, permitting the little bark to drift, while he leisurely took a survey of the state of things. The canoe first sent adrift was floating before the air, quite a quarter of a mile above him, and a little nearer to the shore than he wished, now that he knew more of the savages were so near at hand. The canoe shoved from the point was within a few yards of him, he having directed his own course towards it on quitting the land. The dead Indian lay in grim quiet where he had left him, the warrior who had shown himself from the forest had already vanished, and the woods themselves were as silent and seemingly deserted as the day they came fresh from the hands of their great Creator. This profound stillness, however, lasted but a moment. When time had been given to the scouts of the enemy to reconnoitre, they burst out of the thicket upon the naked point, filling the air with yells of fury at discovering the death of their companion. These cries were immediately succeeded by shouts of delight when they reached the body and clustered eagerly around it. Deerslayer was a sufficient adept in the usages of the natives to understand the reason of the change. The yell was the customary lamentation at the loss of a warrior, the shout a sign of rejoicing that the conqueror had not been able to secure the scalp; the trophy, without which a victory is never considered complete. The distance at which the canoes lay probably prevented any attempts to injure the conqueror, the American Indian, like the panther of his own woods, seldom making any effort against his foe unless tolerably certain it is under circumstances that may be expected to prove effective.

As the young man had no longer any motive to remain near the point, he prepared to collect his canoes, in order to tow them off to the castle. That nearest was soon in tow, when he proceeded in quest of the other, which was all this time floating up the lake. The eye of Deerslayer was no sooner fastened on this last boat, than it struck him that it was nearer to the shore than it would have been had it merely followed the course of the gentle current of air. He began to suspect the influence of some unseen current in the water, and he quickened his exertions in order to regain possession of it before it could drift into a dangerous proximity to the woods. On getting nearer, he thought that the canoe had a perceptible motion through the water, and, as it lay broadside to the air, that this motion was taking it towards the land. A few vigorous strokes of the paddle carried him still nearer, when the mystery was explained. Something was evidently in motion on the off-side of the canoe, or that which was farthest from himself, and closer scrutiny showed that it was a naked human arm. An Indian was lying in the bottom of the canoe, and was propelling it slowly but certainly to the shore, using his hand as a paddle. Deerslayer understood the whole artifice at a glance. A savage had swum off to the boat while he was occupied with his enemy on the point, got possession, and was using these means to urge it to the shore.

Satisfied that the man in the canoe could have no arms, Deerslayer did not hesitate to dash close alongside of the retiring boat, without deeming it necessary to raise his own rifle. As soon as the wash of the water, which he made in approaching, became audible to the prostrate savage, the latter sprang to his feet, and uttered an exclamation that proved how completely he was taken by surprise.

"If you've enj'yed yourself enough in that canoe, redskin," Deerslayer coolly observed, stopping his own career in sufficient time to prevent an absolute collision betweeen the two boats,—"if you've enj'yed yourself enough in that canoe, you'll do a prudent act by taking to the lake ag'in. I'm reasonable in these matters, and don't crave your blood, though there's them about that would look upon you more as a due-bill for the bounty than a human mortal. Take to the lake this minute, afore we get to hot words."

The savage was one of those who did not understand a word of English, and he was indebted to the gestures of Deerslayer, and to the expression of an eye that did not often deceive, for an imperfect comprehension of his meaning. Perhaps, too, the sight of the rifle that lay so near the hand of the white man quickened his decision. At all events, he crouched like a tiger about to take his leap, uttered a yell, and the next instant his naked body disappeared in the water. When he rose to take breath, it was at the distance of several yards from the canoe, and the hasty glance he threw behind him denoted how much he feared the arrival of a fatal messenger from the rifle of his foe. But the young man made no indication of any hostile intention. Deliberately securing the canoe to the others, he began to paddle from the shore; and by the time the Indian reached the land, and had shaken himself, like a spaniel, on quitting the water, his dreaded enemy was already beyond rifle-shot on his way to the castle. As was so much his practice, Deerslayer did not fail to soliloquize on what had just occurred, while steadily pursuing his course towards the point of destination.

"Well, well,"—he commenced,—" 't would have been wrong to kill a human mortal without an object. Scalps are of no account with me, and life is sweet, and ought not to be taken mercilessly by them that have white gifts. The savage was a Mingo, it's true; and I make no doubt he is, and will be as long as he lives, a ra'al riptyle and vagabond; but that's no reason I should forget my gifts and color. No, no,—let him go; if ever we meet ag'in, rifle in hand, why then 't will be seen which has the stoutest heart and the quickest eye. Hawk-eye! That's not a bad name for a warrior, sounding much more manful and valiant than Deerslayer! 'T wouldn't be a bad title to begin with, and it has been fairly 'arned. If 't was Chingachgook, now, he might go home and boast of his deeds, and the chiefs would name him Hawkeye in a minute; but it don't become white blood to brag, and 't isn't easy to see how the matter can be known unless I do. Well, well,—everything is in the hands of Providence; this affair as well as another; I'll trust to that for getting my desarts in all things."

Having thus betrayed what might be termed his weak spot, the young man continued to paddle in silence, making his way dili-gently, and as fast as his tows would allow him, towards the castle. By this time the sun had not only risen, but it had appeared over the eastern mountains, and was shedding a flood of glorious light on this as yet unchristened sheet of water. The whole scene was radiant with beauty; and no one unaccustomed to the ordinary history of the woods would fancy it had so lately witnessed incidents so ruth-less and barbarous.

JOHN STEINBECK

The Promise

IN A MID-AFTERNOON of spring, the little boy Jody walked martially along the brush-lined road toward his home ranch. Banging his knee against the golden lard bucket he used for school lunch, he contrived a good bass drum, while his tongue fluttered sharply against his teeth to fill in snare drums and occasional trumpets. Some time back the other members of the squad that walked so smartly from the school had turned into the various little canyons and taken the wagon roads to their own home ranches. Now Jody marched seemingly alone, with high-lifted knees and pounding feet; but behind him there was a phantom army with great flags and swords, silent but deadly.

The afternoon was green and gold with spring. Underneath the spread branches of the oaks the plants grew pale and tall, and on the hills the feed was smooth and thick. The sagebrushes shone with new silver leaves and the oaks wore hoods of golden green. Over the hills there hung such a green odor that the horses on the flats galloped madly, and then stopped, wondering; lambs, and even old sheep jumped in the air unexpectedly and landed on stiff legs, and went on eating; young clumsy calves butted their heads together and drew back and butted again.

As the gray and silent army marched past, led by Jody, the animals stopped their feeding and their play and watched it go by.

Suddenly Jody stopped. The gray army halted, bewildered and nervous. Jody went down on his knees. The army stood in long uneasy ranks for a moment, and then, with a soft sigh of sorrow, rose up in a faint grey mist and disappeared. Jody had seen the thorny crown of a horny-toad moving under the dust of the road. His grimy hand went out and grasped the spiked halo and held firmly while

From John Steinbeck, *The Long Valley*. (New York: The Viking Press, 1938), pp. 256–279. "The Promise" is the concluding segment of a three-part story, "The Red Pony."

58

the little beast struggled. Then Jody turned the horny-toad over, exposing its pale gold stomach. With a gentle forefinger he stroked the throat and chest until the horny-toad relaxed, until its eyes closed and it lay languorous and asleep.

Jody opened his lunch pail and deposited the first game inside. He moved on now, his knees bent slightly, his shoulders crouched; his bare feet were wise and silent. In his right hand there was a long gray rifle. The brush along the road stirred restively under a new and unexpected population of grey tigers and grey bears. The hunting was very good, for by the time Jody reached the fork of the road where the mail box stood on a post, he had captured two more horny-toads, four little grass lizards, a blue snake, sixteen yellow-winged grasshoppers and a brown damp newt from under a rock. This assortment scrabbled unhappily against the tin of the lunch bucket.

At the road fork the rifle evaporated and the tigers and bears melted from the hillsides. Even the moist and uncomfortable creatures in the lunch pail ceased to exist, for the little red metal flag was up on the mail box, signifying that some postal matter was inside. Jody set his pail on the ground and opened the letter box. There was a Montgomery Ward catalog and a copy of the *Salinas Weekly Journal*. He slammed the box, picked up his lunch pail and trotted over the ridge and down into the cup of the ranch. Past the barn he ran, and past the used-up haystack and the bunkhouse and the cypress tree. He banged through the front screen door of the ranch house calling, "Ma'am, ma'am, there's a catalog."

Mrs. Tiflin was in the kitchen spooning clabbered milk into a cotton bag. She put down her work and rinsed her hands under the tap. "Here in the kitchen, Jody. Here I am."

He ran in and clattered his lunch pail on the sink. "Here it is. Can I open the catalog, ma'am?"

Mrs. Tiflin took up the spoon again and went back to her cottage cheese. "Don't lose it, Jody. Your father will want to see it." She scraped the last of the milk into the bag. "Oh, Jody, your father wants to see you before you go to your chores." She waved a cruising fly from the cheese bag.

Jody closed the new catalog in alarm. "Ma'am?"

"Why don't you ever listen? I say your father wants to see you."

The boy laid the catalog gently on the sink board. "Do you—is it something I did?"

Mrs. Tiflin laughed. "Always a bad conscience. What did you do?"

"Nothing, ma'am," he said lamely. But he couldn't remember, and besides it was impossible to know what action might later be construed as a crime.

His mother hung the full bag on a nail where it could drip into the sink. "He just said he wanted to see you when you got home. He's somewhere down by the barn."

Jody turned and went out the back door. Hearing his mother open the lunch pail and then gasp with rage, a memory stabbed him and he trotted away toward the barn, conscientiously not hearing the angry voice that called him from the house.

Carl Tiflin and Billy Buck, the ranch hand, stood against the lower pasture fence. Each man rested one foot on the lowest bar and both elbows on the top bar. They were talking slowly and aimlessly. In the pasture half a dozen horses nibbled contentedly at the sweet grass. The mare, Nellie, stood backed up against the gate, rubbing her buttocks on the heavy post.

Jody sidled uneasily near. He dragged one foot to give an impression of great innocence and nonchalance. When he arrived beside the men he put one foot on the lowest fence rail, rested his elbows on the second bar and looked into the pasture too. The two men glanced sideways at him.

"I wanted to see you," Carl said in the stern tone he reserved for children and animals.

"Yes, sir," said Jody guiltily.

"Billy, here, says you took good care of the pony before it died." No punishment was in the air. Jody grew bolder. "Yes, sir, I did."

"Billy says you have a good patient hand with horses."

Jody felt a sudden warm friendliness for the ranch hand.

Billy put in, "He trained that pony as good as anybody I ever seen."

Then Carl Tiflin came gradually to the point. "If you could have another horse would you work for it?"

Jody shivered. "Yes, sir."

"Well, look here, then. Billy says the best way for you to be a good hand with horses is to raise a colt."

"It's the *only* good way," Billy interrupted.

"Now, look here, Jody," continued Carl. "Jess Taylor, up to the ridge ranch, has a fair stallion, but it'll cost five dollars. I'll put up the money, but you'll have to work it out all summer. Will you do that?"

Jody felt that his insides were shriveling. "Yes, sir," he said softly.

"And no complaining? And no forgetting when you're told to do something?"

"Yes, sir."

"Well, all right, then. Tomorrow morning you take Nellie up to the ridge ranch and get her bred. You'll have to take care of her, too, till she throws the colt."

"Yes, sir."

"You better get to the chickens and the wood now."

Jody slid away. In passing behind Billy Buck he very nearly put out his hand to touch the blue-jeaned legs. His shoulders swayed a little with maturity and importance.

He went to his work with unprecedented seriousness. This night he did not dump the can of grain to the chickens so that they had to leap over each other and struggle to get it. No, he spread the wheat so far and so carefully that the hens couldn't find some of it at all. And in the house, after listening to his mother's despair over boys who filled their lunch pails with slimy, suffocated reptiles, and bugs, he promised never to do it again. Indeed, Jody felt that all such foolishness was lost in the past. He was far too grown up ever to put horny-toads in his lunch pail any more. He carried in so much wood and built such a high structure with it that his mother walked in fear of an avalanche of oak. When he was done, when he had gathered eggs that had remained hidden for weeks, Jody walked down again past the cypress tree, and past the bunkhouse toward the pasture. A fat warty toad that looked out at him from under the watering trough had no emotional effect on him at all. Carl Tiflin and Billy Buck were not in sight, but from a metallic ringing on the other side of the barn Jody knew that Billy Buck was just starting to milk a cow.

The other horses were eating toward the upper end of the pasture, but Nellie continued to rub herself nervously against the post. Jody walked slowly near, saying, "So, girl, so-o, Nellie." The mare's ears went back naughtily and her lips drew away from her yellow teeth. She turned her head around; her eyes were glazed and mad. Jody climbed to the top of the fence and hung his feet over and looked paternally down on the mare.

The evening hovered while he sat there. Bats and nighthawks flicked about. Billy Buck, walking toward the house carrying a full milk bucket, saw Jody and stopped. "It's a long time to wait," he said gently. "You'll get awful tired waiting."

"No I won't, Billy. How long will it be?"

"Nearly a year."

"Well, I won't get tired."

The triangle at the house rang stridently. Jody climbed down from the fence and walked to supper beside Billy Buck. He even put out his hand and took hold of the milk bucket to help carry it.

The next morning after breakfast Carl Tiflin folded a five-dollar bill in a piece of newspaper and pinned the package in the bib pocket of Jody's overalls. Billy Buck haltered the mare Nellie and led her out of the pasture.

"Be careful now," he warned. "Hold her up short here so she can't bite you. She's crazy as a coot."

Jody took hold of the halter leather itself and started up the hill toward the ridge ranch with Nellie skittering and jerking behind him. In the pasturage along the road the wild oat heads were just clearing their scabbards. The warm morning sun shone on Jody's back so sweetly that he was forced to take a serious stiff-legged hop now and then in spite of his maturity. On the fences the shiny blackbirds with red epaulets clicked their dry call. The meadowlarks sang like water, and the wild doves, concealed among the bursting leaves of the oaks, made a sound of restrained grieving. In the fields the rabbits sat sunning themselves, with only their forked ears showing above the grass heads.

After an hour of steady uphill walking, Jody turned into a narrow road that led up a steeper hill to the ridge ranch. He could see the red roof of the barn sticking up above the oak trees, and he could hear a dog barking unemotionally near the house.

Suddenly Nellie jerked back and nearly freed herself. From the direction of the barn Jody heard a shrill whistling scream and a splintering of wood, and then a man's voice shouting. Nellie reared and whinnied. When Jody held to the halter rope she ran at him with bared teeth. He dropped his hold and scuttled out of the way, into the brush. The high scream came from the oaks again, and Nellie answered it. With hoofs battering the ground the stallion appeared and charged down the hill trailing a broken halter rope. His eyes glittered feverishly. His stiff, erected nostrils were as red as flame. His black, sleek hide shone in the sunlight. The stallion came on so fast that he couldn't stop when he reached the mare. Nellie's ears went back; she whirled and kicked at him as he went by. The stallion spun around and reared. He struck the mare with his front hoof, and while she staggered under the blow, his teeth raked her neck and drew an ooze of blood.

Instantly Nellie's mood changed. She became coquettishly feminine. She nibbled his arched neck with her lips. She edged around and rubbed her shoulder against his shoulder. Jody stood half-hidden in the brush and watched. He heard the step of a horse behind him, but before he could turn, a hand caught him by the overall straps and lifted him off the ground. Jess Taylor sat the boy behind him on the horse.

"You might have got killed," he said. "Sundog's a mean devil sometimes. He busted his rope and went right through a gate."

Jody sat quietly, but in a moment he cried, "He'll hurt her, he'll kill her. Get him away!"

Jess chuckled. "She'll be all right. Maybe you'd better climb off and go up to the house for a little. You could get maybe a piece of pie up there."

But Jody shook his head. "She's mine, and the colt's going to be mine. I'm going to raise it up."

Jess nodded. "Yes, that's a good thing. Carl has good sense sometimes."

In a little while the danger was over. Jess lifted Jody down and then caught the stallion by its broken halter rope. And he rode ahead, while Jody followed, leading Nellie.

It was only after he had unpinned and handed over the five dollars, and after he had eaten two pieces of pie, that Jody started for home again. And Nellie followed docilely after him. She was so quiet that Jody climbed on a stump and rode her most of the way home.

The five dollars his father had advanced reduced Jody to peonage for the whole late spring and summer. When the hay was cut he drove a rake. He led the horse that pulled on the Jackson-fork tackle, and when the baler came he drove the circling horse that put pressure on the bales. In addition, Carl Tiflin taught him to milk and put a cow under his care, so that a new chore was added night and morning.

The bay mare Nellie quickly grew complacent. As she walked about the yellowing hillsides or worked at easy tasks, her lips were curled in a perpetual fatuous smile. She moved slowly, with the calm importance of an empress. When she was put to a team, she pulled steadily and unemotionally. Jody went to see her every day. He studied her with critical eyes and saw no change whatever.

One afternoon Billy Buck leaned the many-tined manure fork against the barn wall. He loosened his belt and tucked in his shirt-tail and tightened the belt again. He picked one of the little straws from his hatband and put it in the corner of his mouth. Jody, who was helping Doubletree Mutt, the big serious dog, to dig out a gopher, straightened up as the ranch hand sauntered out of the barn.

"Let's go up and have a look at Nellie," Billy suggested.

Instantly Jody fell into step with him. Doubletree Mutt watched them over his shoulder; then he dug furiously, growled, sounded little sharp yelps to indicate that the gopher was practically caught. When he looked over his shoulder again, and saw that neither Jody nor Billy was interested, he climbed reluctantly out of the hole and followed them up the hill.

The wild oats were ripening. Every head bent sharply under its load of grain, and the grass was dry enough so that it made a swishing sound as Jody and Billy stepped through it. Halfway up the hill they could see Nellie and the iron-grey gelding, Pete, nibbling the heads from the wild oats. When they approached, Nellie looked at them and backed her ears and bobbed her head up and down rebelliously. Billy walked to her and put his hand under her mane and patted her neck, until her ears came forward again and she nibbled delicately at his shirt.

Jody asked, "Do you think she's really going to have a colt?"

Billy rolled the lids back from the mare's eyes with his thumb and forefinger. He felt the lower lip and fingered the black, leathery teats. "I wouldn't be surprised," he said.

"Well, she isn't changed at all. It's three months gone."

Billy rubbed the mare's flat forehead and his knuckle while she grunted with pleasure. "I told you you'd get tired waiting. It'll be five months more before you can even see a sign, and it'll be at least eight months more before she throws the colt, about next January."

Jody sighed deeply. "It's a long time, isn't it?"

"And then it'll be about two years more before you can ride."

Jody cried out in despair, "I'll be grown up."

"Yep, you'll be an old man," said Billy.

"What color do you think the colt'll be?"

"Why, you can't ever tell. The stud is black and the dam is bay. Colt might be black or bay or gray or dappled. You can't tell. Sometimes a black dam might have a white colt."

"Well, I hope it's black, and a stallion."

"If it's a stallion, we'll have to geld it. Your father wouldn't let you have a stallion."

"Maybe he would," Jody said. "I could train him not to be mean."

Billy pursed his lips, and the little straw that had been in the corner of his mouth rolled down to the center. "You can't ever trust a stallion," he said critically. "They're mostly fighting and making trouble. Sometimes when they're feeling funny they won't work. They make the mares uneasy and kick hell out of the geldings. Your father wouldn't let you keep a stallion."

Nellie sauntered away, nibbling the drying grass. Jody skinned the grain from a grass stem and threw the handful into the air, so that each pointed, feathered seed sailed out like a dart. "Tell me how it'll be, Billy. Is it like when the cows have calves?"

"Just about. Mares are a little more sensitive. Sometimes you have to be there to help the mare. And sometimes if it's wrong, you have to——" he paused.

"Have to what, Billy?"

"Have to tear the colt to pieces to get it out, or the mare'll die."

"But it won't be that way this time, will it, Billy?"

"Oh, no. Nellie's thrown good colts."

"Can I be there, Billy? Will you be certain to call me? It's my colt."

"Sure, I'll call you. Of course I will."

"Tell me how it'll be."

"Why, you've seen the cows calving. It's almost the same. The mare starts groaning and stretching, and then, if it's a good right birth, the head and forefeet come out, and the front hoofs kick a hole just the way the calves do. And the colt starts to breathe. It's good to be there, 'cause if its feet aren't right maybe he can't break the sack, and then he might smother."

Jody whipped his leg with a bunch of grass. "We'll have to be there, then, won't we?"

"Oh, we'll be there, all right."

They turned and walked slowly down the hill toward the barn. Jody was tortured with a thing he had to say, although he didn't want to. "Billy," he began miserably, "Billy, you won't let anything happen to the colt, will you?"

And Billy knew he was thinking of the red pony, Gabilan, and of how it died of strangles. Billy knew he had been infallible before that, and now he was capable of failure. This knowledge made Billy much less sure of himself than he had been. "I can't tell," he said roughly. "All sorts of things might happen, and they wouldn't be my fault. I can't do everything." He felt badly about his lost prestige, and so he said, meanly, "I'll do everything I know, but I won't promise anything. Nellie's a good mare. She's thrown good colts before. She ought to this time." And he walked away from Jody and went into the saddle-room beside the barn, for his feelings were hurt.

Jody traveled often to the brushline behind the house. A rusty iron pipe ran a thin stream of spring water into an old green tub. Where the water spilled over and sank into the ground there was a patch of perpetually green grass. Even when the hills were brown and baked in the summer that little patch was green. The water whined softly into the trough all the year round. This place had grown to be a center-point for Jody. When he had been punished the cool green grass and the singing water soothed him. When he had been mean the biting acid of meanness left him at the brushline. When he sat in the grass and listened to the purling stream, the barriers set up in his mind by the stern day went down to ruin.

On the other hand, the black cypress tree by the bunkhouse was as repulsive as the water-tub was dear; for to this tree all the pigs came, sooner or later, to be slaughtered. Pig killing was fascinating, with the screaming and the blood, but it made Jody's heart beat so fast that it hurt him. After the pigs were scalded in the big iron tripod kettle and their skins were scraped and white, Jody had to go to the water-tub to sit in the grass until his heart grew quiet. The water-tub and the black cypress were opposites and enemies.

When Billy left him and walked angrily away, Jody turned up toward the house. He thought of Nellie as he walked, and of the little colt. Then suddenly he saw that he was under the black cypress, under the very singletree where the pigs were hung. He brushed his dry-grass hair off his forehead and hurried on. It seemed to him an unlucky thing to be thinking of his colt in the very slaughter place, especially after what Billy had said. To counteract any evil result of that bad conjunction he walked quickly past the ranch house, through the chicken yard, through the vegetable patch, until he came at last to the brushline.

He sat down in the green grass. The trilling water sounded in his ears. He looked over the farm buildings and across at the round hills, rich and yellow with grain. He could see Nellie feeding on the slope. As usual the water place eliminated time and distance. Jody saw a black, long-legged colt, butting against Nellie's flanks, demanding milk. And then he saw himself breaking a large colt to halter. All in a few moments the colt grew to be a magnificent animal, deep of chest, with a neck as high and arched as a sea-horse's neck, with a tail that tongued and rippled like black flame. This horse was terrible to everyone but Jody. In the schoolyard the boys begged rides, and Jody smilingly agreed. But no sooner were they mounted than the black demon pitched them off. Why, that was his name, Black Demon! For a moment the trilling water and the grass and the sunshine came back, and then ...

Sometimes in the night the ranch people, safe in their beds, heard a roar of hoofs go by. They said, "It's Jody, on Demon. He's helping out the sheriff again." And then ...

The golden dust filled the air in the arena at the Salinas Rodeo. The announcer called the roping contests. When Jody rode the black horse to the starting chute the other contestants shrugged and gave up first place, for it was well known that Jody and Demon could rope and throw and tie a steer a great deal quicker than any roping team of two men could. Jody was not a boy any more, and Demon was not a horse. The two together were one glorious individual. And then ...

The President wrote a letter and asked them to help catch a bandit in Washington. Jody settled himself comfortably in the grass. The little stream of water whined into the mossy tub.

The year passed slowly on. Time after time Jody gave up his colt for lost. No change had taken place in Nellie. Carl Tiflin still drove her to a light cart, and she pulled on a hay rake and worked the Jackson-fork tackle when the hay was being put into the barn.

The summer passed, and the warm bright autumn. And then the frantic morning winds began to twist along the ground, and a chill came into the air, and the poison oak turned red. One morning in

September, when he had finished his breakfast, Jody's mother called him into the kitchen. She was pouring boiling water into a bucket full of dry midlings and stirring the materials to a steaming paste.

"Yes, ma'am?" Jody asked.

"Watch how I do it. You'll have to do it after this every other morning."

"Well, what is it?"

"Why, it's warm mash for Nellie. It'll keep her in good shape."

Jody rubbed his forehead with a knuckle. "Is she all right?" he asked timidly.

Mrs. Tiflin put down the kettle and stirred the mash with a wooden paddle. "Of course she's all right, only you've got to take better care of her from now on. Here, take this breakfast out to her!" Jody seized the bucket and ran, down past the bunkhouse, past the barn, with the heavy bucket banging against his knees. He found Nellie playing with the water in the trough, pushing waves and tossing her head so that the water slopped out on the ground.

Jody climbed the fence and set the bucket of steaming mash beside her. Then he stepped back to look at her. And she was changed. Her stomach was swollen. When she moved, her feet touched the ground gently. She buried her nose in the bucket and gobbled the hot breakfast. And when she had finished and had pushed the bucket around the ground with her nose a little, she stepped quietly over to Jody and rubbed her cheek against him.

Billy Buck came out of the saddle-room and walked over. "Starts fast when it starts, doesn't it?"

"Did it come all at once?"

"Oh, no, you just stopped looking for a while." He pulled her head around toward Jody. "She's goin' to be nice, too. See how nice her eyes are! Some mares get mean, but when they turn nice, they just love everything." Nellie slipped her head under Billy's arm and rubbed her neck up and down between his arm and his side. "You better treat her awful nice now," Billy said.

"How long will it be?" Jody demanded breathlessly.

The man counted in whispers on his fingers. "About three months," he said aloud. "You can't tell exactly. Sometimes it's eleven months to the day, but it might be two weeks early, or a month late, without hurting anything."

Jody looked hard at the ground. "Billy," he began nervously, "Billy, you'll call me when it's getting born, won't you? You'll let me be there, won't you?"

Billy bit the tip of Nellie's ear with his front teeth. "Carl says he wants you to start right at the start. That's the only way to learn. Nobody can tell you anything. Like my old man did with me about the saddle blanket. He was a government packer when I was your size, and I helped him some. One day I left a wrinkle in my saddle blanket and made a saddle-sore. My old man didn't give me hell at all. But the next morning he saddled me up with a forty-pound stock saddle. I had to lead my horse and carry that saddle over a whole damn mountain in the sun. It darn near killed me, but I never left no wrinkles in a blanket again. I couldn't. I never in my life since then put on a blanket but I felt that saddle on my back."

Jody reached up a hand and took hold of Nellie's mane. "You'll tell me what to do about everything, won't you? I guess you know everything about horses, don't you?"

Billy laughed. "Why I'm half horse myself, you see," he said. "My ma died when I was born, and being my old man was a government packer in the mountains, and no cows around most of the time, why he just gave me mostly mare's milk." He continued seriously, "And horses know that. Don't you know it, Nellie?"

The mare turned her head and looked full into his eyes for a moment, and this is a thing horses practically never do. Billy was proud and sure of himself now. He boasted a little. "I'll see you get a good colt. I'll start you right. And if you do like I say, you'll have the best horse in the county."

That made Jody feel warm and proud, too; so proud that when he went back to the house he bowed his legs and swayed his shoulders as horsemen do. And he whispered, "Whoa, you Black Demon, you! Steady down there and keep your feet on the ground."

The winter fell sharply. A few preliminary gusty showers, and then a strong steady rain. The hills lost their straw color and blackened under the water, and the winter streams scrambled noisily down the canyons. The mushrooms and puffballs popped up and the new grass started before Christmas.

But this year Christmas was not the central day to Jody. Some undetermined time in January had become the axis day around which the months swung. When the rains fell, he put Nellie in a box stall and fed her warm food every morning and curried her and brushed her.

The mare was swelling so greatly that Jody became alarmed. "She'll pop wide open," he said to Billy.

Billy laid his strong square hand against Nellie's swollen abdomen. "Feel here," he said quietly. "You can feel it move. I guess it would surprise you if there were twin colts."

"You don't think so?" Jody cried. "You don't think it will be twins, do you, Billy?"

"No, I don't, but it does happen, sometimes."

During the first two weeks of January it rained steadily. Jody spent most of his time, when he wasn't in school, in the box stall with Nellie. Twenty times a day he put his hand on her stomach to feel the colt move. Nellie became more and more gentle and friendly to him. She rubbed her nose on him. She whinnied softly when he walked into the barn.

Carl Tiflin came to the barn with Jody one day. He looked admiringly at the groomed bay coat, and he felt the firm flesh over ribs and shoulders. "You've done a good job," he said to Jody. And this was the greatest praise he knew how to give. Jody was tight with pride for hours afterward.

The fifteenth of January came, and the colt was not born. And the twentieth came; a lump of fear began to form in Jody's stomach. "Is it all right?" he demanded of Billy.

"Oh, sure."

And again, "Are you sure it's going to be all right?"

Billy stroked the mare's neck. She swayed her head uneasily. "I told you it wasn't always the same time, Jody. You just have to wait."

When the end of the month arrived with no birth, Jody grew frantic. Nellie was so big that her breath came heavily, and her ears were close together and straight up, as though her head ached. Jody's sleep grew restless, and his dreams confused.

On the night of the second of February he awakened crying. His mother called to him, "Jody, you're dreaming. Wake up and start over again."

But Jody was filled with terror and desolation. He lay quietly a few moments, waiting for his mother to go back to sleep, and then he slipped his clothes on, and crept out in his bare feet.

The night was black and thick. A little misting rain fell. The cypress tree and the bunkhouse loomed and then dropped back into the mist. The barn door screeched as he opened it, a thing it never did in the daytime. Jody went to the rack and found a lantern and a tin box of matches. He lighted the wick and walked down the long straw-covered aisle to Nellie's stall. She was standing up. Her whole body weaved from side to side. Jody called to her, "So, Nellie, so-o, Nellie," but she did not stop her swaying nor look around. When he stepped into the stall and touched her on the shoulder she shivered under his hand. Then Billy Buck's voice came from the hayloft right above the stall.

"Jody, what are you doing?"

Jody started back and turned miserable eyes up toward the nest where Billy was lying in the hay. "Is she all right, do you think?"

"Why sure, I think so."

"You won't let anything happen, Billy, you're sure you won't?"

Billy growled down at him, "I told you I'd call you, and I will.

Now you get back to bed and stop worrying that mare. She's got enough to do without you worrying her."

Jody cringed, for he had never heard Billy speak in such a tone. "I only thought I'd come and see," he said. "I woke up."

Billy softened a little then. "Well, you get to bed. I don't want you bothering her. I told you I'd get you a good colt. Get along now."

Jody walked slowly out of the barn. He blew out the lantern and set it in the rack. The blackness of the night, and the chilled mist struck him and enfolded him. He wished he believed everything Billy said as he had before the pony died. It was a moment before his eyes, blinded by the feeble lantern-flame, could make any form of the darkness. The damp ground chilled his bare feet. At the cypress tree the roosting turkeys chattered a little in alarm, and the two good dogs responded to their duty and came charging out, barking to frighten away the coyotes they thought were prowling under the tree.

As he crept through the kitchen, Jody stumbled over a chair. Carl called from his bedroom, "Who's there? What's the matter there?"

And Mrs. Tiflin said sleepily, "What's the matter, Carl?"

The next second Carl came out of the bedroom carrying a candle, and found Jody before he could get into bed. "What are you doing out?"

Jody turned shyly away. "I was down to see the mare."

For a moment anger at being awakened fought with approval in Jody's father. "Listen," he said, finally, "there's not a man in this country that knows more about colts than Billy. You leave it to him."

Words burst out of Jody's mouth. "But the pony died——"

"Don't you go blaming that on him," Carl said sternly. "If Billy can't save a horse, it can't be saved."

Mrs. Tiflin called, "Make him clean his feet and go to bed, Carl. He'll be sleepy all day tomorrow."

It seemed to Jody that he had just closed his eyes to try to go to sleep when he was shaken violently by the shoulder. Billy Buck stood beside him, holding a lantern in his hand. "Get up," he said. "Hurry up." He turned and walked quickly out of the room.

Mrs. Tiflin called, "What's the matter? Is that you, Billy?"

"Yes, ma'am."

"Is Nellie ready?"

"Yes, ma'am."

"All right, I'll get up and heat some water in case you need it."

Jody jumped into his clothes so quickly that he was out the back door before Billy's swinging lantern was half way to the barn. There was a rim of dawn on the mountain-tops, but no light had penetrated into the cup of the ranch yet. Jody ran frantically after the lantern and caught up to Billy just as he reached the barn. Billy hung the lantern to a nail on the stall-side and took off his blue denim coat. Jody saw that he wore only a sleeveless shirt under it.

Nellie was standing rigid and stiff. While they watched, she crouched. Her whole body was wrung with a spasm. The spasm passed. But in a few moments it started over again, and passed.

Billy muttered nervously, "There's something wrong." His bare hand disappeared. "Oh, Jesus," he said. "It's wrong."

The spasm came again, and this time Billy strained, and the muscles stood out on his arm and shoulder. He heaved strongly, his forehead beaded with perspiration. Nellie cried with pain. Billy was muttering, "It's wrong. I can't turn it. It's way wrong. It's turned all around wrong."

He glared wildly toward Jody. And then his fingers made a careful, careful diagnosis. His cheeks were growing tight and grey. He looked for a long questioning minute at Jody standing back of the stall. Then Billy stepped to the rack under the manure window and picked up a horeshoe hammer with his wet right hand.

"Go outside, Jody," he said.

The boy stood still and stared dully at him.

"Go outside, I tell you. It'll be too late."

Jody didn't move.

Then Billy walked quickly to Nellie's head. He cried, "Turn your face away, damn you, turn your face."

This time Jody obeyed. His head turned sideways. He heard Billy whispering hoarsely in the stall. And then he heard a hollow crunch of bone. Nellie chuckled shrilly. Jody looked back in time to see the hammer rise and fall again on the flat forehead. Then Nellie fell heavily to her side and quivered for a moment.

Billy jumped to the swollen stomach; his big pocket-knife was in his hand. He lifted the skin and drove the knife in. He sawed and ripped at the tough belly. The air filled with the sick odor of warm living entrails. The other horses reared back against their halter chains and squealed and kicked.

Billy dropped the knife. Both of his arms plunged into the terrible ragged hole and dragged out a big, white, dripping bundle. His teeth tore a hole in the covering. A little black head appeared through the tear, and little slick, wet ears. A gurgling breath was drawn, and then another. Billy shucked off the sac and found his knife and cut the string. For a moment he held the little black colt in his arms and looked at it. And then he walked slowly over and laid it in the straw at Jody's feet.

Billy's face and arms and chest were dripping red. His body shivered and his teeth chattered. His voice was gone; he spoke in a throaty whisper. "There's your colt. I promised. And there it is. I had to do it—had to." He stopped and looked over his shoulder into the box stall. "Go get hot water and a sponge," he whispered. "Wash him and dry him the way his mother would. You'll have to feed him by hand. But there's your colt, the way I promised."

Jody stared stupidly at the wet, panting foal. It stretched out its chin and tried to raise its head. Its blank eyes were navy blue.

"God damn you," Billy shouted, "will you go now for the water? *Will you go?*"

Then Jody turned and trotted out of the barn into the dawn. He ached from his throat to his stomach. His legs were stiff and heavy. He tried to be glad because of the colt, but the bloody face, and the haunted, tired eyes of Billy Buck hung in the air ahead of him.

H. L. Davis

Open Winter

THE DRYING EAST WIND, which always brought hard luck to Eastern Oregon at whatever season it blew, had combed down the plateau grasslands through so much of the winter that it was hard to see any sign of grass ever having grown on them. Even though March had come, it still blew, drying the ground deep, shrinking the watercourses, beating back the clouds that might have delivered rain, and grinding coarse dust against the fifty-odd head of work horses that Pop Apling, with young Beech Cartwright helping, had brought down from his homestead to turn back into their home pasture while there was still something left of them.

The two men, one past sixty and the other around sixteen, shouldered the horses through the gate of the home pasture about dark, with lights beginning to shine out from the little freighting town across Three Notch Valley, and then they rode for the ranch house, knowing even before they drew up outside the yard that they had picked the wrong time to come. The house was too dark, and the corrals and outbuildings too still, for a place that anybody lived in.

There were sounds, but they were of shingles flapping in the wind, a windmill running loose and sucking noisily at a well that it had already pumped empty, a door that kept banging shut and dragging open again. The haystacks were gone, the stackyard fence had dwindled to a few naked posts, and the entire pasture was as bare and as hard as a floor all the way down into the valley.

The prospect looked so hopeless that the herd horses refused even to explore it, and merely stood with their tails turned to the wind, waiting to see what was to happen to them next.

Old Apling went poking inside the house, thinking somebody might have left a note or that the men might have run down to the saloon in town for an hour or two. He came back, having used up

From H. L. Davis, *Team Bells Woke Me and Other Stories.* (New York: William Morrow and Company, 1953), pp. 3–33. First published in *The Saturday Evening Post,* CCXI (May 6, 1939), 12–13, 112–120.

73

all his matches and stopped the door from banging, and said the place appeared to have been handed back to the Government, or maybe the mortgage company.

"You can trust old Ream Gervais not to be any place where anybody wants him," Beech said. He had hired out to herd for Ream Gervais over the winter. That entitled him to be more critical than old Apling, who had merely contracted to supply the horse herd with feed and pasture for the season at so much per head. "Well, my job was to help herd these steeds while you had 'em, and to help deliver 'em back when you got through with 'em, and here they are. I've put in a week on 'em that I won't ever git paid for, and it won't help anything to sit around and watch 'em try to live on fence pickets. Let's git out."

Old Apling looked at the huddle of horses, at the naked slope with a glimmer of light still on it, and at the lights of the town twinkling in the wind. He said it wasn't his place to tell any man what to do, but that he wouldn't feel quite right to dump the horses and leave.

"I agreed to see that they got delivered back here, and I'd feel better about if if I could locate somebody to deliver 'em to," he said. "I'd like to ride across to town yonder, and see if there ain't somebody that knows something about 'em. You could hold 'em together here till I git back. We ought to look the fences over before we pull out, and you can wait here as well as anywhere else."

"I can't, but go ahead," Beech said. "I don't like to have 'em stand around and look at me when I can't do anything to help 'em out. They'd have been better off if we'd turned 'em out of your homestead and let 'em run loose on the country. There was more grass up there than there is here."

"There wasn't enough to feed 'em, and I'd have had all my neighbors down on me for it," old Apling said. "You'll find out one of these days that if a man aims to live in this world he's got to git along with the people in it. I'd start a fire and thaw out a little and git that pack horse unloaded, if I was you."

He rode down the slope, leaning low and forward to ease the drag of the wind on his tired horse. Beech heard the sound of the road gate being let down and put up again, the beat of hoofs in the hard road, and then nothing but the noises around him as the wind went through its usual process of easing down for the night to make room for the frost. Loose boards settled into place, the windmill clacked to a stop and began to drip water into a puddle, and the herd horses shifted around facing Beech, as if anxious not to miss anything he did.

He pulled off some fence pickets and built a fire, unsaddled his pony and unloaded the pack horse, and got out what was left of a sack of grain and fed them both, standing the herd horses off with a fence picket until they had finished eating.

That was strictly fair, for the pack horse and the saddle pony had worked harder and carried more weight than any of the herd animals, and the grain was little enough to even them up for it. Nevertheless, he felt mean at having to club animals away from food when they were hungry, and they crowded back and eyed the grain sack so wistfully that he carried it inside the yard and stored it down in the root cellar behind the house, so it wouldn't prey on their minds. Then he dumped another armload of fence pickets on to the fire and sat down to wait for old Apling.

The original mistake, he reflected, had been when old Apling took the Gervais horses to feed at the beginning of winter. Contracting to feed them had been well enough, for he had nursed up a stand of bunch grass on his homestead that would have carried an ordinary pack of horses with only a little extra feeding to help out in the roughest weather. But the Gervais horses were all big harness stock, they had pulled in half starved, and they had taken not much over three weeks to clean off the pasture that old Apling had expected would last them at least two months. Nobody would have blamed him for backing out on his agreement then, since he had only undertaken to feed the horses, not to treat them for malnutrition.

Beech wanted him to back out of it, but he refused to, said the stockmen had enough troubles without having that added to them, and started feeding out his hay and insisting that the dry wind couldn't possibly keep up much longer, because it wasn't in Nature.

By the time it became clear that Nature had decided to take in a little extra territory, the hay was all fed out, and, since there couldn't be any accommodation about letting the horses starve to death, he consented to throw the contract over and bring them back where they belonged.

The trouble with most of old Apling's efforts to be accommodating was that they did nobody any good. His neighbors would have been spared all their uneasiness if he had never brought in the horses to begin with. Gervais wouldn't have been any worse off, since he stood to lose them anyway; the horses could have starved to death as gracefully in November as in March, and old Apling would have been ahead a great deal of carefully accumulated bunch grass and two big stacks of extortionately valuable hay. Nobody had gained by his chivalrousness; he had lost by it, and yet he liked it so well that he couldn't stand to leave the horses until he had raked the country for somebody to hand the worthless brutes over to.

Beech fed sticks into the fire and felt out of patience with a man who could stick to his mistakes even after he had been cleaned out by them. He heard the road gate open and shut, and he knew by the draggy-sounding plod of old Apling's horse that the news from town was going to be bad.

Old Apling rode past the fire and over to the picket fence, got off as if he was trying to make it last, tied his horse carefully as if he expected the knot to last a month, and unsaddled and did up his latigo and folded his saddle blanket as if he was fixing them to put in a show window. He remarked that his horse had been given a bait of grain in town and wouldn't need feeding again, and then he began to work down to what he had found out.

"If you think things look bad along this road, you ought to see that town," he said. "All the sheep gone and all the ranches deserted and no trade to run on and their water threatenin' to give out. They've got a little herd of milk cows that they keep up for their children, and to hear 'em talk you'd think it was an ammunition supply that they expected to stand off hostile Indians with. They said Gervais pulled out of here around a month ago. All his men quit him, so he bunched his sheep and took 'em down to the railroad, where he could ship in hay for 'em. Sheep will be a price this year, and you won't be able to buy a lamb for under twelve dollars except at a fire sale. Horses ain't in much demand. There's been a lot of 'em turned out wild, and everybody wants to git rid of 'em."

"I didn't drive this bunch of pelters any eighty miles against the wind to git a market report," Beech said. "You didn't find anybody to turn 'em over to, and Gervais didn't leave any word about what he wanted done with 'em. You've probably got it figured out that you ought to trail 'em a hundred and eighty miles to the railroad, so his feelings won't be hurt, and you're probably tryin' to study how you can work me in on it, and you might as well save your time. I've helped you with your accommodation jobs long enough. I've quit, and it would have been a whole lot better for you if I'd quit sooner."

Old Apling said he could understand that state of feeling, which didn't mean that he shared it.

"It wouldn't be as much of a trick to trail down to the railroad as a man might think," he said, merely to settle a question of fact. "We couldn't make it by the road in a starve-out year like this, but there's old Indian trails back on the ridge where any man has got a right to take livestock whenever he feels like it. Still, as long as you're set against it, I'll meet you halfway. We'll trail these horses down the ridge to a grass patch where I used to corral cattle when I was in the business, and we'll leave 'em there. It'll be enough so they won't starve, and I'll ride on down and notify Gervais where they are, and you can go where you please. It wouldn't be fair to do less than that, to my notion."

Ream Gervais triggered me out of a week's pay," Beech said. "It ain't much, but he swindled you on that pasture contract too. If you expect me to trail his broken-down horses ninety miles down this ridge when they ain't worth anything, you've turned in a poor guess. You'll have to think of a better argument than that if you aim to gain any ground with me."

"Ream Gervais don't count in this," old Apling said. "What does he care about these horses, when he ain't even left word what he wants done with 'em? What counts is you, and I don't have to think up any better argument, because I've already got one. You may not realize it, but you and me are responsible for these horses till they're delivered to their owner, and if we turn 'em loose here to bust fences and overrun that town and starve to death in the middle of it, we'll land in the pen. It's against the law to let horses starve to death, did you know that? If you pull out of here I'll pull out right along with you, and I'll have every man in that town after you before the week's out. You'll have a chance to git some action on that pistol of yours, if you're careful."

Beech said he wasn't intimidated by that kind of talk, and threw a couple of handfuls of dirt on the fire, so it wouldn't look so conspicuous. His pistol was an old single-action relic with its grips tied on with fish line and no trigger, so that it had to be operated by flipping the hammer. The spring was weak, so that sometimes it took several flips to get off one shot. Suggesting that he might use such a thing to stand off any pack of grim-faced pursuers was about the same as saying that he was simple-minded. As far as he could see, his stand was entirely sensible, and even humane.

"It ain't that I don't feel sorry for these horses, but they ain't fit to travel," he said. "They wouldn't last twenty miles. I don't see how it's any worse to let 'em stay here than to walk 'em to death down that ridge."

"They make less trouble for people if you keep 'em on the move," old Apling said. "It's something you can't be cinched for in court, and it makes you feel better afterwards to know that you tried everything you could. Suit yourself about it, though. I ain't beggin' you to do it. If you'd sooner pull out and stand the consequences, it's you for it. Before you go, what did you do with that sack of grain?"

Beech had half a notion to leave, just to see how much of that dark threatening would come to pass. He decided that it wouldn't be worth it. "I'll help you trail the blamed skates as far as they'll last, if you've got to be childish about it," he said. "I put the grain in a root cellar behind the house, so the rats wouldn't git into it. It looked like the only safe place around here. There was about a half a ton of old sprouted potatoes ricked up in it that didn't look like they'd been bothered for twenty years. They had sprouts on 'em—" He stopped, noticing that old Apling kept staring at him as if something was wrong. "Good Lord, potatoes ain't good for horse feed, are they? They had sprouts on 'em a foot long!"

Old Apling shook his head resignedly and got up. "We wouldn't ever find anything if it wasn't for you," he said. "We wouldn't ever git any good out of it if it wasn't for me, so maybe we make a team. Show me where that root cellar is, and we'll pack them spuds out and spread 'em around so the horses can git started on 'em. We'll git this herd through to grassland yet, and it'll be something you'll never be ashamed of. It ain't everybody your age gits a chance to do a thing like this, and you'll thank me for holdin' you to it before you're through."

II

They climbed up by an Indian trail onto a high stretch of tableland, so stony and scored with rock breaks that nobody had ever tried to cultivate it, but so high that it sometimes caught moisture from the atmosphere that the lower elevations missed. Part of it had been doled out among the Indians as allotment lands, which none of them ever bothered to lay claim to, but the main spread of it belonged to the nation, which was too busy to notice it.

The pasture was thin, though reliable, and it was so scantily watered and so rough and broken that in ordinary years nobody bothered to bring stock onto it. The open winter had spoiled most of that seclusion. There was no part of the trail that didn't have at least a dozen new bed grounds for lambed ewes in plain view, easily picked out of the landscape because of the little white flags stuck up around them to keep sheep from straying out and coyotes from straying in during the night. The sheep were pasturing down the draws out of the wind, where they couldn't be seen. There were no herders visible, not any startling amount of grass, and no water except a mud tank thrown up to catch a little spring for one of the camps.

They tried to water the horses in it, but it had taken up the flavor of sheep, so that not a horse in the herd would touch it. It was too near dark to waste time reasoning with them about it, so old Apling headed them down into a long rock break and across it to a tangle of wild cherry and mountain mahogany that lasted for several miles and ended in a grass clearing among some dwarf cottonwoods with a mud puddle in the center of it.

The grass had been grazed over, though not closely, and there were sheep tracks around the puddle that seemed to be fresh, for the horses, after sniffing the water, decided that they could wait a while longer. They spread out to graze, and Beech remarked that he couldn't see where it was any improvement over the tickle-grass homesteads.

"The grass may be better, but there ain't as much of it, and the water ain't any good if they won't drink it," he said. "Well, do you intend to leave 'em here, or have you got some wrinkle figured out to make me help trail 'em on down to the railroad?"

Old Apling stood the sarcasm unresistingly. "It would be better to trail 'em to the railroad, now that we've got this far," he said. "I won't ask you to do that much, because it's outside of what you agreed to. This place has changed since I was here last, but we'll make it do, and that water ought to clear up fit to drink before long. You can settle down here for a few days while I ride around and fix it up with the sheep camps to let the horses stay here. We've got to do that, or they're liable to think it's some wild bunch and start shootin' 'em. Somebody's got to stay with 'em, and I can git along with these herders better than you can."

"If you've got any sense, you'll let them sheep outfits alone," Beech said. "They don't like tame horses on this grass any better than they do wild ones, and they won't make any more bones about shootin' 'em if they find out they're in here. It's a hard place to find, and they'll stay close on account of the water, and you'd better pull out and let 'em have it to themselves. That's what I aim to do."

"You've done what you agreed to, and I ain't got any right to hold you any longer," old Apling said, "I wish I could. You're wrong about them sheep outfits. I've got as much right to pasture this ridge as they have, and they know it, and nobody ever lost anything by actin' sociable with people."

"Somebody will before very long," Beech said. "I've got relatives in the sheep business, and I know what they're like. You'll land yourself in trouble, and I don't want to be around when you do it. I'm pullin' out of here in the morning, and if you had any sense you'd pull out along with me."

There were several things that kept Beech from getting much sleep during the night. One was the attachment that the horses showed for his sleeping place; they stuck so close that he could almost feel their breath on him, could hear the soft breaking sound that the grass made as they pulled it, the sound of their swallowing, the jar of the ground under him when one of the horses changed ground, the peaceful regularity of their eating, as if they didn't have to bother about anything so long as they kept old Apling in sight.

Another irritating thing was old Apling's complete freedom from
uneasiness. He ought by rights to have felt more worried about the
future than Beech did, but he slept, with the hard ground for a bed
and his hard saddle for a pillow and the horses almost stepping on
him every minute or two, as soundly as if the entire trip had come
out exactly to suit him and there was nothing ahead but plain sailing.

His restfulness was so hearty and so unjustifiable that Beech
couldn't sleep for feeling indignant about it, and got up and left
about daylight to keep from being exposed to any more of it. He left
without waking old Apling, because he saw no sense in a leave-tak-
ing that would consist merely in repeating his common-sense warn-
ings and having them ignored, and he was so anxious to get clear of
the whole layout that he didn't even take along anything to eat.
The only thing he took from the pack was his ramshackle old pistol;
there was no holster for it, and, in the hope that he might get a
chance to use it on a loose quail or prairie chicken, he stowed it in
an empty flour sack and hung it on his saddle horn, a good deal like
an old squaw heading for the far blue distances with a bundle of
diapers.

III

There was never anything recreational about traveling a rock desert at any season of the year, and the combination of spring gales,
winter chilliness and summer drought all striking at once brought it
fairly close to hard punishment. Beech's saddle pony, being jaded at
the start with overwork and underfeeding and no water, broke down
in the first couple of miles, and got so feeble and tottery that Beech
had to climb off and lead him, searching likely-looking thickets all
the way down the gully in the hope of finding some little trickle
that he wouldn't be too finicky to drink.

The nearest he came to it was a fair-sized rock sink under some
big half-budded cottonwoods that looked, by its dampness and the
abundance of fresh animal tracks around it, as if it might have held
water recently, but of water there was none, and even digging a hole
in the center of the basin failed to fetch a drop.

The work of digging, hill climbing and scrambling through brush
piles raised Beech's appetite so powerfully that he could scarcely
hold up, and, a little above where the gully opened into the flat
sagebrush plateau, he threw away his pride, pistoled himself a jack
rabbit, and took it down into the sagebrush to cook, where his fire
wouldn't give away which gully old Apling was camped in.

Jack rabbit didn't stand high as a food. It was considered an excellent thing to give men in the last stages of famine, because they weren't likely to injure themselves by eating too much of it, but for ordinary occasions it was looked down on, and Beech covered his trail out of the gully and built his cooking fire in the middle of a high stand of sagebrush, so as not to be embarrassed by inquisitive visitors.

The meat cooked up strong, as it always did, but he ate what he needed of it, and he was wrapping the remainder in his flour sack to take along with him when a couple of men rode past, saw his pony, and turned in to look him over.

They looked him over so closely and with so little concern for his privacy that he felt insulted before they even spoke.

He studied them less openly, judging by their big gallon canteens that they were out on some long scout.

One of them was some sort of hired hand, by his looks; he was broad-faced and gloomy-looking, with a fine white horse, a flower-stamped saddle, an expensive rifle scabbarded under his knee, and a fifteen-dollar saddle blanket, while his own manly form was set off by a yellow hotel blanket and a ninety-cent pair of overalls.

The other man had on a store suit, a plain black hat, fancy stitched boots, and a white shirt and necktie, and rode a burr-tailed Indian pony and an old wrangling saddle with a loose horn. He carried no weapons in sight, but there was a narrow strap across the lower spread of his necktie which indicated the presence of a shoulder holster somewhere within reach.

He opened the conversation by inquiring where Beech had come from, what his business was, where he was going and why he hadn't taken the county road to go there, and why he had to eat jack rabbit when the country was littered with sheep camps where he could get a decent meal by asking for it?

"I come from the upper country," Beech said, being purposely vague about it. "I'm travelin', and I stopped here because my horse give out. He won't drink out of any place that's had sheep in it, and he's gone short of water till he breaks down easy."

"There's a place corralled in for horses to drink at down at my lower camp," the man said, and studied Beech's pony. "There's no reason for you to bum through the country on jack rabbit in a time like this. My herder can take you down to our water hole and see that you get fed and put to work till you can make a stake for yourself. I'll give you a note. That pony looks like he had Ream Gervais' brand on him. Do you know anything about that herd of old work horses he's been pasturing around?"

"I don't know anything about him," Beech said, sidestepping the actual question while he thought over the offer of employment. He could have used a stake, but the location didn't strike him favorably. It was too close to old Apling's camp, he could see trouble ahead over the horse herd, and he didn't want to be around when it started. "If you'll direct me how to find your water, I'll ride on down there, but I don't need anybody to go with me, and I don't need any stake. I'm travelin'."

The man said there wasn't anybody so well off that he couldn't use a stake, and that it would be hardly any trouble at all for Beech to get one. "I want you to understand how we're situated around here, so you won't think we're any bunch of stranglers," he said. "You can see what kind of a year this has been, when we have to run lambed ewes in a rock patch like this. We've got five thousand lambs in here that we're trying to bring through, and we've had to fight the blamed wild horses for this pasture since the day we moved in. A horse that ain't worth hell room will eat as much as two dozen sheep worth twenty dollars, with the lambs, so you can see how it figures out. We've got 'em pretty well thinned out, but one of my packers found a trail of a new bunch that came up from around Three Notch within the last day or two, and we don't want them to feel as if we'd neglected them. We'd like to find out where they lit. You wouldn't have any information about 'em?"

"None that would do you any good to know," Beech said. "I know the man with that horse herd, and it ain't any use to let on that I don't, but it wouldn't be any use to try to deal with him. He don't sell out on a man he works for."

"He might be induced to," the man said. "We'll find him anyhow, but I don't like to take too much time to it. Just for instance, now, suppose you knew that pony of yours would have to go thirsty till you gave us a few directions about that horse herd? You'd be stuck here for quite a spell, wouldn't you?"

He was so pleasant about it that it took Beech a full minute to realize that he was being threatened. The heavy-set herder brought that home to him by edging out into a flank position and hoisting his rifle scabbard so it could be reached in a hurry. Beech removed the cooked jack rabbit from his flour sack carefully, a piece at a time, and, with the same mechanical thoughtfulness, brought out his triggerless old pistol, cut down on the pleasant-spoken man and hauled back on the hammer and held it posed.

"That herder of yours had better go easy on his rifle," he said, trying to keep his voice from trembling. "This pistol shoots if I don't hold back the hammer, and if he knocks me out I'll have to let go of it. You'd better watch him, if you don't want your tack drove. I won't give you no directions about that horse herd, and this pony of mine won't go thirsty for it, either. Loosen them canteens of yours and let 'em drop on the ground. Drop that rifle scabbard back where it belongs, and unbuckle the straps and let go of it. If either of you tries any funny business, there'll be one of you to pack home, heels first."

The quaver in his voice sounded childish and undignified to him, but it had a more businesslike ring to them than any amount of manly gruffness. The herder unbuckled his rifle scabbard, and they both cast loose their canteen straps, making it last as long as they could while they argued with him, not angrily, but as if he was a dull stripling whom they wanted to save from some foolishness that he was sure to regret. They argued ethics, justice, common sense, his future prospects, and the fact that what he was doing amounted to robbery by force and arms and that it was his first fatal step into a probably unsuccessful career of crime. They worried over him, they explained to him, and they ridiculed him.

They managed to make him feel like several kinds of a fool, and they were so pleasant and concerned about it that they came close to breaking him down. What held him steady was the thought of old Apling waiting up the gully.

"That herder with the horses never sold out on any man, and I won't sell out on him," he said. "You've said your say and I'm tired of holdin' this pistol on cock for you, so move along out of here. Keep to open ground, so I can be sure you're gone, and don't be in too much of a hurry to come back. I've got a lot of things I want to think over, and I want to be let alone while I do it."

IV

He did have some thinking that needed tending to, but he didn't take time for it. When the men were well out of range, he emptied their canteens into his hat and let his pony drink. Then he hung the canteens and the scabbarded rifle on a bush and rode back up the gully where the horse camp was, keeping to shaly ground so as not to leave any tracks. It was harder going up than it had been coming down.

He had turned back from the scene of his run-in with the two sheepmen about noon, and he was still a good two miles from the camp when the sun went down, the wind lulled and the night frost began to bite at him so hard that he dismounted and walked to get warm. That raised his appetite again, and, as if by some special considerateness of Nature, the cottonwoods around him seemed to be alive with jack rabbits heading down into the pitch-dark gully where he had fooled away valuable time trying to find water that morning.

They didn't stimulate his hunger much; for a time they even made him feel less like eating anything. Then his pony gave out and had to rest, and noticing that the cottonwoods around him were beginning to bud out, he remembered that peeling the bark off in the budding season would fetch out a foamy, sweet-tasting sap which, among children of the plateau country, was considered something of a delicacy.

He cut a blaze on a fair-sized sapling, waited ten minutes or so, and touched his finger to it to see how much sap had accumulated. None had; the blaze was moist to his touch, but scarcely more so than when he had whittled it.

It wasn't important enough to do any bothering about, and yet a whole set of observed things began to draw together in his mind and form themselves into an explanation of something he had puzzled over: the fresh animal tracks he had seen around the rock sink when there wasn't any water; the rabbits going down into the gully; the cottonwoods in which the sap rose enough during the day to produce buds and got driven back at night when the frost set in. During the day, the cottonwoods had drawn the water out of the ground for themselves; at night they stopped drawing it, and it drained out into the rock sink for the rabbits.

It all worked out so simply that he led his pony down into the gully to see how much there was in it, and, losing his footing on the steep slope, coasted down into the rock sink in the dark and landed in water and thin mud up to his knees. He led his pony down into it to drink, which seemed little enough to get back for the time he had fooled away on it, and then he headed for the horse camp, which was all too easily discernible by the plume of smoke rising, white and ostentatious, against the dark sky from old Apling's campfire.

He made the same kind of entrance that old Apling usually affected when bringing some important item of news. He rode past the campfire and pulled up at a tree, got off deliberately, knocked an accumulation of dead twigs from his hat, took off his saddle and bridle and balanced them painstakingly in the tree fork, and said it was affecting to see how widespread the shortage of pasture was.

"It generally is," old Apling said. "I had a kind of a notion you'd be back after you'd had time to study things over. I suppose you got into some kind of a rumpus with some of them sheep outfits. What was it? Couldn't you git along with them, or couldn't they hit it off with you?"

"There wasn't any trouble between them and me," Beech said. "The only point we had words over was you. They wanted to know where you was camped, so they could shoot you up, and I didn't think it was right to tell 'em. I had to put a gun on a couple of 'em before they'd believe I meant business, and that was all there was to it. They're out after you now, and they can see the smoke of this fire of yours for twenty miles, so they ought to be along almost any time now. I thought I'd come back and see you work your sociability on 'em."

"You probably kicked up a squabble with 'em yourself," old Apling said. He looked a little uneasy. "You talked right up to 'em, I'll bet, and slapped their noses with your hat to show 'em that they couldn't run over you. Well, what's done is done. You did come back, and maybe they'd have jumped us anyway. There ain't much that we can do. The horses have got to have water before they can travel, and they won't touch that seep. It ain't cleared up a particle."

"You can put that fire out, not but what the whole country has probably seen the smoke from it already," Beech said. "If you've got to tag after these horses, you can run 'em off down the draw and keep 'em to the brush where they won't leave a trail. There's some young cottonwood bark that they can eat if they have to, and there's water in a rock sink under some big cottonwood trees. I'll stay here and hold off anybody that shows up, so you'll have time to git your tracks covered."

Old Apling went over and untied the flour-sacked pistol from Beech's saddle, rolled it into his blankets, and sat down on it. "If there's any holdin' off to be done, I'll do it," he said. "You're a little too high-spirited to suit me, and a little too hasty about your conclusions. I looked over that rock sink down the draw today, and there wasn't anything in it but mud, and blamed little of that. Somebody had dug for water, and there wasn't none."

"There is now," Beech said. He tugged off one of his wet boots and poured about a pint of the disputed fluid on the ground. "There wasn't any in the daytime because the cottonwoods took it all. They let up when it turns cold, and it runs back in. I waded in it."

He started to put his boot back on. Old Apling reached out and took it, felt of it inside and out, and handed it over as if performing some ceremonial presentation.

"I'd never have figured out a thing like that in this world," he said. "If we git them horses out of here, it'll be you that done it. We'll bunch 'em and work 'em down there. It won't be no picnic, but we'll make out to handle it somehow. We've got to, after a thing like this."

Beech remembered what had occasioned the discovery, and said he would have to have something to eat first. "I want you to keep in mind that it's you I'm doin' this for," he said. "I don't owe that old groundhog of a Ream Gervais anything. The only thing I hate about this is that it'll look like I'd done him a favor."

"He won't take it for one, I guess," old Apling said. "We've got to git these horses out because it'll be a favor to you. You wouldn't want to have it told around that you'd done a thing like findin' that water, and then have to admit that we'd lost all the horses anyhow. We can't lose 'em. You've acted like a man tonight, and I'll be blamed if I'll let you spoil it for any childish spite."

They got the horses out none too soon. Watering them took a long time, and when they finally did consent to call it enough and climb back up the side hill, Beech and old Apling heard a couple of signal shots from the direction of their old camping place, and saw a big glare mount up into the sky from it as the visitors built up their campfire to look the locality over. The sight was almost comforting; if they had to keep away from a pursuit, it was at least something to know where it was.

V

From then on they followed a grab-and-run policy, scouting ahead before they moved, holding to the draws by day and crossing open ground only after dark, never pasturing over a couple of hours in any one place, and discovering food value in outlandish substances —rock lichens, the sprouts of wild plum and serviceberry, the moss of old trees and the bark of some young ones—that neither they nor the horses had ever considered fit to eat before. When they struck Boulder River Canyon they dropped down and toenailed their way along one side of it where they could find grass and water with less likelihood of having trouble about it.

The breaks of the canyon were too rough to run new-lambed sheep in, and they met with so few signs of occupancy that old Apling got overconfident, neglected his scouting to tie back a break they had been obliged to make in a line fence, and ran the horse herd right over the top of a camp where some men were branding calves, tearing down a cook tent and part of a corral and scattering cattle and bedding from the river all the way to the top of the canyon.

By rights, they should have sustained some damage for that piece of carelessness, but they drove through fast, and they were out of sight around a shoulder of rimrock before any of the men could get themselves picked up. Somebody did throw a couple of shots after them as they were pulling into a thicket of mock orange and chokecherry, but it was only with a pistol, and he probably did it more to relieve his feelings than with any hope of hitting anything.

They were so far out of range that they couldn't even hear where the bullets landed.

Neither of them mentioned that unlucky run-in all the rest of that day. They drove hard, punished the horses savagely when they lagged, and kept them at it until, a long time after dark, they struck an old rope ferry that crossed Boulder River at a place called, in memory of its original founders, Robbers' Roost.

The ferry wasn't a public carrier, and there was not even any main road down to it. It was used by the ranches in the neighborhood as the only means of crossing the river for fifty miles in either direction, and it was tied in to a log with a good solid chain and padlock. It was a way to cross, and neither of them could see anything else but to take it.

Beech favored waiting for daylight for it, pointing out that there was a ranch light half a mile up the slope, and that if anybody caught them hustling a private ferry in the dead of night they would probably be taken for criminals on the dodge. Old Apling said it was altogether likely, and drew Beech's pistol and shot the padlock apart with it.

"They could hear that up at that ranch house," Beech said. "What if they come pokin' down here to see what we're up to?"

Old Apling tossed the fragments of padlock into the river and hung the pistol in the waistband of his trousers. "Let 'em come," he said. "They'll go back again with their fingers in their mouths. This is your trip, and you put in good work on it, and I like to ruined the whole thing stoppin' to patch an eighty-cent fence so some scissorbill wouldn't have his feelings hurt, and that's the last accommodation anybody gits out of me till this is over with. I can take about six horses at a trip, it looks like. Help me to bunch 'em."

Six horses at a trip proved to be an overestimate. The best they could do was five, and the boat rode so deep with them that Beech refused to risk handling it. He stayed with the herd, and old Apling cut it loose, let the current sweep it across into slack water, and hauled it in to the far bank by winding in its cable on an old home made capstan. Then he turned the horses into a counting pen and came back for another load.

He worked at it fiercely, as if he had a bet up that he could wear the whole ferry rig out, but it went with infernal slowness, and when the wind began to move for daylight there were a dozen horses still to cross and no place to hide them in case the ferry had other customers.

Beech waited and fidgeted over small noises until, hearing voices and the clatter of hoofs on shale far up the canyon behind him, he gave way, drove the remaining horses into the river, and swam them

across, letting himself be towed along by his saddle horn and floating his clothes ahead of him on a board.

He paid for that flurry of nervousness before he got out. The
water was so cold it paralyzed him, and so swift it whisked him a
mile downstream before he could get his pony turned to breast it.
He grounded on a gravel bar in a thicket of dwarf willows, with
numbness striking clear to the center of his diaphragm and deaden-
ing his arms so he couldn't pick his clothes loose from the bundle to
put on. He managed it, by using his teeth and elbows, and warmed
himself a little by driving the horses afoot through the brush till he
struck the ferry landing.

It had got light enough to see things in outline, and old Apling
was getting ready to shove off for another crossing when the procession came lumbering at him out of the shadows. He came ashore,
counted the horses into the corral to make sure none had drowned,
and laid Beech under all the blankets and built up a fire to limber
him out by. He got breakfast and got packed to leave, and he did
some rapid expounding about the iniquity of risking the whole trip
on such a wild piece of foolhardiness.

"That was the reason I wanted you to work this boat," he said. "I
could have stood up to anybody that come projectin' around, and if
they wanted trouble I could have filled their order for 'em. They
won't bother us now, anyhow; it don't matter how bad they want
to."

"I could have stood up to 'em if I'd had anything to do it with,"
Beech said. "You've got that pistol of mine, and I couldn't see to
throw rocks. What makes you think they won't bother us? You know
it was that brandin' crew comin' after us, don't you?"

"I expect that's who it was," old Apling agreed. "They ought to
be out after the cattle we scattered, but you can trust a bunch of
cowboys to pick out the most useless things to tend to first. I've got
that pistol of yours because I don't aim for you to git in trouble
with it while this trip is on. There won't anybody bother us because I've cut all the cables on the ferry, and it's lodged downstream
on a gravel spit. If anybody crosses after us within fifty miles of here,
he'll swim, and the people around here ain't as reckless around cold
water as you are."

Beech sat up "We got to git out of here," he said. "There's people
on this side of the river that use that ferry, you old fool, and they'll
have us up before every grand jury in the country from now on. The
horses ain't worth it."

"What the horses is worth ain't everything," old Apling said.
"There's a part of this trip ahead that you'll be glad you went
through. You're entitled to that much out of it, after the work

you've put in, and I aim to see that you git it. It ain't any use tryin' to explain to you what it is. You'll notice it when the time comes."

VI

They worked north, following the breaks of the river canyon, finding the rock breaks hard to travel, but easy to avoid observation in, and the grass fair in stand, but so poor and washy in body that the horses had to spend most of their time eating enough to keep up their strength so they could move.

They struck a series of gorges, too deep and precipitous to be crossed at all, and had to edge back into milder country where there were patches of plowed ground, some being harrowed over for summer fallow and others venturing out with a bright new stand of dark-green wheat.

The pasture was patchy and scoured by the wind, and all the best parts of it were under fence, which they didn't dare cut for fear of getting in trouble with the natives. Visibility was high in that section; the ground lay open to the north as far as they could see, the wind kept the air so clear that it hurt to look at the sky, and they were never out of sight of wheat ranchers harrowing down summer fallow.

A good many of the ranchers pulled up and stared after the horse herd as it went past, and two or three times they waved and rode down toward the road, as if they wanted to make it an excuse for stopping work. Old Apling surmised that they had some warning they wanted to deliver against trespassing, and he drove on without waiting to hear it.

They were unable to find a camping place anywhere among those wheat fields, so they drove clear through to open country and spread down for the night alongside a shallow pond in the middle of some new grass not far enough along to be pastured, though the horses made what they could out of it. There were no trees or shrubs anywhere around, not even sagebrush. Lacking fuel for a fire, they camped without one, and since there was no grass anywhere except around the pond, they left the horses unguarded, rolled in to catch up sleep, and were awakened about daylight by the whole herd stampeding past them at a gallop.

They both got up and moved fast. Beech ran for his pony, which was trying to pull loose from its picket rope to go with the bunch. Old Apling ran out into the dust afoot, waggling the triggerless old pistol and trying to make out objects in the half-light by hard squinting. The herd horses fetched a long circle and came back past him, with a couple of riders clouting along behind trying to turn them back into open country. One of the riders opened up a rope and swung it, the other turned in and slapped the inside flankers with his hat, and old Apling hauled up the old pistol, flipped the hammer a couple of rounds to get it warmed up, and let go at them twice.

The half darkness held noise as if it had been a cellar. The two shots banged monstrously, Beech yelled to old Apling to be careful who he shot at, and the two men shied off sideways and rode away into the open country. One of them yelled something that sounded threatening in tone as they went out of sight, but neither of them seemed in the least inclined to bring on any general engagement. The dust blew clear, the herd horses came back to grass, old Apling looked at the pistol and punched the two exploded shells out of it, and Beech ordered him to hand it over before he got in trouble with it.

"How do you know but what them men had a right here?" he demanded sternly. "We'd be in a fine jack pot if you'd shot one of 'em and it turned out he owned this land we're on, wouldn't we?"

Old Apling looked at him, holding the old pistol poised as if he was getting ready to lead a band with it. The light strengthened and shed a rose-colored radiance over him, so he looked flushed and joyous and lifted up. With some of the dust knocked off him, he could have filled in easily as a day star and son of the morning, whiskers and all.

"I wouldn't have shot them men for anything you could buy me!" he said, and faced north to a blue line of bluffs that came up out of the shadows, a blue gleam of water that moved under them, a white steamboat that moved upstream, glittering as the first light struck it. "Them men wasn't here because we was trespassers. Them was horse thieves, boy! We've brought these horses to a place where they're worth stealin', and we've brought 'em through! The railroad is under them bluffs, and that water down there is the old Columbia River!"

They might have made it down to the river that day, but having it in sight and knowing that nothing could stop them from reaching it, there no longer seemed any object in driving so unsparingly. They ate breakfast and talked about starting, and they even got partly packed up for it. Then they got occupied with talking to a couple of wheat ranchers who pulled in to inquire about buying some of the horse herd; the drought had run up wheat prices at a time when the country's livestock had been allowed to run down, and so many horses had been shot and starved out that they were having to take pretty much anything they could get.

Old Apling swapped them a couple of the most jaded herd horses for part of a haystack, referred other applicants to Gervais down at the railroad, and spent the remainder of the day washing, patching clothes and saddlery, and watching the horses get acquainted once more with a conventional diet.

The next morning a rancher dropped off a note from Gervais urging them to come right on down, and adding a kind but firm admonition against running up any feed bills without his express permission. He made it sound as if there might be some hurry about catching the horse market on the rise, so they got ready to leave, and Beech looked back over the road they had come, thinking of all that had happened on it.

"I'd like it better if old Gervais didn't have to work himself in on the end of it," he said. "I'd like to step out on the whole business right now."

"You'd be a fool to do that," old Apling said. "This is outside your work contract, so we can make the old gopher pay you what it's worth. I'll want to go in ahead and see about that and about the money that he owes me and about corral space and feed and one thing and another, so I'll want you to bring 'em in alone. You ain't seen everything there is to a trip like this, and you won't unless you stay with it."

VII

There would be no ending to this story without an understanding of what that little river town looked like at the hour, a little before sundown of a windy spring day, when Beech brought the desert horse herd down into it. On the wharf below town, some men were unloading baled hay from a steamboat, with some passengers watching from the saloon deck, and the river beyond them hoisting into white-capped peaks that shone and shed dazzling spray over the darkening water.

A switch engine was handling stock cars on a spur track, and the brakeman flagged it to a stop and stood watching the horses, leaning into the wind to keep his balance while the engineer climbed out on the tender to see what was going on.

The street of the town was lined with big leafless poplars that looked as if they hadn't gone short of moisture a day of their lives; the grass under them was bright green, and there were women working around flower beds and pulling up weeds, enough of them so that a horse could have lived on them for two days.

There was a Chinaman clipping grass with a pair of sheep shears to keep it from growing too tall, and there were lawn sprinklers running clean water on the ground in streams. There were stores with windows full of new clothes, and stores with bright hardware, and stores with strings of bananas and piles of oranges, bread and crackers and candy and rows of hams, and there were groups of anxious-faced men sitting around stoves inside who came out to watch Beech pass and told one another hopefully that the back country might make a good year out of it yet, if a youngster could bring that herd of horses through it.

There were women who hauled back their children and cautioned them not to get in the man's way, and there were boys and girls, some near Beech's own age, who watched him and stood looking after him, knowing that he had been through more than they had ever seen and not suspecting that it had taught him something that they didn't know about the things they saw every day. None of them knew what it meant to be in a place where there were delicacies to eat and new clothes to wear and look at, what it meant to be warm and out of the wind for a change, what it could mean merely to have water enough to pour on the ground and grass enough to cut down and throw away.

For the first time, seeing how the youngsters looked at him, he understood what that amounted to. There wasn't a one of them who wouldn't have traded places with him. There wasn't one that he would have traded places with, for all the haberdashery and fancy groceries in town. He turned down to the corrals, and old Apling held the gate open for him and remarked that he hadn't taken much time to it.

"You're sure you had enough of that ridin' through town?" he said. "It ain't the same when you do it a second time, remember."

"It'll last me," Beech said. "I wouldn't have missed it, and I wouldn't want it to be the same again. I'd sooner have things the way they run with us out in the high country. I'd sooner not have anything be the same a second time."

3

Disenchantment

THE WORD "DISENCHANTMENT" may have a negative, even cynical connotation, suggesting disillusionment and the destruction of values. Yet sloughing off the illusions that enclose and protect a child's world is an inevitable part of growing up. In most initiation stories, and especially in the kind illustrated in this section, a young man moves from innocence to knowledge. The process was described by St. Paul almost 2000 years ago: "When I was a child, I spoke as a child, I understood as a child, I thought as a child; but when I became a man, I put away childish things." The narratives that follow involve the putting away of such "childish things" as fascination with a colorful profession, belief in a family's love and responsibility, admiration for an older playmate, trust in a father's invariable wisdom, respect for the values of white society, and enjoyment of upper-middle-class affluence California-style. In each story, the main character takes a step toward maturity as he sees through or beyond an illusion. Each of the stories represents the *process* of disillusionment. For instance, although Benjamin Braddock, the "anti-hero" of "Homecoming," has already lost many illusions, the reader senses that further disenchantment awaits him.

The surrender or rejection of illusions can be salutary, resulting in the acquisition, however painful, of self-knowledge. If John Steinbeck's *Grapes of Wrath* (1939) is analyzed in terms of Tom Joad, a self-discovery theme becomes evident. When the book opens, Tom has just been released from prison; he is tough and defiant and acknowledges no emotional ties except a casual affection for his family. The struggle to reach California, oppression by the authorities, and the murder of Jim Casy open his eyes; and at the close of the novel he resolves to devote his life to combatting injustice on behalf of his fellowmen. Similarly, *Intruder in the Dust,* though one of Faulkner's weaker novels, effectively portrays young Chick Mallison's gradual rejection of the presuppositions of white supremacy and his

eventual recognition of the humanity of the Negro, Lucas Beau-
champ.

Huckleberry Finn (1884), a novel of many facets, can be interpreted from the point of view suggested in this section. At the beginning of the novel, Huck accepts the romantic make-believe of Tom
Sawyer's world and the myths that safeguard the institution of slavery. From the threat to sell Jim away from his family to the tar-and-
feathering of the King and the Duke, he witnesses a broad spectrum
of Southern (or human) hypocrisy and cruelty. The effect on him is
left largely to conjecture; at the close of the novel he still acquiesces
in Tom's play-acting without believing in it, but he plans to "light
out for the territory" because Aunt Sally wants to civilize him and
he has "been there before."

Although Henry James's heroes are usually mature rather than
youthful, the disenchantment theme is frequently employed in his
"international" novels, such as *Roderick Hudson* (1875), *The American* (1877), and *The Ambassadors* (1903). An inexperienced and unsophisticated American encounters the entrenched conventions of
European society. His eyes are gradually opened to the injustice and
corruption beneath the glittering surface, and he emerges from the
experience chastened but wiser in the ways of the world.

In Stephen Crane's *The Red Badge of Courage* (1895), as in much
war fiction, the main character casts off illusions nurtured by inexperience. Henry Fleming has dreamed of "vague and bloody conflicts";
but he finds army life to be mostly mud and boredom, and during
his first battle he discovers within himself unsuspected depths of
cowardice and of heroism. When the battle is over, he feels "a quiet
manhood, non-assertive but of sturdy and strong blood," and he re-
calls with contempt his delusive dreams. He may later be deluded by
other fantasies, but he has outgrown his false notions of military
glory.

Ernest Hemingway in *A Farewell to Arms* (1929) treats the same
theme somewhat more subtly. Frederic Henry has enlisted in the
Italian army, apparently out of idealistic motives that he will not
even try to explain to anyone. He finds war to be "like the stock-
yards in Chicago if nothing was done with the meat except to bury
it." Resolving to "make a separate peace," he deserts from the army
and escapes to Switzerland with Catherine Barkley. Before she dies
in childbirth, he learns the truth of advice given him earlier by the
regimental priest: "When you love you wish to do things for. You
wish to sacrifice for." The theme of self-knowledge is not emphasized, but there are occasional brief statements like "I did not know
that then, although I learned it later." In Hemingway's short stories,
Nick Adams, an autobiographical character, watches his father per-

form a Caesarian operation on an Indian woman ("Indian Camp"), realizes the gulf of misunderstanding between his parents ("The Doctor and the Doctor's Wife"), breaks off a puppy love affair ("The End of Something"), is thrown off a freight car and confronts a punchdrunk prizefighter in a hobo jungle ("The Battler"). In these stories and others, Hemingway portrays the dispelling of illusions as a step toward maturity. This maturity, which is continually tested, entails acceptance of the tragic nature of human life and the stoical philosophy that a man can be destroyed but not defeated.

Fitzgerald's *The Great Gatsby* (1925) is narrated in the first person by Nick Carraway, a naive Midwesterner who seems considerably younger than his thirty years. After army service and a broken engagement, he has come to New York to work as a bond salesman. He is fascinated at first by the glamorous world of the fashionable rich. His neighbor on Long Island, Jay Gatsby, seems "an elegant young roughneck" until he comes to know him and discovers the scope of his romantic dreams. Nick finally realizes that Gatsby's crudity is preferable to the callous cruelty of wealthy society, and he is horrified by "what foul dust floated in the wake of his dreams."

In first person narratives like *A Farewell to Arms, The Great Gatsby,* and several of the stories in this volume, the narrator describes an experience in retrospect. If the author is skillful, he can establish a kind of dual perspective as the "I" looks back at his former self. This sort of double-vision narrative at its best merges cause and effect as it conveys the immediacy of an experience like Nick's acquaintance with Gatsby and simultaneously suggests the emotional aftermath of that experience.

In "The Magic Barrel," Leo Finkle sheds illusions about himself and achieves self-awareness in a flash of mystical insight that is beyond the scope of precise verbal description. The character himself cannot analyze the change that has occurred, but a commonplace, even ugly sight has given him a sense of his share in the commonalty of mankind's suffering and guilt, and thereafter he will not be altogether the same. A similar example of this kind of story is J. D. Salinger's "De Daumier-Smith's Blue Period," published in *Nine Stories* (1953). A mystical revelation comes to the self-deluding young hero as he watches an overweight window trimmer adjusting a truss on a display dummy in the window of an orthopedic appliances shop. The amused tone in which the narrator describes this grotesquely absurd scene ten years after it occurred suggests that he has achieved a resolution of his frustrations and fears. As in other stories of this type, he has become a man and put away childish things.

MARK TWAIN

Old Times on the Mississippi

I

WHEN I WAS A BOY, there was but one permanent ambition among my comrades in our village on the west bank of the Mississippi River. That was, to be a steamboatman. We had transient ambitions of other sorts, but they were only transient. When a circus came and went, it left us all burning to become clowns; the first negro minstrel show that came to our section left us all suffering to try that kind of life; now and then we had a hope that if we lived and were good, God would permit us to be pirates. These ambitions faded out, each in its turn; but the ambition to be a steamboatman always remained.

Once a day a cheap, gaudy packet arrived upward from St. Louis, and another downward from Keokuk. Before these events had transpired, the day was glorious with expectancy; after they had transpired, the day was a dead and empty thing. Not only the boys, but the whole village, felt this. After all these years I can picture that old time to myself now, just as it was then: the white town drowsing in the sunshine of a summer's morning; the streets empty, or pretty nearly so; one or two clerks sitting in front of the Water Street stores, with their splint-bottomed chairs tilted back against the wall, chins on breasts, hats slouched over their faces, asleep—with shingle-shavings enough around to show what broke them down; a sow and a litter of pigs loafing along the sidewalk, doing a good business in water-melon rinds and seeds; two or three lonely little freight piles scattered about the "levee;" a pile of "skids" on the slope of the stone-paved wharf, and the fragrant town drunkard asleep in the shadow of them; two or three wood flats at the head of the wharf,

From Mark Twain, "Old Times on the Mississippi." *The Atlantic Monthly*, XXXV, (January-March, 1875), 69–73, 217–224, 283–289. Further installments appeared in the *Atlantic* in April, May, June, and August. Twain later included these articles in his book *Life on the Mississippi* (1883).

but nobody to listen to the peaceful lapping of the wavelets against them; the great Mississippi, the majestic, the magnificent Mississippi, rolling its mile-wide tide along, shining in the sun; the dense forest away on the other side; the "point" above the town, and the "point" below, bounding the river-glimpse and turning it into a sort of sea, and withal a very still and brilliant and lonely one. Presently a film of dark smoke appears above one of those remote "points;" instantly a negro drayman, famous for his quick eye and prodigious voice, lifts up the cry, "S-t-e-a-m-boat a-comin'!" and the scene changes! The town drunkard stirs, the clerks wake up a furious clatter of drays follows, every house and store pours out a human contribution, and all in a twinkling the dead town is alive and moving. Drays, carts, men, boys, all go hurrying from many quarters to a common centre, the wharf. Assembled there, the people fasten their eyes upon the coming boat as upon a wonder they are seeing for the first time. And the boat *is* rather a handsome sight, too. She is long and sharp and trim and pretty; she has two tall, fancy-topped chimneys, with a gilded device of some kind swung between them; a fanciful pilot-house, all glass and "gingerbread," perched on top of the "texas" deck behind them; the paddle-boxes are gorgeous with a picture or with gilded rays above the boat's name; the boiler deck, the hurricane deck, and the texas deck are fenced and ornamented with clean white railings; there is a flag gallantly flying from the jackstaff; the furnace doors are open and the fires glaring bravely; the upper decks are black with passengers; the captain stands by the big bell, calm, imposing, the envy of all; great volumes of the blackest smoke are rolling and tumbling out of the chimneys—a husbanded grandeur created with a bit of pitch pine just before arriving at a town; the crew are grouped on the forecastle; the broad stage is run far out over the port bow, and an envied deck-hand stands picturesquely on the end of it with a coil of rope in his hand; the pent steam is screaming through the gauge-cocks; the captain lifts his hand, a bell rings, the wheels stop; then they turn back, churning the water to foam, and the steamer is at rest. Then such a scramble as there is to get aboard, and to get ashore and to take in freight and to discharge freight, all at one and the same time; and such a yelling and cursing as the mates facilitate it all with! Ten minutes later the steamer is under way again, with no flag on the jack-staff and no black smoke issuing from the chimneys. After ten more minutes the town is dead again, and the town drunkard asleep by the skids once more.

My father was a justice of the peace, and I supposed he possessed the power of life and death over all men and could hang anybody that offended him. This was distinction enough for me as a general thing; but the desire to be a steamboatman kept intruding, nevertheless. I first wanted to be a cabin-boy, so that I could come out with a white apron on and shake a table-cloth over the side, where all my old comrades could see me; later I thought I would rather be the deck-hand who stood on the end of the stage-plank with the coil of rope in his hand, because he was particularly conspicuous. But these were only daydreams—they were too heavenly to be contemplated as real possibilities. By and by one of our boys went away. He was not heard of for a long time. At last he turned up as apprentice engineer or "striker" on a steamboat. This thing shook the bottom out of all my Sunday-school teachings. That boy had been notoriously worldly, and I just the reverse; yet he was exalted to this eminence, and I left in obscurity and misery. There was nothing generous about this fellow in his greatness. He would always manage to have a rusty bolt to scrub while his boat tarried at our town, and he would sit on the inside guard and scrub it, where we could all see him and envy him and loathe him. And whenever his boat was laid up he would come home and swell around the town in his blackest and greasiest clothes, so that nobody could help remembering that he was a steamboatman; and he used all sorts of steamboat technicalities in his talk, as if he were so used to them that he forgot common people could not understand them. He would speak of the "labboard" side of a horse in an easy, natural way that would make one wish he was dead. And he was always talking about "St. Looy" like an old citizen; he would refer casually to occasions when he "was coming down Fourth Street," or when he was "passing by the Planter's House," or when there was a fire and he took a turn on the brakes of "the old Big Missouri;" and then he would go on and lie about how many towns the size of ours were burned down there that day. Two or three of the boys had long been persons of consideration among us because they had been to St. Louis once and had a vague general knowledge of its wonders, but the day of their glory was over now. They lapsed into a humble silence, and learned to disappear when the ruthless "cub"-engineer approached. This fellow had money, too, and hair oil. Also an ignorant silver watch and a showy brass watch chain. He wore a leather belt and used no suspenders. If ever a youth was cordially admired and hated by his comrades, this one was. No girl could withstand his charms. He "cut out" every boy in the village. When his boat blew up at last, it diffused a tranquil contentment among us such as we had not known for months. But when he came home the next week, alive, renowned, and appeared in church all battered up and bandaged, a shining hero, stared at and wondered over by everybody, it seemed to us that the partiality of Providence for an undeserving reptile had reached a point where it was open to criticism.

This creature's career could produce but one result, and it speedily followed. Boy after boy managed to get on the river. The minister's son became an engineer. The doctor's and the postmaster's sons became "mud clerks;" the wholesale liquor dealer's son became a bar-keeper on a boat; four sons of the chief merchant, and two sons of the county judge, became pilots. Pilot was the grandest position of all. The pilot, even in those days of trivial wages, had a princely salary—from a hundred and fifty to two hundred and fifty dollars a month, and no board to pay. Two months of his wages would pay a preacher's salary for a year. Now some of us were left disconsolate. We could not get on the river—at least our parents would not let us.

So by and by I ran away. I said I never would come home again till I was a pilot and could come in glory. But somehow I could not manage it. I went meekly aboard a few of the boats that lay packed together like sardines at the long St. Louis wharf, and very humbly inquired for the pilots, but got only a cold shoulder and short words from mates and clerks. I had to make the best of this sort of treatment for the time being, but I had comforting day-dreams of a future when I should be a great and honored pilot, with plenty of money, and could kill some of these mates and clerks and pay for them.

Months afterward the hope within me struggled to a reluctant death, and I found myself without an ambition. But I was ashamed to go home. I was in Cincinnati, and I set to work to map out a new career. I had been reading about the recent exploration of the river Amazon by an expedition sent out by our government. It was said that the expedition owing to difficulties, had not thoroughly explored a part of the country lying about the head-waters, some four thousand miles from the mouth of the river. It was only about fifteen hundred miles from Cincinnati to New Orleans, where I could doubtless get a ship. I had thirty dollars left; I would go and complete the exploration of the Amazon. This was all the thought I gave to the subject. I never was great in matters of detail. I packed my valise, and took passage on an ancient tub called the Paul Jones, for New Orleans. For the sum of sixteen dollars I had the scarred and tarnished splendors of "her" main saloon principally to myself, for she was not a creature to attract the eye of wiser travelers.

When we presently got under way and went poking down the broad Ohio, I became a new being, and the subject of my own admiration. I was a traveler! A word never had tasted so good in my mouth before. I had an exultant sense of being bound for mysterious lands and distant climes which I never have felt in so uplifting a degree since. I was in such a glorified condition that all ignoble feelings departed out of me, and I was able to look down and pity the untraveled with a compassion that had hardly a trace of contempt in it. Still, when we stopped at villages and wood-yards, I could not help lolling carelessly upon the railings of the boiler deck to enjoy the envy of the country boys on the bank. If they did not seem to discover me, I presently sneezed to attract their attention, or moved to a position where they could not help seeing me. And as soon as I knew they saw me I gaped and stretched, and gave other signs of being mightily bored with traveling.

I kept my hat off all the time, and stayed where the wind and the sun could strike me, because I wanted to get the bronzed and weather-beaten look of an old traveler. Before the second day was half gone, I experienced a joy which filled me with the purest gratitude; for I saw that the skin had begun to blister and peel off my face and neck. I wished that the boys and girls at home could see me now.

We reached Louisville in time—at least the neighborhood of it. We stuck hard and fast on the rocks in the middle of the river and lay there four days. I was now beginning to feel a strong sense of being a part of the boat's family, a sort of infant son to the captain and younger brother to the officers. There is no estimating the pride I took in this grandeur, or the affection that began to swell and grow in me for those people. I could not know how the lordly steamboatman scorns that sort of presumption in a mere landsman. I particularly longed to acquire the least trifle of notice from the big stormy mate, and I was on the alert for an opportunity to do him a service to that end. It came at last. The riotous powwow of setting a spar was going on down on the forecastle, and I went down there and stood around in the way—or mostly skipping out of it—till the mate suddenly roared a general order for somebody to bring him a capstan bar. I sprang to his side and said: "Tell me where it is—I'll fetch it!"

If a rag-picker had offered to do a diplomatic service for the Emperor of Russia, the monarch could not have been more astounded than the mate was. He even stopped swearing. He stood and stared down at me. It took him ten seconds to scrape his disjointed remains together again. Then he said impressively: "Well, if this don't beat hell!" and turned to his work with the air of a man who had been confronted with a problem too abstruse for solution.

I crept away, and courted solitude for the rest of the day. I did not go to dinner; I stayed away from supper until everybody else had finished. I did not feel so much like a member of the boat's family now as before. However, my spirits returned, in installments, as we pursued our way down the river. I was sorry I hated the mate so, because it was not in (young) human nature not to admire him. He was huge and muscular, his face was bearded and whiskered all over; he had a red woman and a blue woman tattooed on his right arm,— one on each side of a blue anchor with a red rope to it; and in the matter of profanity he was perfect. When he was getting out cargo at a landing, I was always where I could see and hear. He felt all the sublimity of his great position, and made the world feel it, too. When he gave even the simplest order, he discharged it like a blast of lightning, and sent a long, reverberating peal of profanity thundering after it. I could not help contrasting the way in which the average landsman would give an order, with the mate's way of doing it. If the landsman should wish the gangplank moved a foot farther forward, he would probably say: "James, or William, one of you push that plank forward, please;" but put the mate in his place, and he would roar out: "Here, now, start that gang-plank for'ard! Lively, now. *What*'re you about! Snatch it! *snatch* it! There! there! Aft again! aft again! Don't you hear me? Dash it to dash! are you going to *sleep* over it! '*Vast* heaving. 'Vast heaving, I tell you! Going to heave it clear astern? WHERE're you going with the barrel! *for'ard* with it 'fore I make you swallow it, you dash-dash-dash-*dashed* split between a tired mud-turtle and a crippled hearse-horse!"

I wished I could talk like that.

When the soreness of my adventure with the mate had somewhat worn off, I began timidly to make up to the humblest official connected with the boat—the night watchman. He snubbed my advances at first, but I presently ventured to offer him a new chalk pipe, and that softened him. So he allowed me to sit with him by the big bell on the hurricane deck, and in time he melted into conversation. He could not well have helped it, I hung with such homage on his words and so plainly showed that I felt honored by his notice. He told me the names of dim capes and shadowy islands as we glided by them in the solemnity of the night, under the winking stars, and by and by got to talking about himself. He seemed oversentimental for a man whose salary was six dollars a week—or rather he might have seemed so to an older person than I. But I drank in his words hungrily, and with a faith that might have moved mountains if it had been applied judiciously. What was it to me that he was soiled and seedy and fragrant with gin? What was it to me that his grammar was bad, his construction worse, and his profanity so void of art that it was an element of weakness rather than strength in his conversation? He was a wronged man, a man who had seen trouble, and that was enough for me. As he mellowed into his plaintive history his tears dripped upon the lantern in his lap, and I cried, too, from sympathy. He said he was the son of an English nobleman—either an earl or an alderman, he could not remember which, but believed he was both; his father, the nobleman, loved him, but his mother hated him from the cradle; and so while he was still a little boy he was sent to "one of them old, ancient colleges"—he couldn't remember which; and by and by his father died and his mother seized the property and "shook" him, as he phrased it. After his mother shook him, members of the nobility with whom he was acquainted used their influence to get him the position of "lob-lolly-boy in a ship;" and from that point my watchman threw off all trammels of date and locality and branched out into a narrative that bristled all along with incredible adventures; a narrative that was so reeking with bloodshed and so crammed with hair-breadth escapes and the most engaging and unconscious personal villainies, that I sat speechless, enjoying, shuddering, wondering, worshiping.

It was a sore blight to find out afterwards that he was a low, vulgar, ignorant, sentimental, half-witted humbug, an untraveled native of the wilds of Illinois, who had absorbed wildcat literature and appropriated its marvels, until in time he had woven odds and ends of the mess into this yarn, and then gone on telling it to fledglings like me, until he had come to believe it himself.

II

What with lying on the rocks four days at Louisville, and some other delays, the poor old Paul Jones fooled away about two weeks in making the voyage from Cincinnati to New Orleans. This gave me a chance to get acquainted with one of the pilots, and he taught me how to steer the boat, and thus made the fascination of river life more potent than ever for me.

It also gave me a chance to get acquainted with a youth who had taken deck passage—more's the pity; for he easily borrowed six dollars of me on a promise to return to the boat and pay it back to me the day after we should arrive. But he probably died or forgot, for he never came. It was doubtless the former, since he had said his parents were wealthy, and he only traveled deck passage because it was cooler.[1]

I soon discovered two things. One was that a vessel would not be likely to sail for the mouth of the Amazon under ten or twelve years; and the other was that the nine or ten dollars still left in my pocket would not suffice for so imposing an exploration as I had planned, even if I could afford to wait for a ship. Therefore it followed that I

---

[1] "Deck" passage—i.e., steerage passage. (Mark Twain's note)

must contrive a new career. The Paul Jones was now bound for St. Louis, I planned a siege against my pilot, and at the end of three hard days he surrendered. He agreed to teach me the Mississippi River from New Orleans to St. Louis for five hundred dollars, payable out of the first wages I should receive after graduating. I entered upon the small enterprise of "learning" twelve or thirteen hundred miles of the great Mississippi River with the easy confidence of my time of life. If I had really known what I was about to require of my faculties, I should not have had the courage to begin. I supposed that all a pilot had to do was to keep his boat in the river, and I did not consider that that could be much of a trick, since it was so wide.

The boat backed out from New Orleans at four in the afternoon, and it was "our watch" until eight. Mr. B——, my chief, "straightened her up," plowed her along past the sterns of the other boats that lay at the Levee, and then said, "Here, take her; shave those steamships as close as you'd peel an apple." I took the wheel, and my heart went down into my boots; for it seemed to me that we were about to scrape the side off every ship in the line, we were so close. I held my breath and began to claw the boat away from the danger; and I had my own opinion of the pilot who had known no better than to get us into such peril, but I was too wise to express it. In half a minute I had a wide margin of safety intervening between the Paul Jones and the ships; and within ten seconds more I was set aside in disgrace, and Mr. B—— was going into danger again and flaying me alive with abuse of my cowardice. I was stung, but I was obliged to admire the easy confidence with which my chief loafed from side to side of his wheel, and trimmed the ships so closely that disaster seemed ceaselessly imminent. When he had cooled a little he told me that the easy water was close ashore and the current outside, and therefore we must hug the bank, up-stream, to get the benefit of the former, and stay well out, downstream, to take advantage of the latter. In my own mind I resolved to be a down-stream pilot and leave the up-streaming to people dead to prudence.

Now and then Mr. B—— called my attention to certain things. Said he, "This is Six-Mile Point." I assented. It was pleasant enough information, but I could not see the bearing of it. I was not conscious that it was a matter of any interest to me. Another time he said, "This is Nine-Mile Point." Later he said, "This is Twelve-Mile Point." They were all about level with the water's edge; they all looked about alike to me; they were monotonously unpicturesque. I hoped Mr. B—— would change the subject. But no; he would crowd up around a point, hugging the shore with affection, and then say: "The slack water ends here, abreast this bunch of China-trees; now we cross over." So he crossed over. He gave me the wheel once or twice, but I had no luck. I either came near chipping off the edge of a sugar plantation, or else I yawed too far from shore, and so I dropped back into disgrace again and got abused.

The watch was ended at last, and we took supper and went to bed. At midnight the glare of a lantern shone in my eyes, and the night watchman said:—

"Come! turn out!"

And then he left. I could not understand this extraordinary procedure; so I presently gave up trying to, and dozed off to sleep. Pretty soon the watchman was back again, and this time he was gruff. I was annoyed. I said:—

"What do you want to come bothering around here in the middle of the night for? Now as like as not I'll not get to sleep again to-night."

The watchman said:—

"Well, if this an't good, I'm blest."

The "off-watch" was just turning in, and I heard some brutal laughter from them, and such remarks as "Hello, watchman! an't the new cub turned out yet? He's delicate, likely. Give him some sugar in a rag and send for the chambermaid to sing rock-a-by-baby to him."

About this time Mr. B—— appeared on the scene. Something like a minute later I was climbing the pilot-house steps with some of my clothes on and the rest in my arms. Mr. B—— was close behind, commenting. Here was something fresh—this thing of getting up in the middle of the night to go to work. It was a detail in piloting that had never occurred to me at all. I knew that boats ran all night, but somehow I had never happened to reflect that somebody had to get up out of a warm bed to run them. I began to fear that piloting was not quite so romantic as I had imagined it was; there was something very real and work-like about this new phase of it.

It was a rather dingy night, although a fair number of stars were out. The big mate was at the wheel, and he had the old tub pointed at a star and was holding her straight up the middle of the river. The shores on either hand were not much more than a mile apart, but they seemed wonderfully far away and ever so vague and indistinct. The mate said:—

"We've got to land at Jones's plantation, sir."

The vengeful spirit in me exulted. I said to myself, I wish you joy of your job, Mr. B——; you'll have a good time finding Mr. Jones's plantation such a night as this; and I hope you never *will* find it as long as you live.

Mr. B—— said to the mate:—

"Upper end of the plantation, or the lower?"

"Upper."

"I can't do it. The stumps there are out of the water at this stage. It's no great distance to the lower, and you'll have to get along with that."

"All right, sir. If Jones don't like it he'll have to lump it, I reckon."

And then the mate left. My exultation began to cool and my wonder to come up. Here was a man who not only proposed to find this plantation on such a night, but to find either end of it you preferred. I dreadfully wanted to ask a question, but I was carrying about as many short answers as my cargoroom would admit of, so I held my peace. All I desired to ask Mr. B—— was the simple question whether he was ass enough to really imagine he was going to find that plantation on a night when all plantations were exactly alike and all the same color. But I held in. I used to have fine inspirations of prudence in those days.

Mr. B—— made for the shore and soon was scraping it, just the same as if it had been daylight. And not only that, but singing—"Father in heaven the day is declining," etc.

It seemed to me that I had put my life in the keeping of a peculiarly reckless outcast. Presently he turned on me and said:—

"What's the name of the first point above New Orleans?"

I was gratified to be able to answer promptly, and I did. I said I didn't know.

"Don't *know?*"

This manner jolted me. I was down at the foot again, in a moment. But I had to say just what I had said before.

"Well, you're a smart one," said Mr. B——. "What's the name of the *next* point?"

Once more I didn't know.

"Well this beats anything. Tell me the name of *any* point or place I told you."

I studied a while and decided that I couldn't.

"Look-a-here! What do you start out from, above Twelve-Mile, Point, to cross over?"

"I—I—don't know."

"You—you—don't know?" mimicking my drawling manner of speech. "What *do* you know?"

"I—I—nothing, for certain."

"By the great Cæsar's ghost I believe you! You're the stupidest dunderhead I ever saw or ever heard of, so help me Moses! The idea of *you* being a pilot—*you!* Why, you don't know enough to pilot a cow down a lane."

Oh, but his wrath was up! He was a nervous man, and he shuffled from one side of his wheel to the other as if the floor was hot. He would boil a while to himself, and then overflow and scald me again.

"Look-a-here! What do you suppose I told you the names of those points for?"

I tremblingly considered a moment, and then the devil of temptation provoked me to say:—

"Well—to—to—be entertaining, I thought."

This was a red rag to the bull. He raged and stormed so (he was crossing the river at the time) that I judge it made him blind, because he ran over the steering-oar of a trading-scow. Of course the traders sent up a volley of red-hot profanity. Never was a man so grateful as Mr. B—— was: because he was brim full, and here were subjects who would *talk back*. He threw open a window, thrust his head out, and such an irruption followed as I never had heard before. The fainter and farther the scowmen's curses drifted, the higher Mr. B—— lifted his voice and the weightier his adjectives grew. When he closed the window he was empty. You could have drawn a seine through his system and not caught curses enough to disturb your mother with. Presently he said to me in the gentlest way:—

"My boy, you must get a little memorandum-book, and every time I tell you a thing, put it down right away. There's only one way to be a pilot, and that is to get this entire river by heart. You have to know it just like A B C."

That was a dismal revelation to me; for my memory was never loaded with anything but blank cartridges. However, I did not feel discouraged long. I judged that it was best to make some allowances, for doubtless Mr. B—— was "stretching." Presently he pulled a rope and struck a few strokes on the big bell. The stars were all gone, now, and the night was as black as ink. I could hear the wheels churn along the bank, but I was not entirely certain that I could see the shore. The voice of the invisible watchman called up from the hurricane deck:—

"What's this, sir?"

"Jones's plantation."

I said to myself, I wish I might venture to offer a small bet that it isn't. But I did not chirp. I only waited to see. Mr. B—— handled the engine bells, and in due time the boat's nose came to the land, a torch glowed from the forecastle, a man skipped ashore, a darky's voice on the bank said, "Gimme de carpet-bag, Mars' Jones," and the next moment we were standing up the river again, all serene. I reflected deeply a while, and then said,—but not aloud,—Well, the finding of that plantation was the luckiest accident that ever happened; but it couldn't happen again in a hundred years. And I fully believed it *was* an accident, too.

By the time we had gone seven or eight hundred miles up the river, I had learned to be a tolerably plucky upstream steersman, in daylight, and before we reached St. Louis I had made a trifle of progress in night-work, but only a trifle. I had a note-book that fairly bristled with the names of towns, "points," bars, islands, bends, reaches, etc.; but the information was to be found only in the note-book—none of it was in my head. It made my heart ache to think I had only got half of the river set down; for as our watch was four hours off and four hours on, day and night, there was a long four-hour gap in my book every time I had slept since the voyage began.

My chief was presently hired to go on a big New Orleans boat, and I packed my satchel and went with him. She was a grand affair. When I stood in her pilot-house I was so far above the water that I seemed perched on a mountain; and her decks stretched so far away, fore and aft, below me, that I wondered how I could ever have considered the little Paul Jones a large craft. There were other differences, too. The Paul Jones's pilot-house was a cheap, dingy, battered rattle-trap, cramped for room: but here was a sumptuous glass temple; room enough to have a dance in; showy red and gold window-curtains; an imposing sofa; leather cushions and a back to the high bench where visiting pilots sit, to spin yarns and "look at the river;" bright, fanciful "cuspadores" instead of a broad wooden box filled with sawdust; nice new oil-cloth on the floor; a hospitable big stove for winter; a wheel as high as my head, costly with inlaid work; a wire tiller-rope; bright brass knobs for the bells; and a tidy, white-aproned, black "texas-tender," to bring up tarts and ices and coffee during mid-watch, day and night. Now this was "something like;" and so I began to take heart once more to believe that piloting was a romantic sort of occupation after all. The moment we were under way I began to prowl about the great steamer and fill myself with joy. She was as clean and as dainty as a drawing-room; when I looked down her long, gilded saloon, it was like gazing through a splendid tunnel; she had an oil-picture, by some gifted sign-painter, on every state-room door; she glittered with no end of prism-fringed chandeliers; the clerk's office was elegant, the bar was marvelous, and the bar-keeper had been barbered and upholstered at incredible cost. The boiler deck (*i.e.*, the second story of the boat, so to speak) was as spacious as a church, it seemed to me; so with the forecastle; and there was no pitiful handful of deckhands, firemen, and roust-abouts down there, but a whole battalion of men. The fires were fiercely glaring from a long row of furnaces, and over them were eight huge boilers! This was unutterable pomp. The mighty engines—but enough of this. I had never felt so fine before. And when I found that the regiment of natty servants respectfully "sir'd" me, my satisfaction was complete.

When I returned to the pilot-house St. Louis was gone and I was lost. Here was a piece of river which was all down in my book, but I could make neither head nor tail of it: you understand, it was turned around. I had seen it, when coming up-stream, but I had never faced about to see how it looked when it was behind me. My heart broke again, for it was plain that I had got to learn this troublesome river *both ways*.

The pilot-house was full of pilots, going down to "look at the river." What is called the "upper river" (the two hundred miles between St. Louis and Cairo, where the Ohio comes in) was low; and the Mississippi changes its channel so constantly that the pilots used to always find it necessary to run down to Cairo to take a fresh look, when their boats were to lie in port a week, that is, when the water was at a low stage. A deal of this "looking at the river" was done by poor fellows who seldom had a berth, and whose only hope of getting one lay in their being always freshly posted and therefore ready to drop into the shoes of some reputable pilot, for a single trip, on account of such pilot's sudden illness, or some other necessity. And a good many of them constantly ran up and down inspecting the river, not because they ever really hoped to get a berth, but because (they being guests of the boat) it was cheaper to "look at the river" than stay ashore and pay board. In time these fellows grew dainty in their tastes, and only infested boats that had an established reputation for setting good tables. All visiting pilots were useful, for they were always ready and willing, winter or summer, night or day, to go out in the yawl and help buoy the channel or assist the boat's pilots in any way they could. They were likewise welcome because all pilots are tireless talkers, when gathered together, and as they talk only about the river they are always understood and are always interesting. Your true pilot cares nothing about anything on earth but the river, and his pride in his occupation surpasses the pride of kings.

We had a fine company of these river-inspectors along, this trip. There were eight or ten; and there was abundance of room for them in our great pilot-house. Two or three of them wore polished silk hats, elaborate shirt-fronts, diamond breastpins, kid gloves, and patent-leather boots. They were choice in their English, and bore themselves with a dignity proper to men of solid means and prodigious reputation as pilots. The others were more or less loosely clad, and wore upon their heads tall felt cones that were suggestive of the days of the Commonwealth.

I was a cipher in this august company, and felt subdued, not to say torpid. I was not even of sufficient consequence to assist at the wheel when it was necessary to put the tiller hard down in a hurry; the guest that stood nearest did that when occasion required—and this was pretty much all the time, because of the crookedness of the channel and the scant water. I stood in a corner; and the talk I listened to took the hope all out of me. One visitor said to another:—

"Jim, how did you run Plum Point, coming up?"

"It was in the night, there, and I ran it the way one of the boys on the Diana told me; started out about fifty yards above the wood pile on the false point, and held on the cabin under Plum Point till I raised the reef—quarter less twain—then straigthened up for the middle bar till I got well abreast the old one-limbed cotton-wood in the bend, then got my stern on the cottonwood and head on the low place above the point, and came through a-booming—nine and a half."

"Pretty square crossing, an't it?"

"Yes, but the upper bar's working down fast."

Another pilot spoke up and said:—

"I had better water than that, and ran it lower down; started out from the false point—mark twain—raised the second reef abreast the big snag in the bend, and had quarter less twain."

One of the gorgeous ones remarked: "I don't want to find fault with your leadsmen, but that's a good deal of water for Plum Point, it seems to me."

There was an approving nod all around as this quiet snub dropped on the boaster and "settled" him. And so they went on talk-talk-talking. Meantime, the thing that was running in my mind was, "Now if my ears hear right, I have not only to get the names of all towns and islands and bends, and so on, by heart, but I must even get up a warm personal acquaintanceship with every old snag and one-limbed cotton-wood and obscure wood pile that ornaments the banks of this river for twelve hundred miles; and more than that, I must actually know where these things are in the dark, unless these guests are gifted with eyes that can pierce through two miles of solid blackness; I wish the piloting business was in Jericho and I had never thought of it."

At dusk Mr. B—— tapped the big bell three times (the signal to land), and the captain emerged from his drawing-room in the forward end of the texas, and looked up inquiringly. Mr. B—— said:—

"We will lay up here all night, captain."

"Very well, sir."

That was all. The boat came to shore and was tied up for the night. It seemed to me a fine thing that the pilot could do as he pleased without asking so grand a captain's permission. I took my supper and went immediately to bed, discouraged by my day's observations and experiences. My late voyage's note-booking was but a confusion of meaningless names. It had tangled me all up in a knot every time I had looked at it in the daytime. I now hoped for respite in sleep; but no, it reveled all through my head till sunrise again, a frantic and tireless nightmare.

Next morning I felt pretty rusty and low-spirited. We went booming along, taking a good many chances, for we were anxious to "get out of the river" (as getting out to Cairo was called) before night should overtake us. But Mr. B——'s partner, the other pilot, presently grounded the boat, and we lost so much time getting her off that it was plain the darkness would overtake us a good long way above the mouth. This was a great misfortune, especially to certain of our visiting pilots, whose boats would have to wait for their return, no matter how long that might be. It sobered the pilot-house talk a good deal. Coming up-stream, pilots did not mind low water or any kind of darkness; nothing stopped them but fog. But downstream work was different; a boat was too nearly helpless, with a stiff current pushing behind her; so it was not customary to run downstream at night in low water.

There seemed to be one small hope, however: if we could get through the intricate and dangerous Hat Island crossing before night, we could venture the rest, for we would have plainer sailing and better water. But it would be insanity to attempt Hat Island at night. So there was a deal of looking at watches all the rest of the day, and a constant ciphering upon the speed we were making; Hat Island was the eternal subject; sometimes hope was high and sometimes we were delayed in a bad crossing, and down it went again. For hours all hands lay under the burden of this suppressed excitement; it was even communicated to me, and I got to feeling so solicitous about Hat Island, and under such an awful pressure of responsibility, that I wished I might have five minutes on shore to draw a good, full, relieving breath, and start over again. We were standing no regular watches. Each of our pilots ran such portions of the river as he had run when coming up-stream, because of his greater familiarity with it; but both remained in the pilot-house constantly.

An hour before sunset, Mr. B—— took the wheel and Mr. W—— stepped aside. For the next thirty minutes every man held his watch in his hand and was restless, silent, and uneasy. At last somebody said, with a doomful sigh.

"Well, yonder's Hat Island—and we can't make it."

All the watches closed with a snap, everybody sighed and muttered something about its being "too bad, too bad—ah, if we could *only* have got here half an hour sooner!" and the place was thick with the atmosphere of disappointment. Some started to go out, but loitered, hearing no bell-tap to land. The sun dipped behind the horizon, the boat went on. Inquiring looks passed from one guest to another; and one who had his hand on the doorknob, and had turned it, waited, then presently took away his hand and let the knob turn back again. We bore steadily down the bend. More looks were exchanged, and nods of surprised admiration—but no words. Insensibly the men drew together behind Mr. B—— as the sky darkened and one or two dim stars came out. The dead silence and sense of waiting became oppressive. Mr. B—— pulled the cord, and two deep, mellow notes from the big bell floated off on the night. Then a pause, and one more note was struck. The watchman's voice followed, from the hurricane deck:—

"Labboard lead, there! Stabboard lead!"

The cries of the leadsmen began to rise out of the distance, and were gruffly repeated by the word-passers on the hurricane deck.

"M-a-r-k three! M-a-r-k three! Quarter-less-three! Half twain! Quarter twain! M-a-r-k twain! Quarter-less"—

Mr. B—— pulled two bell-ropes, and was answered by faint jinglings far below in the engine-room, and our speed slackened. The steam began to whistle through the gauge-cocks. The cries of the leadsmen went on—and it is a weird sound, always, in the night. Every pilot in the lot was watching, now, with fixed eyes, and talking under his breath. Nobody was calm and easy but Mr. B——. He would put his wheel down and stand on a spoke, and as the steamer swung into her (to me) utterly invisible marks—for we seemed to be in the midst of a wide and gloomy sea—he would meet and fasten her there. Talk was going on, now, in low voices:—

"There; she's over the first reef all right!"

After a pause, another subdued voice:—

"Her stern's coming down just *exactly* right, by *George!* Now she's in the marks; over she goes!"

Somebody else muttered:—

"Oh, it was done beautiful—*beautiful!*"

Now the engines were stopped altogether, and we drifted with the current. Not that I could see the boat drift, for I could not, the stars being all gone by this time. This drifting was the dismalest work; it held one's heart still. Presently I discovered a blacker gloom than that which surrounded us. It was the head of the island. We were closing right down upon it. We entered its deeper shadow, and so imminent seemed the peril that I was likely to suffocate; and I had the strongest impulse to do *something*, anything, to save the vessel. But still Mr. B—— stood by his wheel, silent, intent as a cat, and all the pilots stood shoulder to shoulder at his back.

"She'll not make it !" somebody whispered.

The water grew shoaler and shoaler by the leadsmen's cries, till it was down to—

"Eight-and-a-half! E-i-g-h-t feet! E-i-g-h-t feet! Seven-and" —

Mr. B—— said warningly through his speaking tube to the engineer:—

"Stand by, now!"

"Aye-aye, sir."

"Seven-and-a-half! Seven feet! *Six*-and"—

We touched bottom! Instantly Mr. B—— set a lot of bells ringing, shouted through the tube, "*Now* let her have it—every ounce you've got!" then to his partner, "Put her hard down! snatch her! snatch her!" The boat rasped and ground her way through the sand, hung upon the apex of disaster a single tremendous instant, and then over she went! And such a shout as went up at Mr. B——'s back never loosened the roof of a pilot-house before!

There was no more trouble after that. Mr. B—— was a hero that night; and it was some little time, too before his exploit ceased to be talked about by river men.

Fully to realize the marvelous precision required in laying the great steamer in her marks in that murky waste of water, one should know that not only must she pick her intricate way through snags and blind reefs, and then shave the head of the island so closely as to brush the overhanging foliage with her stern, but at one place she must pass almost within arm's reach of a sunken and invisible wreck that would snatch the hull timbers from under her if she should strike it, and destroy a quarter of a million dollars' worth of steamboat and cargo in five minutes, and maybe a hundred and fifty human lives into the bargain.

The last remark I heard that night was a compliment to Mr. B——, uttered in soliloquy and with unction by one of our guests. He said:—

"By the Shadow of Death, but he's a lightning pilot!"

III

At the end of what seemed a tedious while, I had managed to pack my head full of islands, town, bars, "points," and bends; and a curiously inanimate mass of lumber it was, too. However, inasmuch as I could shut my eyes and reel off a good long string of these names without leaving out more than ten miles of river in every fifty, I began to feel that I could take a boat down to New Orleans if I could make her skip those little gaps. But of course my complacency could hardly get start enough to lift my nose a trifle into the air, before Mr. B—— would think of something to fetch it down again. One day he turned on me suddenly with this settler:—

"What is the shape of Walnut Bend?"

He might as well have asked me my grandmother's opinion of protoplasm. I reflected respectfully, and then said I didn't know it had any particular shape. My gunpowdery chief went off with a bang, of course, and then went on loading and firing until he was out of adjectives.

I had learned long ago that he only carried just so many rounds of ammunition, and was sure to subside into a very placable and even remorseful old smooth-bore as soon as they were all gone. That word "old" is merely affectionate; he was not more than thirty-four. I waited. By and by he said,—

"My boy, you've got to know the *shape* of the river perfectly. It is all there is left to steer by on a very dark night. Everything else is blotted out and gone. But mind you, it hasn't the same shape in the night that it has in the day-time."

"How on earth am I ever going to learn it, then?"

"How do you follow a hall at home in the dark? Because you know the shape of it. You can't see it."

"Do you mean to say that I've got to know all the million trifling variations of shape in the banks of this interminable river as well as I know the shape of the front hall at home?"

"On my honor you've got to know them *better* than any man ever did know the shapes of the halls in his own house."

"I wish was dead!"

"Now I don't want to discourage you, but"—

"Well, pile it on me; I might as well have it now as another time."

"You see, this has got to be learned; there isn't any getting around it. A clear starlight night throws such heavy shadows that if you didn't know the shape of a shore perfectly you would claw away from every bunch of timber, because you would take the black shadow of it for a solid cape; and you see you would be getting scared to death every fifteen minutes by the watch. You would be fifty yards from shore all the time when you ought to be within twenty feet of it. You can't see a snag in one of those shadows, but you know exactly where it is, and the shape of the river tells you when you are coming to it. Then there's your pitch dark night; the river is a very different shape on a pitch dark night from what it is on a starlight night. All shores seem to be straight lines, then, and mighty dim ones, too; and you'd *run* them for straight lines, only you know better. You boldly drive your boat right into what seems to be a solid, straight wall (you knowing very well that in reality there is a curve there), and that wall falls back and makes way for you. Then there's your gray mist. You take a night when there's one of these grisly, drizzly, gray mists, and then there isn't *any* particular shape to a shore. A gray mist would tangle the head of the oldest man that ever lived. Well, then, different kinds of *moonlight* change the shape of the river in different ways. You see"—

"Oh, don't say any more, please! Have I got to learn the shape of the river according to all these five hundred thousand different ways? If I tried to carry all that cargo in my head it would make me stoop-shouldered."

"*No!* you only learn *the* shape of the river; and you learn it with such absolute certainty that you can always steer by the shape that's *in your head,* and never mind the one that's before your eyes."

"Very well, I'll try it; but after I have learned it can I depend on it? Will it keep the same form and not go on fooling around?"

Before Mr. B—— could answer, Mr. W—— came in to take the watch, and he said,—

"B——, you'll have to look out for President's Island and all that country clear away up above the Old Hen and Chickens. The banks are caving and the shape of the shores changing like everything. Why, you wouldn't know the point above 40. You can go up inside the old sycamore snag, now."[2]

So that question was answered. Here were leagues of shore changing shape. My spirits were down in the mud again. Two things seemed pretty apparent to me. One was, that in order to be a pilot a man had got to learn more than any one man ought to be allowed to know; and the other was, that he must learn it all over again in a different way every twenty-four hours.

That night we had the watch until twelve. Now it was an ancient river custom for the two pilots to chat a bit when the watch changed. While the relieving pilot put on his gloves and lit his cigar, his partner, the retiring pilot, would say something like this:

"I judge the upper bar is making down a little at Hale's Point; had quarter twain with the lower head and mark twain[3] with the other."

"Yes, I thought it was making down a little, last trip. Meet any boats?"

"Met one abreast of the head of 21, but she was away over hug-

[2] It may not be necessary, but still it can do no harm to explain that "inside" means between the snag and the shore. (M.T.)

[3] Two fathoms. Quarter twain is 2¼ fathoms, 13½ feet. Mark three is three fathoms. (M.T.)

ging the bar, and I couldn't make her out entirely. I took her for the Sunny South—hadn't any skylights forward of the chimneys."

And so on. And as the relieving pilot took the wheel his partner[4] would mention that we were in such-and-such a bend, and say we were abreast of such-and-such a man's wood-yard or plantation. This was courtesy; I supposed it was *necessity*. But Mr. W—— came on watch full twelve minutes late, on this particular night—a tremendous breach of etiquette; in fact, it is the unpardonable sin among pilots. So Mr. B—— gave him no greeting whatever, but simply surrendered the wheel and marched out of the pilot-house without a word. I was appalled; it was a villainous night for blackness, we were in a particularly wide and blind part of the river, where there was no shape or substance to anything, and it seemed incredible that Mr. B—— should have left that poor fellow to kill the boat trying to find out where he was. But I resolved that I would stand by him any way. He should find that he was not wholly friendless. So I stood around, and waited to be asked where we were. But Mr. W——plunged on serenely through the solid firmament of black cats that stood for an atmosphere, and never opened his mouth. Here is a proud devil, thought I; here is a limb of Satan that would rather send us all to destruction than put himself under obligations to me, because I am not yet one of the salt of the earth and privileged to snub captains and lord it over everything dead and alive in a steamboat. I presently climbed up on the bench; I did not think it was safe to go to sleep while this lunatic was on watch.

However, I must have gone to sleep in the course of time, because the next thing I was aware of was the fact that day was breaking, Mr. W—— gone, and Mr. B—— at the wheel again. So it was four o'clock and all well—but me; I felt like a skinful of dry bones and all of them trying to ache at once.

Mr. B—— asked me what I had stayed up there for. I confessed that it was to do Mr. W—— a benevolence: tell him where he was. It took five minutes for the entire preposterousness of the thing to filter into Mr. B's system, and then I judge it filled him nearly up to the chin; because he paid me a compliment—and not much of a one either. He said,—

"Well, taking you by-and-large, you do seem to be more different kinds of an ass than any creature I ever saw before. What did you suppose he wanted to know for?"

I said I thought it might be a convenience to him.

"Convenience! Dash! Didn't I tell you that a man's got to know the river in the night the same as he'd know his own front hall?"

---

[4] "Partner" is technical for "the other pilot." (M.T.)

"Well, I can follow the front hall in the dark if I know it *is* the front hall; but suppose you set me down in the middle of it in the dark and not tell me which hall it is; how am *I* to know?"

"Well, you've *got* to, on the river!"

"All right. Then I'm glad I never said anything to Mr. W—."

"I should say so. Why, he'd have slammed you through the window and utterly ruined a hundred dollars' worth of window-sash and stuff."

I was glad this damage had been saved, for it would have made me unpopular with the owners. They always hated anybody who had the name of being careless, and injuring things.

I went to work, now, to learn the shape of the river; and of all the eluding and ungraspable objects that ever I tried to get mind or hands on, that was the chief. I would fasten my eyes upon a sharp, wooded point that projected far into the river some miles ahead of me, and go to laboriously photographing its shape upon my brain; and just as I was beginning to succeed to my satisfaction, we would draw up toward it and the exasperating thing would begin to melt away and fold back into the bank! If there had been a conspicuous dead tree standing upon the very point of the cape, I would find that tree inconspicuously merged into the general forest, and occupying the middle of a straight shore, when I got abreast of it! No prominent hill would stick to its shape long enough for me to make up my mind what its form really was, but it was as dissolving and changeful as if it had been a mountain of butter in the hottest corner of the tropics. Nothing ever had the same shape when I was coming down-stream that it had borne when I went up. I mentioned these little difficulties to Mr. B——. He said,—

"That's the very main virtue of the thing. If the shapes didn't change every three seconds they wouldn't be of any use. Take this place where we are now, for instance. As long as that hill over yonder is only one hill, I can boom right along the way I'm going; but the moment it splits at the top and forms a V, I know I've got to scratch to starboard in a hurry, or I'll bang this boat's brains out against a rock; and then the moment one of the prongs of the V swings behind the other, I've got to waltz to larboard again, or I'll have a misunderstanding with a snag that would snatch the keelson out of this steamboat as neatly as if it were a sliver in your hand. If that hill didn't change its shape on bad nights there would be an awful steamboat grave-yard around here inside of a year."

It was plain that I had got to learn the shape of the river in all the different ways that could be thought of,—upside down, wrong end first, inside out, fore-and-aft, and "thortships,"—and then know what to do on gray nights when it hadn't any shape at all. So I set about it. In the course of time I began to get the best of this knotty lesson, and my self-complacency moved to the front once more. Mr. B—— was all fixed, and ready to start it to the rear again. He opened on me after this fashion:—

"How much water did we have in the middle crossing at Hole-in-the-Wall, trip before last?"

I considered this an outrage. I said:

"Every trip, down and up, the leadsmen are singing through that tangled place for three quarters of an hour on a stretch. How do you reckon I can remember such a mess as that?"

"My boy, you've got to remember it. You've got to remember the exact spot and the exact marks the boat lay in when we had the shoalest water, in every one of the two thousand shoal places between St. Louis and New Orleans; and you mustn't get the shoal soundings and marks of one trip mixed up with the shoal soundings and marks of another, either, for they're not often twice alike. You must keep them separate."

When I came to myself again, I said,—

"When I get so that I can do that, I'll be able to raise the dead, and then I won't have to pilot a steamboat in order to make a living. I want to retire from this business. I want a slushbucket and a brush; I'm only fit for a roustabout. I haven't got brains enough to be a pilot; and if I had I wouldn't have strength enough to carry them around, unless I went on crutches."

"Now drop that! When I say I'll learn[5] a man the river, I mean it. And you can depend on it I'll learn him or kill him."

There was no use in arguing with a person like this. I promptly put such a strain on my memory that by and by even the shoal water and the countless crossing-marks began to stay with me. But the result was just the same. I never could more than get one knotty thing learned before another presented itself. Now I had often seen pilots gazing at the water and pretending to read it as if it were a book; but it was a book that told me nothing. A time came at last, however, when Mr. B—— seemed to think me far enough advanced to bear a lesson on water-reading. So he began:—

"Do you see that long slanting line on the face of the water? Now that's a reef. Moreover, it's a bluff reef. There is a solid sand-bar under it that is nearly as straight up and down as the side of a house. There is plenty of water close up to it, but mighty little on top of it. If you were to hit it you would knock the boat's brains out. Do you see where the line fringes out at the upper end and begins to fade away?"

---

[5] "Teach" is not in the river vocabulary. (M.T.)

"Yes, sir."

"Well, that is a low place; that is the head of the reef. You can climb over there, and not hurt anything. Cross over, now, and follow along close under the reef—easy water there—not much current."

I followed the reef along till I approached the fringed end. Then Mr. B——said,—

"Now get ready. Wait till I give the word. She won't want to mount the reef; a boat hates shoal water. Stand by—wait—wait—keep her well in hand. *Now* cramp her down! Snatch her! snatch her!"

He seized the other side of the wheel and helped to spin it around until it was hard down, and then we held it so. The boat resisted and refused to answer for a while, and next she came surging to starboard, mounted the reef, and sent a long, angry ridge of water foaming away from her bows.

"Now watch her; watch her like a cat, or she'll get away from you. When she fights strong and the tiller slips a little, in a jerky, greasy sort of way, let up on her a trifle; it is the way she tells you at night that the water is too shoal; but keep edging her up, little by little, toward the point. You are well up on the bar, now; there is a bar under every point, because the water that comes down around it forms an eddy and allows the sediment to sink. Do you see those fine lines on the face of the water that branch out like the ribs of a fan? Well, those are little reefs; you want to just miss the ends of them, but run them pretty close. Now look out—look out! Don't you crowd that slick, greasy-looking place; there ain't nine feet there; she won't stand it. She begins to smell it; look sharp, I tell you! Oh blazes, there you go! Stop the starboard wheel! Quick! Ship up to back! Set her back!"

The engine bells jingled and the engines answered promptly, shooting white columns of steam far aloft out of the scape pipes, but it was too late. The boat had "smelt" the bar in good earnest; the foamy ridges that radiated from her bows suddenly disappeared, a great dead swell came rolling forward and swept ahead of her, she careened far over to larboard, and went tearing away toward the other shore as if she were about scared to death. We were a good mile from where we ought to have been, when we finally got the upper hand of her again.

During the afternoon watch the next day, Mr. B—— asked me if I knew how to run the next few miles. I said:—

"Go inside the first snag above the point, outside the next one, start out from the lower end of Higgins's woodyard, make a square crossing and"—

"That's all right. I'll be back before you close up on the next point."

But he wasn't. He was still below when I rounded it and entered upon a piece of river which I had some misgivings about. I did not know that he was hiding behind a chimney to see how I would perform. I went gayly along, getting prouder and prouder, for he had never left the boat in my sole charge such a length of time before. I even got to "setting" her and letting the wheel go, entirely, while I vain-gloriously turned my back and inspected the stern marks and hummed a tune, a sort of easy indifference which I had prodigiously admired in B—— and other great pilots. Once I inspected rather long, and when I faced to the front again my heart flew into my mouth so suddenly that if I hadn't clapped my teeth together I would have lost it. One of those frightful bluff reefs was stretching its deadly length right across our bows! My head was gone in a moment; I did not know which end I stood on; I gasped and could not get my breath; I spun the wheel down with such rapidity that it wove itself together like a spider's web; the boat answered and turned square away from the reef, but the reef followed her! I fled, and still it followed—still it kept right across my bows! I never looked to see where I was going, I only fled. The awful crash was imminent—why didn't that villain come! If I committed the crime of ringing a bell, I might get thrown overboard. But better that than kill the boat. So in blind desperation I started such a rattling "shivaree" down below as never had astounded an engineer in this world before, I fancy. Amidst the frenzy of the bells the engines began to back and fill in a furious way, and my reason forsook its throne—we were about to crash into the woods on the other side of the river. Just then Mr. B—— stepped calmly into view on the hurricane deck. My soul went out to him in gratitude. My distress vanished; I would have felt safe on the brink of Niagara, with Mr. B—— on the hurricane deck. He blandly and sweetly took his tooth-pick out of his mouth between his fingers, as if it were a cigar, we were just in the act of climbing an overhanging big tree, and the passengers were scudding astern like rats,—and lifted up these commands to me ever so gently:—

"Stop the starboard. Stop the larboard. Set her back on both."

The boat hesitated, halted, pressed her nose among the boughs a critical instant, then reluctantly began to back away.

"Stop the larboard. Come ahead on it. Stop the starboard. Come ahead on it. Point her for the bar."

I sailed away as serenely as a summer's morning. Mr. B—— came in and said, with mock simplicity,—

"When you have a hail, my boy, you ought to tap the big bell three times before you land, so that the engineers can get ready."

I blushed under the sarcasm, and said I hadn't had any hail.

"Ah! Then it was for wood, I suppose. The officer of the watch will tell you when he wants to wood up."

I went on consuming, and said I wasn't after wood.

"Indeed? Why, what could you want over here in the bend, then? Did you ever know of a boat following a bend up-stream at this stage of the river?"

"No, sir,—and *I* wasn't trying to follow it. I was getting away from a bluff reef."

"No, it wasn't a bluff reef; there isn't one within three miles of where you were."

"But I saw it. It was as bluff as that one yonder."

"Just about. Run over it!"

"Do you give it as an order?"

"Yes. Run over it."

"If I don't, I wish I may die."

"All right; I am taking the responsibility."

I was just as anxious to kill the boat, now, as I had been to save her before. I impressed my orders upon my memory, to be used at the inquest, and made a straight break for the reef. As it disappeared under our bows I held my breath; but we slid over it like oil.

"Now don't you see the difference? It wasn't anything but a wind reef. The wind does that."

"So I see. But it is exactly like a bluff reef. How am I ever going to tell them apart?"

"I can't tell you. It is an instinct. By and by you will just naturally *know* one from the other, but you never will be able to explain why or how you know them apart."

It turned out to be true. The face of the water, in time, became a wonderful book—a book that was a dead language to the uneducated passenger, but which told its mind to me without reserve, delivering its most cherished secrets as clearly as if it uttered them with a voice. And it was not a book to be read once and thrown aside, for it had a new story to tell every day. Throughout the long twelve hundred miles there was never a page that was void of interest, never one that you could leave unread without loss, never one that you would want to skip, thinking you could find higher enjoyment in some other thing. There never was so wonderful a book written by man; never one whose interest was so absorbing, so unflagging, so sparklingly renewed with every re-perusal. The passenger who could not read it was charmed with a peculiar sort of faint dimple in its surface (on the rare occasions when he did not overlook it altogether); but to the pilot that was an *italicized* passage; indeed, it was more than that, it was a legend of the largest capitals with a string of shouting exclamation points at the end of it; for it meant that a wreck or a rock was buried here that could tear the life out of the strongest vessel that ever floated. It is the faintest and simplest expression the water ever makes, and the most hideous to a pilot's eye. In truth, the passenger who could not read this book saw nothing but all manner of pretty pictures in it, painted by the sun and shaded by the clouds, whereas to the trained eye these were not pictures at all, but the grimmest and most dead-earnest of reading-matter.

Now when I had mastered the language of this water and had come to know every trifling feature that bordered the great river as familiarly as I knew the letters of the alphabet, I had made a valuable acquisition. But I had lost something, too. I had lost something which could never be restored to me while I lived. All the grace, the beauty, the poetry had gone out of the majestic river! I still keep in mind a certain wonderful sunset which I witnessed when steamboating was new to me. A broad expanse of the river was turned to blood; in the middle distance the red hue brightened into gold, through which a solitary log came floating, black and conspicuous; in one place a long, slanting mark lay sparkling upon the water; in another the surface was broken by boiling, tumbling rings, that were as many-tinted as an opal; where the ruddy flush was faintest, was a smooth spot that was covered with graceful circles and radiating lines, ever so delicately traced; the shore on our left was densely wooded, and the sombre shadow that fell from this forest was broken in one place by a long, ruffled trail that shone like silver; and high above the forest wall a clean-stemmed dead tree waved a single leafy bough that glowed like a flame in the unobstructed splendor that was flowing from the sun. There were graceful curves, reflected images, woody heights, soft distances; and over the whole scene, far and near, the dissolving lights drifted steadily, enriching it, every passing moment, with new marvels of coloring.

I stood like one bewitched. I drank it in, in a speechless rapture. The world was new to me, and I had never seen anything like this at home. But as I have said, a day came when I began to cease noting the glories and the charms which the moon and the sun and the twilight wrought upon the river's face; another day came when I ceased altogether to note them. Then, if that sunset scene had been repeated, I would have looked upon it without rapture, and would have commented upon it, inwardly, after this fashion: This sun means that we are going to have wind to-morrow; that floating log means that the river is rising, small thanks to it; that slanting mark on the water refers to a bluff reef which is going to kill somebody's steamboat one of these nights, if it keeps on stretching out like that; those tumbling "boils" show a dissolving bar and a changing channel there; the lines and circles in the slick water over yonder are a warning that that execrable place is shoaling up dangerously; that silver streak in the shadow of the forest is the "break" from a new snag, and he has located himself in the very best place he could have found to fish for steamboats; that tall, dead tree, with a single living branch, is not going to last long, and then how is a body ever going to get through this blind place at night without the friendly old landmark?

No, the romance and the beauty were all gone from the river. All the value any feature of it had for me now was the amount of usefulness it could furnish toward compassing the safe piloting of a steamboat. Since those days, I have pitied doctors from my heart. What does the lovely flush in a beauty's cheek mean to a doctor but a "break" that ripples above some deadly disease? Are not all her visible charms sown thick with what are to him the signs and symbols of hidden decay? Does he ever see her beauty at all, or doesn't he simply view her professionally, and comment upon her unwholesome condition all to himself? And doesn't he sometimes wonder whether he has gained most or lost most by learning his trade?

HENRY JAMES

The Pupil

I

THE POOR YOUNG MAN hesitated and procrastinated: it cost him such an effort to broach the subject of terms, to speak of money to a person who spoke only of feelings and, as it were, of the aristocracy. Yet he was unwilling to take leave, treating his engagement as settled, without some more conventional glance in that direction than he could find an opening for in the manner of the large, affable lady who sat there drawing a pair of soiled *gants de Suède*[1] through a fat, jewelled hand and, at once pressing and gliding, repeated over and over everything but the thing he would have liked to hear. He would have liked to hear the figure of his salary; but just as he was nervously about to sound that note the little boy came back—the little boy Mrs. Moreen had sent out of the room to fetch her fan. He came back without the fan, only with the casual observation that he couldn't find it. As he dropped this cynical confession he looked straight and hard at the candidate for the honour of taking his education in hand. This personage reflected, somewhat grimly, that the first thing he should have to teach his little charge would be to appear to address himself to his mother when he spoke to her—especially not to make her such an improper answer as that.

When Mrs. Moreen bethought herself of this pretext for getting rid of their companion, Pemberton supposed it was precisely to approach the delicate subject of his remuneration. But it had been only to say some things about her son which it was better that a boy of eleven shouldn't catch. They were extravagantly to his advantage, save when she lowered her voice to sigh, tapping her left side famil-

From Henry James, *The Lesson of the Master*. (New York and London: Macmillan and Co., 1892), pp. 123–179. First published in *Longman's Magazine*, (March-April, 1891); revised and included in Vol. XI of James's collected works (1909).

[1] Suede gloves.

124 THE YOUNG MAN IN AMERICAN LITERATURE

iarly: "And all overclouded by *this,* you know—all at the mercy of a weakness—!" Pemberton gathered that the weakness was in the region of the heart. He had known the poor child was not robust: this was the basis on which he had been invited to treat, through an English lady, an Oxford acquaintance, then at Nice, who happened to know both his needs and those of the amiable American family looking out for something really superior in the way of a resident tutor.

The young man's impression of his prospective pupil, who had first come into the room, as if to see for himself, as soon as Pemberton was admitted, was not quite the soft solicitation the visitor had taken for granted. Morgan Moreen was, somehow, sickly without being delicate, and that he looked intelligent (it is true Pemberton wouldn't have enjoyed his being stupid), only added to the suggestion that, as with his big mouth and big ears he really couldn't be called pretty, he might be unpleasant. Pemberton was modest—he was even timid; and the chance that his small scholar might prove cleverer than himself had quite figured, to his nervousness, among the dangers of an untried experiment. He reflected, however, that these were risks one had to run when one accepted a position, as it was called, in a private family; when as yet one's University honours had, pecuniarily speaking, remained barren. At any rate, when Mrs. Moreen got up as if to intimate that, since it was understood he would enter upon his duties within the week she would let him off now, he succeeded, in spite of the presence of the child, in squeezing out a phrase about the rate of payment. It was not the fault of the conscious smile which seemed a reference to the lady's expensive identity, if the allusion did not sound rather vulgar. This was exactly because she became still more gracious to reply: "Oh! I can assure you that all that will be quite regular."

Pemberton only wondered, while he took up his hat, what "all that" was to amount to—people had such different ideas. Mrs. Moreen's words, however, seemed to commit the family to a pledge definite enough to elicit from the child a strange little comment, in the shape of the mocking, foreign ejaculation, "Oh, là-là!"

Pemberton, in some confusion, glanced at him as he walked slowly to the window with his back turned, his hands in his pockets and the air in his elderly shoulders of a boy who didn't play. The young man wondered if he could teach him to play, though his mother had said it would never do and that this was why school was impossible. Mrs. Moreen exhibited no discomfiture; she only continued blandly: "Mr. Moreen will be delighted to meet your wishes. As I told you, he has been called to London for a week. As soon as he comes back you shall have it out with him."

This was so frank and friendly that the young man could only reply, laughing as his hostess laughed: "Oh! I don't imagine we shall have much of a battle."

"They'll give you anything you like," the boy remarked unexpectedly, returning from the window. "We don't mind what anything costs—we live awfully well."

"My darling, you're too quaint!" his mother exclaimed, putting out to caress him a practiced but ineffectual hand. He slipped out of it, but looked with intelligent, innocent eyes at Pemberton, who had already had time to notice that from one moment to the other his small satiric face seemed to change its time of life. At this moment it was infantine; yet it appeared also to be under the influence of curious intuitions and knowledges. Pemberton rather disliked precocity, and he was disappointed to find gleams of it in a disciple not yet in his teens. Nevertheless he divined on the spot that Morgan wouldn't prove a bore. He would prove on the contrary a kind of excitement. This idea held the young man, in spite of a certain repulsion.

"You pompous little person! We're not extravagant!" Mrs. Moreen gayly protested, making another unsuccessful attempt to draw the boy to her side. "You must know what to expect," she went on to Pemberton.

"The less you expect the better!" her companion interposed. "But we *are* people of fashion."

"Only so far as *you* make us so!" Mrs. Moreen mocked, tenderly. "Well, then, on Friday—don't tell me you're superstitious—and mind you don't fail us. Then you'll see us all. I'm so sorry the girls are out. I guess you'll like the girls. And, you know, I've another son, quite different from this one."

"He tries to imitate me," said Morgan to Pemberton.

"He tries? Why, he's twenty years old!" cried Mrs. Moreen.

"You're very witty," Pemberton remarked to the child—a proposition that his mother echoed with enthusiasm, declaring that Morgan's sallies were the delight of the house. The boy paid no heed to this; he only inquired abruptly of the visitor, who was surprised afterwards that he hadn't struck him as offensively forward: "Do you *want* very much to come?"

"Can you doubt it, after such a description of what I shall hear?" Pemberton replied. Yet he didn't want to come at all; he was coming because he had to go somewhere, thanks to the collapse of his fortune at the end of a year abroad, spent on the system of putting his tiny patrimony into a single full wave of experience. He had had his full wave, but he couldn't pay his hotel bill. Moreover, he had caught in the boy's eyes the glimpse of a far-off appeal.

"Well, I'll do the best I can for you," said Morgan; with which he turned away again. He passed out of one of the long windows; Pemberton saw him go and lean on the parapet of the terrace. He remained there while the young man took leave of his mother, who, on Pemberton's looking as if he expected a farewell from him, interposed with: "Leave him, leave him; he's so strange!" Pemberton suspected she was afraid of something he might say. "He's a genius—you'll love him," she added. "He's much the most interesting person in the family." And before he could invent some civility to oppose to this, she would up with: "But we're all good, you know!"

"He's a genius—you'll love him!" were words that recurred to Pemberton before the Friday, suggesting, among other things that geniuses were not invariably lovable. However, it was all the better if there was an element that would make tutorship absorbing: he had perhaps taken too much for granted that it would be dreary. As he left the villa after his interview, he looked up at the balcony and saw the child leaning over it. "We shall have great larks!" he called up.

Morgan hesitated a moment; then he answered, laughing: "By the time you come back I shall have thought of something witty!"

This made Pemberton say to himself: "After all he's rather nice."

II

On the Friday he saw them all, as Mrs. Moreen had promised, for her husband had come back and the girls and the other son were at home. Mr. Moreen had a white moustache, a confiding manner and, in his buttonhole, the ribbon of a foreign order—bestowed, as Pemberton eventually learned, for services. For what services he never clearly ascertained: this was a point—one of a large number—that Mr. Moreen's manner never confided. What it emphatically did confide was that he was a man of the world. Ulick, the firstborn, was in visible training for the same profession—under the disadvantage as yet, however, of a buttonhole only feebly floral and a moustache with no pretensions to type. The girls had hair and figures and manners and small fat feet, but had never been out alone. As for Mrs. Moreen, Pemberton saw on a nearer view that her elegance was intermittent and her parts didn't always match. Her husband, as she had promised, met with enthusiasm Pemberton's ideas in regard to a salary. The young man had endeavoured to make them modest, and Mr. Moreen confided to him that *he* found them positively meagre. He further assured him that he aspired to be intimate with his children, to be their best friend, and that he was always looking out for them. That was what he went off for, to London and other places—to look out; and this vigilance was the theory of life, as well as the real occupation, of the whole family. They all looked out, for they were very frank on the subject of its being necessary. They desired it to be understood that they were earnest people, and also that their fortune, though quite adequate for earnest people, required the most careful administration. Mr. Moreen, as the parent bird, sought sustenance for the nest. Ulick found sustenance mainly at the club, where Pemberton guessed that it was usually served on green cloth. The girls used to do up their hair and their frocks themselves, and our young man felt appealed to to be glad, in regard to Morgan's education, that, though it must naturally be of the best, it didn't cost too much. After a little he *was* glad, forgetting at times his own needs in the interest inspired by the child's nature and education and the pleasure of making easy terms for him.

During the first weeks of their acquaintance Morgan had been as puzzling as a page in an unknown language—altogether different from the obvious little Anglo-Saxons who had misrepresented child-hood to Pemberton. Indeed the whole mystic volume in which the boy had been bound demanded some practice in translation. To-day, after a considerable interval, there is something phantasmagoric, like a prismatic reflection or a serial novel, in Pemberton's memory of the queerness of the Moreens. If it were not for a few tangible tokens—a lock of Morgan's hair, cut by his own hand, and the half-dozen letters he got from him when they were separated—the whole episode and the figures peopling it would seem too inconsequent for anything but dreamland. The queerest thing about them was their success (as it appeared to him for a while at the time), for he had never seen a family so brilliantly equipped for failure. Wasn't it suc-cess to have kept him so hatefully long? Wasn't it success to have drawn him in that first morning at *déjeuner,*[2] the Friday he came—it was enough to *make* one superstitious—so that he utterly committed himself, and this not by calculation or a *mot d' ordre,*[3] but by a happy instinct which made them, like a band of gipsies, work so neatly together? They amused him as much as if they had really been a band of gipsies. He was still young and had not seen much of the world—his English years had been intensely usual; therefore the reversed conventions of the Moreens (for they had their standards), struck him as topsyturvy. He had encountered nothing like them at Oxford; still less had any such note been struck to his younger American ear during the four years at Yale in which he had richly supposed himself to be reacting against Puritanism. The reaction of the Moreens, at any rate, went ever so much further. He had thought himself very clever that first day in hitting them all off in

[2] Lunch.
[3] Password.

his mind with the term "cosmopolite." Later, it seemed feeble and colourless enough—confessedly, helplessly provisional.

However, when he first applied it to them he had a degree of joy —for an instructor he was still empirical—as if from the apprehension that to live with them would really be to see life. Their sociable strangeness was an intimation of that—their chatter of tongues, their gaiety and good humour, their infinite dawdling (they were always getting themselves up, but it took forever, and Pemberton had once found Mr. Moreen shaving in the drawing-room), their French, their Italian and, in the spiced fluency, their cold, tough slices of American. They lived on macaroni and coffee (they had these articles prepared in perfection), but they knew recipes for a hundred other dishes. They overflowed with music and song, were always humming and catching each other up, and had a kind of professional acquaintance with continental cities. They talked of "good places" as if they had been strolling players. They had at Nice a villa, a carriage, a piano and a banjo, and they went to official parties. They were a perfect calendar of the "days" of their friends, which Pemberton knew them, when they were indisposed, to get out of bed to go to, and which made the week larger than life when Mrs. Moreen talked of them with Paula and Amy. Their romatic initiations gave their new inmate at first an almost dazzling sense of culture. Mrs. Moreen had translated something, at some former period—an author whom it made Pemberton feel *borné*[4] never to have heard of. They could imitate Venetian and sing Neapolitan, and when they wanted to say something very particular they communicated with each other in an ingenious dialect of their own—a sort of spoken cipher, which Pemberton at first took for Volapuk, but which he learned to understand as he would not have understood Volapuk.

"It's the family language—Ultramoreen." Morgan explained to him drolly enough; but the boy rarely condescended to use it himself, though he attempted colloquial Latin as if he had been a little prelate.

Among all the "days" with which Mrs. Moreen's memory was taxed she managed to squeeze in one of her own, which her friends sometimes forgot. But the house derived a frequented air from the number of fine people who were freely named there and from several mysterious men with foreign titles and English clothes whom Morgan called the princes and who, on sofas with the girls, talked French very loud, as if to show they were saying nothing improper. Pemberton wondered how the princes could ever propose in that tone and so publicly: he took for granted cynically that this was

[4] Unimportant.

what was desired of them. Then he acknowledged that even for the chance of such an advantage Mrs. Moreen would never allow Paula and Amy to receive alone. These young ladies were not at all timid, but it was just the safeguards that made them so graceful. It was a houseful of Bohemians who wanted tremendously to be Philistines.

In one respect, however, certainly, they achieved no rigour—they were wonderfully amiable and ecstatic about Morgan. It was a genuine tenderness, an artless admiration, equally strong in each. They even praised his beauty, which was small, and were rather afraid of him, as if they recognised that he was of a finer clay. They called him a little angel and a little prodigy and pitied his want of health effusively. Pemberton feared at first that their extravagance would make him hate the boy, but before this happened he had become extravagant himself. Later, when he had grown rather to hate the others, it was a bribe to patience for him that they were at any rate nice about Morgan, going on tiptoe if they fancied he was showing symptoms, and even giving up somebody's "day" to procure him a pleasure. But mixed with this was the oddest wish to make him independent, as if they felt that they were not good enough for him. They passed him over to Pemberton very much as if they wished to force a constructive adoption on the obliging bachelor and shirk altogether a responsibility. They were delighted when they perceived that Morgan liked his preceptor, and could think of no higher praise for the young man. It was strange how they contrived to reconcile the appearance, and indeed the essential fact, of adoring the child with their eagerness to wash their hands of him. Did they want to get rid of him before he should find them out? Pemberton was finding them out month by month. At any rate, the boy's relations turned their backs with exaggerated delicacy, as if to escape the charge of interfering. Seeing in time how little he had in common with them (it was by *them* he first observed it—they proclaimed it with complete humility), his preceptor was moved to speculate on the mysteries of transmission, the far jumps of heredity. Where his detachment from most of the things they represented had come from was more than an observer could say—it certainly had burrowed under two or three generations.

As for Pemberton's own estimate of his pupil, it was a good while before he got the point of view, so little had he been prepared for it by the smug young barbarians to whom the tradition of tutorship, as hitherto revealed to him, had been adjusted. Morgan was scrappy and surprising, deficient in many properties supposed common to the *genus* and abounding in others that were the portion only of the supernaturally clever. One day Pemberton made a great stride: it cleared up the question to perceive that Morgan *was* supernaturally clever and that, though the formula was temporarily meagre, this would be the only assumption on which one could successfully deal with him. He had the general quality of a child for whom life had not been simplified by school, a kind of homebred sensibility which might have been bad for himself but was charming for others, and a whole range of refinement and perception—little musical vibrations as taking as picked-up airs—begotten by wandering about Europe at the tail of his migratory tribe. This might not have been an education to recommend in advance, but its results with Morgan were as palpable as a fine texture. At the same time he had in his composition a sharp spice of stoicism, doubtless the fruit of having had to begin early to bear pain, which produced the impression of pluck and made it of less consequence that he might have been thought at school rather a polyglot little beast. Pemberton indeed quickly found himself rejoicing that school was out of the question: in any million of boys it was probably good for all but one, and Morgan was that millionth. It would have made him comparative and superior—it might have made him priggish. Pemberton would try to be school himself—a bigger seminary than five hundred grazing donkeys; so that, winning no prizes, the boy would remain unconscious and irresponsible and amusing—amusing, because, though life was already intense in his childish nature, freshness still made there a strong draught for jokes. It turned out that even in the still air of Morgan's various disabilities jokes flourished greatly. He was a pale, lean, acute, undeveloped little cosmopolite, who liked intellectual gymnastics and who, also, as regards the behaviour of mankind, had noticed more things than you might suppose, but who nevertheless had his proper playroom of superstitions, where he smashed a dozen toys a day.

III

At Nice once, towards evening, as the pair sat resting in the open air after a walk, looking over the sea at the pink western lights, Morgan said suddenly to his companion: "Do you like it—you know, being with us all in this intimate way?"

"My dear fellow, why should I stay if I didn't?"

"How do I know you will stay? I'm almost sure you won't, very long."

"I hope you don't mean to dismiss me," said Pemberton.

Morgan considered a moment, looking at the sunset. "I think if I did right I ought to."

"Well, I know I'm supposed to instruct you in virtue; but in that case don't do right."

"You're very young—fortunately," Morgan went on, turning to him again.

"Oh yes, compared with you!"

"Therefore, it won't matter so much if you do lose a lot of time."

"That's the way to look at it," said Pemberton accommodatingly.

They were silent a minute; after which the boy asked: "Do you like my father and mother very much?"

"Dear me, yes. They're charming people."

Morgan received this with another silence; then, unexpectedly, familiarly, but at the same time affectionately, he remarked: "You're a jolly old humbug!"

For a particular reason the words made Pemberton change colour. The boy noticed in an instant that he had turned red, whereupon he turned red himself and the pupil and the master exchanged a longish glance in which there was a consciousness of many more things than are usually touched upon, even tacitly, in such a relation. It produced for Pemberton an embarrassment; it raised, in a shadowy form, a question (this was the first glimpse of it), which was destined to play as singular and, as he imagined, owing to the altogether peculiar conditions, an unprecedented part in his intercourse with his little companion. Later, when he found himself talking with this small boy in a way in which few small boys could ever have been talked with, he thought of that clumsy moment on the bench at Nice as the dawn of an understanding that had broadened. What had added to the clumsiness then was that he thought it his duty to declare to Morgan that he might abuse him (Pemberton) as much as he liked, but must never abuse his parents. To this Morgan had the easy reply that he hadn't dreamed of abusing them; which appeared to be true: it put Pemberton in the wrong.

"Then why am I a humbug for saying *I* think them charming?" the young man asked, conscious of a certain rashness.

"Well—they're not *your* parents."

"They love you better than anything in the world—never forget that," said Pemberton.

"Is that why you like them so much?"

"They're very kind to me," Pemberton replied, evasively.

"You *are* a humbug!" laughed Morgan, passing an arm into his tutor's. He leaned against him, looking off at the sea again and swinging his long, thin legs.

"Don't kick my shins," said Pemberton, while he reflected: "Hang it, I can't complain of them to the child!"

"There's another reason, too," Morgan went on, keeping his legs still.

"Another reason for what?"

"Besides their not being your parents."

"I don't understand you," said Pemberton.

"Well, you will before long. All right!"

Pemberton did understand, fully, before long; but he made a fight even with himself before he confessed it. He thought it the oddest thing to have a struggle with the child about. He wondered he didn't detest the child for launching him in such a struggle. But by the time it began the resource of detesting the child was closed to him. Morgan was a special case, but to know him was to accept him on his own odd terms. Pemberton had spent his aversion to special cases before arriving at knowledge. When at last he did arrive he felt that he was in an extreme predicament. Against every interest he had attached himself. They would have to meet things together. Before they went home that evening, at Nice, the boy had said, clinging to his arm:

"Well, at any rate you'll hang on to the last."

"To the last?"

"Till you're fairly beaten."

"*You* ought to be fairly beaten!" cried the young man, drawing him closer.

IV

A year after Pemberton had come to live with them Mr. and Mrs. Moreen suddenly gave up the villa at Nice. Pemberton had got used to suddenness, having seen it practiced on a considerable scale during two jerky little tours—one in Switzerland the first summer, and the other late in the winter, when they all ran down to Florence and then, at the end of ten days, liking it much less than they had intended, straggled back in mysterious depression. They had returned to Nice "for ever," as they said; but this didn't prevent them from squeezing, one rainy, muggy May night, into a second-class railway-carriage—you could never tell by which class they would travel—where Pemberton helped them to stow away a wonderful collection of bundles and bags. The explanation of this manœuvre was that they had determined to spend the summer "in some bracing place;" but in Paris they dropped into a small furnished apartment—a fourth floor in a third-rate avenue, where there was a smell on the staircase and the *portier* was hateful—and passed the next four months in blank indigence.

The better part of this baffled sojourn was for the preceptor and his pupil, who, visiting the Invalides and Notre Dame, the Conciergerie and all the museums, took a hundred remunerative rambles. They learned to know their Paris, which was useful, for they came back another year for a longer stay, the general character of which in Pemberton's memory to-day mixes pitiably and confusedly with that of the first. He sees Morgan's shabby knickerbockers—the everlasting pair that didn't match his blouse and that as he grew longer could only grow faded. He remembers the particular holes in his three or four pair of coloured stockings.

Morgan was dear to his mother, but he never was better dressed than was absolutely necessary—partly, no doubt, by his own fault, for he was as indifferent to his appearance as a German philosopher. "My dear fellow, you *are* coming to pieces," Pemberton would say to him in sceptical remonstrance; to which the child would reply, looking at him serenely up and down: "My dear fellow, so are you! I don't want to cast you in the shade." Pemberton could have no rejoinder for this—the assertion so closely represented the fact. If however the deficiencies of his own wardrobe were a chapter by themselves he didn't like his little charge to look too poor. Later he used to say: "Well, if we are poor, why, after all, shouldn't we look it?" and he consoled himself with thinking there was something rather elderly and gentlemanly in Morgan's seediness—it differed from the untidiness of the urchin who plays and spoils his things. He could trace perfectly the degrees by which, in proportion as her little son confined himself to his tutor for society, Mrs. Moreen shrewdly forbore to renew his garments. She did nothing that didn't show, neglected him because he escaped notice, and then, as she illustrated this clever policy, discouraged at home his public appearances. Her position was logical enough—those members of her family who did show had to be showy.

During this period and several others Pemberton was quite aware of how he and his comrade might strike people; wandering languidly through the Jardin des Plantes as if they had nowhere to go, sitting, on the winter days, in the galleries of the Louvre, so splendidly ironical to the homeless, as if for the advantage of the *calorifère*.[5] They joked about it sometimes: it was the sort of joke that was perfectly within the boy's compass. They figured themselves as part of the vast, vague, hand-to-mouth multitude of the enormous city and pretended they were proud of their position in it—it showed them such a lot of life and made them conscious of a sort of democratic brotherhood. If Pemberton could not feel a sympathy in destitution with his small companion (for after all Morgan's fond parents would never have let him really suffer), the boy would at least feel it with him, so it came to the same thing. He used sometimes to wonder what people would think they were—fancy they were looked

[5] Heating.

askance at, as if it might be a suspected case of kidnapping. Morgan wouldn't be taken for a young patrician with a preceptor—he wasn't smart enough; though he might pass for his companion's sickly little brother. Now and then he had a five-franc piece, and except once, when they bought a couple of lovely neckties, one of which he made Pemberton accept, they laid it out scientifically in old books. It was a great day, always spent on the quays, rummaging among the dusty boxes that garnish the parapets. These were occasions that helped them to live, for their books ran low very soon after the beginning of their acquaintance. Pemberton had a good many in England, but he was obliged to write to a friend and ask him kindly to get some fellow to give him something for them.

If the bracing climate was untasted that summer the young man had an idea that at the moment they were about to make a push the cup had been dashed from their lips by a movement of his own. It had been his first blow-out, as he called it, with his patrons; his first successful attempt (though there was little other success about it), to bring them to a consideration of his impossible position. As the ostensible eve of a costly journey the moment struck him as a good one to put in a signal protest—to present an ultimatum. Ridiculous as it sounded he had never yet been able to compass an uninterrupted private interview with the elder pair or with either of them singly. They were always flanked by their elder children, and poor Pemberton usually had his own little charge at his side. He was conscious of its being a house in which the surface of one's delicacy got rather smudged; neverthless he had kept the bloom of his scruple against announcing to Mr. and Mrs. Moreen with publicity that he couldn't go on longer without a little money. He was still simple enough to suppose Ulick and Paula and Amy might not know that since his arrival he had only had a hundred and forty francs; and he was magnanimous enough to wish not to compromise their parents in their eyes. Mr. Moreen now listened to him, as he listened to every one and to everything, like a man of the world, and seemed to appeal to him —though not of course too grossly—to try and be a little more of one himself. Pemberton recognised the importance of the character from the advantage it gave Mr. Moreen. He was not even confused, whereas poor Pemberton was more so than there was any reason for. Neither was he surprised—at least any more than a gentleman had to be who freely confessed himself a little shocked, though not, strictly, at Pemberton.

"We must go into this, mustn't we, dear?" he said to his wife. He assured his young friend that the matter should have his very best attention; and he melted into space as elusively as if, at the door, he were taking an inevitable but deprecatory precedence. When, the next moment, Pemberton found himself alone with Mrs. Moreen it was to hear her say: "I see, I see," stroking the roundness of her chin and looking as if she were only hesitating between a dozen easy remedies. If they didn't make their push Mr. Moreen could at least disappear for several days. During his absence his wife took up the subject again spontaneously, but her contribution to it was merely that she had thought all the while they were getting on so beautifully. Pemberton's reply to this revelation was that unless they immediately handed him a substantial sum he would leave them for ever. He knew she would wonder how he would get away, and for a moment expected her to inquire. She didn't, for which he was almost grateful to her, so little was he in a position to tell.

"You won't, you know you won't—you're too interested," she said. "You *are* interested, you know you are, you dear, kind man!" She laughed, with almost condemnatory archness, as if it were a reproach (but she wouldn't insist), while she flirted a soiled pocket-handkerchief at him.

Pemberton's mind was fully made up to quit the house the following week. This would give him time to get an answer to a letter he had dispatched to England. If he did nothing of the sort—that is, if he stayed another year and then went away only for three months —it was not merely because before the answer to his letter came (most unsatisfactory when it did arrive), Mr. Moreen generously presented him—again with all the precautions of a man of the world —three hundred francs. He was exasperated to find that Mrs. Moreen was right, that he couldn't bear to leave the child. This stood out clearer for the very reason that, the night of his desperate appeal to his patrons, he had seen fully for the first time where he was. Wasn't it another proof of the success with which those patrons practiced their arts that they had managed to avert for so long the illuminating flash? It descended upon Pemberton with a luridness which perhaps would have struck a spectator as comically excessive, after he had returned to his little servile room, which looked into a close court where a bare, dirty opposite wall took, with the sound of shrill clatter, the reflection of lighted back-windows. He had simply given himself away to a band of adventurers. The idea, the word itself, had a sort of romantic horror for him—he had always lived on such safe lines. Later it assumed a more interesting, almost a soothing, sense: it pointed a moral, and Pemberton could enjoy a moral. The Moreens were adventurers not merely because they didn't pay their debts, because they lived on society, but because their whole view of life, dim and confused and instinctive, like that of clever colour-blind animals, was speculative and rapacious and mean. Oh, they were "respectable," and that only made them more *immondes*.[6]

[6] Disgusting.

The young man's analysis of them put it at last very simply—they were adventurers because they were abject snobs. That was the completest account of them—it was the law of their being. Even when this truth became vivid to their ingenious inmate he remained unconscious of how much his mind had been prepared for it by the extraordinary little boy who had now become such a complication in his life. Much less could he then calculate on the information he was still to owe to the extraordinary little boy.

V

But it was during the ensuing time that the real problem came up —the problem of how far it was excusable to discuss the turpitude of parents with a child of twelve, of thirteen, of fourteen. Absolutely inexcusable and quite impossible it of course at first appeared; and indeed the question didn't press for a while after Pemberton had received his three hundred francs. They produced a sort of lull, a relief from the sharpest pressure. Pemberton frugally amended his wardrobe and even had a few francs in his pocket. He thought the Moreens looked at him as if he were almost too smart, as if they ought to take care not to spoil him. If Mr. Moreen hadn't been such a man of the world he would perhaps have said something to him about his neckties. But Mr. Moreen was always enough a man of the world to let things pass—he had certainly shown that. It was singular how Pemberton guessed that Morgan, though saying nothing about it, knew something had happened. But three hundred francs, especially when one owed money, couldn't last for ever; and when they were gone—the boy knew when they were gone—Morgan did say something. The party had returned to Nice at the beginning of the winter, but not to the charming villa. They went to an hotel, where they stayed three months, and then they went to another hotel, explaining that they had left the first because they had waited and waited and couldn't get the rooms they wanted. These apartments, the rooms they wanted, were generally very splendid; but fortunately they never *could* get them—fortunately, I mean, for Pemberton, who reflected always that if they had got them there would have been still less for educational expenses. What Morgan said at last was said suddenly, irrelevantly, when the moment came, in the middle of a lesson, and consisted of the apparently unfeeling words: "You ought to *filer,* you know—you really ought."

Pemberton stared. He had learnt enough French slang from Morgan to know that to *filer* meant to go away. "Ah, my dear fellow, don't turn me off!"

Morgan pulled a Greek lexicon toward him (he used a Greek-German), to look out a word, instead of asking it of Pemberton. "You can't go on like this, you know."

"Like what, my boy?"

"You know they don't pay you up," said Morgan, blushing and turning his leaves.

"Don't pay me?" Pemberton stared again and feigned amazement. "What on earth put that into your head?"

"It has been there a long time," the boy replied, continuing his search.

Pemberton was silent, then he went on: "I say, what are you hunting for? They pay me beautifully."

"I'm hunting for the Greek for transparent fiction," Morgan dropped.

"Find that rather for gross impertinence, and disabuse your mind. What do I want of money?"

"Oh, that's another question!"

Pemberton hesitated—he was drawn in different ways. The severely correct thing would have been to tell the boy that such a matter was none of his business and bid him to go on with his lines. But they were really too intimate for that; it was not the way he was in the habit of treating him; there had been no reason it should be. On the other hand Morgan had quite lighted on the truth—he really shouldn't be able to keep it up much longer; therefore why not let him know one's real motive for forsaking him? At the same time it wasn't decent to abuse to one's pupil the family of one's pupil; it was better to misrepresent than to do that. So in reply to Morgan's last exclamation he just declared, to dismiss the subject, that he had received several payments.

"I say—I say!" the boy ejaculated, laughing.

"That's all right," Pemberton insisted. "Give me your written rendering."

Morgan pushed a copybook across the table, and his companion began to read the page, but with something running in his head that made it no sense. Looking up after a minute or two he found the child's eyes fixed on him, and he saw something strange in them. Then Morgan said: "I'm not afraid of the reality."

"I haven't yet seen the thing that you *are* afraid of —I'll do you that justice!"

This came out with a jump (it was perfectly true), and evidently gave Morgan pleasure. "I've thought of it a long time," he presently resumed.

"Well, don't think of it any more."

The child appeared to comply, and they had a comfortable and even an amusing hour. They had a theory that they were very thor-

ough, and yet they seemed always to be in the amusing part of lessons, the intervals between the tunnels, where there were waysides
and views. Yet the morning was brought to a violent end by Morgan's suddenly leaning his arms on the table, burying his head in
them and bursting into tears. Pemberton would have been startled
at any rate; but he was doubly startled because, as it then occurred
to him, it was the first time he had ever seen the boy cry. It was
rather awful.

The next day, after much thought, he took a decision and, believing it to be just, immediately acted upon it. He cornered Mr. and
Mrs. Moreen again and informed them that if, on the spot, they
didn't pay him all they owed him, he would not only leave their
house, but would tell Morgan exactly what had brought him to it.

"Oh, you *haven't* told him?" cried Mrs. Moreen, with a pacifying
hand on her well-dressed bosom.

"Without warning you? For what do you take me?"

Mr. and Mrs. Moreen looked at each other, and Pemberton could
see both that they were relieved and that there was a certain alarm
in their relief. "My dear fellow," Mr. Moreen demanded, "what use
can you have, leading the quiet life we all do, for such a lot of money?"—an inquiry to which Pemberton made no answer, occupied as
he was in perceiving that what passed in the mind of his patrons was
something like: "Oh, then, if we've felt that the child, dear little
angel, has judged us and how he regards us, and we haven't been
betrayed, he must have guessed—and, in short, it's *general!*" an idea
that rather stirred up Mr. and Mrs. Moreen, as Pemberton had desired that it should. At the same time, if he had thought that his
threat would do something towards bringing them round, he was
disappointed to find they had taken for granted (how little they appreciated his delicacy!) that he had already given them away to his
pupil. There was a mystic uneasiness in their parental breasts, and
that was the way they had accounted for it. None the less his threat
did touch them; for if they had escaped it was only to meet a new
danger. Mr. Moreen appealed to Pemberton, as usual, as a man of
the world; but his wife had recourse, for the first time since the arrival of their inmate, to a fine *hauteur*, reminding him that a devoted mother, with her child, had arts that protected her against
gross misrepresentation.

"I should misrepresent you grossly if I accused you of common
honesty!" the young man replied; but as he closed the door behind
him sharply, thinking he had not done himself much good, while
Mr. Moreen lighted another cigarette, he heard Mrs. Moreen shout
after him, more touchingly:

"Oh, you do, you *do*, put the knife to one's throat!"

The next morning, very early, she came to his room. He recognised her knock, but he had no hope that she brought him money; as to which he was wrong, for she had fifty francs in her hand. She squeezed forward in her dressing-gown, and he received her in his own, between his bath-tub and his bed. He had been tolerably schooled by this time to the "foreign ways" of his hosts. Mrs. Moreen was zealous, and when she was zealous she didn't care what she did; so she now sat down on his bed, his clothes being on the chairs, and, in her preoccupation, forgot, as she glanced round, to be ashamed of giving him such a nasty room. What Mrs. Moreen was zealous about on this occasion was to persuade him that in the first place she was very good-natured to bring him fifty francs, and, in the second, if he would only see it, he was really too absurd to expect to be *paid*. Wasn't he paid enough, without perpetual money—wasn't he paid by the comfortable, luxurious home that he enjoyed with them all, without a care, an anxiety, a solitary want? Wasn't he sure of his position, and wasn't that everything to a young man like him, quite unknown, with singularly little to show, the ground of whose exorbitant pretensions it was not easy to discover? Wasn't he paid, above all, by the delightful relation he had established with Morgan—quite ideal, as from master to pupil—and by the simple privilege of knowing and living with so amazingly gifted a child, than whom really—she meant literally what she said—there was no better company in Europe? Mrs. Moreen herself took to appealing to him as a man of the world; she said "Voyons, mon cher," and "My dear sir, look here now;" and urged him to be reasonable, putting it before him that it was really a chance for him. She spoke as if, according as he *should* be reasonable, he would prove himself worthy to be her son's tutor and of the extraordinary confidence they had placed in him.

After all, Pemberton reflected, it was only a difference of theory, and the theory didn't matter much. They had hitherto gone on that of renumerated, as now they would go on that of gratuitous, service; but why should they have so many words about it? Mrs. Moreen, however, continued to be convincing; sitting there with her fifty francs she talked and repeated, as women repeat, and bored and irritated him, while he leaned against the wall with his hands in the pockets of his wrapper, drawing it together round his legs and looking over the head of his visitor at the grey negations of his window. She wound up with saying: "You see I bring you a definite proposal."

"A definite proposal?"

"To make our relations regular, as it were—to put them on a comfortable footing."

"I see—it's a system," said Pemberton. "A kind of blackmail."

Mrs. Moreen bounded up, which was what the young man wanted.

"What do you mean by that?"

"You practice on one's fears—one's fears about the child if one should go away."

"And, pray, what would happen to him in that event?" demanded Mrs. Moreen, with majesty.

"Why, he'd be alone with *you*."

"And pray, with whom *should* a child be but with those whom he loves most?"

"If you think that, why don't you dismiss me?"

"Do you pretend that he loves you more than he loves *us?*" cried Mrs. Moreen.

"I think he ought to. I make sacrifices for him. Though I've heard of those *you* make, I don't see them."

Mrs. Moreen stared a moment; then, with emotion, she grasped Pemberton's hand. "*Will* you make it—the sacrifice?"

Pemberton ·burst out laughing. "I'll see—I'll do what I can—I'll stay a little longer. Your calculation is just—I *do* hate intensely to give him up; I'm fond of him and he interests me deeply, in spite of the inconvenience I suffer. You know my situation perfectly; I haven't a penny in the world, and, occupied as I am with Morgan, I'm unable to earn money."

Mrs. Moreen tapped her undressed arm with her folded bank-note. "Can't you write articles? Can't you translate, as *I* do?"

"I don't know about translating; it's wretchedly paid."

"I am glad to earn what I can," said Mrs. Moreen virtuously, with her head high.

"You ought to tell me who you do it for." Pemberton paused a moment, and she said nothing; so he added: "I've tried to turn off some little sketches, but the magazines won't have them—they're declined with thanks."

"You see then you're not such a phœnix—to have such pretensions," smiled his interlocutress.

"I haven't time to do things properly," Pemberton went on. Then as it came over him that he was almost abjectly good-natured to give these explanations he added: "If I stay on longer it must be on one condition—that Morgan shall know distinctly on what footing I am."

Mrs. Moreen hesitated. "Surely you don't want to show off to a child?"

"To show *you* off, do you mean?"

Again Mrs. Moreen hesitated, but this time it was to produce a still finer flower. "And *you* talk of blackmail!"

"You can easily prevent it," said Pemberton.

"And *you* talk of practicing on fears," Mrs. Moreen continued.

"Yes, there's no doubt I'm a great scoundrel."

His visitor looked at him a moment—it was evident that she was sorely bothered. Then she thrust out her money at him. "Mr. Moreen desired me to give you this on account."

"I'm much obliged to Mr. Moreen; but we have no account."

"You won't take it?"

"That leaves me more free," said Pemberton.

"To poison my darling's mind?" groaned Mrs. Moreen.

"Oh, your darling's mind!" laughed the young man.

She fixed him a moment, and he thought she was going to break out tormentedly, pleadingly: "For God's sake, tell me what *is* in it!" But she checked this impulse—another was stronger. She pocketed the money—the crudity of the alternative was comical—and swept out of the room with the desperate concession: "You may tell him any horror you like!"

VI

A couple of days after this, during which Pemberton had delayed to profit by Mrs. Moreen's permission to tell her son any horror, the two had been for a quarter of an hour walking together in silence when the boy became sociable again with the remark: "I'll tell you how I know it; I know it through Zénobie."

"Zénobie? Who in the world is *she?*"

"A nurse I used to have—ever so many years ago. A charming woman. I liked her awfully, and she liked me."

"There's no accounting for tastes. What is it you know through her?"

"Why, what their idea is. She went away because they didn't pay her. She did like me awfully, and she stayed two years. She told me all about it—that at last she could never get her wages. As soon as they saw how much she liked me they stopped giving her anything. They thought she'd stay for nothing, out of devotion. And she did stay ever so long—as long as she could. She was only a poor girl. She used to send money to her mother. At last she couldn't afford it any longer, and she went away in a fearful rage one night—I mean of course in a rage against *them*. She cried over me tremendously, she hugged me nearly to death. She told me all about it," Morgan repeated. "She told me it was their idea. So I guessed, ever so long ago, that they have had the same idea with you."

"Zénobie was very shrewd," said Pemberton. "And she made you so."

"Oh, that wasn't Zénobie; that was nature. And experience!" Morgan laughed.

"Well, Zénobie was a part of your experience."

"Certainly I was a part of hers, poor dear!" the boy exclaimed. "And I'm a part of yours."

"A very important part. But I don't see how you know that I've been treated like Zénobie."

"Do you take me for an idiot?" Morgan asked. "Havn't I been conscious of what we've been through together?"

"What we've been through?"

"Our privations—our dark days."

"Oh, our days have been bright enough."

Morgan went on in silence for a moment. Then he said: "My dear fellow, you're a hero!"

"Well, you're another!" Pemberton retorted.

"No, I'm not; but I'm not a baby. I won't stand it any longer. You must get some occupation that pays. I'm ashamed, I'm ashamed!" quavered the boy in a little passionate voice that was very touching to Pemberton.

"We ought to go off and live somewhere together," said the young man.

"I'll go like a shot if you'll take me."

"I'd get some work that would keep us both afloat," Pemberton continued.

"So would I. Why shouldn't *I* work? I ain't such a *crétin!*"[1]

"The difficulty is that your parents wouldn't hear of it," said Pemberton. "They would never part with you; they worship the ground you tread on. Don't you see the proof of it? They don't dislike me; they wish me no harm; they're very amiable people; but they're perfectly ready to treat me badly for your sake."

The silence in which Morgan received this graceful sophistry struck Pemberton somehow as expressive. After a moment Morgan repeated: "You *are* a hero!" Then he added: "They leave me with you altogether. You've all the responsibility. They put me off on you from morning till night. Why, then, should they object to my taking up with you completely? I'd help you."

"They're not particularly keen about my being helped, and they delight in thinking of you as *theirs*. They're tremendously proud of you."

"I'm not proud of them. But you know *that*," Morgan returned.

"Except for the little matter we speak of they're charming people," said Pemberton, not taking up the imputation of lucidity, but

[1] Idiot.

wondering greatly at the child's own, and especially at this fresh reminder of something he had been conscious of from the first—the strangest thing in the boy's large little composition, a temper, a sensibility, even a sort of ideal, which made him privately resent the general quality of his kinsfolk. Morgan had in secret a small loftiness which begot an element of reflection, a domestic scorn not imperceptible to his companion (though they never had any talk about it), and absolutely anomalous in a juvenile nature, especially when one noted that it had not made this nature "old-fashioned," as the word is of children—quaint or wizened or offensive. It was as if he had been a little gentleman and had paid the penalty by discovering that he was the only such person in the family. This comparison didn't make him vain; but it could make him melancholy and a trifle austere. When Pemberton guessed at these young dimnesses he saw him serious and gallant, and was partly drawn on and partly checked, as if with a scruple, by the charm of attempting to sound the little cool shallows which were quickly growing deeper. When he tried to figure to himself the morning twilight of childhood, so as to deal with it safely, he perceived that it was never fixed, never arrested, that ignorance, at the instant one touched it, was already flushing faintly into knowledge, that there was nothing that at a given moment you could say a clever child didn't know. It seemed to him that *he* both knew too much to imagine Morgan's simplicity and too little to disembroil his tangle.

The boy paid no heed to his last remark; he only went on: "I should have spoken to them about their idea, as I call it, long ago, if I hadn't been sure what they would say."

"And what would they say?"

"Just what they said about what poor Zénobie told me—that it was a horrid, dreadful story, that they had paid her every penny they owed her."

"Well, perhaps they had," said Pemberton.

"Perhaps they've paid you!"

"Let us pretend they have, and *n'en parlons plus*.⁸"

"They accused her of lying and cheating," Morgan insisted perversely. "That's why I don't want to speak to them."

"Lest they should accuse me, too?"

To this Morgan made no answer, and his companion, looking down at him (the boy turned his eyes, which had filled, away), saw that he couldn't have trusted himself to utter.

"You're right. Don't squeeze them," Pemberton pursued. "Except for that, they *are* charming people."

⁸ Let's not talk about it any more.

"Except for *their* lying and *their* cheating?"

"I say—I say!" cried Pemberton, imitating a little tone of the lad's which was itself an imitation.

"We must be frank, at the last; we *must* come to an understanding," said Morgan, with the importance of the small boy who lets himself think he is arranging great affairs—almost playing at shipwreck or at Indians. "I know all about everything," he added.

"I daresay your father has his reasons," Pemberton observed, too vaguely, as he was aware.

"For lying and cheating?"

"For saving and managing and turning his means to the best account. He has plenty to do with his money. You're an expensive family."

"Yes, I'm very expensive," Morgan rejoined, in a manner which made his preceptor burst out laughing.

"He's saving for *you*," said Pemberton. "They think of you in everything they do."

"He might save a little——" The boy paused. Pemberton waited to hear what. Then Morgan brought out oddly: "A little reputation."

"Oh, there's plenty of that. That's all right!"

"Enough of it for the people they know, no doubt. The people they know are awful."

"Do you mean the princes? We mustn't abuse the princes."

"Why not? They haven't married Paula—they haven't married Amy. They only clean out Ulick."

"You *do* know everything!" Pemberton exclaimed.

"No, I don't, after all. I don't know what they live on, or how they live, or *why* they live! What have they got and how did they get it? Are they rich, are they poor, or have they a *modeste aisance*[9]? Why are they always chiveying about—living one year like ambassadors and the next like paupers? Who are they, any way, and what are they? I've thought of all that—I've thought of a lot of things. They're so beastly worldly. That's what I hate most—oh, I've *seen* it! All they care about is to make an appearance and to pass for something or other. What do they want to pass for? What *do* they, Mr. Pemberton?"

"You pause for a reply," said Pemberton, treating the inquiry as a joke, yet wondering too, and greatly struck with the boy's intense, if imperfect, vision. "I haven't the least idea."

"And what good does it do? Haven't I seen the way people treat them—the "nice" people, the ones they want to know? They'll take anything from them—they'll lie down and be trampled on. The nice

9 Moderate means.

ones hate that—they just sicken them. You're the only really nice person we know."

"Are you sure? They don't lie down for me!"

"Well, you shan't lie down for them. You've got to go—that's what you've got to do," said Morgan.

"And what will become of you?"

"Oh, I'm growing up. I shall get off before long. I'll see you later."

"You had better let me finish you," Pemberton urged, lending himself to the child's extraordinarily competent attitude.

Morgan stopped in their walk, looking up at him. He had to look up much less than a couple of years before—he had grown, in his loose leanness, so long and high. "Finish me?" he echoed.

"There are such a lot of jolly things we can do together yet. I want to turn you out—I want you to do me credit."

Morgan continued to look at him. "To give you credit—do you mean?"

"My dear fellow, you're too clever to live."

"That's just what I'm afraid you think. No, no; it isn't fair—I can't endure it. We'll part next week. The sooner it's over the sooner to sleep."

"If I hear of anything—any other chance, I promise to go," said Pemberton.

Morgan consented to consider this. "But you'll be honest," he demanded; "you won't pretend you haven't heard?"

"I'm much more likely to pretend I have."

"But what can you hear of, this way, stuck in a hole with us? You ought to be on the spot, to go to England—you ought to go to America."

"One would think you were *my* tutor!" said Pemberton.

Morgan walked on, and after a moment he began again: "Well, now that you know that I know and that we look at the facts and keep nothing back—it's much more comfortable, isn't it?"

"My dear boy, it's so amusing, so interesting, that it surely will be quite impossible for me to forego such hours as these."

This made Morgan stop once more. "You *do* keep something back. Oh, you're not straight—*I* am!"

"Why am I not straight?"

"Oh, you've got your idea!"

"My idea?"

"Why, that I probably sha'n't live, and that you can stick it out till I'm removed."

"You *are* too clever to live!" Pemberton repeated.

"I call it a mean idea," Morgan pursued. "But I shall punish you by the way I hang on."

"Look out or I'll poison you!" Pemberton laughed.

"I'm stronger and better every year. Haven't you noticed that there hasn't been a doctor near me since you came?"

"*I'm* your doctor," said the young man, taking his arm and drawing him on again.

Morgan proceeded; and after a few steps he gave a sigh of mingled weariness and relief. "Ah, now that we look at the facts, it's all right!"

VII

They looked at the facts a good deal after this; and one of the first consequences of their doing so was that Pemberton stuck it out, as it were, for the purpose. Morgan made the facts so vivid and so droll, and at the same time so bald and so ugly, that there was fascination in talking them over with him, just as there would have been heartlessness in leaving him alone with them. Now that they had such a number of perceptions in common it was useless for the pair to pretend that they didn't judge such people; but the very judgment, and the exchange of perceptions, created another tie. Morgan had never been so interesting as now that he himself was made plainer by the sidelight of these confidences. What came out in it most was the soreness of his characteristic pride. He had plenty of that, Pemberton felt—so much that it was perhaps well it should have had to take some early bruises. He would have liked his people to be gallant, and he had waked up too soon to the sense that they were perpetually swallowing humble-pie. His mother would consume any amount, and his father would consume even more than his mother. He had a theory that Ulick had wriggled out of an "affair" at Nice: there had once been a flurry at home, a regular panic, after which they all went to bed and took medicine, not to be accounted for on any other supposition. Morgan had a romantic imagination, fed by poetry and history, and he would have liked those who "bore his name" (as he used to say to Pemberton with the humour that made his sensitiveness manly), to have a proper spirit. But their one idea was to get in with people who didn't want them and to take snubs as if they were honourable scars. Why people didn't want them more he didn't know—that was people's own affair; after all they were not superficially repulsive—they were a hundred times cleverer than most of the dreary grandees, the "poor swells" they rushed about Europe to catch up with. "After all, they *are* amusing—they are!" Morgan used to say, with the wisdom of the ages. To which Pemberton always replied: "Amusing—the great Moreen troupe? Why, they're altogether delightful; and if it were not for the hitch that you and I

(feeble performers!) make in the *ensemble,* they would carry everything before them."

What the boy couldn't get over was that this patricular blight
seemed, in a tradition of self-respect, so undeserved and so arbitrary.
No doubt people had a right to take the line they liked; but why
should *his* people have liked the line of pushing and toadying and
lying and cheating? What had their forefathers—all decent folk, so
far as he knew—done to them, or what had *he* done to them? Who
had poisoned their blood with the fifth-rate social ideal, the fixed
idea of making smart acquaintances and getting into the *monde
chic*,[10] especially when it was foredoomed to failure and exposure?
They showed so what they were after; that was what made the people they wanted not want *them.* And never a movement of dignity,
never a throb of shame at looking each other in the face, never an
independence or resentment or disgust. If his father or his brother
would only knock some one down once or twice a year! Clever as
they were they never guessed how they appeared. They were good-
natured, yes—as good-natured as Jews at the doors of clothing-shops!
But was that the model one wanted one's family to follow? Morgan
had dim memories of an old grandfather, the maternal, in New
York, whom he had been taken across the ocean to see, at the age of
five: a gentleman with a high neckcloth and a good deal of pronun-
ciation, who wore a dress-coat in the morning, which made one wonder what he wore in the evening, and had, or was supposed to have,
"property" and something to do with the Bible Society. It couldn't
have been but that *he* was a good type. Pemberton himself remembered Mrs. Clancy, a widowed sister of Mr. Moreen's, who was as irritating as a moral tale and had paid a fortnight's visit to the family
at Nice shortly after he came to live with them. She was "pure and
refined," as Amy said, over the banjo, and had the air of not knowing what they meant and of keeping something back. Pemberton
judged that what she kept back was an approval of many of their
ways; therefore it was to be supposed that she too was of a good type,
and that Mr. and Mrs. Moreen and Ulick and Paula and Amy might
easily have been better if they would.

But that they wouldn't was more and more perceptible from day
to day. They continued to "chivey," as Morgan called it, and in due
time became aware of a variety of reasons for proceeding to Venice.
They mentioned a great many of them—they were always strikingly
frank, and had the brightest friendly chatter, at the late foreign
breakfast in especial, before the ladies had made up their faces,
when they leaned their arms on the table, had something to follow

[10] Fashionable world.

the *demi-tasse,* and, in the heat of familiar discussion as to what they
"really ought" to do, fell inevitably into the languages in which they
could *tutoyer*.[11] Even Pemberton liked them, then; he could endure
even Ulick when he heard him give his little flat voice for the "sweet
sea-city." That was what made him have a sneaking kindness for
them—that they were so out of the workaday world and kept him so
out of it. The summer had waned when, with cries of ecstasy, they
all passed out on the balcony that overhung the Grand Canal; the
sunsets were splendid—the Dorringtons had arrived. The Dorringtons were the only reason they had not talked of at breakfast; but
the reasons that they didn't talk of at breakfast always came out in
the end. The Dorringtons, on the other hand, came out very little;
or else, when they did, they stayed—as was natural—for hours, during
which periods Mrs. Moreen and the girls sometimes called at their
hotel (to see if they had returned) as many as three times running.
The gondola was for the ladies; for in Venice too there were "days,"
which Mrs. Moreen knew in their order an hour after she arrived.
She immediately took one herself, to which the Dorringtons never
came, though on a certain occasion when Pemberton and his pupil
were together at St. Mark's—where, taking the best walks they had
ever had and haunting a hundred churches, they spent a great deal
of time—they saw the old lord turn up with Mr. Moreen and Ulick,
who showed him the dim basilica as if it belonged to them. Pemberton noted how much less, among its curiosities, Lord Dorrington carried himself as a man of the world; wondering too whether, for such
services, his companions took a fee from him. The autumn, at any
rate, waned, the Dorringtons departed, and Lord Verschoyle, the el-
dest son, had proposed neither for Amy nor for Paula.

One sad November Day, while the wind roared round the old pal-
ace and the rain lashed the lagoon, Pemberton, for exercise and even
somewhat for warmth (The Moreens were horribly frugal about fires
—it was a cause of suffering to their inmate), walked up and down
the big bare *sala*[12] with his pupil. The scagliola floor was cold, the
high battered casements shook in the storm, and the stately decay of
the place was unrelieved by a particle of furniture. Pemberton's spirits were low, and it came over him that the fortune of the Moreens
was now even lower. A blast of desolation, a prophecy of disaster
and disgrace, seemed to draw through the comfortless hall. Mr. Moreen and Ulick were in the Piazza, looking out for something, strolling drearily, in mackintoshes, under the arcades; but still, in spite of
mackintoshes, unmistakable men of the world. Paula and Amy

---

[11] Use the intimate second person singular form of address.
[12] Room.

were in bed—it might have been thought they were staying there to keep warm. Pemberton looked askance at the boy at his side, to see to what extent he was conscious of these portents. But Morgan, luckily for him, was now mainly conscious of growing taller and stronger and indeed of being in his fifteenth year. This fact was intensely interesting to him—it was the basis of a private theory (which, however, he had imparted to his tutor) that in a little while he should stand on his own feet. He considered that the situation would change—that, in short, he should be "finished," grown up, producible in the world of affairs and ready to prove himself of sterling ability. Sharply as he was capable, at times, of questioning his circumstances, there were happy hours when he was as superficial as a child; the proof of which was his fundamental assumption that he should presently go to Oxford, to Pemberton's college, and, aided and abetted by Pemberton, do the most wonderful things. It vexed Pemberton to see how little, in such a project, he took account of ways and means: on other matters he was so sceptical about them. Pemberton tried to imagine the Moreens at Oxford, and fortunately failed; yet unless they were to remove there as a family there would be no *modus vivendi*[13] for Morgan. How could he live without an allowance, and where was the allowance to come from? He (Pemberton) might live on Morgan; but how could Morgan live on him? What was to become of him anyhow? Somehow, the fact that he was a big boy now, with better prospects of health, made the question of his future more difficult. So long as he was frail the consideration that he inspired seemed enough of an answer to it. But at the bottom of Pemberton's heart was the recognition of his probably being strong enough to live and not strong enough to thrive. He himself, at any rate, was in a period of a natural, boyish rosiness about all this, so that the beating of the tempest seemed to him only the voice of life and the challenge of fate. He had on his shabby little overcoat, with the collar up, but he was enjoying his walk.

It was interrupted at last by the appearance of his mother at the end of the *sala*. She beckoned to Morgan to come to her, and while Pemberton saw him, complacent, pass down the long vista, over the damp false marble, he wondered what was in the air. Mrs. Moreen said a word to the boy and made him go into the room she had quitted. Then, having closed the door after him, she directed her steps swiftly to Pemberton. There *was* something in the air, but his wildest flight of fancy wouldn't have suggested what it proved to be. She signified that she had made a pretext to get Morgan out of the way, and then she inquired—without hesitation—if the young man could

---

[13] Mode of living.

lend her sixty francs. While, before bursting into a laugh, he stared at her with surprise, she declared that she was awfully pressed for the money; she was desperate for it—it would save her life.

"Dear lady, *c'est trop fort!*"[14] Pemberton laughed. "Where in the world do you suppose I should get sixty francs, *du train dont vous allez?*"[15]

"I thought you worked—wrote things; don't they pay you?"

"Not a penny."

"Are you such a fool as to work for nothing?"

"You ought surely to know that."

Mrs. Moreen stared an instant, then she coloured a little. Pemberton saw she had quite forgotten the terms—if "terms" they could be called—that he had ended by accepting from herself; they had burdened her memory as little as her conscience. "Oh, yes, I see what you mean—you have been very nice about that; but why go back to it so often?" She had been perfectly urbane with him ever since the rough scene of explanation in his room, the morning he made her accept *his* "terms"—the necessity of his making his case known to Morgan. She had felt no resentment, after seeing that there was no danger of Morgan's taking the matter up with her. Indeed, attributing this immunity to the good taste of his influence with the boy, she had once said to Pemberton: "My dear fellow; it's an immense comfort you're a gentleman." She repeated this, in substance, now. "Of course you're a gentleman—that's a bother the less!" Pemberton reminded her that he had not "gone back" to anything; and she also repeated her prayer that, somewhere and somehow, he would find her sixty francs. He took the liberty of declaring that if he could find them it wouldn't be to lend them to *her*—as to which he consciously did himself injustice, knowing that if he had them he would certainly place them in her hand. He accused himself, at bottom and with some truth, of a fantastic, demoralised sympathy with her. If misery made strange bedfellows it also made strange sentiments. It was moreover a part of the demoralisation and of the general bad effect of living with such people that one had to make rough retorts, quite out of the tradition of good manners. "Morgan, Morgan, to what pass have I come for you?" he privately exclaimed, while Mrs. Moreen floated voluminously down the *sala* again, to liberate the boy; groaning, as she went, that everything was too odious.

Before the boy was liberated there came a thump at the door communicating with the staircase, followed by the apparition of a dripping youth who poked in his head. Pemberton recognised him as the

[14] This is too much.
[15] Considering your behavior.

bearer of a telegram and recognised the telegram as addressed to himself. Morgan came back as, after glancing at the signature (that of a friend in London), he was reading the words: "Found jolly job for you—engagement to coach opulent youth on own terms. Come immediately." The answer, happily, was paid, and the messenger waited. Morgan, who had drawn near, waited too, and looked hard at Pemberton; and Pemberton, after a moment, having met his look, handed him the telegram. It was really by wise looks (they knew each other so well), that, while the telegraph-boy, in his waterproof cape, made a great puddle on the floor, the thing was settled between them. Pemberton wrote the answer with a pencil against the frescoed wall, and the messenger departed. When he had gone Pemberton said to Morgan:

"I'll make a tremendous charge; I'll earn a lot of money in a short time, and we'll live on it."

"Well, I hope the opulent youth will be stupid—he probably will —" Morgan parenthesised, "and keep you a long time."

"Of course, the longer he keeps me the more we shall have for our old age."

"But suppose *they* don't pay you!" Morgan awfully suggested.

"Oh, there are not two such—!" Pemberton paused, he was on the point of using an invidious term. Instead of this he said "two such chances."

Morgan flushed—the tears came to his eyes. "*Dites toujours,*[16] two such rascally crews!" Then, in a different tone, he added: "Happy opulent youth!"

"Not if he's stupid!"

"Oh, they're happier then. But you can't have everything, can you?" the boy smiled.

Pemberton held him, his hands on his shoulders. "What will become of *you,* what will you do?" He thought of Mrs. Moreen, desperate for sixty francs.

"I shall turn into a man." And then, as if he recognised all the bearings of Pemberton's allusion: "I shall get on with them better when you're not here."

"Ah, don't say that—it sounds as if I set you against them!"

"You do—the sight of you. It's all right; you know what I mean. I shall be beautiful. I'll take their affairs in hand; I'll marry my sisters."

"You'll marry yourself!" joked Pemberton; as high, rather tense pleasantry would evidently be the right, or the safest, tone for their separation.

[16] Speak frankly.

It was, however, not purely in this strain that Morgan suddenly asked: "But I say—how will you get to your jolly job? You'll have to telegraph to the opulent youth for money to come on."

Pemberton bethought himself. "They won't like that, will they?"

"Oh, look out for them!"

Then Pemberton brought out his remedy. "I'll go to the American Consul; I'll borrow some money of him—just for the few days, on the strength of the telegram."

Morgan was hilarious. "Show him the telegram—then stay and keep the money!"

Pemberton entered into the joke enough to reply that, for Morgan, he was really capable of that; but the boy, growing more serious, and to prove that he hadn't meant what he said, not only hurried him off to the Consulate (since he was to start that evening, as he had wired to his friend), but insisted on going with him. They splashed through the tortuous perforations and over the hump-backed bridges, and they passed through the Piazza, where they saw Mr. Moreen and Ulick go into a jeweller's shop. The Consul proved accommodating (Pemberton said it wasn't the letter, but Morgan's grand air), and on their way back they went into St. Mark's for a hushed ten minutes. Later they took up and kept up the fun of it to the very end; and it seemed to Pemberton a part of that fun that Mrs. Moreen, who was very angry when he had announced to her his intention, should charge him, grotesquely and vulgarly, and in reference to the loan she had vainly endeavoured to effect, with bolting lest they should "get something out" of him. On the other hand he had to do Mr. Moreen and Ulick the justice to recognise that when, on coming in, *they* heard the cruel news, they took it like perfect men of the world.

VIII

When Pemberton got at work with the opulent youth, who was to be taken in hand for Balliol, he found himself unable to say whether he was really an idiot or it was only, on his own part, the long association with an intensely living little mind that made him seem so. From Morgan he heard half-a-dozen times: the boy wrote charming young letters, a patchwork of tongues, with indulgent postscripts in the family Volapuk and, in little squares and rounds and crannies of the text, the drollest illustrations—letters that he was divided between the impulse to show his present disciple, as a kind of wasted incentive, and the sense of something in them that was profanable by publicity. The opulent youth went up, in due course, and failed to pass; but it seemed to add to the presumption that brilliancy was not expected of him all at once that his parents, condoning the lapse, which they good-naturedly treated as little as possible as if were Pemberton's, should have sounded the rally again, begged the young coach to keep his pupil in hand another year.

The young coach was now in a position to lend Mrs. Moreen sixty francs, and he sent her a post-office order for the amount. In return for this favour he received a frantic, scribbled line from her: "Implore you to come back instantly—Morgan dreadfully ill." They were on the rebound, once more in Paris—often as Pemberton had seen them depressed he had never seen them crushed—and communication was therefore rapid. He wrote to the boy to ascertain the state of his health, but he received no answer to his letter. Accordingly he took an abrupt leave of the opulent youth and, crossing the Channel, alighted at the small hotel, in the quarter of the Champs Elysées, of which Mrs. Moreen had given him the address. A deep if dumb dissatisfaction with this lady and her companions bore him company: they couldn't be vulgarly honest, but they could live at hotels, in velvety *entresols*,[17] amid a smell of burnt pastilles, in the most expensive city in Europe. When he had left them, in Venice, it was with an irrepressible suspicion that something was going to happen; but the only thing that had happened was that they succeeded in getting away. "How is he? where is he?" he asked of Mrs. Moreen; but before she could speak, these questions were answered by the pressure round his neck of a pair of arms, in shrunken sleeves, which were perfectly capable of an effusive young foreign squeeze.

"Dreadfully ill—I don't see it!" the young man cried. And then, to Morgan: "Why on earth didn't you relieve me? Why didn't you answer my letter?"

Mrs. Moreen declared that when she wrote he was very bad, and Pemberton learned at the same time from the boy that he had answered every letter he had received. This led to the demonstration that Pemberton's note had been intercepted. Mrs. Moreen was prepared to see the fact exposed, as Pemberton perceived, the moment he faced her, that she was prepared for a good many other things. She was prepared above all to maintain that she had acted from a sense of duty, that she was enchanted she had got him over, whatever they might say; and that it was useless of him to pretend that he didn't *know*, in all his bones, that his place at such a time was with Morgan. He had taken the boy away from them, and now he had no right to abandon him. He had created for himself the gravest responsibilities; he must at least abide by what he had done.

"Taken him away from you?" Pemberton exclaimed indignantly.

[17] Lobbies.

"Do it—do it, for pity's sake; that's just what I want. I can't stand *this*—and such scenes. They're treacherous!" These words broke from Morgan, who had intermitted his embrace, in a key which made Pemberton turn quickly to him, to see that he had suddenly seated himself, was breathing with evident difficulty and was very pale.

"*Now* do you say he's not ill—my precious pet?" shouted his mother, dropping on her knees before him with clasped hands, but touching him no more than if he had been a gilded idol. "It will pass—it's only for an instant; but don't say such dreadful things!"

"I'm all right—all right," Morgan panted to Pemberton, whom he sat looking up at with a strange smile, his hands resting on either side on the sofa.

"Now do you pretend I've been treacherous—that I've deceived?" Mrs. Moreen flashed at Pemberton as she got up.

"It isn't *he* says it, it's I!" the boy returned, apparently easier, but sinking back against the wall; while Pemberton, who had sat down beside him, taking his hand, bent over him.

"Darling child, one does what one can; there are so many things to consider," urged Mrs. Moreen. "It's his *place*—his only place. You see *you* think it is now."

"Take me away—take me away," Morgan went on, smiling to Pemberton from his white face.

"Where shall I take you, and how—oh, *how*, my boy?" the young man stammered, thinking of the rude way in which his friends in London held that, for his convenience, and without a pledge of instantaneous return, he had thrown them over; of the just resentment with which they would already have called in a successor, and of the little help as regarded finding fresh employment that resided for him in the flatness of his having failed to pass his pupil.

"Oh, we'll settle that. You used to talk about it," said Morgan. "If we can only go, all the rest's a detail."

"Talk about it as much as you like, but don't think you can attempt it. Mr. Moreen would never consent—it would be so precarious," Pemberton's hostess explained to him. Then to Morgan she explained: "I would destroy our peace, it would break our hearts. Now that he's back it will be all the same again. You'll have your life, your work and your freedom, and we'll all be happy as we used to be. You'll bloom and grow perfectly well, and we won't have any more silly experiments, will we? They're too absurd. It's Mr. Pemberton's place—every one in his place. You in yours, your papa in his, me in mine—*n'est-ce pas, chéri?*[18] We'll all forget how foolish we've been, and we'll have lovely times."

[18] Isn't it so, dear?

She continued to talk and to surge vaguely about the little draped, stuffy *salon,* while Pemberton sat with the boy, whose colour gradually came back; and she mixed up her reasons, dropping that there were going to be changes, that the other children might scatter (who knew?—Paula had her ideas), and that then it might be fancied how much the poor old parent-birds would want the little nestling. Morgan looked at Pemberton, who wouldn't let him move; and Pemberton knew exactly how he felt at hearing himself called a little nestling. He admitted that he had had one or two bad days, but he protested afresh against the iniquity of his mother's having made them the ground of an appeal to poor Pemberton. Poor Pemberton could laugh now, apart from the comicality of Mrs. Moreen's producing so much philosophy for her defence (she seemed to shake it out of her agitated petticoats, which knocked over the light gilt chairs), so little did the sick boy strike him as qualified to repudiate any advantage.

He himself was in for it, at any rate. He should have Morgan on his hands again indefinitely; though indeed he saw the lad had a private theory to produce which would be intended to smooth this down. He was obliged to him for it in advance; but the suggested amendment didn't keep his heart from sinking a little, any more than it prevented him from accepting the prospect on the spot, with some confidence moreover that he would do so even better if he could have a little supper. Mrs. Moreen threw out more hints about the changes that were to be looked for, but she was such a mixture of smiles and shudders (she confessed she was very nervous), that he couldn't tell whether she were in high feather or only in hysterics. If the family were really at last going to pieces why shouldn't she recognise the necessity of pitching Morgan into some sort of lifeboat? This presumption was fostered by the fact that they were established in luxurious quarters in the capital of pleasure; that was exactly where they naturally *would* be established in view of going to pieces. Moreover didn't she mention that Mr. Moreen and the others were enjoying themselves at the opera with Mr. Granger, and wasn't *that* also precisely where one would look for them on the eve of a smash? Pemberton gathered that Mr. Granger was a rich, vacant American —a big bill with a flourishy heading and no items; so that one of Paula's "ideas" was probably that this time she had really done it, which was indeed an unprecedented blow to the general cohesion. And if the cohesion was to terminate what was to become of poor Pemberton? He felt quite enough bound up with them to figure, to his alarm, as a floating spar in case of a wreck.

It was Morgan who eventually asked if no supper had been ordered for him; sitting with him below, later, at the dim, delayed meal, in the presence of a great deal of corded green plush, a plate of ornamental biscuit and a languor marked on the part of the waiter. Mrs. Moreen had explained that they had been obliged to secure a room for the visitor out of the house; and Morgan's consolation (he offered it while Pemberton reflected on the nastiness of lukewarm sauces), proved to be, largely, that this circumstance would facilitate their escape. He talked of their escape (recurring to it often afterwards), as if they were making up a "boy's book" together. But he likewise expressed his sense that there was something in the air, that the Moreens couldn't keep it up much longer. In point of fact, as Pemberton was to see, they kept it up for five or six months. All the while, however, Morgan's contention was designed to cheer him. Mr. Moreen and Ulick, whom he had met the day after his return, accepted that return like perfect men of the world. If Paula and Amy treated it even with less formality an allowance was to be made for them, inasmuch as Mr. Granger had not come to the opera after all. He had only placed his box at their service, with a bouquet for each of the party; there was even one apiece, embittering the thought of his profusion, for Mr. Moreen and Ulick. "They're all like that," was Morgan's comment; "at the very last, just when we think we've got them fast, we're chucked!"

Morgan's comments, in these days, were more and more free; they even included a large recognition of the extraordinary tenderness with which he had been treated while Pemberton was away. Oh, yes, they couldn't do enough to be nice to him, to show him they had him on their mind and make up for his loss. That was just what made the whole thing so sad, and him so glad, after all, of Pemberton's return—he had to keep thinking of their affection less, had less sense of obligation. Pemberton laughed out at this last reason, and Morgan blushed and said: "You know what I mean." Pemberton knew perfectly what he meant; but there were a good many things it didn't make any clearer. This episode of his second sojourn in Paris stretched itself out wearily, with their resumed readings and wanderings and maunderings, their potterings on the quays, their hauntings of the museums, their occasional lingerings in the Palais Royal, when the first sharp weather came on and there was a comfort in warm emanations, before Chevet's wonderful succulent window. Morgan wanted to hear a great deal about the opulent youth—he took an immense interest in him. Some of the details of his opulence —Pemberton could spare him none of them—evidently intensified the boy's appreciation of all his friend had given up to come back to him; but in addition to the greater reciprocity established by such a renunciation he had always his little brooding theory, in which there was a frivolous gaiety too, that their long probation was drawing to a close. Morgan's conviction that the Moreens couldn't go on much longer kept pace with the unexpended impetus with which, from month to month, they did go on. Three weeks after Pemberton had rejoined them they went on to another hotel, a dingier one than the first; but Morgan rejoiced that his tutor had at least still not sacrificed the advantage of a room outside. He clung to the romantic utility of this when the day, or rather the night, should arrive for their escape.

For the first time, in this complicated connection, Pemberton felt sore and exasperated. It was, as he had said to Mrs. Moreen in Venice, *trop fort*—everything was *trop fort*. He could neither really throw off his blighting burden nor find it the benefit of a pacified conscience or of a rewarded affection. He had spent all the money that he had earned in England, and he felt that his youth was going and that he was getting nothing back for it. It was all very well for Morgan to seem to consider that he would make up to him for all inconveniences by settling himself upon him permanently—there was an irritating flaw in such a view. He saw what the boy had in his mind; the conception that as his friend had had the generosity to come back to him he must show his gratitude by giving him his life. But the poor friend didn't desire the gift—what could he do with Morgan's life? Of course at the same time that Pemberton was irritated he remembered the reason, which was very honourable to Morgan and which consisted simply of the fact that he was perpetually making one forget that he was after all only a child. If one dealt with him on a different basis one's misadventures were one's own fault. So Pemberton waited in a queer confusion of yearning and alarm for the catastrophe which was held to hang over the house of Moreen, of which he certainly at moments felt the symptoms brush his cheek and as to which he wondered much in what form it would come.

Perhaps it would take the form of dispersal—a frightened *sauve qui peut*,[19] a scuttling into selfish corners. Certainly they were less elastic than of yore; they were evidently looking for something they didn't find. The Dorringtons hadn't reappeared, the princes had scattered; wasn't that the beginning of the end? Mrs. Moreen had lost her reckoning of the famous "days;" her social calendar was blurred—it had turned its face to the wall. Pemberton suspected that the great, the cruel, discomfiture had been the extraordinary behaviour of Mr. Granger, who seemed not to know what he wanted, or, what was much worse, what *they* wanted. He kept sending flowers, as if to bestrew the path of his retreat, which was never the path of return. Flowers were all very well, but—Pemberton could complete the

[19] Every man for himself.

proposition. It was now positively conspicuous that in the long run
the Moreens were a failure; so that the young man was almost grateful the run had not been short. Mr. Moreen, indeed, was still occasionally able to get away on business, and, what was more surprising,
he was also able to get back. Ulick had no club, but you could not
have discovered it from his appearance, which was as much as ever
that of a person looking at life from the window of such an institution; therefore Pemberton was doubly astonished at an answer he
once heard him make to his mother, in the desperate tone of a man
familiar with the worst privations. Her question Pemberton had not
quite caught; it appeared to be an appeal for a suggestion as to
whom they could get to take Amy. "Let the devil take her!" Ulick
snapped; so that Pemberton could see that not only they had lost
their amiability, but had ceased to believe in themselves. He could
also see that if Mrs. Moreen was trying to get people to take her children she might be regarded as closing the hatches for the storm. But
Morgan would be the last she would part with.

One winter afternoon—it was a Sunday—he and the boy walked
far together in the Bois de Boulogne. The evening was so splendid,
the cold lemon-coloured sunset so clear, the stream of carriages and
pedestrians so amusing and the fascination of Paris so great, that
they stayed out later than usual and became aware that they would
have to hurry home to arrive in time for dinner. They hurried accordingly, arm-in-arm, good-humoured and hungry, agreeing that
there was nothing like Paris after all and that after all, too, that had
come and gone they were not yet sated with innocent pleasures.
When they reached the hotel they found that, though scandalously
late, they were in time for all the dinner they were likely to sit down
to. Confusion reigned in the apartments of the Moreens (very
shabby ones this time, but the best in the house), and before the interrupted service of the table (with objects displaced almost as if
there had been a scuffle, and a great wine stain from an overturned
bottle), Pemberton could not blink the fact that there had been a
scene of proprietary mutiny. The storm had come—they were all
seeking refuge. The hatches were down—Paula and Amy were invisible (they had never tried the most casual art upon Pemberton, but
he felt that they had enough of an eye to him not to wish to meet
him as young ladies whose frocks had been confiscated), and Ulick
appeared to have jumped overboard. In a word, the host and his
staff had ceased to "go on" at the pace of their guests, and the air of
embarrassed detention, thanks to a pile of gaping trunks in the passage, was strangely commingled with the air of indignant withdrawal.

When Morgan took in all this—and he took it in very quickly—he blushed to the roots of his hair. He had walked, from his infancy, among difficulties and dangers, but he had never seen a public exposure. Pemberton noticed, in a second glance at him, that the tears had rushed into his eyes and that they were tears of bitter shame. He wondered for an instant, for the boy's sake, whether he might successfully pretend not to understand. Not successfully, he felt, as Mr. and Mrs. Moreen, dinnerless by their extinguished hearth, rose before him in their little dishonoured *salon*, considering apparently with much intensity what lively capital would be next on their list. They were not prostrate, but they were very pale, and Mrs. Moreen had evidently been crying. Pemberton quickly learned however that her grief was not for the loss of her dinner, much as she usually enjoyed it, but on account of a necessity much more tragic. She lost no time in laying this necessity bare, in telling him how the change had come, the bolt had fallen, and how they would all have to turn themselves about. Therefore cruel as it was to them to part with their darling she must look to him to carry a little further the influence he had so fortunately acquired with the boy—to induce his young charge to follow him into some modest retreat. They depended upon him, in a word, to take their delightful child temporarily under his protection—it would leave Mr. Moreen and herself so much more free to give the proper attention (too little, alas! had been given), to the readjustment of their affairs.

"We trust you—we feel that we can," said Mrs. Moreen, slowly rubbing her plump white hands and looking, with compunction, hard at Morgan, whose chin, not to take liberties, her husband stroked with a tentative paternal forefinger.

"Oh, yes; we feel that we can. We trust Mr. Pemberton fully, Morgan," Mr. Moreeen conceded.

Pemberton wondered again if he might pretend not to understand; but the idea was painfully complicated by the immediate perception that Morgan had understood.

"Do you mean that he may take me to live with him—for ever and ever?" cried the boy. "Away, away, anywhere he likes?"

"For ever and ever? *Comme vous-y-allez!*"[20] Mr. Moreen laughed indulgently. "For as long as Mr. Pemberton may be so good."

"We've struggled, we've suffered," his wife went on; "but you've made him so your own that we've already been through the worst of the sacrifice."

Morgan had turned away from his father—he stood looking at Pemberton with a light in his face. His blush had died out, but something had come that was brighter and more vivid. He had a moment

---

[20] How you go on!

of boyish joy, scarcely mitigated by the reflection that, with this unexpected consecration of his hope—too sudden and too violent; the
thing was a good deal less like a boy's book—the "escape" was left on
their hands. The boyish joy was there for an instant, and Pemberton
was almost frightened at the revelation of gratitude and affection
that shone through his humiliation. When Morgan stammered "My
dear fellow, what do you say to *that?*" he felt that he should say
something enthusiastic. But he was still more frightened at something else that immediately followed and that made the lad sit down
quickly on the nearest chair. He had turned very white and had
raised his hand to his left side. They were all three looking at him,
but Mrs. Moreen was the first to bound forward. "Ah, his darling
little heart!" she broke out; and this time, on her knees before him
and without respect for the idol, she caught him ardently in her
arms. "You walked him too far, you hurried him too fast!" she
tossed over her shoulder at Pemberton. The boy made no protest,
and the next instant his mother, still holding him, sprang up with
her face convulsed and with the terrified cry "Help, help! he's going,
he's gone!" Pemberton saw, with equal horror, by Morgan's own
stricken face, that he *was* gone. He pulled him half out of his mother's hands, and for a moment, while they held him together, they
looked, in their dismay, into each other's eyes. "He couldn't stand it,
with his infirmity," said Pemberton—"the shock, the whole scene, the
violent emotion."

"But I thought he *wanted* to go to you!" wailed Mrs. Moreen.

"I *told* you he didn't, my dear," argued Mr. Moreen. He was trembling all over, and he was, in his way, as deeply affected as his wife.
But, after the first, he took his bereavement like a man of the world.

HAROLD FREDERIC

The Eve of the Fourth

IT WAS WELL ON TOWARD EVENING before this Third of July all at
once made itself gloriously different from other days in my mind.

There was a very long afternoon, I remember, hot and overcast,
with continual threats of rain, which never came to anything. The
other boys were too excited about the morrow to care for present
play. They sat instead along the edge of the broad platform-stoop in
front of Delos Ingersoll's grocery-store, their brown feet swinging at
varying heights above the sidewalk, and bragged about the manner
in which they contemplated celebrating the anniversary of their
Independence. Most of the elder lads were very independent indeed;
they were already secure in the parental permission to stay up all
night, so that the Fourth might be ushered in with its full quota of
ceremonial. The smaller urchins pretended that they also had this
permission, or were sure of getting it. Little Denny Cregan attracted
admiring attention by vowing that he should remain out, even if his
father chased him with a policeman all around the ward, and he had
to go and live in a cave in the gulf until he was grown up.

My inferiority to these companions of mine depressed me. They
were allowed to go without shoes and stockings; they wore loose and
comfortable old clothes, and were under no responsibility to keep
them dry or clean or whole; they had their pockets literally bulging
now with all sorts of portentous engines of noise and racket—huge
brown "double-enders," bound with waxed cord; long, slim, vicious-
looking "nigger-chasers;" big "Union torpedoes," covered with clay,
which made a report like a horse-pistol, and were invaluable for
frightening farmers' horses; and so on through an extended catalogue of recondite and sinister explosives upon which I looked with
awe, as their owners from time to time exhibited them with the
proud simplicity of those accustomed to greatness. Several of these

From Harold Frederic, *In the Sixties*. (New York: Charles Scribner's Sons, 1897),
pp. 273–298. First published in *St. Nicholas Magazine*, XX, (July, 1893), 644–655.

boys also possessed toy cannons, which would be brought forth at twilight. They spoke firmly of ramming them to the muzzle with grass, to produce a greater noise—even if it burst them and killed everybody.

By comparison, my lot was one of abasement. I was a solitary child, and a victim to conventions. A blue necktie was daily pinned under my Byron collar, and there were gilt buttons on my zouave jacket. When we were away in the pasture playground near the gulf, and I ventured to take off my foot-gear, every dry old thistle-point in the whole territory seemed to arrange itself to be stepped upon by my whitened and tender soles. I could not swim; so, while my lithe bold comrades dived out of sight under the deep water, and darted about chasing one another far beyond their depth, I paddled ignobly around the "baby-hole" close to the bank, in the warm and muddy shallows.

Especially apparent was my state of humiliation on this July afternoon. I had no "double-enders," nor might hope for any. The mere thought of a private cannon seemed monstrous and unnatural to me. By some unknown process of reasoning my mother had years before reached the theory that a good boy ought to have two ten-cent packs of small fire-crackers on the Fourth of July. Four or five succeeding anniversaries had hardened this theory into an orthodox tenet of faith, with all its observances rigidly fixed. The fire-crackers were bought for me overnight, and placed on the hall table. Beside them lay a long rod of punk. When I hastened down and out in the morning, with these ceremonial implements in my hands, the hired girl would give me, in an old kettle, some embers from the wood-fire in the summer kitchen. Thus furnished, I went into the front yard, and in solemn solitude fired off these crackers one by one. Those which, by reason of having lost their tails, were only fit for "fizzes," I saved till after breakfast. With the exhaustion of these, I fell reluctantly back upon the public for entertainment. I could see the soldiers, hear the band and the oration, and in the evening, if it didn't rain, enjoy the fireworks; but my own contribution to the patriotic noise was always before the breakfast dishes had been washed.

My mother scorned the little paper torpedoes as flippant and wasteful things. You merely threw one of them, and it went off, she said, and there you were. I don't know that I ever grasped this objection in its entirety; but it impressed my whole childhood with its unanswerableness. Years and years afterward, when my own children asked for torpedoes, I found myself unconsciously advising against them on quite the maternal lines. Nor was it easy to budge the good lady from her position on the great two-packs issue. I seem to recall having successfully undermined it once or twice, but two was the rule. When I called her attention to the fact that our neighbor, Tom Hemingway, thought nothing of exploding a whole pack at a time inside their wash-boiler, she was not dazzled, but only replied: "Wilful waste makes woful want."

Of course the idea of the Hemingways ever knowing what want meant was absurd. They lived a dozen doors or so from us, in a big white house with stately white columns rising from veranda to gable across the whole front, and a large garden, flowers and shrubs in front, fruit-trees and vegetables behind. Squire Hemingway was the most important man in our part of the town. I know now that he was never anything more than United States Commissioner of Deeds, but in those days, when he walked down the street with his gold-headed cane, his blanket-shawl folded over his arm, and his severe, dignified, close-shaven face held well up in the air, I seemed to behold a companion of Presidents.

This great man had two sons. The elder of them, De Witt Hemingway, was a man grown, and was at the front. I had seen him march away, over a year before, with a bright drawn sword, at the side of his company. The other son, Tom, was my senior by only a twelvemonth. He was by nature proud, but often consented to consort with me when the selection of other available associates was at low ebb.

It was to this Tom that I listened with most envious eagerness, in front of the grocery-store, on the afternoon of which I speak. He did not sit on the stoop with the others—no one expected quite that degree of condescension—but leaned nonchalantly against a post, whittling out a new ramrod for his cannon. He said that this year he was not going to have any ordinary fire-crackers at all; they, he added with a meaning glance at me, were only fit for girls. He might do a little in "double-enders," but his real point would be in "ringers"—an incredible giant variety of cracker, Turkey-red like the other, but in size almost a rolling-pin. Some of these he would fire off singly, between volleys from his cannon. But a good many he intended to explode, in bunches say of six, inside the tin wash-boiler, brought out into the middle of the road for that purpose. It would doubtless blow the old thing sky-high, but that didn't matter. They could get a new one.

Even as he spoke, the big bell in the tower of the town-hall burst forth in a loud clangor of swift-repeated strokes. It was half a mile away, but the moist air brought the urgent, clamorous sounds to our ears as if the belfry had stood close above us. We sprang off the stoop and stood posed, waiting to hear the number of the ward struck, and ready to scamper off on the instant if the fire was anywhere in our part of the town. But the excited peal went on and on, without a pause. It became obvious that this meant something besides a fire. Perhaps some of us wondered vaguely what that something might be, but as a body our interest had lapsed. Billy Norris, who was the son of poor parents, but could whip even Tom Hemingway, said he had been told that the German boys on the other side of the gulf were coming over to "rush" us on the following day, and that we ought all to collect nails to fire at them from our cannon. This we pledged ourselves to do—the bell keeping up its throbbing tumult ceaselessly.

Suddenly we saw the familiar figure of Johnson running up the street toward us. What his first name was I never knew. To every one, little or big, he was just Johnson. He and his family had moved into our town after the war began; I fancy they moved away again before it ended. I do not even know what he did for a living. But he seemed always drunk, always turbulently good-natured, and always shouting out the news at the top of his lungs. I cannot pretend to guess how he found out everything as he did, or why, having found it out, he straightway rushed homeward, scattering the intelligence as he ran. Most probably Johnson was moulded by Nature as a town-crier, but was born by accident some generations after the race of bellmen had disappeared. Our neighborhood did not like him; our mothers did not know Mrs. Johnson, and we boys behaved with snobbish roughness to his children. He seemed not to mind this at all, but came up unwearyingly to shout out the tidings of the day for our benefit.

"Vicksburg's fell! Vicksburg's fell!" was what we heard him yelling as he approached.

Delos Ingersoll and his hired boy ran out of the grocery. Doors opened along the street and heads were thrust inquiringly out.

"Vicksburg's fell!" he kept hoarsely proclaiming, his arms waving in the air, as he staggered along at a dog-trot past us, and went into the saloon next to the grocery.

I cannot say how definite an idea these tidings conveyed to our boyish minds. I have a notion that at the time I assumed that Vicksburg had something to do with Gettysburg, where I knew, from the talk of my elders, that an awful fight had been proceeding since the middle of the week. Doubtless this confusion was aided by the fact that an hour or so later, on that same wonderful day, the wire brought us word that this terrible battle on Pennsylvanian soil had at last taken the form of a Union victory. It is difficult now to see how we could have known both these things on the Third of July— that is to say, before the people actually concerned seemed to have been sure of them. Perhaps it was only inspired guesswork, but I know that my town went wild over the news, and that the clouds overhead cleared away as if by magic.

The sun did well to spread that summer sky at eventide with all the pageantry of color the spectrum knows. It would have been preposterous that such a day should slink off in dull, Quaker drabs. Men were shouting in the streets now. The old cannon left over from the Mexican war had been dragged out on to the rickety covered river-bridge, and was frightening the fishes, and shaking the dry, worm-eaten rafters, as fast as the swab and rammer could work. Our town bandsmen were playing as they had never played before, down in the square in front of the post-office. The management of the Universe could not hurl enough wild fireworks into the exultant sunset to fit our mood.

The very air was filled with the scent of triumph—the spirit of conquest. It seemed only natural that I should march off to my mother and quite collectedly tell her that I desired to stay out all night with the other boys. I had never dreamed of daring to prefer such a request in other years. Now I was scarcely conscious of surprise when she gave her permission, adding with a smile that I would be glad enough to come in and go to bed before half the night was over.

I steeled my heart after supper with the proud resolve that if the night turned out to be as protracted as one of those Lapland winter nights we read about in the geography, I still would not surrender.

The boys outside were not so excited over the tidings of my unlooked-for victory as I had expected them to be. They received the news, in fact, with a rather mortifying stoicism. Tom Hemingway, however, took enough interest in the affair to suggest that, instead of spending my twenty cents in paltry fire-crackers, I might go down town and buy another can of powder for his cannon. By doing so, he pointed out, I would be a part-proprietor, as it were, of the night's performance, and would be entitled to occasionally touch the cannon off. This generosity affected me, and I hastened down the long hill-street to show myself worthy of it, repeating the instruction of "Kentucky Bear-Hunter-coarse-grain" over and over again to myself as I went.

Half-way on my journey I overtook a person whom, even in the gathering twilight, I recognized as Miss Stratford, the school-teacher. She also was walking down the hill and rapidly. It did not need the sight of a letter in her hand to tell me that she was going to the post-office. I myself went regularly to get our mail, and to exchange shin-plasters for one-cent stamps with which to buy yeast and other commodities that called for minute fractional currency.

Although I was very fond of Miss Stratford—I still recall her gentle eyes, and pretty, rounded, dark face, in its frame of long, black curls, with tender liking—I now coldly resolved to hurry past, pretending not to know her. It was a mean thing to do; Miss Stratford had always been good to me, shining in that respect in brilliant contrast to my other teachers, whom I hated bitterly. Still, the "Kentucky-Bear-Hunter-coarse-grain" was too important a matter to wait upon any mere female friendships, and I quickened my pace into a trot, hoping to scurry by unrecognized.

"Oh, Andrew! is that you?" I heard her call out as I ran past. For the instant I thought of rushing on, quite as if I had not heard. Then I stopped and walked beside her.

"I am going to stay up all night: mother says I may; and I am going to fire off Tom Hemingway's big cannon every fourth time, straight through till breakfast time," I announced to her loftily.

"Dear me! I ought to be proud to be seen walking with such an important citizen," she answered, with kindly playfulness. She added more gravely, after a moment's pause: "Then Tom is out playing with the other boys, is he?"

"Why, of course!" I responded. "He always lets us stand around when he fires off his cannon. He's got some 'ringers' this year too."

I heard Miss Stratford murmur an impulsive "Thank God!" under her breath.

Full as the day had been of surprises, I could not help wondering that the fact of Tom's ringers should stir up such profound emotions in the teacher's breast. Since the subject so interested her, I went on with a long catalogue of Tom's other pyrotechnic possessions, and from that to an account of his almost supernatural collection of postage-stamps. In a few minutes more I am sure I should have revealed to her the great secret of my life, which was my determination, in case I came to assume the victorious rôle and rank of Napoleon, to immediately make Tom a Marshal of the Empire.

But we had reached the post-office square. I had never before seen it so full of people.

Even to my boyish eyes the tragic line of division which cleft this crowd in twain was apparent. On one side, over by the Seminary, the youngsters had lighted a bonfire, and were running about it— some of the bolder ones jumping through it in frolicsome recklessness. Close by stood the band, now valiantly thumping out "John Brown's Body" upon the noisy night air. It was quite dark by this time, but the musicians knew the tune by heart. So did the throng about them, and sang it with lusty fervor. The doors of the saloon toward the corner of the square were flung wide open. Two black streams of men kept in motion under the radiance of the big reflector-lamp over these doors—one going in, one coming out. They slapped one another on the back as they passed, with exultant screams and shouts. Every once in a while, when movement was for the instant blocked, some voice lifted above the others would begin "Hip-hip-hip-hip—" and then would come a roar that fairly drowned the music.

On the post-office side of the square there was no bonfire. No one raised a cheer. A densely packed mass of men and women stood in front of the big square stone building, with its closed doors, and curtained windows upon which, from time to time, the shadow of some passing clerk, bareheaded and hurried, would be momentarily thrown. They waited in silence for the night mail to be sorted. If they spoke to one another, it was in whispers—as if they had been standing with uncovered heads at a funeral service in a graveyard. The dim light reflected over from the bonfire, or down from the shaded windows of the post-office, showed solemn, hard-lined, anxious faces. Their lips scarcely moved when they muttered little low-toned remarks to their neighbors. They spoke from the side of the mouth, and only on one subject.

"He went all through Fredericksburg without a scratch—"

"He looks so much like me—General Palmer told my brother he'd have known his hide in a tanyard—"

"He's been gone—let's see—it was a year some time last April—"

"He was counting on a furlough the first of this month. I suppose nobody got one as things turned out—"

"He said, 'No; it ain't my style. I'll fight as much as you like, but I won't be nigger-waiter for no man, captain or no captain'—"

Thus I heard the scattered murmurs among the grown-up heads above me, as we pushed into the outskirts of the throng, and stood there, waiting for the rest. There was no sentence without a "he" in it. A stranger might have fancied that they were all talking of one man. I knew better. They were the fathers and mothers, the sisters, brothers, wives of the men whose regiments, had been in that horrible three days' fight at Gettysburg. Each was thinking and speaking of his own, and took it for granted the others would understand. For that matter, they all did understand. The town knew the name and family of every one of the twelve-score sons she had in this battle.

It is not very clear to me now why people all went to the post-office to wait for the evening papers that came in from the nearest big city. Nowadays they would be brought in bulk and sold on the street before the mail-bags had reached the post-office. Apparently that had not yet been thought of in our slow old town.

The band across the square had started up afresh with "Annie Lisle"—the sweet old refrain of "Wave willows, murmur waters," comes back to me now after a quarter-century of forgetfulness—when all at once there was a sharp forward movement of the crowd. The doors had been thrown open, and the hallway was on the instant filled with a swarming multitude. The band had stopped as suddenly as it began, and no more cheering was heard. We could see whole troops of dark forms scudding toward us from the other side of the square.

"Run in for me—that's a good boy—ask for Dr. Stratford's mail," the teacher whispered, bending over me.

It seemed an age before I finally got back to her, with the paper in its postmarked wrapper buttoned up inside my jacket. I had never been in so fierce and determined a crowd before, and I emerged from it at last, confused in wits and panting for breath. I was still looking about through the gloom in a foolish way for Miss Stratford, when I felt her hand laid sharply on my shoulder.

"Well—where is it?—did nothing come?" she asked, her voice trembling with eagerness, and the eyes which I had thought so soft and dove-like flashing down upon me as if she were Miss Pritchard, and I had been caught chewing gum in school.

I drew the paper out from under my roundabout, and gave it to her. She grasped it, and thrust a finger under the cover to tear it off. Then she hesitated for a moment, and looked about her. "Come where there is some light," she said, and started up the street. Although she seemed to have spoken more to herself than to me, I followed her in silence, close to her side.

For a long way the sidewalk in front of every lighted store-window was thronged with a group of people clustered tight about some one who had a paper, and was reading from it aloud. Beside broken snatches of this monologue, we caught, now groans of sorrow and horror, now exclamations of proud approval, and even the beginnings of cheers, broken in upon by a general " 'Sh-h-" as we hurried past outside the curb.

It was under a lamp in the little park nearly half-way up the hill that Miss Stratford stopped, and spread the paper open. I see her still, white-faced, under the flickering gaslight, her black curls making a strange dark bar between the pale-straw hat and the white of her shoulder shawl and muslin dress, her hands trembling as they held up the extended sheet. She scanned the columns swiftly, skimmingly for a time, as I could see by the way she moved her round chin up and down. Then she came to a part which called for closer reading. The paper shook perceptibly now, as she bent her eyes upon it. Then all at once it fell from her hands, and without a sound she walked away.

I picked the paper up and followed her along the gravelled path.

It was like pursuing a ghost, so weirdly white did her summer attire now look to my frightened eyes, with such a swift and deathly silence did she move. The path upon which we were described a circle touching the four sides of the square. She did not quit it when the intersection with our street was reached, but followed straight round again toward the point where we had entered the park. This, too, in turn, she passed, gliding noiselessly forward under the black arches of the overhanging elms. The suggestion that she did not know she was going round and round in a ring startled my brain. I would have run up to her now if I had dared.

Suddenly she turned, and saw that I was behind her. She sank slowly into one of the garden-seats, by the path, and held out for a moment a hesitating hand toward me. I went up at this and looked into her face. Shadowed as it was, the change I saw there chilled my blood. It was like the face of some one I had never seen before, with fixed, wide-open, staring eyes which seemed to look beyond me through the darkness, upon some terrible sight no other could see.

"Go—run and tell—Tom—to go home! His brother—his brother has been killed," she said to me, choking over the words as if they hurt her throat, and still with the same strange dry-eyed, far-away gaze covering yet not seeing me.

I held out the paper for her to take, but she made no sign, and I gingerly laid it on the seat beside her. I hung about for a minute or two longer, imagining that she might have something else to say— but no word came. Then, with a feebly inopportune "Well, good-by," I started off alone up the hill.

It was a distinct relief to find that my companions were congregated at the lower end of the common, instead of their accustomed haunt farther up near my home, for the walk had been a lonely one, and I was deeply depressed by what had happened. Tom, it seems, had been called away some quarter of an hour before. All the boys knew of the calamity which had befallen the Hemingways. We talked about it, from time to time, as we loaded and fired the cannon which Tom had obligingly turned over to my friends. It had been out of deference to the feelings of the stricken household that they had betaken themselves and their racket off to the remote corner of the common. The solemnity of the occasion silenced criticism upon my conduct in forgetting to buy the powder. "There would be enough as long as it lasted," Billy Norris said, with philosophic decision.

We speculated upon the likelihood of De Witt Hemingway's being given a military funeral. These mournful pageants had by this time become such familiar things to us that the prospect of one more had no element of excitement in it, save as it involved a gloomy sort of distinction for Tom. He would ride in the first mourning-carriage with his parents, and this would associate us, as we walked along ahead of the band, with the most intimate aspects of the demonstration. We regretted now that the soldier company which we had so long projected remained still unorganized. Had it been otherwise we would probably have been awarded the right of the line in the procession. Some one suggested that it was not too late—and we promptly bound ourselves to meet after breakfast next day to organize and begin drilling. If we worked at this night and day, and our parents instantaneously provided us with uniforms and guns, we should be in time. It was also arranged that we should be called the De Witt C. Hemingway Fire Zouaves, and that Billy Norris should be side captain. The chief command would, of course, be reserved for Tom. We would specially salute him as he rode past in the closed carriage, and then fall in behind, forming his honorary escort.

None of us had known the dead officer closely, owing to his advanced age. He was seven or eight years older than even Tom. But the more elderly among our group had seen him play base-ball in the academy nine, and our neighborhood was still alive with legends of his early audacity and skill in collecting barrels and dry-goods boxes at night for election bonfires. It was remembered that once he carried away a whole front-stoop from the house of a little German tailor on one of the back streets. As we stood around the heated cannon, in the great black solitude of the common, our fancies pictured this redoubtable young man once more among us—not in his blue uniform, with crimson sash and sword laid by his side, and the gauntlets drawn over his lifeless hands, but as a taller and glorified Tom, in a roundabout jacket and copper-toed boots, giving the law on this his playground. The very cannon at our feet had once been his. The night air became peopled with ghosts of his contemporaries —handsome boys who had grown up before us, and had gone away to lay down their lives in far-off Virginia or Tennessee.

These heroic shades brought drowsiness in their train. We lapsed into long silences, punctuated by yawns, when it was not our turn to ram and touch off the cannon. Finally some of us stretched ourselves out on the grass, in the warm darkness, to wait comfortably for this turn to come.

What did come instead was daybreak—finding Billy Norris and myself alone constant to our all-night vow. We sat up and shivered as we rubbed our eyes. The morning air had a chilling freshness that went to my bones—and these, moreover, were filled with those novel aches and stiffnesses which beds were invented to prevent. We stood up, stretching out our arms, and gaping at the pearl-and-rose beginnings of the sunrise in the eastern sky. The other boys had all gone home, and taken the cannon with them. Only scraps of torn paper and tiny patches of burnt grass marked the site of our celebration.

My first weak impulse was to march home without delay, and get into bed as quickly as might be. But Billy Norris looked so finely resolute and resourceful that I hesitated to suggest this, and said nothing, leaving the initiative to him. One could see, by the most casual glance, that he was superior to mere considerations of unseasonableness in hours. I remembered now that he was one of that remarkable body of boys, the paper-carriers, who rose when all others were asleep in their warm nests, and trudged about long before breakfast distributing the *Clarion* among the well-to-do households. This fact had given him position in our neighborhood as quite the next in leadership to Tom Hemingway.

He presently outlined his plans to me, after having tried the centre of light on the horizon, where soon the sun would be, by an old brass compass he had in his pocket—a process which enabled him, he said, to tell pretty well what time it was. The paper wouldn't be out for nearly two hours yet— and if it were not for the fact of a great battle, there would have been no paper at all on this glorious anniversary—but he thought we would go downtown and see what was going on around about the newspaper office. Forthwith we started. He cheered my faint spirits by assuring me that I would soon cease to be sleepy, and would, in fact, feel better than usual. I dragged my feet along at his side, waiting for this revival to come, and meantime furtively yawning against my sleeve.

Billy seemed to have dreamed a good deal, during our nap on the common, about the De Witt C. Hemingway Fire Zouaves. At least he had now in his head a marvellously elaborated system of organization, which he unfolded as we went along. I felt that I had never before realized his greatness, his born genius for command. His scheme halted nowhere. He allotted offices with discriminating firmness; he treated the question of uniforms and guns as a trivial detail which would settle itself; he spoke with calm confidence of our offering our services to the Republic in the autumn; his clear vision saw even the materials for a fife-and-drum corps among the German boys in the back streets. It was true that I appeared personally to play a meagre part in these great projects; the most that was said about me was that I might make a fair third-corporal. But Fate had thrown in my way such a wonderful chance of becoming intimate with Billy that I made sure I should swiftly advance in rank—the more so as I discerned in the background of his thoughts, as it were, a grim determination to make short work of Tom Hemingway's aristocratic pretensions, once the funeral was over.

We were forced to make a detour of the park on our way down,

because Billy observed some half-dozen Irish boys at play with a cannon inside, whom he knew to be hostile. If there had been only
four, he said, he would have gone in and routed them. He could
whip any two of them, he added, with one hand tied behind his
back. I listened with admiration. Billy was not tall, but he possessed great thickness of chest and length of arm. His skin was so
dark that we canvassed the theory from time to time of his having
Indian blood. He did not discourage this, and he admitted himself
that he was double-jointed.

The streets of the business part of the town, into which we now
made our way, were quite deserted. We went around into the yard
behind the printing-office, where the carrier-boys were wont to wait
for the press to get to work; and Billy displayed some impatience at
discovering that here too there was no one. It was now broad daylight, but through the windows of the composing-room we could see
some of the printers still setting type by kerosene lamps.

We seated ourselves at the end of the yard on a big, flat, smooth-
faced stone, and Billy produced from his pocket a number of "em"
quads, so he called them, and with which the carriers had learned
from the printers' boys to play a very beautiful game. You shook the
pieces of metal in your hands and threw them on the stone; your
score depended upon the number of nicked sides that were turned
uppermost. We played this game in the interest of good-fellowship
for a little. Then Billy told me that the carriers always played it for
pennies, and that it was unmanly for us to do otherwise. He had no
pennies at that precise moment, but would pay at the end of the
week what he had lost; in the meantime there was my twenty cents
to go on with. After this Billy threw so many nicks uppermost that
my courage gave way, and I made an attempt to stop the game; but
a single remark from him as to the military destiny which he was
reserving for me, if I only displayed true soldierly nerve and grit,
sufficed to quiet me once more, and the play went on. I had now
only five cents left.

Suddenly a shadow interposed itself between the sunlight and the
stone. I looked up, to behold a small boy with bare arms and a
blackened apron standing over me, watching our game. There was a
great deal of ink on his face and hands, and a hardened, not to say
rakish expression in his eye.

"Why don't you 'jeff' with somebody of your own size?" he demanded of Billy after having looked me over critically.

He was not nearly so big as Billy, and I expected to see the latter
instantly rise and crush him, but Billy only laughed and said we
were playing for fun; he was going to give me all my money back. I

was rejoiced to hear this, but still felt surprised at the propitiatory manner Billy adopted toward this diminutive inky boy. It was not the demeanor befitting a side-captain—and what made it worse was that the strange boy loftily declined to be cajoled by it. He sniffed when Billy told him about the military company we were forming; he coldly shook his head, with a curt "Nixie!" when invited to join it; and he laughed aloud at hearing the name our organization was to bear.

"He ain't dead at all—that De Witt Hemingway," he said, with jeering contempt.

"Hain't he though!" exclaimed Billy. "The news come last night. Tom had to go home—his mother sent for him—on account of it!"

"I'll bet you a quarter he ain't dead," responded the practical inky boy. "Money up, though!"

"I've only got fifteen cents. I'll bet you that, though," rejoined Billy, producing my torn and dishevelled shin-plasters.

"All right! Wait here!" said the boy, running off to the building and disappearing through the door. There was barely time for me to learn from my companion that this printer's apprentice was called "the devil," and could not only whistle between his teeth and crack his fingers, but chew tobacco, when he reappeared, with a long narrow strip of paper in his hand. This he held out for us to see, indicating with an ebon forefinger the special paragraph we were to read. Billy looked at it sharply, for several moments in silence. Then he said to me: "What does it say there? I must 'a' got some powder in my eyes last night."

I read this paragraph aloud, not without an unworthy feeling that the inky boy would now respect me deeply:

"CORRECTION. Lieutenant De Witt C. Hemingway, of Company A, —th New York, reported in earlier despatches among the killed, is uninjured. The officer killed is Lieutenant Carl Heinninge, Company F, same regiment."

Billy's face visibly lengthened as I read this out, and he felt us both looking at him. He made a pretence of examining the slip of paper again, but in a half-hearted way. Then he ruefully handed over the fifteen cents and, rising from the stone, shook himself.

"Them Dutchmen never was no good!" was what he said.

The inky boy had put the money in the pocket under his apron, and grinned now with as much enjoyment as dignity would permit him to show. He did not seem to mind any longer the original source of his winnings, and it was apparent that I could not with decency recall it to him. Some odd impulse prompted me, however, to ask him if I might have the paper he had in his hand. He was magnanimous enough to present me with the proof-sheet on the spot. Then with another grin he turned and left us.

Billy stood sullenly kicking with his bare toes into a sand-heap by the stone. He would not answer me when I spoke to him. It flashed across my perceptive faculties that he was not such a great man, after all, as I had imagined. In another instant or two it had become quite clear to me that I had no admiration for him whatever. Without a word I turned on my heel and walked determinedly out of the yard and into the street, homeward bent.

All at once I quickened my pace; something had occurred to me. The purpose thus conceived grew so swiftly that soon I found myself running. Up the hill I sped, and straight through the park. If the Irish boys shouted after me I knew it not, but dashed on heedless of all else save the one idea. I only halted, breathless and panting, when I stood on Dr. Stratford's doorstep, and heard the night-bell inside jangling shrilly in response to my excited pull.

As I waited, I pictured to myself the old doctor as he would presently come down, half-dressed and pulling on his coat as he advanced. He would ask, eagerly, "Who is sick? Where am I to go?" and I would calmly reply that he unduly alarmed himself, and that I had a message for his daughter. He would, of course, ask me what it was, and I, politely but firmly, would decline to explain to any one but the lady in person. Just what might ensue was not clear—but I beheld myself throughout commanding the situation, at once benevolent, polished, and inexorable.

The door opened with unlooked-for promptness, while my self-complacent vision still hung in mid-air. Instead of the bald and spectacled old doctor, there confronted me a white-faced, solemn-eyed lady in a black dress, whom I did not seem to know. I stared at her, tongue-tied, till she said, in a low, grave voice, "Well, Andrew, what is it?"

Then of course I saw that it was Miss Stratford, my teacher, the person whom I had come to see. Some vague sense of what the sleepless night had meant in this house came to me as I gazed confusedly at her mourning, and heard the echo of her sad tones in my ears.

"Is some one ill?" she asked again.

"No; some one—some one is very well!" I managed to reply, lifting my eyes again to her wan face. The spectacle of its drawn lines and pallor all at once assailed my wearied and overtaxed nerves with crushing weight. I felt myself beginning to whimper, and rushing tears scalded my eyes. Something inside my breast seemed to be dragging me down through the stoop.

I have now only the recollection of Miss Stratford's kneeling by my side, with a supporting arm around me, and of her thus unrolling and reading the proof-paper I had in my hand. We were in the hall now, instead of on the stoop, and there was a long silence. Then she put her head on my shoulder and wept. I could hear and feel her sobs as if they were my own.

"I—I didn't think you'd cry—that you'd be so sorry," I heard myself saying, at last, in despondent self-defence.

Miss Stratford lifted her head and, still kneeling as she was, put a finger under my chin to make me look her in her face. Lo! the eyes were laughing through their tears; the whole countenance was radiant once more with the light of happy youth and with that other glory which youth knows only once.

"Why, Andrew, boy," she said, trembling, smiling, sobbing, beaming all at once, "didn't you know that people cry for very joy sometimes?"

And as I shook my head she bent down and kissed me.

JAMES GOULD COZZENS

Total Stranger

CLAD IN A LONG GRAY DUSTER, wearing a soft gray cap, my father, who was short and strong, sat bolt upright. Stiffly, he held his gauntleted hands straight on the wheel. The car jiggled scurrying along the narrow New England country road. Sometimes, indignant, my father drove faster. Then, to emphasize what he was saying, and for no other reason, he drove much slower. Though he was very fond of driving, he drove as badly as most people who had grown up before there were cars to drive.

"Well," I said, "I can't help it."

"Of course you can help it!" my father said, adding speed. His severe, dark mustache seemed to bristle a little. He had on tinted sunglasses, and he turned them on me.

"For heaven's sake, look what you're doing!" I cried. He looked just in time, but neither his dignity nor his train of thought was shaken. He continued: "Other boys help it, don't they?"

"If you'd just let me finish," I began elaborately. "If you'd just give me a chance to—"

"Go on, go on," he said. "Only don't tell me you can't help it! I'm very tired of hearing—"

"Well, it's mostly Mr. Clifford," I said. "He has it in for me. And if you want to know why, it's because I'm not one of his gang of bootlickers, who hang around his study to bum some tea, every afternoon practically." As I spoke, I could really feel that I would spurn an invitation so dangerous to my independence. The fact that Mr. Clifford rarely spoke to me except to give me another hour's detention became a point in my favor. "So, to get back at me, he tells the Old Man—"

"Do you mean Doctor Holt?"

"Everyone calls him that. Why shouldn't I?"

From James Gould Cozzens, *Children and Others*. (New York: Harcourt, Brace & World, 1964), pp. 74–89. First published in *The Saturday Evening Post*, CCVIII, (February 15, 1936), 8–9, 96–100.

"If you were a little more respectful, perhaps you wouldn't be in trouble all the time."

"I'm not in trouble all the time. I'm perfectly respectful. This year I won't be in the dormitory any more, so Snifty can't make up a lot of lies about me."

My father drove dashing past a farmhouse in a billow of dust and flurry of panic-struck chickens. "Nonsense!" he said. "Sheer nonsense! Doctor Holt wrote that after a long discussion in faculty meeting he was satisfied that your attitude—"

"Oh, my attitude!" I groaned. "For heaven's sake, a fellow's attitude! Of course, I don't let Snifty walk all over me. What do you think I am? That's what that means. It means that I'm not one of Snifty's little pets, hanging around to bum some tea."

"You explained about the tea before," my father said. "I don't feel that it quite covers the case. How about the other masters? Do they also expect you to come around and take tea with them? When they tell the headmaster that you make no effort to do your work, does that mean that they are getting back at you?"

I drew a deep breath in an effort to feel less uncomfortable. Though I was experienced in defending myself, and with my mother could do it very successfully, there was a certain remote solemnity about my father which made me falter. From my standpoint, talking to my father was a risky business, since he was only interested in proved facts. From his standpoint, I had reason to know, my remarks would form nothing but a puerile exhibition of sorry nonsense. The result was that he avoided, as long as he could, these serious discussions; and I avoided, as long as I could, any discussions at all.

I said laboriously, "Well, I don't think they told him that. Not all of them. And I can prove it, because didn't I get promoted with my form? What did I really flunk except maybe algebra? I suppose Mr. Blackburn was the one who said it." I nodded several times, as though it confirmed my darkest suspicions.

My father said frigidly, "In view of the fact that your grade for the year was forty-four, I wouldn't expect him to be exactly delighted with you."

"Well, I can tell you something about that," I said, ill at ease, but sufficiently portentous. "You can ask anyone. He's such a bum teacher that you don't learn anything in his courses. He can't even explain the simplest thing. Why, once he was working out a problem on the board, and I had to laugh, he couldn't get it himself. Until finally one of the fellows who is pretty good in math had to show him where he made a mistake even a first former wouldn't make. And that's how good he is."

My father said, "Now, I don't want any more argument. I simply want you to understand that this fall term will be your last chance. Doctor Holt is disgusted with you. I want you to think how your mother would feel if you disgrace her by being dropped at Christmas. I want you to stop breaking rules and wasting time."

He let the car slow down for emphasis. He gave me a look, at once penetrating and baffled. He could see no sense in breaking the simple, necessary rules of any organized society; and wasting time was worse than wrong, it was mad and dissolute. Time lost, he very well knew, can never be recovered. Left to himself, my father's sensible impulse would probably have been to give me a thrashing I'd remember. But this was out of the question; for my mother had long ago persuaded him that he, too, believed in reasoning with a child.

Looking at me, he must have found the results of reasoning as unimpressive as ever. He said, with restrained grimness: "And if you're sent home, don't imagine that you can go back to the academy. You'll go straight into the public school and stay there. So just remember that."

"Oh, I'll remember all right," I nodded significantly. I had not spent the last two years without, on a number of occasions, having to think seriously about what I'd do if I were expelled. I planned to approach a relative of mine connected with a steamship company and get a job on a boat.

"See that you do!" said my father. We looked at each other with mild antagonism. Though I was still full of arguments, I knew that none of them would get me anywhere, and I was, as always, a little alarmed and depressed by my father's demonstrable rightness about everything. In my position, I supposed that he would always do his lessons, never break any rules, and probably end up a prefect, with his rowing colors and a football letter—in fact, with everything that I would like, if only the first steps toward them did not seem so dull and difficult. Since they did, I was confirmed in my impression that it was impossible to please him. Since it was impossible, I had long been resolved not to care whether I pleased him or not. Practice had made not caring fairly easy.

As for my father, surely he viewed me with much the same resentful astonishment. My mother was accustomed to tell him that he did not understand me. He must have been prepared to believe it; indeed, he must have wondered if he understood anything when he tried to reconcile such facts as my marks with such contentions as my mother's that I had a brilliant mind. At the moment he could doubtless think of nothing else to say, so he drove faster, as if he wanted to get away from the whole irksome matter; but suddenly the movement of the car was altered by a series of heavy, jolting bumps.

"Got a flat," I said with satisfaction and relief. "Didn't I tell you? Everybody knows those tires pick up nails. You can ask anybody."

My father edged the limping car to the side of the road. In those days you had to expect punctures if you drove any distance, so my father was not particularly put out. He may have been glad to get his mind off a discussion which was not proving very profitable. When we had changed the tire—we had demountable rims, which made it wonderfully easy, as though you were putting something over on a puncture—we were both in better spirits and could resume our normal, polite and distant attitudes. That is, what I said was noncommittal, but not impertinent; and what he said was perfunctory, but not hostile. We got into Sansbury at five o'clock, having covered one hundred and three miles, which passed at the time for a long, hard drive.

When my father drove me up to school, we always stopped at Sansbury. The hotel was not a good or comfortable one, but it was the only convenient place to break the journey. Sansbury was a fair-sized manufacturing town, and the hotel got enough business from traveling salesmen—who, of course, traveled by train—to operate in a shabby way something like a metropolitan hotel. It had a gloomy little lobby with rows of huge armchairs and three or four imitation-marble pillars. There were two surly bellboys, one about twelve, the other about fifty. The elevator, already an antique, was made to rise by pulling on a cable. In the dark dining room a few sad, patient, middle-aged waitresses distributed badly cooked food, much of it, for some reason, served in separate little dishes of the heaviest possible china. It was all awful.

But this is in retrospect. At the time I thought the hotel more pleasant than not. My father had the habit, half stoical, half insensitive, of making the best of anything there was. Though he acted with promptness and decision when it was in his power to change circumstances, he did not grumble when it wasn't. If the food was bad, favored by an excellent digestion, he ate it anyway. If his surroundings were gloomy and the company either boring to him or nonexistent, he did not fidget.

When he could find one of the novels at the moment seriously regarded, he would read it critically. When he couldn't, he would make notes on business affairs in a shorthand of his own invention nobody else could read. When he had no notes to make, he would retire, without fuss or visible regret, into whatever his thoughts were.

I had other ideas of entertainment. At home I was never allowed to go to the moving pictures, for my mother considered the films themselves silly and cheap, and the theaters likely to be infested with germs. Away from home, I could sometimes pester my father

into taking me. As we moved down the main street of Sansbury—my
father serenely terrorizing all the rest of the traffic—I was watching
to see what was at the motion-picture theater. To my chagrin, it
proved to be Annette Kellerman in "A Daughter of the Gods," and I
could be sure I wouldn't be taken to that.

The hotel garage was an old stable facing the kitchen wing across
a yard of bare dirt forlornly stained with oil. My father halted in the
middle of it and honked the horn until finally the fifty-year-old bellboy appeared, scowling. While my father had an argument with him
over whether luggage left in the car would be safe, I got out. Not far
away there stood another car. The hood was up and a chauffeur in his
shirt sleeves had extracted and spread out on a sheet of old canvas
an amazing array of parts. The car itself was a big impressive landaulet with carriage lamps at the doorposts. I moved toward it and
waited until the chauffeur noticed me.

"What's the trouble?" I inquired professionally.

Busy with a wrench, he grunted, "Camshaft."

"Oh! How much'll she do?"

"Hundred miles an hour."

"Ah, go on!"

"Beat it," he said. "I got no time."

My father called me, and, aggrieved, I turned away, for I felt sure
that I had been treated with so little respect because I had been
compelled to save my clothes by wearing for the trip an old knicker-
bocker suit and a gray cloth hat with the scarlet monogram of a
summer camp I used to go to on it. Following the aged bellboy
through the passage toward the lobby I said to my father, "Well, I
guess I'll go up and change."

My father said, "There's no necessity for that. Just see that you
wash properly, and you can take a bath before you go to bed."

"I don't see how I can eat in a hotel, looking like this," I said. "I
should think you'd want me to look halfway respectable. I—"

"Nonsense!" said my father. "If you wash your face and hands,
you'll look perfectly all right."

The aged bellboy dumped the bags indignantly and my father
went up to the imitation-marble desk to register. The clerk turned
the big book around and gave him a pen. I wanted to sign for myself, so I was standing close to him, watching him write in his
quick, scratchy script, when suddenly the pen paused. He held his
hand, frowning a little.

"Come on," I said, "I want to—"

"Now, you can just wait until I finish," he answered. When he
had finished, he let me have the pen. To the clerk he said, "Curious
coincidence! I used to know someone by that name." He stopped
short, gave the clerk a cold, severe look, as though he meant to indi-

cate that the fellow would be well advised to attend to his own business, and turned away.

The elevator was upstairs. While we stood listening to its creep-
ing, creaky descent, my father said "Hm!" and shook his head several times. The lighted cage came into view. My father gazed at it a
moment. Then he said "Hm!" again. It came shaking to a halt in
front of us. The door opened and a woman walked out. Her eyes
went over us in a brief, impersonal glance. She took two steps,
pulled up short, and looked at us again. Then, with a sort of gasp,
she said, "Why, Will!"

She came right up to him. She put her hand on his arm. "Will!"
she repeated. "Well, now, honestly!" She gave his arm a quick
squeeze, tapped it and dropped her hand. "Will, I can't believe it!
Isn't it funny! You know, I never planned to stop here. If that
wretched car hadn't broken down—"

I was looking at her with blank curiosity, and I saw at once that
she was pretty—though not in the sense in which you applied pretty
to a girl, exactly. In a confused way, she seemed to me to look more
like a picture—the sort of woman who might appear on a completed
jigsaw puzzle, or on the back of a pack of cards. Her skin had a
creamy, powdered tone. Her eyes had a soft, gay shine which I knew
from unconscious observation was not usual in a mature face. Her
hair was just so. Very faint, yet very distinct, too, a smell of roses
reached me. Although she was certainly not wearing anything resembling evening dress, and, in fact, had a hat on, something about
her made me think of my mother when she was ready to go to one of
the dances they called assemblies, or of the mothers of my friends
who came to dinner looking not at all as they usually looked. I was
so absorbed in this feeling of strangeness—I neither liked it nor disliked it; it simply bewildered me—that I didn't hear anything until
my father said rather sharply, "John! Say how do you do to Mrs.
Prentice!"

"I can't get over it!" she was saying. She broke into a kind of bubbling laughter. "Why, he's grown up, Will! Oh, dear, doesn't it
make you feel queer?"

Ordinarily, I much resented that adult trick of talking about you
as if you weren't there, but the "grown up" was all right, and she
looked at me without a trace of the customary patronage; as though,
of course, I saw the joke too. She laughed again. I would not have
had the faintest idea why, yet I was obliged to laugh in response.

She asked brightly, "Where's Hilda?"

My father answered, with slight constraint, that my mother was
not with us, that he was just driving me up to school.

Mrs. Prentice said, "Oh, that's too bad. I'd so like to see her." She
smiled at me again and said, "Will, I can't face that dreadful dining

room. I was going to have something sent up. They've given me what must be the bridal suite." She laughed. "You should see it! Why don't we all have supper up there?"

"Capital!" my father said.

The word astonished me. I was more or less familiar with most of my father's expressions, and that certainly was not one of them. I thought it sounded funny, but Mrs. Prentice said, "Will, you haven't changed a bit! But then, you wouldn't. It comes from having such a wonderful disposition."

The aged bellboy had put our luggage in the elevator and shuffled his feet beside it, glowering at us. "Leave the supper to me," my father said. "I'll see if something fit to eat can be ordered. We'll be down in about an hour."

In our room, my father gave the aged bellboy a quarter. It was more than a bellboy in a small-town hotel would ever expect to get, and so, more than my father would normally give, for he was very exact in money matters and considered lavishness not only wasteful but rather common, and especially bad for the recipient, since it made him dissatisfied when he was given what he really deserved. He said to me, "You can go in the bathroom first, and see that you wash your neck and ears. If you can get your blue suit out without un-packing everything else, change to that."

While I was splashing around I could hear him using the tele-phone. It did not work very well, but he must eventually have pre-vailed over it, for when I came out he had unpacked his shaving kit. With the strop hung on a clothes hook, he was whacking a razor up and down. Preoccupied, he sang, or, rather, grumbled, to himself, for he was completely tone-deaf: "I am the monarch of the sea, the ruler of the Queen's—"

The room where we found Mrs. Prentice was quite a big one, with a large dark-green carpet on the floor, and much carved furniture, upholstered where possible in green velvet of the color of the carpet. Long full glass curtains and green velvet drapes shrouded the win-dows, so the lights—in brass wall brackets and a wonderfully coiled and twisted chandelier—were on. There was also an oil painting in a great gold frame showing a group of red-trousered French soldiers defending a farmhouse against the Prussians—the type of art I liked most. It all seemed to me tasteful and impressive, but Mrs. Prentice said, "Try not to look at it!" She and my father both laughed.

"I don't know what we'll get," my father said. "I did what I could."

"Anything will do," she said. "Will, you're a godsend! I was expir-ing for a cocktail, but I hated to order one by myself."

I was startled. My father was not a drinking man. At home I could tell when certain people were coming to dinner, for a tray with glasses and a decanter of sherry would appear in the living room about the time I was going upstairs, and a bottle of sauterne would be put in the icebox.

My mother usually had a rehearsal after the table was set, to make sure that the maid remembered how wine was poured.

Sometimes, when I was at the tennis club, my father would bring me into the big room with the bar and we would both have lemonades. I had never actually seen him drink anything else, so I had an impression that drinking was unusual and unnecessary. I even felt that it was reprehensible, since I knew that the man who took care of the garden sometimes had to be spoken to about it.

To my astonishment, my father said, as though it were the most natural thing in the world, "Well, we can't let you expire, May. What'll it be?"

She said, "I'd love a Clover Club, Will. Do you suppose they could make one?"

My father said, "We'll soon find out! But I think I'd better go down and superintend it myself. That bar looks the reverse of promising."

Left alone with Mrs. Prentice, still feeling that astonishment, I was uncomfortable. I studied the exciting details of the fight for the farmhouse, but I was self-conscious, for I realized that she was looking at me. When I looked at her, she was lighting a gold-tipped cigarette which she had taken from a white cardboard box on the table. She seemed to understand something of my confusion. She said, "Many years ago your father and I were great friends, John. After I was married, I went to England to live—to London. I was there until my husband died, so we didn't see each other. That's why we were both so surprised."

I could not think of anything to say. Mrs. Prentice tried again. "You two must have wonderful times together," she said. "He's lots of fun, isn't he?"

Embarrassed, I inadvertently nodded; and thinking that she had found the right subject, she went on warmly, "He was always the most wonderful swimmer and tennis player, and a fine cyclist. I don't know how many cups he took for winning the century run."

Of course, I had often seen my father play tennis. He played it earnestly, about as well as a strong but short-legged amateur who didn't have much time for it could. He was a powerful swimmer, but he did not impress me particularly, even when he swam, as he was fond of doing, several miles; for he never employed anything but a measured, monotonous breast stroke which moved him through the water with unbending dignity. It was very boring to be in the boat accompanying him across some Maine lake. I had no idea what a century run was, but I guessed it meant bicycling, so my confusion and amazing were all the greater. The fad for bicycling wasn't within my memory. I could as easily imagine my father playing tag or trading cigarette pictures as riding a bicycle.

Mrs. Prentice must have wondered what was wrong with me. She could see that I ought to be past the stage when overpowering shyness would be natural. She must have known, too, that she had a more than ordinary gift for attracting people and putting them at ease. No doubt, her failure with me mildly vexed and amused her.

She arose, saying, "Oh, I forgot! I have something." She swept into the room beyond. In a moment she came back with a box in her hands. I had stood up awkwardly when she stood up. She brought the box to me. It was very elaborate. A marvelous arrangement of candied fruits and chocolates filled it. I said, "Thank you very much." I took the smallest and plainest piece of chocolate I could see.

"You mustn't spoil your appetitie, must you?" she said, her eyes twinkling. "You take what you want. We won't tell your father."

Her air of cordial conspiracy really warmed me. I tried to smile, but I didn't find myself any more articulate. I said again, "Thank you. This is really all I want."

"All right, John," she said, "We'll leave it on the desk there, in case you change your mind."

The door, which had stood ajar, swung open. In came my father, carrying a battered cocktail shaker wrapped in a napkin. He headed a procession made up of the young bellboy, with a folding table; the old bellboy, with a bunch of roses in a vase; and a worried-looking waitress, with a tray of silver and glasses and folded linen.

"Why, Will," Mrs. Prentice cried, "it's just like magic!"

My father said, "What it will be just like, I'm afraid, is the old Ocean House."

"Oh, oh!" Mrs. Prentice laughed. "The sailing parties! You know, I haven't thought of those—and those awful buffet suppers!"

"Very good," my father said, looking at the completed efforts of his procession. "Please try to see that the steak is rare, and gets here hot. That's all." He filled two glasses with pink liquid from the cocktail shaker. He brought one of them to Mrs. Prentice, and, lifting the other, said, "Well, May. Moonlight Bay!"

She looked at him, quick and intent. She began quizzically to smile. It seemed to me she blushed a little. "All right, Will," she said and drank.

They were both silent for an instant. Then, with a kind of energetic abruptness, she said, "Lottie Frazer! Oh, Will, do you know, I saw Lottie a month or two ago."

I sat quiet, recognizing adult conversation, and knowing that it would be dull. I fixed my eyes on the battle picture. I tried to imagine myself behind the mottled stone wall with the French infantrymen, but constantly I heard Mrs. Prentice laugh. My father kept responding, but with an odd, light, good-humored inflection, as though he knew that she would laugh again as soon as he finished speaking. I could not make my mind stay on the usually engrossing business of thinking myself into a picture.

". . . you were simply furious," I heard Mrs. Prentice saying. "I didn't blame you."

My father said, "I guess I was."

"You said you'd break his neck."

They had my full attention, but I had missed whatever it was, for my father only responded, "Poor old Fred!" and looked thoughtfully at his glass. "So you're going back?"

Mrs. Prentice nodded. "This isn't really home to me. Becky and I are—well, I can hardly believe we're sisters. She disapproves of me so."

"I don't remember Becky ever approving of anything," my father said. "There's frankness for you."

"Oh, but she approved of you!" Mrs. Prentice looked at him a moment.

"I never knew it," said my father. "She had a strange way of showing it. I had the impression that she thought I was rather wild, and hanging would be too good—"

"Oh, Will, the things you never knew!" Mrs. Prentice shook her head. "And of course, the person Becky really couldn't abide was Joe. They never spoke to each other. Not even at the wedding." Mrs. Prentice gazed at me, but abstractedly, without expression. She started to look back to my father, stopped herself, gave me a quick little smile, and then looked back. My father was examining his glass.

"Ah, well," he said, "there is a divinity that shapes our ends, rough-hew them—"

Mrs. Prentice smiled. "Do you still write poetry?" she asked.

My father looked at her as though taken aback. "No," he said. He chuckled, but not with composure. "And what's more, I never did."

"Oh, but I think I could say some of it to you."

"Don't," said my father. "I'm afraid I was a very pretentious young man." At that moment, dinner arrived on two trays under a number of metal covers.

I thought the dinner was good and ate all that was offered me; yet eating seemed to form no more than a pleasant, hardly noticed undercurrent to my thoughts. From time to time I looked at the empty cocktail glasses or the great box of candied fruit and chocolates. I stole glances at Mrs. Prentice's pretty, lively face. Those fragments of conversation repeated themselves to me.

Intently, vainly, I considered "century run," "Ocean House," "Moonlight Bay." I wondered about Fred, whose neck, it seemed, my father thought of breaking; about this Becky and what she approved of; and about the writing of poetry. My mother had done a good deal to acquaint me with poetry. She read things like "Adonais," and the "Ode to a Nightingale," to me; and though I did not care much for them, I knew enough about poets to know that my father had little in common with pictures of Shelley and Keats.

Thus I had already all I could handle; and though talk went on during the meal, I hardly heard what they were saying. My attention wasn't taken until Mrs. Prentice, pouring coffee from a little pot, said something about the car.

My father accepted the small cup and answered, "I don't know that it's wise."

"But I've just got to," she said. "I can't make the boat unless—"

"Well, if you've got to, you've got to," my father said. "Are you sure he knows the roads? There are one or two places where you can easily make the wrong turn. I think I'd better get a map I have and mark it for you. It will only take a moment."

"Oh, Will," she said, "that would be such a help."

My father set his cup down and arose with decision. When we were alone, Mrs. Prentice got up too. As I had been taught to, I jumped nervously to my feet. She went and took the box from the desk and brought it to me again.

"Thank you very much," I said. I found another small piece of chocolate. "I'm going to put the cover on," she said, "and you take it with you."

I made a feeble protesting sound. I was aware that I ought not to accept such a considerable present from a person I did not know, but I realized that, with it, I was bound to be very popular on my arrival—at least, until the evening school meeting, when anything left would have to be turned in.

She could see my painful indecision. She set the box down. She gave a clear warm laugh, extended a hand and touched me on the chin. "John, you're a funny boy!" she said. My mother had sometimes addressed those very words to me, but with an air of great regret; meaning that the way I had just spoken or acted, while not quite deserving punishment, saddened her. Mrs. Prentice's tone was delighted, as though the last thing she meant to do was reprove me. "You don't like strangers to bother you, do you?"

The touch of her hand so astonished me that I hadn't moved a muscle. "I didn't think you were, at first," she said, "but you are! You don't look very much like him, but you can't imagine how exactly—" She broke into that delighted little laugh again. Without warning, she bent forward and kissed my cheek.

I was frightfully embarrassed. My instant reaction was a sense of deep outrage, for I thought that I had been made to look like a child and a fool. Collecting my wits took me a minute, however; and I found then that I was not angry at all. My first fear—that she might mean to imply that I was just a baby or a little boy—was too clearly unfounded. I was not sure just what she did mean, but part of it, I realized, was that I had pleased her somehow, that she had suddenly felt a liking for me, and that people she liked, she kissed.

I stood rigid, my face red. She went on at once: "Will you do something for me, John? Run down and see if you can find my chauffeur. His name is Alex. Tell him to bring the car around as soon as he can. Would you do that?"

"Yes, Mrs. Prentice," I said.

I left the room quickly. It was only the second floor, so I found the stairs instead of waiting for the elevator. I went down slowly, gravely and bewildered, thinking of my father and how extraordinary it all was; how different he seemed, and yet I could see, too, that he really hadn't changed. What he said and did was new to me, but not new to him. Somehow it all fitted together. I could feel that.

I came into the lobby and went down the back passage and out to the yard. It was now lighted by an electric bulb in a tin shade over the stable door. A flow of thin light threw shadows upon the bare earth. The hood of the big landaulet was down in place, and the man was putting some things away. "Alex!" I said authoritatively.

He turned sharp, and I said, "Mrs. Prentice wants you to bring the car around at once." He continued to look at me a moment. Then he smiled broadly. He touched his cap and said, "Very good, sir."

When I got back upstairs, my father had returned. The old bellboy was taking out a couple of bags. After a moment Mrs. Prentice came from the other room with a coat on and a full veil pinned over her face and hat. "Thank you, John," she said to me. "Don't forget this." She nodded at the big box on the table. I blushed and took it.

"Aren't you going to thank Mrs. Prentice?" my father asked.

She said, "Oh, Will, he's thanked me already. Don't bother him."

"Bother him!" said my father. "He's not bothered. Why, I can remember my father saying to me, 'Step up here, sir, and I'll mend your manners!' and for less than not saying thank you. I'm slack, but I know my parental duties."

They both laughed, and I found myself laughing too. We all went out to the elevator.

In front of the hotel, at the bottom of the steps, the car stood. "Just see he follows the map," my father said. "You can't miss it." He looked at the sky. "Fine moonlight night! I wouldn't mind driving myself."

"Will," said Mrs. Prentice, "Will!" She took his hand in both of hers and squeezed it. "Oh, I hate to say good-by like this! Why, I've hardly seen you at all!"

"There," said my father. "It's wonderful to have seen you, May."

She turned her veiled face toward me. "Well, John! Have a grand time at school!"

I said, "Good-by, Mrs. Prentice. Thank you very much for the—"

The chauffeur held the door open and my father helped her in. There was a thick click of the latch closing. The chauffeur went around to his seat. We stood on the pavement, waiting while he started the engine. The window was down a little and I could hear Mrs. Prentice saying, "Good-by, good-by."

My father waved a hand and the car drew away with a quiet, powerful drone. It passed, the sound fading, lights glinting on it, down the almost empty street.

"Well, that's that!" said my father. He looked at me at last and said, "I think you might send a postcard to your mother to tell her we got here all right."

I was feeling strangely cheerful and obedient. I thought fleetingly of making a fuss about the movies, but I decided not to. At the newsstand inside, my father bought me a postcard showing a covered bridge near the town. I took it to one of the small writing tables by the wall.

"Dear Mother," I wrote with the bad pen, "arrived here safely." I paused. My father had bought a paper and, putting on his glasses, had settled in one of the big chairs. He read with close, critical attention, light shining on his largely bald head, his mustache drawn down sternly. I had seen him reading like that a hundred times, but tonight he did not look quite the same to me. I thought of Mrs. Prentice a moment, but when I came to phrase it, I could not think of anything to say. Instead, I wrote: "We drove over this bridge." I paused again for some time, watching my father read, while I pondered. I wrote: "Father and I had a serious talk. Mean to do better at school—"

Unfortunately, I never did do much better at school. But that year and the year following, I would occasionally try to, for I thought it would please my father.

RALPH ELLISON

———•——•——

Battle Royal

.

IT GOES A LONG WAY BACK, some twenty years. All my life I had
been looking for something, and everywhere I turned someone tried
to tell me what it was. I accepted their answers too, though they
were often in contradiction and even self-contradictory. I was naïve.
I was looking for myself and asking everyone except myself questions which I, and only I, could answer. It took me a long time and
much painful boomeranging of my expectations to achieve a realization everyone else appears to have been born with: That I am
nobody but myself. But first I had to discover that I am an invisible
man!

And yet I am no freak of nature, nor of history. I was in the cards,
other things having been equal (or unequal) eighty-five years ago. I
am not ashamed of my grandparents for having been slaves. I am
only ashamed of myself for having at one time been ashamed. About
eighty-five years ago they were told that they were free, united with
others of our country in everything pertaining to the common good,
and, in everything social, separate like the fingers of the hand. And
they believed it. They exulted in it. They stayed in their place,
worked hard, and brought up my father to do the same. But my
grandfather is the one. He was an odd old guy, my grandfather, and
I am told I take after him. It was he who caused the trouble. On his
deathbed he called my father to him and said, "Son, after I'm gone I
want you to keep up the good fight. I never told you, but our life is
a war and I have been a traitor all my born days, a spy in the enemy's country ever since I give up my gun back in the Reconstruc-
tion. Live with your head in the lion's mouth. I want you to overcome 'em with yeses, undermine 'em with grins, agree 'em to death
and destruction, let 'em swoller you till they vomit or bust wide
open." They thought the old man had gone out of his mind. He had
been the meekest of men. The younger children were rushed from

From Ralph Ellison, *Invisible Man*. (New York: Random House, 1952), pp. 13–
26. The narrative reprinted here is the opening chapter of the novel.

the room, the shades drawn and the flame of the lamp turned so low that it sputtered on the wick like the old man's breathing. "Learn it to the younguns," he whispered fiercely; then he died.

But my folks were more alarmed over his last words than over his dying. It was as though he had not died at all, his words caused so much anxiety. I was warned emphatically to forget what he had said and, indeed, this is the first time it has been mentioned outside the family circle. It had a tremendous effect upon me, however. I could never be sure of what he meant. Grandfather had been a quiet old man who never made any trouble, yet on his deathbed he had called himself a traitor and a spy, and he had spoken of his meekness as a dangerous activity. It became a constant puzzle which lay unanswered in the back of my mind. And whenever things went well for me I remembered my grandfather and felt guilty and uncomfortable. It was as though I was carrying out his advice in spite of myself. And to make it worse, everyone loved me for it. I was praised by the most lily-white men of the town. I was considered an example of desirable conduct—just as my grandfather had been. And what puzzled me was that the old man had defined it as *treachery*. When I was praised for my conduct I felt a guilt that in some way I was doing something that was really against the wishes of the white folks, that if they had understood they would have desired me to act just the opposite, that I should have been sulky and mean, and that that really would have been what they wanted, even though they were fooled and thought they wanted me to act as I did. It made me afraid that some day they would look upon me as a traitor and I would be lost. Still I was more afraid to act any other way because they didn't like that at all. The old man's words were like a curse. On my graduation day I delivered an oration in which I showed that humility was the secret, indeed, the very essence of progress. (Not that I believed this—how could I, remembering my grandfather?—I only believed that it worked.) It was a great success. Everyone praised me and I was invited to give the speech at a gathering of the town's leading white citizens. It was a triumph for our whole community.

It was in the main ballroom of the leading hotel. When I got there I discovered that it was on the occasion of a smoker, and I was told that since I was to be there anyway I might as well take part in the battle royal to be fought by some of my schoolmates as part of the entertainment. The battle royal came first.

All of the town's big shots were there in their tuxedoes, wolfing down the buffet foods, drinking beer and whiskey and smoking black cigars. It was a large room with a high ceiling. Chairs were arranged in neat rows around three sides of a portable boxing ring.

The fourth side was clear, revealing a gleaming space of polished floor. I had some misgivings over the battle royal, by the way. Not from a distaste for fighting, but because I didn't care too much for the other fellows who were to take part. They were tough guys who seemed to have no grandfather's curse worrying their minds. No one could mistake their toughness. And besides, I suspected that fighting a battle royal might detract from the dignity of my speech. In those pre-invisible days I visualized myself as a potential Booker T. Washington. But the other fellows didn't care too much for me either, and there were nine of them. I felt superior to them in my way, and I didn't like the manner in which we were all crowded together into the servants' elevator. Nor did they like my being there. In fact, as the warmly lighted floors flashed past the elevator we had words over the fact that I, by taking part in the fight, had knocked one of their friends out of a night's work.

We were led out of the elevator through a rococo hall into an anteroom and told to get into our fighting togs. Each of us was issued a pair of boxing gloves and ushered out into the big mirrored hall, which we entered looking cautiously about us and whispering, lest we might accidentally be heard above the noise of the room. It was foggy with cigar smoke. And already the whiskey was taking effect. I was shocked to see some of the most important men of the town quite tipsy. They were all there—bankers, lawyers, judges, doctors, fire chiefs, teachers, merchants. Even one of the more fashionable pastors. Something we could not see was going on up front. A clarinet was vibrating sensuously and the men were standing up and moving eagerly forward. We were a small tight group, clustered together, our bare upper bodies touching and shining with anticipatory sweat; while up front the big shots were becoming increasingly excited over something we still could not see. Suddenly I heard the school superintendent, who had told me to come, yell, "Bring up the shines, gentlemen! Bring up the little shines!"

We were rushed up to the front of the ballroom, where it smelled even more strongly of tobacoo and whiskey. Then we were pushed into place. I almost wet my pants. A sea of faces, some hostile, some amused, ringed around us, and in the center, facing us, stood a magnificent blonde—stark naked. There was dead silence. I felt a blast of cold air chill me. I tried to back away, but they were behind me and around me. Some of the boys stood with lowered heads, trembling. I felt a wave of irrational guilt and fear. My teeth chattered, my skin turned to goose flesh, my knees knocked. Yet I was strongly attracted and looked in spite of myself. Had the price of looking been blindness, I would have looked. The hair was yellow like that of a circus kewpie doll, the face heavily powdered and rouged, as though to form an abstract mask, the eyes hollow and smeared a cool blue, the color of a baboon's butt. I felt a desire to spit upon her as my eyes brushed slowly over her body. Her breasts were firm and round as the domes of East Indian temples, and I stood so close as to see the fine texture and beads of pearly perspiration glistening like dew around the pink and erected buds of her nipples. I wanted at one and the same time to run from the room, to sink through the floor, or go to her and cover her from my eyes and the eyes of the others with my body; to feel the soft thighs, to caress her and destroy her, to love her and murder her, to hide from her, and yet to stroke where below the small American flag tattooed upon her belly her thighs formed a capital V. I had a notion that of all in the room she saw only me with her impersonal eyes.

And then she began to dance, a slow sensuous movement; the smoke of a hundred cigars clinging to her like the thinnest of veils. She seemed like a fair bird-girl girdled in veils calling to me from the angry surface of some gray and threatening sea. I was transported. Then I became aware of the clarinet playing and the big shots yelling at us. Some threatened us if we looked and others if we did not. On my right I saw one boy faint. And now a man grabbed a silver pitcher from a table and stepped close as he dashed ice water upon him and stood him up and forced two of us to support him as his head hung and moans issued from his thick bluish lips. Another boy began to plead to go home. He was the largest of the group, wearing dark red fighting trunks much too small to conceal the erection which projected from him as though in answer to the insinuating low-registered moaning of the clarinet. He tried to hide himself with his boxing gloves.

And all the while the blond continued dancing, smiling faintly at the big shots who watched her with fascination, and faintly smiling at our fear. I noticed a certain merchant who followed her hungrily, his lips loose and drooling. He was a large man who wore diamond studs in a shirtfront which swelled with the ample paunch underneath, and each time the blonde swayed her undulating hips he ran his hand through the thin hair of his bald head and, with his arms upheld, his posture clumsy like that of an intoxicated panda, wound his belly in a slow and obscene grind. This creature was completely hypnotized. The music had quickened. As the dancer flung herself about with a detached expression on her face, the men began reaching out to touch her. I could see their beefy fingers sink into the soft flesh. Some of the others tried to stop them and she began to move around the floor in graceful circles, as they gave chase, slipping and sliding over the polished floor. It was mad. Chairs went crashing, drinks were spilt, as they ran laughing and howling after her. They caught her just as she reached a door, raised her from the floor, and tossed her as college boys are tossed at a hazing, and above her red, fixed-smiling lips I saw the terror and disgust in her eyes, almost like my own terror and that which I saw in some of the other boys. As I watched, they tossed her twice and her soft breasts seemed to flatten against the air and her legs flung wildly as she spun. Some of the more sober ones helped her to escape. And I started off the floor, heading for the anteroom with the rest of the boys.

Some were still crying and in hysteria. But as we tried to leave we were stopped and ordered to get into the ring. There was nothing to do but what we were told. All ten of us climbed under the ropes and allowed ourselves to be blindfolded with broad bands of white cloth. One of the men seemed to feel a bit sympathetic and tried to cheer us up as we stood with our backs against the ropes. Some of us tried to grin. "See that boy over there?" one of the men said. "I want you to run across at the bell and give it to him right in the belly. If you don't get him, I'm going to get you. I don't like his looks." Each of us was told the same. The blindfolds were put on. Yet even then I had been going over my speech. In my mind each word was as bright as flame. I felt the cloth pressed into place, and frowned so that it would be loosened when I relaxed.

But now I felt a sudden fit of blind terror. I was unused to darkness. It was as though I had suddenly found myself in a dark room filled with poisonous cottonmouths. I could hear the bleary voices yelling insistently for the battle royal to begin.

"Get going in there!"

"Let me at that big nigger!"

I strained to pick up the school superintendent's voice, as though to squeeze some security out of that slightly more familiar sound.

"Let me at those black sonsabitches!" someone yelled.

"No, Jackson, no!" another voice yelled. "Here, somebody, help me hold Jack."

"I want to get at that ginger-colored nigger. Tear him limb from limb," the first voice yelled.

"I stood against the ropes trembling. For in those days I was what they called ginger-colored, and he sounded as though he might crunch me between his teeth like a crisp ginger cookie.

Quite a struggle was going on. Chairs were being kicked about and I could hear voices grunting as with a terrific effort. I wanted to see, to see more desperately than ever before. But the blindfold was tight as a thick skin-puckering scab and when I raised my gloved hands to push the layers of white aside a voice yelled, "Oh, no you don't, black bastard! Leave that alone!"

"Ring the bell before Jackson kills him a coon!" someone boomed in the sudden silence. And I heard the bell clang and the sound of the feet scuffling forward.

A glove smacked against my head. I pivoted, striking out stiffly as someone went past, and felt the jar ripple along the length of my arm to my shoulder. Then it seemed as though all nine of the boys had turned upon me at once. Blows pounded me from all sides while I struck out as best I could. So many blows landed upon me that I wondered if I were not the only blindfolded fighter in the ring, or if the man called Jackson hadn't succeeded in getting me after all.

Blindfolded, I could no longer control my motions. I had no dignity. I stumbled about like a baby or a drunken man. The smoke had become thicker and with each new blow it seemed to sear and further restrict my lungs. My saliva became like hot bitter glue. A glove connected with my head, filling my mouth with warm blood. It was everywhere. I could not tell if the moisture I felt upon my body was sweat or blood. A blow landed hard against the nape of my neck. I felt myself going over, my head hitting the floor. Streaks of blue light filled the black world behind the blindfold. I lay prone, pretending that I was knocked out, but felt myself seized by hands and yanked to my feet. "Get going, black boy! Mix it up!" My arms were like lead, my head smarting from blows. I managed to feel my way to the ropes and held on, trying to catch my breath. A glove landed in my mid-section and I went over again, feeling as though the smoke had become a knife jabbed into my guts. Pushed this way and that by the legs milling around me, I finally pulled erect and discovered that I could see the black, sweat-washed forms weaving in the smoky-blue atmosphere like drunken dancers weaving to the rapid drum-like thuds of blows.

Everyone fought hysterically. It was complete anarchy. Everybody fought everybody else. No group fought together for long. Two, three, four, fought one, then turned to fight each other, were themselves attacked. Blows landed below the belt and in the kidney, with the gloves open as well as closed, and with my eye partly opened now there was not so much terror. I moved carefully, avoiding blows, although not too many to attract attention, fighting from group to group. The boys groped about like blind, cautious crabs crouching to protect their mid-sections, their heads pulled in short against their shoulders, their arms stretched nervously before them, with their fists testing the smoke-filled air like the knobbed feelers of hypersensitive snails. In one corner I glimpsed a boy violently punching the air and heard him scream in pain as he smashed his hand against a ring post. For a second I saw him bent over holding his hand, then going down as a blow caught his unprotected head. I played one group against the other, slipping and throwing a punch then stepping out of range while pushing the others into the melee to take the blows blindly aimed at me. The smoke was agonizing and there were no rounds, no bells at three minutes intervals to relieve our exhaustion. The room spun round me, a swirl of lights, smoke, sweating bodies surrounded by tense white faces. I bled from both nose and mouth, the blood spattering upon my chest.

The men kept yelling, "Slug him, black boy! Knock his guts out!"

"Uppercut him! Kill him! Kill that big boy!"

Taking a fake fall, I saw a boy going down heavily beside me as though we were felled by a single blow, saw a sneaker-clad foot shoot into his groin as the two who had knocked him down stumbled upon him. I rolled out of range, feeling a twinge of nausea.

The harder we fought the more threatening the men became. And yet, I had begun to worry about my speech again. How would it go? Would they recognize my ability? What would they give me?

I was fighting automatically when suddenly I noticed that one after another of the boys was leaving the ring. I was surprised, filled with panic, as though I had been left alone with an unknown danger. Then I understood. The boys had arranged it among themselves. It was the custom for the two men left in the ring to slug it out for the winner's prize. I discovered this too late. When the bell sounded two men in tuxedoes leaped into the ring and removed the blindfold. I found myself facing Tatlock, the biggest of the gang. I felt sick at my stomach. Hardly had the bell stopped ringing in my ears than it clanged again and I saw him moving swiftly toward me. Thinking of nothing else to do I hit him smash on the nose. He kept coming, bringing the rank sharp violence of stale sweat. His face was a black blank of a face, only his eyes alive—with hate of me and aglow with a feverish terror from what had happened to us all. I became anxious. I wanted to deliver my speech and he came at me as though he meant to beat it out of me. I smashed him again and again, taking his blows as they came. Then on a sudden impulse I struck him lightly and as we clinched, I whispered, "Fake like I knocked you out, you can have the prize."

"I'll break your behind," he whispered hoarsely.

"For *them*?"

"For *me*, sonofabitch!"

They were yelling for us to break it up and Tatlock spun me half around with a blow, and as a joggled camera sweeps in a reeling scene, I saw the howling red faces crouching tense beneath the cloud of blue-gray smoke. For a moment the world wavered, unraveled, flowed, then my head cleared and Tatlock bounced before me. That fluttering shadow before my eyes was his jabbing left hand. Then falling forward, my head against his damp shoulder, I whispered,

"I'll make it five dollars more."

"Go to hell!"

But his muscles relaxed a trifle beneath my pressure and I breathed, "Seven?"

"Give it to your ma," he said, ripping me beneath the heart.

And while I still held him I butted him and moved away. I felt myself bombarded with punches. I fought back with hopeless desperation. I wanted to deliver my speech more than anything else in the world, because I felt that only these men could judge truly my ability, and now this stupid clown was ruining my chances. I began fighting carefully now, moving in to punch him and out again with my greater speed. A lucky blow to his chin and I had him going too— until I heard a loud voice yell, "I got my money on the big boy."

Hearing this, I almost dropped my guard. I was confused: Should I try to win against the voice out there? Would not this go against my speech, and was not this a moment for humility, for nonresistance? A blow to my head as I danced about sent my right eye popping like a jack-in-the-box and settled my dilemma. The room went red as I fell. It was a dream fall, my body languid and fastidious as to where to land, until the floor became impatient and smashed up to meet me. A moment later I came to. An hypnotic voice said FIVE emphatically. And I lay there, hazily watching a dark red spot of my own blood shaping itself into a butterfly, glistening and soaking into the soiled gray world of the canvas.

When the voice drawled TEN I was lifted up and dragged to a chair. I sat dazed. My eye pained and swelled with each throb of my pounding heart and I wondered if now I would be allowed to speak. I was wringing wet, my mouth still bleeding. We were grouped along the wall now. The other boys ignored me as they congratulated Tatlock and speculated as to how much they would be paid. One boy whimpered over his smashed hand. Looking up front, I saw attendants in white jackets rolling the portable ring away and placing a small square rug in the vacant space surrounded by chairs. Perhaps, I thought, I will stand on the rug to deliver my speech.

Then the M.C. called to us, "Come on up here boys and get your money."

We ran forward to where the men laughed and talked in their chairs, waiting. Everyone seemed friendly now.

"There it is on the rug," the man said. I saw the rug covered with coins of all dimensions and a few crumpled bills. But what excited me, scattered here and there, were the gold pieces.

"Boys, it's all yours," the man said. "You get all you grab."

"That's right, Sambo," a blond man said, winking at me confidentially.

I trembled with excitement, forgetting my pain. I would get the gold and the bills, I thought. I would use both hands. I would throw my body against the boys nearest me to block them from the gold.

"Get down around the rug now," the man commanded, "and don't anyone touch it until I give the signal."

"This ought to be good," I heard.

As told, we got around the square rug on our knees. Slowly the man raised his freckled hand as we followed it upward with our eyes.

I heard, "These niggers look like they're about to pray!"

Then, "Ready," the man said. "Go!"

I lunged for a yellow coin lying on the blue design of the carpet, touching it and sending a surprised shriek to join those rising around me. I tried frantically to remove my hand but could not let go. A hot, violent force tore through my body, shaking me like a wet rat. The rug was electrified. The hair bristled up on my head as I shook myself free. My muscles jumped, my nerves jangled, writhed. But I saw that this was not stopping the other boys. Laughing in fear and embarrassment, some were holding back and scooping up the coins knocked off by the painful contortions of the others. The men roared above us as we struggled.

"Pick it up, goddamnit, pick it up!" someone called like a bass-voiced parrot. "Go on, get it!"

I crawled rapidly around the floor, picking up the coins, trying to avoid the coppers and to get greenbacks and the gold. Ignoring the shock by laughing, as I brushed the coins off quickly, I discovered that I could contain the electricity—a contradiction, but it works. Then the men began to push us onto the rug. Laughing embarrassedly we struggled out of their hands and kept after the coins. We were all wet and slippery and hard to hold. Suddenly I saw a boy lifted into the air, glistening with sweat like a circus seal, and dropped, his wet back landing flush upon the charged rug, heard him yell and saw him literally dance upon his back, his elbows beating a frenzied tattoo upon the floor, his muscles twitching like the flesh of a horse stung by many flies. When he finally rolled off, his face was gray and no one stopped him when he ran from the floor amid booming laughter.

"Get the money," the M.C. called. "That's good hard American cash!"

And we snatched and grabbed, snatched and grabbed. I was careful not to come too close to the rug now, and when I felt the hot whiskey breath descend upon me like a cloud of foul air I reached out and grabbed the leg of a chair. It was occupied and I held on desperately.

"Leggo, nigger! Leggo!"

The huge face wavered down to mine as he tried to push me free. But my body was slippery and he was too drunk. It was Mr. Colcord, who owned a chain of movie houses and "entertainment palaces." Each time he grabbed me I slipped out of his hands. It became a real struggle. I feared the rug more than I did the drunk, so I held on, surprising myself for a moment by trying to topple *him* upon the rug. It was such an enormous idea that I found myself actually carrying it out. I tried not to be obvious, yet when I grabbed his leg, trying to tumble him out of the chair, he raised up roaring with laughter, and, looking at me with soberness dead in the eye, kicked me viciously in the chest. The chair leg flew out of my hand and I felt myself going and rolled. It was as though I had rolled through a bed of hot coals. It seemed a whole century would pass before I would roll free, a century in which I was seared through the deepest levels of my body to the fearful breath within me and the breath seared and heated to the point of explosion. It'll all be over in a flash, I thought as I rolled clear. It'll all be over in a flash.

But not yet, the men on the other side were waiting, red faces swollen as though from apoplexy as they bent forward in their chairs. Seeing their fingers coming toward me I rolled away as a fumbled football rolls off the receiver's fingertips, back into the coals. That time I luckily sent the rug sliding out of place and heard the coins ringing against the floor and the boys scuffling to pick them up and the M.C. calling, "All right, boys, that's all. Go get dressed and get your money."

I was limp as a dish rag. My back felt as though it had been beaten with wires.

When we had dressed the M.C. came in and gave us each five dollars, except Tatlock, who got ten for being last in the ring. Then he told us to leave. I was not to get a chance to deliver my speech, I thought. I was going out into the dim alley in despair when I was stopped and told to go back. I returned to the ballroom, where the men were pushing back their chairs and gathering in groups to talk.

The M.C. knocked on a table for quiet. "Gentlemen," he said, "we almost forgot an important part of the program. A most serious part, gentlemen. This boy was brought here to deliver a speech which he made at his graduation yesterday . . ."

"Bravo!"

"I'm told that he is the smartest boy we've got out there in Greenwood. I'm told that he knows more big words than a pocket-sized dictionary."

Much applause and laughter.

"So now, gentlemen, I want you to give him your attention."

There was still laughter as I faced them, my mouth dry, my eye throbbing. I began slowly, but evidently my throat was tense, because they began shouting, "Louder! Louder!"

"We of the younger generation extol the wisdom of that great leader and educator," I shouted, "who first spoke these flaming words of wisdom: 'A ship lost at sea for many days suddenly sighted a friendly vessel. From the mast of the unfortunate vessel was seen a signal: "Water, water; we die of thirst!" The answer from the friendly vessel came back: "Cast down your bucket where you are." The captain of the distressed vessel, at last heeding the injunction cast down his bucket, and it came up full of fresh sparkling water from the mouth of the Amazon River.' And like him I say, and in his words, 'To those of my race who depend upon bettering their condition in a foreign land, or who underestimate the importance of cultivating friendly relations with the Southern white man, who is his next-door neighbor, I would say: "Cast down your bucket where you are"—cast it down in making friends in every manly way of the people of all races by whom we are surrounded...'"

I spoke automatically and with such fervor that I did not realize that the men were still talking and laughing until my dry mouth, filling up with blood from the cut, almost strangled me. I coughed, wanting to stop and go to one of the tall brass, sand-filled spittoons to relieve myself, but a few of the men, especially the superintendent, were listening and I was afraid. So I gulped it down, blood, saliva and all, and continued. (What powers of endurance I had during those days! What enthusiasm! What a belief in the rightness of things!) I spoke even louder in spite of the pain. But still they talked and still they laughed, as though deaf with cotton in dirty ears. So I spoke with greater emotional emphasis. I closed my ears and swallowed blood until I was nauseated. The speech seemed a hundred times as long as before, but I could not leave out a single word. All had to be said, each memorized nuance considered, rendered. Nor was that all. Whenever I uttered a word of three or more syllables a group of voices would yell for me to repeat it. I used the phrase "social responsibility" and they yelled:

"What's that word you say, boy?"

"Social responsibility," I said.

"What?"

"Social..."

"Louder."

"...responsibility."

"More!"

"Respon—"

"Repeat!"

"—sibility."

The room filled with the uproar of laughter until, no doubt, distracted by having to gulp down my blood, I made a mistake and yelled a phrase I had often seen denounced in newspaper editorials, heard debated in private.

"Social . . ."

"What?" they yelled.

". . . equality—"

The laughter hung smokelike in the sudden stillness. I opened my eyes, puzzled. Sounds of displeasure filled the room. The M.C. rushed forward. They shouted hostile phrases at me. But I did not understand.

A small dry mustached man in the front row blared out, "Say that slowly, son!"

"What, sir?"

"What you just said!"

"Social responsibility, sir," I said.

"You weren't being smart, were you, boy?" he said, not unkindly.

"No, sir!"

"You sure that about 'equality' was a mistake?"

"Oh, yes, sir," I said. "I was swallowing blood."

"Well, you had better speak more slowly so we can understand. We mean to do right by you, but you've got to know your place at all times. All right, now, go on with your speech."

I was afraid. I wanted to leave but I wanted also to speak and I was afraid they'd snatch me down.

"Thank you, sir," I said, beginning where I had left off, and having them ignore me as before.

Yet when I finished there was a thunderous applause. I was surprised to see the superintendent come forth with a package wrapped in white tissue paper, and, gesturing for quiet, address the men.

"Gentlemen, you see that I did not overpraise this boy. He makes a good speech and some day he'll lead his people in the proper paths. And I don't have to tell you that that is important in these days and times. This is a good, smart boy, and so to encourage him in the right direction, in the name of the Board of Education I wish to present him a prize in the form of this . . ."

He paused, removing the tissue paper and revealing a gleaming calfskin brief case.

". . . in the form of this first-class article from Shad Whitmore's shop."

"Boy," he said, addressing me, "take this prize and keep it well. Consider it a badge of office. Prize it. Keep developing as you are and some day it will be filled with important papers that will help shape the destiny of your people."

I was so moved that I could hardly express my thanks. A rope of bloody saliva forming a shape like an undiscovered continent drooled upon the leather and I wiped it quickly away. I felt an importance that I had never dreamed.

"Open it and see what's inside," I was told.

My fingers a-tremble, I complied, smelling the fresh leather and finding an official-looking document inside. It was a scholarship to the state college for Negroes. My eyes filled with tears and I ran awkwardly off the floor.

I was overjoyed; I did not even mind when I discovered that the gold pieces I had scrambled for were brass pocket tokens advertising a certain make of automobile.

When I reached home everyone was excited. Next day the neighbors came to congratulate me. I even felt safe from grandfather, whose deathbed curse usually spoiled my triumphs. I stood beneath his photograph with my brief case in hand and smiled triumphantly into his stolid black peasant's face. It was a face that fascinated me. The eyes seemed to follow everywhere I went.

That night I dreamed I was at a circus with him and that he refused to laugh at the clowns no matter what they did. Then later he told me to open my brief case and read what was inside and I did, finding an official envelope stamped with the state seal; and inside the envelope I found another and another, endlessly, and I thought I would fall of weariness. "Them's years," he said. "Now open that one." And I did and in it I found an engraved document containing a short message in letters of gold. "Read it," my grandfather said. "Out loud!"

"To Whom It May Concern," I intoned. "Keep This Nigger-Boy Running."

I awoke with the old man's laughter ringing in my ears.

(It was a dream I was to remember and dream again for many years after. But at that time I had no insight into its meaning. First I had to attend college.)

BERNARD MALAMUD

The Magic Barrel

NOT LONG AGO there lived in uptown New York, in a small, almost
meager room, though crowded with books, Leo Finkle, a rabbinical
student in the Yeshivah University. Finkle, after six years of study,
was to be ordained in June and had been advised by an acquaintance that he might find it easier to win himself a congregation if he
were married. Since he had no present prospects of marriage, after
two tormented days of turning it over in his mind, he called in
Pinye Salzman, a marriage broker whose two-line advertisement he
had read in the *Forward*.

The matchmaker appeared one night out of the dark fourth-floor
hallway of the graystone rooming house where Finkle lived, grasping
a black, strapped portfolio that had been worn thin with use.
Salzman, who had been long in the business, was of slight but dignified build, wearing an old hat, and an overcoat too short and tight
for him. He smelled frankly of fish, which he loved to eat, and although he was missing a few teeth, his presence was not displeasing,
because of an amiable manner curiously contrasted with mournful
eyes. His voice, his lips, his wisp of beard, his bony fingers were animated, but give him a moment of repose and his mild blue eyes revealed a depth of sadness, a characteristic that put Leo a little at ease
although the situation, for him, was inherently tense.

He at once informed Salzman why he had asked him to come, explaining that his home was in Cleveland, and that but for his parents, who had married comparatively late in life, he was alone in the
world. He had for six years devoted himself almost entirely to his
studies, as a result of which, understandably, he had found himself
without time for a social life and the company of young women.
Therefore he thought it the better part of trial and error—of embar-
rassing fumbling—to call in an experienced person to advise him on

From Bernard Malamud, *The Magic Barrel*. (New York: Farrar, Straus & Cudahy,
1958), pp. 193–214. First published in *Partisan Review*, XXI (November, 1954),
587–603.

these matters. He remarked in passing that the function of the marriage broker was ancient and honorable, highly approved in the Jewish community, because it made practical the necessary without hindering joy. Moreover, his own parents had been brought together by a matchmaker. They had made, if not a financially profitable marriage—since neither had possessed any worldly goods to speak of—at least a successful one in the sense of their everlasting devotion to each other. Salzman listened in embarrassed surprise, sensing a sort of apology. Later, however, he experienced a glow of pride in his work, an emotion that had left him years ago, and he heartily approved of Finkle.

The two went to their business. Leo had led Salzman to the only clear place in the room, a table near a window that overlooked the lamp-lit city. He seated himself at the matchmaker's side but facing him, attempting by an act of will to suppress the unpleasant tickle in his throat. Salzman eagerly unstrapped his portfolio and removed a loose rubber band from a thin packet of much-handled cards. As he flipped through them, a gesture and sound that physically hurt Leo, the student pretended not to see and gazed steadfastly out the window. Although it was still February, winter was on its last legs, signs of which he had for the first time in years begun to notice. He now observed the round white moon, moving high in the sky through a cloud menagerie, and watched with half-open mouth as it penetrated a huge hen, and dropped out of her like an egg laying itself. Salzman, though pretending through eyeglasses he had just slipped on, to be engaged in scanning the writing on the cards, stole occasional glances at the young man's distinguished face, noting with pleasure the long, severe scholar's nose, brown eyes heavy with learning, sensitive yet ascetic lips, and a certain, almost hollow quality of the dark cheeks. He gazed around at shelves upon shelves of books and let out a soft, contented sigh.

When Leo's eyes fell upon the cards, he counted six spread out in Salzman's hand.

"So few?" he asked in disappointment.

"You wouldn't believe me how much cards I got in my office," Salzman replied. "The drawers are already filled to the top, so I keep them now in a barrel, but is every girl good for a new rabbi?"

Leo blushed at this, regretting all he had revealed of himself in a curriculum vitae he had sent to Salzman. He had thought it best to acquaint him with his strict standards and specifications, but in having done so, felt he had told the marriage broker more than was absolutely necessary.

He hesitantly inquired, "Do you keep photographs of your clients on file?"

"First comes family, amount of dowry, also what kind promises," Salzman replied, unbuttoning his tight coat and settling himself in the chair. "After comes pictures, rabbi."

"Call me Mr. Finkle. I'm not yet a rabbi."

Salzman said he would, but instead called him doctor, which he changed to rabbi when Leo was not listening too attentively.

Salzman adjusted his horn-rimmed spectacles, gently cleared his throat and read in an eager voice the contents of the top card:

"Sophie P. Twenty four years. Widow one year. No children. Educated high school and two years college. Father promises eight thousand dollars. Has wonderful wholesale business. Also real estate. On the mother's side comes teachers, also one actor. Well known on Second Avenue."

Leo gazed up in surprise. "Did you say a widow?"

"A widow don't mean spoiled, rabbi. She lived with her husband maybe four months. He was a sick boy she made a mistake to marry him."

"Marrying a widow has never entered my mind."

"This is because you have no experience. A widow, especially if she is young and healthy like this girl, is a wonderful person to marry. She will be thankful to you the rest of her life. Believe me, if I was looking now for a bride, I would marry a widow."

Leo reflected, then shook his head.

Salzman hunched his shoulders in an almost imperceptible gesture of disappointment. He placed the card down on the wooden table and began to read another:

"Lily H. High school teacher. Regular. Not a substitute. His savings and new Dodge car. Lived in Paris one year. Father is successful dentist thirty-five years. Interested in professional man. Well Americanized family. Wonderful opportunity."

"I knew her personally," said Salzman. "I wish you could see this girl. She is a doll. Also very intelligent. All day you could talk to her about books and theyater and what not. She also knows current events."

"I don't believe you mentioned her age?"

"Her age?" Salzman said, raising his brows. "Her age is thirty-two years."

Leo said after a while, "I'm afraid that seems a little too old."

Salzman let out a laugh. "So how old are you, rabbi?"

"Twenty-seven."

"So what is the difference, tell me, between twenty-seven and thirty-two? My own wife is seven years older than me. So what did I suffer?—Nothing. If Rothschild's a daughter wants to marry you, would you say on account her age, no?"

"Yes," Leo said dryly.

Salzman shook off the no in the yes. "Five years don't mean a thing. I give you my word that when you will live with her for one week you will forget her age. What does it mean five years—that she lived more and knows more than somebody who is younger? On this girl, God bless her, years are not wasted. Each one that it comes makes better the bargain."

"What subject does she teach in high school?"

"Languages. If you heard the way she speaks French, you will think it is music. I am in the business twenty-five years, and I recommend her with my whole heart. Believe me, I know what I'm talking, rabbi."

"What's on the next card?" Leo said abruptly.

Salzman reluctantly turned up the third card:

"Ruth K. Nineteen years. Honor student. Father offers thirteen thousand cash to the right bridegroom. He is a medical doctor. Stomach specialist with marvelous practice. Brother in law owns own garment business. Particular people."

Salzman looked as if he had read his trump card.

"Did you say nineteen?" Leo asked with interest.

"On the dot."

"Is she attractive?" He blushed. "Pretty?"

Salzman kissed his finger tips. "A little doll. On this I give you my word. Let me call the father tonight and you will see what means pretty."

But Leo was troubled. "You're sure she's that young?"

"This I am positive. The father will show you the birth certificate."

"Are you positive there isn't something wrong with her?" Leo insisted.

"Who says there is wrong?"

"I don't understand why an American girl her age should go to a marriage broker."

A smile spread over Salzman's face.

"So for the same reason you went, she comes."

Leo flushed. "I am pressed for time."

Salzman, realizing he had been tactless, quickly explained. "The father came, not her. He wants she should have the best, so he looks around himself. When we will locate the right boy he will introduce him and encourage. This makes a better marriage than if a young girl without experience takes for herself. I don't have to tell you this."

"But don't you think this young girl believes in love?" Leo spoke uneasily.

Salzman was about to guffaw but caught himself and said soberly, "Love comes with the right person, not before."

Leo parted dry lips but did not speak. Noticing that Salzman had snatched a glance at the next card, he cleverly asked, "How is her health?"

"Perfect," Salzman said, breathing with difficulty. "Of course, she is a little lame on her right foot from an auto accident that it happened to her when she was twelve years, but nobody notices on account she is so brilliant and also beautiful."

Leo got up heavily and went to the window. He felt curiously bitter and upbraided himself for having called in the marriage broker. Finally, he shook his head.

"Why not?" Salzman persisted, the pitch of his voice rising.

"Because I detest stomach specialists."

"So what do you care what is his business? After you marry her do you need him? Who says he must come every Friday night in your house?"

Ashamed of the way the talk was going, Leo dismissed Salzman, who went home with heavy, melancholy eyes.

Though he had felt only relief at the marriage broker's departure, Leo was in low spirits the next day. He explained it as arising from Salzman's failure to produce a suitable bride for him. He did not care for his type of clientele. But when Leo found himself hesitating whether to seek out another matchmaker, one more polished than Pinye, he wondered if it could be—his protestations to the contrary, and although he honored his father and mother—that he did not, in essence, care for the matchmaking institution? This thought he quickly put out of mind yet found himself still upset. All day he ran around in the woods—missed an important appointment, forgot to give out his laundry, walked out of a Broadway cafeteria without paying and had to run back with the ticket in his hand; had even not recognized his landlady in the street when she passed with a friend and courteously called out, "A good evening to you, Doctor Finkle." By nightfall, however, he had regained sufficient calm to sink his nose into a book and there found peace from his thoughts.

Almost at once there came a knock on the door. Before Leo could say enter, Salzman, commercial cupid, was standing in the room. His face was gray and meager, his expression hungry, and he looked as if he would expire on his feet. Yet the marriage broker managed, by some trick of the muscles, to display a broad smile.

"So good evening. I am invited?"

Leo nodded, disturbed to see him again, yet unwilling to ask the man to leave.

Beaming still, Salzman laid his portfolio on the table. "Rabbi, I got for you tonight good news."

"I've asked you not to call me rabbi. I'm still a student."

"Your worries are finished. I have for you a first-class bride."

"Leave me in peace concerning this subject." Leo pretended lack of interest.

"The world will dance at your wedding."

"Please, Mr. Salzman, no more."

"But first must come back my strength," Salzman said weakly. He fumbled with the portfolio straps and took out of the leather case an oily paper bag, from which he extracted a hard, seeded roll and a small, smoked white fish. With a quick motion of his hand he stripped the fish out of its skin and began ravenously to chew. "All day in a rush," he muttered.

Leo watched him eat.

"A sliced tomato you have maybe?" Salzman hesitantly inquired.

"No."

The marriage broker shut his eyes and ate. When he had finished he carefully cleaned up the crumbs and rolled up the remains of the fish, in the paper bag. His spectacled eyes roamed the room until he discovered, amid some piles of books, a one-burner gas stove. Lifting his hat he humbly asked, "A glass tea you got, rabbi?"

Conscience-stricken, Leo rose and brewed the tea. He served it with a chunk of lemon and two cubes of lump sugar, delighting Salzman.

After he had drunk his tea, Salzman's strength and good spirits were restored.

"So tell me, rabbi," he said amiably, "you considered some more the three clients I mentioned yesterday?"

"There was no need to consider."

"Why not?"

"None of them suits me."

"What then suits you?"

Leo let it pass because he could give only a confused answer.

Without waiting for a reply, Salzman asked, "You remember this girl I talked to you—the high school teacher?"

"Age thirty-two?"

But, surprisingly, Salzman's face lit in a smile. "Age twenty-nine."

Leo shot him a look. "Reduced from thirty-two?"

"A mistake," Salzman avowed. "I talked today with the dentist. He took me to his safety deposit box and showed me the birth certificate. She was twenty-nine years last August. They made her a party in the mountains where she went for her vacation. When her father spoke to me the first time I forgot to write the age and I told you thirty-two, but now I remember this was a different client, a widow."

"The same one you told me about? I thought she was twenty-four?"

"A different. Am I responsible that the world is filled with widows?"

"No, but I'm not interested in them, nor for that matter, in school teachers."

Salzman pulled his clasped hands to his breast. Looking at the ceiling he devoutly exclaimed, "Yiddishe kinder, what can I say to somebody that he is not interested in high-school teachers? So what then you are interested?"

Leo flushed but controlled himself.

"In what else will you be interested," Salzman went on, "if you not interested in this fine girl that she speaks four languages and has personally in the bank ten thousand dollars? Also her father guarantees further twelve thousand. Also she has a new car, wonderful clothes, talks on all subjects, and she will give you a first-class home and children. How near do we come in our life to paradise?"

"If she's so wonderful, why wasn't she married ten years ago?"

"Why?" said Salzman with a heavy laugh. "—Why? Because she is *partikiler*. That is why. She wants the *best*."

Leo was silent, amused at how he had entangled himself. But Salzman had aroused his interest in Lily H., and he began seriously to consider calling on her. When the marriage broker observed how intently Leo's mind was at work on the facts he had supplied, he felt certain they would soon come to an agreement.

Late Saturday afternoon, conscious of Salzman, Leo Finkle walked with Lily Hirschorn along Riverside Drive. He walked briskly and erectly, wearing with distinction the black fedora he had that morning taken with trepidation out of the dusty hat box on his closet shelf, and the heavy black Saturday coat he had thoroughly whisked clean. Leo also owned a walking stick, a present from a distant relative, but quickly put temptation aside and did not use it. Lily, petite and not unpretty, had on something signifying the approach of spring. She was au courant, animatedly, with all sorts of subjects, and he weighed her words and found her surprisingly sound—score another for Salzman, whom he uneasily sensed to be somewhere around, hiding perhaps high in a tree along the street, flashing the lady signals with a pocket mirror; or perhaps a cloven-hoofed Pan, piping nuptial ditties as he danced his invisible way before them, strewing wild buds on the walk and purple grapes in their path, symbolizing fruit of a union, though there was of course still none.

Lily startled Leo by remarking, "I was thinking of Mr. Salzman, a curious figure, wouldn't you say?"

Not certain what to answer, he nodded.

She bravely went on, blushing, "I for one am grateful for his introducing us. Aren't you?"

He courteously replied, "I am."

"I mean," she said with a little laugh—and it was all in good taste, or at least gave the effect of being not in bad—"do you mind that we came together so?"

He was not displeased with her honesty, recognizing that she meant to set the relationship aright, and understanding that it took a certain amount of experience in life, and courage, to want to do it quite that way. One had to have some sort of past to make that kind of beginning.

He said that he did not mind. Salzman's function was traditional and honorable—valuable for what it might achieve, which, he pointed out, was frequently nothing.

Lily agreed with a sigh. They walked on for a while and she said after a long silence, again with a nervous laugh, "Would you mind if I asked you something a little bit personal? Frankly, I find the subject fascinating." Although Leo shrugged, she went on half embarrassedly, "How was it that you came to your calling? I mean was it a sudden passionate inspiration?"

Leo, after a time, slowly replied, "I was always interested in the Law."

"You saw revealed in it the presence of the Highest?"

He nodded and changed the subject. "I understand that you spent a little time in Paris, Miss Hirschorn?"

"Oh, did Mr. Salzman tell you, Rabbi Finkle?" Leo winced but she went on, "It was ages ago and almost forgotten. I remember I had to return for my sister's wedding."

And Lily would not be put off. "When," she asked in a trembly voice, "did you become enamored of God?"

He stared at her. Then it came to him that she was talking not about Leo Finkle, but of a total stranger, some mystical figure, perhaps even passionate prophet that Salzman had dreamed up for her —no relation to the living or dead. Leo trembled with rage and weakness. The trickster had obviously sold her a bill of goods, just as he had him, who'd expected to become acquainted with a young lady of twenty-nine, only to behold, the moment he laid eyes upon her strained and anxious face, a woman past thirty-five and aging rapidly. Only his self control had kept him this long in her presence.

"I am not," he said gravely, "a talented religious person," and in seeking words to go on, found himself possessed by shame and fear.

"I think," he said in a strained manner, "that I came to God not because I loved Him, but because I did not."

This confession he spoke harshly because its unexpectedness shook him.

Lily wilted. Leo saw a profusion of loaves of bread go flying like ducks high over his head, not unlike the winged loaves by which he had counted himself to sleep last night. Mercifully, then, it snowed, which he would not put past Salzman's machinations.

He was infuriated with the marriage broker and swore he would throw him out of the room the minute he reappeared. But Salzman did not come that night, and when Leo's anger had subsided, an unaccountable despair grew in its place. At first he thought this was caused by his disappointment in Lily, but before long it became evident that he had involved himself with Salzman without a true knowledge of his own intent. He gradually realized—with an emptiness that seized him with six hands—that he had called in the broker to find him a bride because he was incapable of doing it himself. This terrifying insight he had derived as a result of his meeting and conversation with Lily Hirschorn. Her probing questions had somehow irritated him into revealing—to himself more than her—the true nature of his relationship to God, and from that it had come upon him, with shocking force, that apart from his parents, he had never loved anyone. Or perhaps it went the other way, that he did not love God so well as he might, because he had not loved man. It seemed to Leo that his whole life stood starkly revealed and he saw himself for the first time as he truly was—unloved and loveless. This bitter but somehow not fully unexpected revelation brought him to a point of panic, controlled only by extraordinary effort. He covered his face with his hands and cried.

The week that followed was the worst of his life. He did not eat and lost weight. His beard darkened and grew ragged. He stopped attending seminars and almost never opened a book. He seriously considered leaving the Yeshivah, although he was deeply troubled at the thought of the loss of all his years of study—saw them like pages torn from a book, strewn over the city—and at the devastating effect of this decision upon his parents. But he had lived without knowledge of himself, and never in the Five Books and all the Commentaries—mea culpa—had the truth been revealed to him. He did not know where to turn, and in all this desolating loneliness there was no *to whom,* although he often thought of Lily but not once could bring himself to go downstairs and make the call. He became touchy and irritable, especially with his landlady, who asked him all manner of personal questions; on the other hand, sensing his own disagreeableness, he waylaid her on the stairs and apologized abjectly, until mortified, she ran from him. Out of this, however, he drew the consolation that he was a Jew and that a Jew suffered. But gradually, as the long and terrible week drew to a close, he regained his composure and some idea of purpose in life: to go on as planned. Although he was imperfect, the ideal was not. As for his quest of a bride, the thought of continuing afflicted him with anxiety and heartburn, yet perhaps with this new knowledge of himself he would be more successful than in the past. Perhaps love would now come to him and a bride to that love. And for this sanctified seeking who needed a Salzman?

The marriage broker, a skeleton with haunted eyes, returned that very night. He looked, withal, the picture of frustrated expectancy— as if he had steadfastly waited the week at Miss Lily Hirschorn's side for a telephone call that never came.

Casually coughing, Salzman came immediately to the point: "So how did you like her?"

Leo's anger rose and he could not refrain from chiding the matchmaker: "Why did you lie to me, Salzman?"

Salzman's pale face went dead white, the world had snowed on him.

"Did you not state that she was twenty-nine?" Leo insisted.

"I give you my word—"

"She was thirty-five, if a day. *At least* thirty-five."

"Of this don't be too sure. Her father told me—"

"Never mind. The worst of it was that you lied to her."

"How did I lie to her, tell me?"

"You told her things about me that weren't true. You made me out to be more, consequently less than I am. She had in mind a totally different person, a sort of semi-mystical Wonder Rabbi."

"All I said, you was a religious man."

"I can imagine."

Salzman sighed. "This is my weakness that I have," he confessed. "My wife says to me I shouldn't be a salesman, but when I have two fine people that they would be wonderful to be married, I am so happy that I talk too much." He smiled wanly. "This is why Salzman is a poor man."

Leo's anger left him. "Well, Salzman, I'm afraid that's all."

The marriage broker fastened hungry eyes on him.

"You don't want any more a bride?"

"I do," said Leo, "but I have decided to seek her in a different way. I am no longer interested in an arranged marriage. To be frank, I now admit the necessity of premarital love. That is, I want to be in love with the one I marry."

"Love?" said Salzman, astounded. After a moment he remarked, "For us, our love is our life, not for the ladies. In the ghetto they—"

"I know, I know," said Leo. "I've thought of it often. Love, I have said to myself, should be a by-product of living and worship rather than its own end. Yet for myself I find it necessary to establish the level of my need and fulfill it."

Salzman shrugged but answered, "Listen, rabbi, if you want love, this I can find for you also. I have such beautiful clients that you will love them the minute your eyes will see them."

Leo smiled unhappily. "I'm afraid you don't understand."

But Salzman hastily unstrapped his portfolio and withdrew a manila packet from it.

"Pictures," he said, quickly laying the envelope on the table.

Leo called after him to take the pictures away, but as if on the wings of the wind, Salzman had disappeared.

March came. Leo had returned to his regular routine. Although he felt not quite himself yet—lacked energy—he was making plans for a more active social life. Of course it would cost something, but he was an expert in cutting corners; and when there were no corners left he would make circles rounder. All the while Salzman's pictures had lain on the table, gathering dust. Occasionally as Leo sat studying, or enjoying a cup of tea, his eyes fell on the manila envelope, but he never opened it.

The days went by and no social life to speak of developed with a member of the opposite sex—it was difficult, given the circumstances of his situation. One morning Leo toiled up the stairs to his room and stared out the window at the city. Although the day was bright his view of it was dark. For some time he watched the people in the street below hurrying along and then turned with a heavy heart to his little room. On the table was the packet. With a sudden relentless gesture he tore it open. For a half-hour he stood by the table in a state of excitement, examining the photographs of the ladies Salzman had included. Finally, with a deep sigh he put them down. There were six, of varying degrees of attractiveness, but look at them long enough and they all became Lily Hirschorn: all past their prime, all starved behind bright smiles, not a true personality in the lot. Life, despite their frantic yoohooings, had passed them by; they were pictures in a brief case that stank of fish. After a while, however, as Leo attempted to return the photographs into the envelope, he found in it another, a snapshot of the type taken by a machine for a quarter. He gazed at it a moment and let out a cry.

Her face deeply moved him. Why, he could at first not say. It

gave him the impression of youth—spring flowers, yet age—a sense of
having been used to the bone, wasted; this came from the eyes,
which were hauntingly familiar, yet absolutely strange. He had a
vivid impression that he had met her before, but try as he might he
could not place her although he could almost recall her name, as if
he had read it in her own handwriting. No, this couldn't be; he
would have remembered her. It was not, he affirmed, that she had
an extraordinary beauty—no, though her face was attractive
enough; it was that *something* about her moved him. Feature for
feature, even some of the ladies of the photographs could do better;
but she leaped forth to his heart—had *lived*, or wanted to—more
than just wanted, perhaps regretted how she had lived—had somehow deeply suffered: it could be seen in the depths of those reluctant eyes, and from the way the light enclosed and shone from her,
and within her, opening realms of possibility: this was her own. Her
he desired. His head ached and eyes narrowed with the intensity of
his gazing, then as if an obscure fog had blown up in the mind, he
experienced fear of her and was aware that he had received an
impression, somehow, of evil. He shuddered, saying softly, it is thus
with us all. Leo brewed some tea in a small pot and sat sipping it
without sugar, to calm himself. But before he had finished drinking,
again with excitement he examined the face and found it good:
good for Leo Finkle. Only such a one could understand him and
help him seek whatever he was seeking. She might, perhaps, love
him. How she had happened to be among the discards in Salzman's
barrel he could never guess, but he knew he must urgently go find
her.

Leo rushed downstairs, grabbed up the Bronx telephone book,
and searched for Salzman's home address. He was not listed, nor was
his office. Neither was he in the Manhattan book. But Leo remembered having written down the address on a slip of paper after he
had read Salzman's advertisement in the "personals" column of the
Forward. He ran up to his room and tore through his papers, without luck. It was exasperating. Just when he needed the matchmaker
he was nowhere to be found. Fortunately Leo remembered to look
in his wallet. There on a card he found his name written and a
Bronx address. No phone number was listed, the reason—Leo now
recalled—he had originally communicated with Salzman by letter.
He got on his coat, put a hat on over his skull cap and hurried to
the subway station. All the way to the far end of the Bronx he sat
on the edge of his seat. He was more than once tempted to take out
the picture and see if the girl's face was as he remembered it, but he
refrained, allowing the snapshot to remain in his inside coat pocket,

content to have her so close. When the train pulled into the station he was waiting at the door and bolted out. He quickly located the street Salzman had advertised.

The building he sought was less than a block from the subway, but it was not an office building, nor even a loft, nor a store in which one could rent office space. It was a very old tenement house. Leo found Salzman's name in pencil on a soiled tag under the bell and climbed three dark flights to his apartment. When he knocked, the door was opened by a thin, asthmatic, gray-haired woman, in felt slippers.

"Yes?" she said, expecting nothing. She listened without listening. He could have sworn he had seen her, too, before but knew it was an illusion.

"Salzman—does he live here? Pinye Salzman," he said, "the matchmaker?"

She stared at him a long minute. "Of course."

He felt embarrassed. "Is he in?"

"No." Her mouth, though left open, offered nothing more.

"The matter is urgent. Can you tell me where his office is?"

"In the air." She pointed upward.

"You mean he has no office?" Leo asked.

"In his socks."

He peered into the apartment. It was sunless and dingy, one large room divided by a half-open curtain, beyond which he could see a sagging metal bed. The near side of a room was crowded with rickety chairs, old bureaus, a three-legged table, racks of cooking utensils, and all the apparatus of a kitchen. But there was no sign of Salzman or his magic barrel, probably also a figment of the imagination. An odor of frying fish made Leo weak to the knees.

"Where is he?" he insisted. "I've got to see your husband."

At length she answered, "So who knows where he is? Every time he thinks a new thought he runs to a different place. Go home, he will find you."

"Tell him Leo Finkle."

She gave no sign she had heard.

He walked downstairs, depressed.

But Salzman, breathless, stood waiting at his door.

Leo was astounded and overjoyed. "How did you get here before me?"

"I rushed."

"Come inside."

They entered. Leo fixed tea, and a sardine sandwich for Salzman. As they were drinking he reached behind him for the packet of pictures and handed them to the marriage broker.

MALAMUD: *The Magic Barrel* 215

Salzman put down his glass and said expectantly, "You found somebody you like?"

"Not among these."

The marriage broker turned away.

"Here is the one I want." Leo held forth the snapshot.

Salzman slipped on his glasses and took the picture into his trembling hand. He turned ghastly and let out a groan.

"What's the matter?" cried Leo.

"Excuse me. Was an accident this picture. She isn't for you."

Salzman frantically shoved the manila packet into his portfolio. He thrust the snapshot into his pocket and fled down the stairs.

Leo, after momentary paralysis, gave chase and cornered the marriage broker in the vestibule. The landlady made hysterical outcries but neither of them listened.

"Give me back the picture, Salzman."

"No." The pain in his eyes was terrible.

"Tell me who she is then."

"This I can't tell you. Excuse me."

He made to depart, but Leo, forgetting himself, seized the matchmaker by his tight coat and shook him frenziedly.

"Please," sighed Salzman. *"Please."*

Leo ashamedly let him go. "Tell me who she is," he begged. "It's very important for me to know."

"She is not for you. She is a wild one—wild, without shame. This is not a bride for a rabbi."

"What do you mean wild?"

"Like an animal. Like a dog. For her to be poor was a sin. This is why to me she is dead now."

"In God's name, what do you mean?"

"Her I can't introduce to you," Salzman cried.

"Why are you so excited?"

"Why, he asks," Salzman said, bursting into tears. "This is my baby, my Stella, she should burn in hell."

Leo hurried up to bed and hid under the covers. Under the covers he thought his life through. Although he soon fell asleep he could not sleep her out of his mind. He woke, beating his breast. Though he prayed to be rid of her, his prayers went unanswered. Through days of torment he endlessly struggled not to love her; fearing success, he escaped it. He then concluded to convert her to goodness, himself to God. The idea alternately nauseated and exalted him.

He perhaps did not know that he had come to a final decision until he encountered Salzman in a Broadway cafeteria. He was sitting alone at a rear table, sucking the bony remains of a fish. The marriage broker appeared haggard, and transparent to the point of vanishing.

Salzman looked up at first without recognizing him. Leo had grown a pointed beard and his eyes were weighted with wisdom.

"Salzman," he said, "love has at last come to my heart."

"Who can love from a picture?" mocked the marriage broker.

"It is not impossible."

"If you can love her, then you can love anybody. Let me show you some new clients that they just sent me their photographs. One is a little doll."

"Just her I want," Leo murmured.

"Don't be a fool, doctor. Don't bother with her."

"Put me in touch with her, Salzman," Leo said humbly. "Perhaps I can be of service."

Salzman had stopped eating and Leo understood with emotion that it was now arranged.

Leaving the cafeteria, he was, however, afflicted by a tormenting suspicion that Salzman had planned it all to happen this way.

Leo was informed by letter that she would meet him on a certain corner, and she was there one spring night, waiting under a street lamp. He appeared, carrying a small bouquet of violets and rosebuds. Stella stood by the lamp post, smoking. She wore white with red shoes, which fitted his expectations, although in a troubled moment he had imagined the dress red, and only the shoes white. She waited uneasily and shyly. From afar he saw that her eyes—clearly her father's—were filled with desperate innocence. He pictured, in her, his own redemption. Violins and lit candles revolved in the sky. Leo ran forward with flowers outthrust.

Around the corner, Salzman, leaning against a wall, chanted prayers for the dead.

CHARLES WEBB

Homecoming

BENJAMIN BRADDOCK GRADUATED from a small eastern college on a day in June. Then he flew home. The following evening a party was given for him by his parents. By eight o'clock most of the guests had arrived but Benjamin had not yet come down from his room. His father called up from the foot of the stairs but there was no answer. Finally he hurried up the stairs and to the end of the hall.

"Ben?" he said, opening his son's door.

"I'll be down later," Benjamin said.

"Ben, the guests are all here," his father said. "They're all waiting."

"I said I'll be down later."

Mr. Braddock closed the door behind him. "What is it," he said. Benjamin shook his head and walked to the window.

"What is it, Ben."

"Nothing."

"Then why don't you come on down and see your guests."

Benjamin didn't answer.

"Ben?"

"Dad," he said, turning around, "I have some things on my mind right now."

"What things."

"Just some things."

"Well can't you tell me what they are?"

"No."

Mr. Braddock continued frowning at his son a few more moments, glanced at his watch, then looked back at Benjamin. "Ben, these are our friends down there," he said. "My friends. Your mother's friends. You owe them a little courtesy."

"Tell them I have to be alone right now."

From Charles Webb, *The Graduate*. (New York: New American Library, 1963), pp. 9–37.

218 THE YOUNG MAN IN AMERICAN LITERATURE

"Mr. Robinson's out in the garage looking at your new sports car. Now go on down and give him a ride in it."

Benjamin reached into his pocket for a pair of shiny keys on a small chain. "Here," he said.

"What?"

"Give him the keys. Let him drive it."

"But he wants to see you."

"Dad, I don't want to see him right now," Benjamin said. "I don't want to see the Robinsons, I don't want to see the Pearsons, I don't want to see the . . . the Terhunes."

"Ben, Mr. Robinson and I have been practicing law together in this town for seventeen years. He's the best friend I have."

"I realize that."

"He has a client over in Los Angeles that he's put off seeing so he could be here and welcome you home from college."

"Dad—"

"Do you appreciate that?"

"I'd appreciate it if I could be alone!"

His father shook his head. "I don't know what's got into you," he said, "but whatever it is I want you to snap out of it and march right on down there."

Suddenly the door opened and Benjamin's mother stepped into the room. "Aren't you ready yet?" she said.

"No."

"We'll be right down," his father said.

"Well what's wrong," she said, closing the door behind her.

"I am trying to think!"

"Come on, Ben," his father said. He took his arm and began leading him toward the door.

"Goddammit will you leave me alone!" Benjamin said. He pulled away and stood staring at him.

"Ben?" Mr. Braddock said quietly, staring back at him, "don't you ever swear at your mother or me again."

Benjamin shook his head. Then he walked between them and to the door. "I'm going for a walk," he said. He stepped out into the hall and closed the door behind him.

He hurried to the head of the stairs and down but just as he had gotten to the front door and was about to turn the knob Mr. Terhune appeared out of the living room.

"Ben" he said. "I want to shake your hand."

Benjamin shook it.

"Goddammit I'm proud of you," Mr. Terhune said, still holding his hand.

Benjamin nodded. "Thank you," he said. "Now if you'll excuse me I'm going for a walk. I'll be back later."

Mrs. Pearson appeared at the end of the hall. "Oh Benjamin," she said, smiling at him. She hurried to where he was standing and reached up to pull his head down and kiss him. "Benjamin?" she said. "I'm just speechless."

Benjamin nodded.

"Golly you did a fine job back there."

"I'm sorry to seem rude," Benjamin said, "but I'm trying to go on a walk right now."

Mr. Robinson appeared at the end of the hall with a drink in his hand. He began grinning when he saw Benjamin and walked into the group of people surrounding him to shake his hand. "Ben, how in hell are you," he said. "You look swell."

"I'm fine."

"Say, that's something out in the garage. That little Italian job your old man gave you for graduation?"

"Oh how exciting," Mrs. Pearson said.

"Let's go for a spin," Mr. Robinson said.

Benjamin reached into his pocket and pulled out the keys. "Can you work a foreign gearshift?" he said, holding them out.

"What?"

"Do you know how to operate a foreign gearshift."

"Well sure," Mr. Robinson said. "But I thought you'd take me for a little spin yourself."

"I can't right now," Benjamin said. "Excuse me." He reached for the doorknob and turned it, then pulled open the door. Just as he was about to step outside Mr. and Mrs. Carlson walked up onto the front porch.

"Well here he is himself," Mrs. Carlson said. She wrapped her arms around Benjamin and hugged him. "Ben?" she said, patting one of his shoulders, "I hope you won't be embarrassed if I tell you I'm just awfully awfully proud to know you."

"I won't," Benjamin said. "But I have some things on my mind at the moment and I'm—"

"Here's something for you," Mr. Carlson said. He handed Benjamin a bottle wrapped with a red ribbon. "I hope they taught you to hold your liquor back there." He threw his arm around Benjamin's shoulder and swept him back inside the house.

Benjamin ducked under his arm and set the bottle of liquor beside the door. "Look," he said. "Could you please let me go for my walk!"

"What?"

"I'm sorry not to be more sociable," Benjamin said. "I appreciate everybody coming over but—"

"Now Ben," Mrs. Carlson said as her husband removed her coat, "I want you to tell me all about this prize you won. It was for teaching, wasn't it?"

Benjamin grabbed the doorknob but before he could turn it his father appeared beside him and put his arm around him. "Let's get you fixed up with a drink," he said.

"Dad?"

"Come on, Ben," his father said quietly. "You're making kind of a scene here."

"Then let me out!"

"Here we go," Mr. Braddock said. He began leading him away from the door.

"All right!" Benjamin said. He walked ahead of his father and into the living room, shaking his head.

"Well Benjamin," a woman said.

Benjamin nodded.

"Aren't you just thrilled to death?"

He walked on through the room, nodding at several more guests, and into the dining room where there was a tray of bottles on the dining-room table and a bucket of ice and some glasses. He selected one of the largest and poured it full of bourbon. Then he took several swallows, closed his eyes a moment and took several more. He refilled the glass to the top and turned around to see his mother standing in front of him.

"What's that," she said, frowning at the glass in his hand.

"This?"

"Yes."

"I don't know," he said. "Maybe it's a drink."

His mother turned her frown up to his face. "Ben, what's the trouble," she said.

"The trouble is I'm trying to get out of this house!"

"But what's on your mind."

"Different things, Mother."

"Well, can't you worry about them another time?"

"No."

Mrs. Braddock reached for his drink. "Here," she said, taking it. "Come out to the kitchen for a minute."

Benjamin shook his head but followed her through the swinging door and into the kitchen. Mrs. Braddock walked to the sink and poured out most of the drink, then filled the glass with water.

"Can't you tell me what you're worried about?" she said, drying off the glass with a dish towel beside the sink.

"Mother, I'm worried about different things. I'm a little worried about my future."

"About what you're going to do?"

"That's right."

She handed him back the glass. "Well you still plan to teach don't you," she said.

"No."

"You don't?" she said. "Well what about your award."

"I'm not taking it."

"You're not?"

"No."

"Well Ben," she said, "that doesn't sound very wise, to pass up something you've spent four years working for."

Mr. Terhune pushed into the kitchen carrying his drink. "I thought I saw you duck in here," he said. "Now let's have the low-down on that prize of yours."

"I'm not—"

"Tell him about it, Ben," his mother said.

"It's called the Frank Halpingham Education Award," Benjamin said. "It's given by the college. It puts me through two years of graduate school if I decide to go into teaching."

"Well now why did they pick you," Mr. Terhune said.

Benjamin didn't answer.

"He did some practice teaching back there," his mother said. "He's been an assistant teacher for two years. Last term they let him take a junior seminar in American History."

Mr. Terhune sipped at his drink. "Well, have you got in any graduate schools yet?" he said.

"Yes."

"He's in Harvard and Yale," his mother said. "And what's that other one?"

"Columbia."

Mr. Terhune sipped at his drink again. "It sounds like you've got things pretty well sewed up," he said.

Benjamin turned and walked quickly across the room to the back door. He opened it and walked out and to the edge of the swimming pool in the back yard. He stood staring down at the blue light rising up through the water for several moments before hearing the door open and bang shut behind him and someone walk across to where he was standing.

"Ben?" Mrs. McQuire said. "I think your yearbook is just unbelievable."

Benjamin nodded.

"Was there anyone who got his picture in there more times than you did?"

"Abe Frankel did."

Mrs. McQuire shook her head. "What a fantastic record you made for yourself."

"Ben?" Mr. Calendar came out beside the pool and shook Benjamin's hand. "Congratulations to you," he said.

"Have you seen Ben's yearbook?" Mrs. McQuire said.

"Why no."

"Let's see if I can remember all the different things," she said. "Ben, you tell me if I miss any." She cleared her throat and counted them off on her fingers as she talked. "Captain of the cross-country team. Head of the debating club. First in his class."

"I wasn't first."

"Oh?"

"I tied Abe Frankel for first."

"Oh," she said. "Now let's see what else. One of the editors of the school newspaper. Student teacher. I'm running out of fingers. Social chairman of his house. And that wonderful teaching award."

"Could I ask you a question," Benjamin said, turning suddenly toward her.

"Of course."

"Why are you so impressed with all those things."

"All the things you did?"

"Excuse me," Mr. Calendar said, holding up his glass. "I think I'll find a refill." He turned around and walked back into the house.

"Could you tell me that, Mrs. McQuire?"

She was frowning down into the bright blue water beside them. "Well," she said, "aren't you awfully proud of yourself? Of all those things?"

"No."

"What?" she said, looking up. "You're not?"

"I want to know why you're so impressed, Mrs. McQuire."

"Well," she said, shaking her head. "I'm afraid—I'm afraid I don't quite see what you're driving at."

"You don't know what I'm talking about, do you."

"Well not exactly. No."

"Then why do you—why do you—" He shook his head. "Excuse me," he said. He turned around and walked back toward the house.

"Ben?" she called after him. "I'm afraid I haven't been much help, but if it makes any difference I just want to say I'm thrilled to pieces by all your wonderful achievements and I couldn't be prouder if you were my own son."

Benjamin opened the door leading into the living room. He walked through the room keeping his eyes ahead of him on the carpet until Mrs. Calendar took his elbow.

"Ben?" she said. "I just think it's too terrific for words."

He walked past her and into the hall. Just as he got to the foot of the stairs his father came up behind him.

"Leave me alone."

"Ben, for God's sake what is it."

"I don't know what it is."

"Come here," Mr. Braddock said. He took his arm and led him down the hall and into a bedroom. "Son?" he said, closing the door and locking it. "Now what is it."

"I don't know."

"Well something seems pretty wrong."

"Something is."

"Well what."

"I don't know!" Benjamin said. "But everything—everything is grotesque all of a sudden."

"Grotesque?"

"Those people in there are grotesque. You're grotesque."

"Ben."

"I'm grotesque. This house is grotesque. It's just this feeling I have all of a sudden. And I don't know why!"

"Ben, it's because you're all tied up in knots."

Benjamin shook his head.

"Now I want you to relax."

"I can't seem to."

"Ben, you've just had four of the most strenuous years of your life back there."

"They were nothing," Benjamin said.

"What?"

"The whole four years," he said, looking up at his father. "They were nothing. All the things I did are nothing. All the distinctions. The things I learned. All of a sudden none of it seems to be worth anything to me."

His father was frowning. "Why do you say that."

"I don't know," Benjamin said. He walked across the room to the door. "But I've got to be alone. I've got to think until I know what's happening to me."

"Ben?"

"Dad, I've got to figure this thing out before I go crazy," he said, unlocking the door. "I'm not just joking around either." He stepped back out into the hall.

"Ben?" Mr. Robinson said, holding out his hand. "I've got a client waiting for me over in Los Angeles."

Benjamin nodded and shook his hand.

"Real proud of you boy," Mr. Robinson said.

Benjamin waited till he had gone out the door, then turned around and walked upstairs and into his room. He closed the door behind him and sat down at his desk. For a long time he sat looking down at the rug, then he got up and walked to the window. He was staring out at a light over the street when the door opened and Mrs. Robinson stepped inside, carrying a drink and her purse.

"Oh," she said. "I guess this isn't the bathroom is it."

"It's down the hall," Benjamin said.

She nodded but instead of leaving the room stood in the doorway looking at him.

"It's right at the end of the hall," Benjamin said.

Mrs. Robinson was wearing a shiny green dress cut very low across her chest, and over one of her breasts was a large gold pin.

"Don't I get to kiss the graduate?" she said.

"What?"

She smiled at him.

"Mrs. Robinson," Benjamin said, shaking his head. "I'm kind of distraught at the moment. Now I'm sorry to be rude but I have some things on my mind."

She walked across the room to where he was standing and kissed one of his cheeks.

"It's good to see you," Benjamin said. "The bathroom's at the end of the hall."

Mrs. Robinson stood looking at him a moment longer, then turned around and walked to his bed. She seated herself on the edge of it and sipped at her drink. "How are you," she said.

"Look," Benjamin said. "I'm sorry not to be more congenial but I'm trying to think."

Mrs. Robinson had set her glass down on the rug. She reached into her purse for a package of cigarettes and held it out to Benjamin.

"No."

She took one for herself.

"Is there an ash tray in here?"

"No."

"Oh," she said, "I forgot. The track star doesn't smoke." She blew out her match and set it down on the bedspread.

Benjamin walked to his desk for a wastebasket and carried it to the bed. He picked up the match and dropped it in.

"Thank you."

He walked back to the window.

"What are you upset about," she said.

"Some personal things."

"Don't you want to talk about them?"

"Well they wouldn't be of much interest to you, Mrs. Robinson."

She nodded and sat quietly on the bed smoking her cigarette and dropping ashes into the wastebasket beside her.

"Girl trouble?" she said.

"What?"

"Do you have girl trouble?"

"Look," Benjamin said. "Now I'm sorry to be this way but I can't help it. I'm just sort of disturbed about things."

"In general," she said.

"That's right," Benjamin said. "So please." He shook his head and looked back out through the glass of the window.

Mrs. Robinson picked up her drink to take a swallow from it, then set it down and sat quietly until she was finished with her cigarette.

"Shall I put this out in the wastebasket?"

Benjamin nodded.

Mrs. Robinson ground it out on the inside of the wastebasket, then sat back up and folded her hands in her lap. It was quiet for several moments.

"The bathroom's at the end of the hall," Benjamin said.

"I know."

She didn't move from the bed but sat watching him until finally Benjamin turned around and walked to the door. "Excuse me," he said. "I think I'll go on a walk."

"Benjamin?"

"What."

"Come here a minute."

"Look I'm sorry to be rude, Mrs. Robinson. But I'm . . ."

She held out her hands. "Just for a minute," she said.

Benjamin shook his head and walked back to the bed. She took both his hands in hers and looked up into his face for several moments.

"What do you want," he said.

"Will you take me home?"

"What?"

"My husband took the car. Will you drive me home?"

Benjamin reached into one of his pockets for the keys. "Here," he said. "You take the car."

"What?"

"Borrow the car. I'll come and get it tomorrow."

"Don't you want to take me home?" she said, raising her eyebrows.

"I want to be alone, Mrs. Robinson. Now do you know how to work a foreign shift?"

She shook her head.

"You don't?"

"No."

Benjamin waited a few moments, then returned the keys to his pocket. "Let's go," he said.

Mr. Braddock was standing in the front doorway saying goodbye to the Terhunes. "Mrs. Robinson needs a ride home," Benjamin said. "I'll be right back."

"Wonderful party," Mrs. Robinson said. She took her coat from a closet beside the front door, put it on and followed Benjamin back through the house and out to the garage. He got into the car and started the engine and she got in beside him.

"What kind of car is this," she said.

"I don't know."

He backed out the driveway and they drove without speaking the several miles between the Braddocks' home and the Robinsons'. Benjamin stopped by the curb in front of her house. Mrs. Robinson reached up to push some hair away from her forehead and turned in her seat to smile at him.

"Thank you," she said.

"Right."

She didn't move from her seat. Finally Benjamin turned off the engine, got out and walked around to open the door for her.

"Thank you," she said, getting out.

"You're welcome."

"Will you come in, please?"

"What?"

"I want you to come in till I get the lights on."

"What for."

"Because I don't feel safe until I get the lights on."

Benjamin frowned at her, then followed her up a flagstone walk to the front porch. She found a key in her purse. When the door was opened she reached up to the wall just inside and turned on a hall light.

"Would you mind walking ahead of me to the sun porch?" she said.

"Can't you see now?"

"I feel funny about coming into a dark house," she said.

"But it's light in there now."

"Please?"

Benjamin waited a moment but then walked ahead of her down the hall and toward the rear of the house.

"To your left," she said.

Benjamin walked to his left and down three steps leading to the sun porch. Mrs. Robinson came in behind him and turned on a lamp beside a long couch against one of the walls.

"Thank you," she said.

"You're welcome."

"What do you drink," she said, "bourbon?"

Benjamin shook his head. "Look," he said. "I drove you home. I was glad to do it. But for God's sake I have some things on my mind. Can you understand that?"

She nodded.

"All right then."

"What do you drink," she said.

"What?"

"Benjamin, I'm sorry to be this way," she said. "But I don't want to be alone in this house."

"Why not."

"Please wait till my husband gets home."

"Lock the doors," Benjamin said. "I'll wait till you have all the doors locked."

"I want you to sit down till Mr. Robinson comes back."

"But I want to be alone!" Benjamin said.

"Well I know you do," she said. "But I don't."

"Are you afraid to be alone in your own house?"

"Yes."

"Can't you just lock the doors?"

Mrs. Robinson nodded at a chair behind him.

"When's he coming back," Benjamin said.

"I don't know."

Benjamin sat down in the chair. "I'll sit here till he gets back," he said. "Then I'll go. Good night."

"Don't you want some company?"

"No."

"A drink?"

"No."

Mrs. Robinson turned and walked up the three stairs leading

from the porch. Benjamin folded his hands in his lap and looked at his reflection in one of the large panels of glass enclosing the room. Several moments later music began playing in another part of the house. He turned and frowned at the doorway. Then Mrs. Robinson walked back into the room carrying two drinks.

"Look. I said I didn't want any."

She handed it to him, then went to the side of the room and pulled a cord. Two large curtains slid closed across the windows. Benjamin shook his head and looked at the drink. Mrs. Robinson seated herself on a couch beside his chair. Then it was quiet.

"Are you always this much afraid of being alone?"

She nodded.

"You are."

"Yes."

"Well why can't you just lock the doors and go to bed."

"I'm very neurotic," she said.

Benjamin frowned at her a few moments, then tasted his drink and set it down on the floor.

"May I ask you a question?" Mrs. Robinson said.

He nodded.

"What do you think of me."

"What?"

"What do you think of me."

He shook his head.

"You've known me nearly all your life," she said. "Haven't you formed any—"

"Look. This is kind of a strange conversation. Now I told my father I'd be right back."

"Don't you have any opinions at all?"

"No," he said. He glanced at his watch. "Look, I'm sure Mr. Robinson will be here any minute. So please lock your doors and let me go."

"Benjamin?"

"What."

"Did you know I was an alcoholic?"

Benjamin shook his head. "Mrs. Robinson," he said, "I don't want to talk about this."

"Did you know that?"

"No."

"You never suspected?"

"Mrs. Robinson, this is none of my business," Benjamin said, rising from the chair. "Now excuse me because I've got to go."

"You never suspected I was an alcoholic."

"Goodbye, Mrs. Robinson."

"Sit down," she said.

"I'm leaving now."

She stood and walked to where he was standing to put one of her hands on his shoulder. "Sit down," she said.

"I'm leaving, Mrs. Robinson."

"Why."

"Because I want to be alone."

"My husband will probably be back quite late," she said.

Benjamin frowned at her.

"Mr. Robinson probably won't be here for several hours."

Benjamin took a step backwards. "Oh my God," he said.

"What?"

"Oh no, Mrs. Robinson. Oh no."

"What's wrong."

Benjamin looked at her a few moments longer, then turned around and walked to one of the curtains. "Mrs. Robinson," he said, "you didn't—I mean you didn't expect . . ."

"What?"

"I mean you—you didn't really think I would do something like that."

"Like what?"

"What do you think!" he said.

"Well I don't know."

"Come Mrs. Robinson."

"What?"

"For God's sake, Mrs. Robinson. Here we are. You've got me in your house. You put on music. You give me a drink. We've both been drinking already. Now you start opening up your personal life to me and tell me your husband won't be home for hours."

"So?"

"Mrs. Robinson," he said, turning around, "you are trying to seduce me."

She frowned at him.

"Aren't you."

She seated herself again on the couch.

"Aren't you?"

"Why no," she said, smiling. "I hadn't thought of it. I feel rather flattered that you . . ."

Suddenly Benjamin put his hands up over his face. "Mrs. Robinson?" he said. "Will you forgive me?"

"What?"

"Will you forgive me for what I just said?"

"It's all right."

"It's not all right! That's the worst thing I've ever said! To anyone!"

"Sit down."

"Please forgive me. Because I like you. I don't think of you that way. But I'm mixed up!"

"All right," she said. "Now finish your drink."

Benjamin sat back down in his chair and lifted his drink up from the floor. "Mrs. Robinson, it makes me sick that I said that to you."

"I forgive you," she said.

"Can you? Can you ever forget that I said that?"

"We'll forget it right now," she said. "Finish your drink."

"What is wrong with me," Benjamin said. He took several large swallows from his drink and set it back on the floor.

"Benjamin?"

"What, Mrs. Robinson."

She cleared her throat. "Have you ever seen Elaine's portrait?"

"Her portrait?"

"Yes."

Benjamin shook his head. "No."

"We had it done last Christmas. Would you like to see it?"

Benjamin nodded. "Very much."

"It's upstairs," she said, standing.

Benjamin followed her back to the front of the house and then up the thickly carpeted stairs to the second story. Mrs. Robinson walked ahead of him along a hall and turned into a room. A moment later dim yellow light spread out the doorway and into the hall. Benjamin walked into the room.

The portrait was hanging by itself on one of the walls and the light was coming from a small tubular lamp fixed at the top of the heavy gold frame. Benjamin looked at it, then nodded. "She's a very good looking girl," he said.

Mrs. Robinson seated herself on the edge of a single bed in a corner of the room.

Benjamin folded his arms across his chest and stepped up closer to the portrait to study some of the detail of the face. "I didn't remember her as having brown eyes," he said. He stepped back again and tilted his head slightly to the side. "She's really—she's really a beautiful girl."

"Benjamin?"

"Yes?"

She didn't answer. Benjamin turned to smile at her.

"Come here," she said quietly.

"What?"

"Will you come over here a minute?"

"Over there?"

She nodded.

"Sure," Benjamin said. He walked over to the bed. Mrs. Robinson reached up to put one of her hands on his sleeve. Then she stood slowly until she was facing him.

"Benjamin?" she said.

"Yes?"

She turned around. "Will you unzip my dress?"

Benjamin unfolded his arms suddenly and took a step backwards.

"I think I'll go to bed," she said.

"Oh," Benjamin said. "Well. Good night." He walked to the door.

"Won't you unzip the dress?"

"I'd rather not, Mrs. Robinson."

She turned around again and frowned at him. "Do you still think I'm trying to . . ."

"No I don't. But I just feel a little funny."

"You still think I'm trying to seduce you."

"I don't," Benjamin said. "But I think I'd better get downstairs now."

"Benjamin," she said, smiling, "you've known me all your life."

"I know that. I know that. But I'm—"

"Come on," she said, turning back to him. "It's hard for me to reach."

Benjamin waited a moment, then walked back to her. He reached for the zipper and pulled it down along her back. The dress split open.

"Thank you."

"Right," Benjamin said. He walked back to the doorway.

"What are you so scared of," she said, smiling at him again.

"I'm not scared, Mrs. Robinson."

"Then why do you keep running away."

"Because you're going to bed," he said. "I don't think I should be up here."

"Haven't you ever seen anybody in a slip before?" she said, letting the dress fall down around her and onto the floor.

"Yes I have," Benjamin said, glancing away from her and at the portrait of Elaine. "But I just—"

"You still think I'm trying to seduce you, don't you."

"No I do not!" He threw his hands down to his sides. "Now I told you I feel terrible about saying that. But I don't feel right up here."

"Why not," she said.

"Why do you think, Mrs. Robinson."

"Well I don't know," she said. "We're pretty good friends I think. I don't see why you should be embarrassed to see me in a slip."

"Look," Benjamin said, pointing in back of him out the door. "What if—what if Mr. Robinson walked in right now."

"What if he did?" she said.

"Well it would look pretty funny, wouldn't it."

"Don't you think he trusts us together?"

"Of course he does. But he might get the wrong idea. Anyone might."

"I don't see why," she said. "I'm twice as old as you are. How could anyone think—"

"But they would! Don't you see?"

"Benjamin," she said, "I'm not trying to seduce you. I wish you'd —"

"I know that. But please, Mrs. Robinson. This is difficult for me."

"Why is it," she said.

"Because I am confused about things. I can't tell what I'm imagining. I can't tell what's real. I can't—"

"Would you like me to seduce you?"

"What?"

"Is that what you're trying to tell me?"

"I'm going home now. I apologize for what I said. I hope you can forget it. But I'm going home right now." He turned around and walked to the stairs and started down.

"Benjamin?" she called after him.

"What."

"Will you bring up my purse before you go?"

Benjamin shook his head.

"Please?" she said.

"I have to go now. I'm sorry."

Mrs. Robinson walked out to the railing holding her green dress across the front of her slip and looked down at Benjamin standing at the foot of the stairs. "I really don't want to put this on again," she said. "Won't you bring it up?"

"Where is it."

"On the sun porch."

Benjamin hurried through the hall and found the purse beside the couch on the sun porch. He returned with it to the foot of the stairs. "Mrs. Robinson?"

"I'm in the bathroom," she called from upstairs.

"Well here's the purse."

"Could you bring it up?"

"Well I'll hand it to you. Come to the railing and I'll hand it up."

"Benjamin?" she called. "I'm getting pretty tired of this."

"What?"

"I am getting pretty tired of all this suspicion. Now if you won't do me a simple favor I don't know what."

Benjamin waited a moment, then carried the purse up to the top of the stairs.

"I'm putting it on the top step," he said.

"For God's sake, Benjamin, will you stop acting this way and bring me the purse?"

He frowned down the hallway. A line of bright light was coming from under the bathroom door. Finally he walked slowly down the hall toward it. "Mrs. Robinson?"

"Did you bring it up?"

"I did," he said. "I'm putting it here by the door."

"Won't you bring it in to me?"

"I'd rather not."

"All right," she said from the other side of the door. "Put it across the hall."

"Where?"

"Across the hall," she said. "In the room where we were."

"Oh," Benjamin said. "Right." He walked quickly back into the room where Elaine's portrait was and set the purse on the end of the bed. Then he turned around and was about to leave the room when Mrs. Robinson stepped in through the door. She was naked.

"Oh God."

She smiled at him.

"Let me out," Benjamin said. He rushed toward the door but she closed it behind her and turned the lock under the handle.

"Don't be nervous," she said.

Benjamin turned around.

"Benjamin?"

"Get away from that door!"

"I want to say something first."

"Jesus Christ!" Benjamin put his hands up over his face.

"Benjamin, I want you to know I'm available to you," she said. "If you won't sleep with me this time—"

"Oh my God."

"If you won't sleep with me this time, Benjamin, I want you to know you can call me up any time you want and we'll make some kind of arrangement."

"Let me out!"

"Do you understand what I said?"

"Yes! Yes! Let me out!"

"Because I find you very attractive and any time—"

Suddenly there was the sound of a car passing along the driveway underneath the window.

Benjamin turned and leaped at the door. He pushed Mrs. Robinson aside, fumbled for the lock then ran out the door and downstairs. He opened the front door of the house but then stepped back inside and hurried back onto the porch. He sat down with his drink and tried to catch his breath. The back door of the house slammed shut.

"Is that Ben's car in front?" Mr. Robinson called.

"Yes sir!" Benjamin said, jumping up from the chair.

Mr. Robinson came into the room.

"I drove—I drove your wife home. She wanted me to drive her home so I—so I drove her home."

"Swell," Mr. Robinson said. "I appreciate it."

"She's upstairs. She wanted me to wait down here till you got home."

"Standing guard over the old castle, are you."

"Yes sir."

"Here," Mr. Robinson said, reaching for Benjamin's glass. "It looks like you need a refill."

"Oh no."

"What?"

"I've got to go."

Mr. Robinson was frowning at him. "Is anything wrong?" he said. "You look a little shaken up."

"No," Benjamin said. "No, I'm just—I'm just—I'm just a little worried about my future. I'm a little upset about my future."

"Come on," Mr. Robinson said, taking the glass. "Let's have a nightcap together. I didn't get much of a chance to talk to you at the party."

Benjamin waited till Mr. Robinson had left the room, then took several deep breaths. When he finished taking the deep breaths he put his hands in his pockets and walked quickly back and forth till Mr. Robinson brought him his drink.

"Thank you very much, sir," he said as he took it.

"Not at all," Mr. Robinson said. He carried his drink to the chair beside Benjamin's and sat. "Well," he said. "I guess I already said congratulations."

"Thank you."

Mr. Robinson nodded and sipped at his drink. "Ben?" he said, "How old are you now."

"Twenty. I'll be twenty-one next week."

Again Mr. Robinson nodded. "I guess you skipped a grade or two back there in high school," he said. "I guess that's why you graduated so young."

"Yes sir."

Mr. Robinson reached into his pocket for a package of cigarettes and held them out to Benjamin. He took one and put it in his mouth. "Ben?" Mr. Robinson said, picking up a book of matches and lighting the cigarette for him. "That's a hell of a good age to be."

"Thank you."

Mr. Robinson lit a cigarette for himself and dropped the match in an ash tray. "I wish I was that age again," he said.

Benjamin nodded.

"Because Ben?"

"What."

"You'll never be young again."

"I know."

"And I think maybe—I think maybe you're a little too worried about things right now."

"That's possible."

"You seem all wrapped up about things," Mr. Robinson said. "You don't seem to be—Ben, can I say something to you?"

"What."

"How long have we known each other now."

Benjamin shook his head.

"How long have you and I known each other. How long have your dad and I been partners."

"Quite a while."

"I've watched you grow up, Ben."

"Yes sir."

"In many ways I feel almost as though you were my own son."

"Thank you."

"So I hope you won't mind my giving you a friendly piece of advice."

"I'd like to hear it."

"Ben?" Mr. Robinson said, settling back in his chair and frowning up over Benjamin's head. "I know as sure as I'm sitting here that you're going to do great things someday."

"I hope you're right."

"Well I am right," he said. "That's something I just know. But Ben?"

"What."

"I think—" He dropped an ash from his cigarette into the ash tray. "I think you ought to be taking it a little easier right now than you seem to."

Benjamin nodded.

"Sow a few wild oats." Mr. Robinson said. "Take things as they come. Have a good time with the girls and so forth."

Benjamin glanced at the door.

"Because Ben, you're going to spend most of your life worrying. That's just the way it is, I'm afraid. But right now you're young. Don't start worrying yet, for God's sake."

"No."

"Before you know it you'll find a nice little girl and settle down and have a damn fine life. But until then I wish you'd try and make up a little for my mistakes by—"

Mrs. Robinson, dressed again in the green dress and the gold pin she had worn to the party, stepped into the room.

"Don't get up," she said.

Benjamin sat back down in the chair. Mrs. Robinson seated herself and picked up her unfinished drink from the floor.

"I was just telling Ben here he ought to sow a few wild oats," Mr. Robinson said. "Have a good time while he can. You think that's sound advice?"

Mrs. Robinson nodded.

"Yes I sure do," her husband said.

Benjamin finished his drink quickly and set it down on the table beside him. "I've got to go." he said.

"Just hang on here, Ben," Mr. Robinson said. "Wait'll I finish my drink, then I'm going to have you spin me around the block in that new car out front."

"Maybe he's tired," Mrs. Robinson said.

"Tired, Ben?"

"Oh no. No." He picked up his glass and held it up to his mouth till the ice cubes clicked down against his teeth. Then he replaced it on the table.

"Do you want another?" Mrs. Robinson said.

"What? No."

"Sure," Mr. Robinson said. "You have yourself a few flings this summer. I bet you're quite the ladies' man."

"Oh no."

"What?" Mr. Robinson said, grinning at him. "You look like the kind of guy that has to fight them off."

Benjamin reached for his glass.

"Are you sure you won't have another?" Mrs. Robinson said.

"No. No."

Mr. Robinson turned to his wife. "Doesn't he look to you like the kind of guy who has trouble keeping the ladies at a distance?"

"Yes he does."

"Oh say," Mr. Robinson said. "When does Elaine get down from Berkeley."

"Saturday," she said.

"Ben, I want you to give her a call."

"I will."

"Because I just know you two would hit it off real well. She's a wonderful girl and I'm just awful sorry you two haven't got to know each other better over the years."

"I am too," Benjamin said. He watched Mr. Robinson until he had taken the last swallow from his glass, then stood. "I'll take you around the block," he said.

"Great."

Benjamin walked ahead of Mr. and Mrs. Robinson through the hall and to the front door and opened it. Mrs. Robinson stepped out onto the front porch after them.

"Benjamin?"

He put his hands in his pockets and walked down across the flagstone path without answering her.

"Benjamin?"

"What."

"Thank you for taking me home."

Benjamin nodded without turning around.

"I'll see you soon, I hope," she said.

"Hey Ben," Mr. Robinson said, opening the door of the car and getting in. "What do you say we hit the freeway with this thing and see what she does."

4

Fearful Confrontations

THE STORIES IN THIS SECTION also involve disenchantment, but give it special force because in each of them a hitherto unsuspected aspect of the adult world is personified in a single individual. Both the personification and the ugliness, corruption, or evil of the world it represents are fearful. For instance, in Stephen Crane's "An Experiment in Misery," the young man of "meagre experience" confronts not only a red-skinned derelict who looks like an assassin, but also the enormous human compost of urban life.

Frequently the symbolic adult is a stranger, as in "Blackberry Winter," but he may be a familiar person (often the father) seen in a new and frightening light, as in "The Disinherited" or "Goin' to Town." A prototype of the first kind of story is Mark Twain's misanthropic and blasphemous short novel *The Mysterious Stranger*, which was first published in 1916, six years after Twain's death. Philip Traum, a nephew of Satan, appears in a medieval village, where he discloses to three boys the hypocrisy and cruelty of man's nature and finally reveals that "life itself is only a vision, a dream." In Hemingway's famous story "The Killers" (1927), Nick Adams is confronted by casual, impersonal cruelty in two hired killers planning to murder a boxer, Ole Andreson. As usual in Hemingway's best fiction, the emotional effect is understated but powerful: Nick merely says when it is over, "It's too damned awful." Holden Caulfield in J. D. Salinger's *The Catcher in the Rye* (1951) is not a totally representative example of the second kind of confrontation because he is on the verge of a neurotic crack-up, but circumstances and his distraught mental state cause him to regard familiar persons in a new way. Holden can ignore the vulgarity of his roommate, Stradlater, until he learns he has a date with Jane Gallagher, Holden's friend during summer vacation. After fighting with Stradlater, leaving school, and wandering around New York, Holden goes to the apartment of Mr. Antolini, the only teacher he has ever trusted. After dropping into an exhausted sleep, he wakes in panic and rushes out of the apartment because he thinks, perhaps mistakenly, that Mr. Antolini has made homosexual advances.

Because of the possible symbolic overtones, this type of story often lends itself to psychological interpretation. Simon Lesser in *Fiction and the Unconscious* (1957) analyzes two of the stories in this section. He believes that in "My Kinsman, Major Molineux," Robin unconsciously is "searching for sexual adventure" and that his uncle symbolizes the restrictive authority of his clergyman-father, which he destroys by laughter "so that, freed from its restraining influence, he can begin life as an adult." In "I Want to Know Why," Lesser finds that the boy unconsciously resents the sexual relations of his parents. At the paddock he idealizes Jerry Tillford as a sympathetic and desexualized father and sees Sunstreak as a pure symbol of his mother. A reader may not accept such thoroughgoing psychoanalytic interpretation, yet recognize that there are psychological implications in many stories of this kind.

Because Hawthorne was preoccupied with questions of guilt and moral responsibility, it may seem strange that he did not write more fiction on the theme of initiation. Perhaps his deep awareness of man's capacity for evil prevented him from creating characters with the requisite preliminary state of innocence. Most of Hawthorne's characters are initiates of evil from birth. At any rate, except for "My Kinsman, Major Molineux," his best example of an initiation story is "Young Goodman Brown." An innocent, as his name suggests, Goodman Brown spends a night in the forest, where he meets a diabolical stranger and witnesses (or dreams that he witnesses) a witches' sabbath, where all of the persons he has reverenced are worshipping the devil. The result is not wisdom or maturity but scepticism and disillusion that blight the remainder of his life.

Perhaps because Herman Melville's own youthful experience as a sailor on trading, whaling, and naval ships marked him so deeply, the theme of initiation is, at the least, a subordinate element in most of his work. The protagonists in *Typee* (1846), *Omoo* (1847), *White Jacket* (1850), *Pierre* (1852), and *Billy Budd* (1892, published in 1924) are naive young men most of them from comfortable homes, who are thrust into a world whose perils they had not suspected. The figure of Captain Ahab dominates Melville's masterpiece, *Moby Dick* (1851), but close examination reveals the significance of the youthful narrator, Ishmael. When the novel opens, he is misanthropic and has been considering suicide; after his experience aboard the *Pequod,* he has learned the meaning of brotherhood and is symbolically reborn.

At the age of nineteen, Melville sailed as a ship's boy on the *St. Lawrence* to Liverpool and back. A native of New York, Robert

Jackson, aged thirty-one, was a member of the crew. Despite these resemblances to actuality, *Redburn* is not literal autobiography. Wellingborough Redburn, the aristocratic hero, is only about fifteen years old, and the log of the *St. Lawrence* reveals no deaths among the crew members. In some episodes Redburn is a comic bungler, offering the mate a pinch of snuff, paying a formal call on the captain, and misinterpreting orders; but in the four chapters reprinted here, he encounters malevolent evil in the person of Jackson. Characters like Jackson representing diabolical malice appear in Melville's narratives almost as frequently as the unsophisticated young man. In *Benito Cereno* (1856), Babo, a Negro mutineer, misrepresents the situation aboard a ship so that he completely deceives the American captain, Amasa Delano. Bland, the master-at-arms in *White Jacket,* is a handsome "irreclaimable scoundrel" who tyrannizes over the crew. In *Billy Budd,* the title character is destroyed by the master-at-arms, Claggart, who feels "an antipathy spontaneous and profound" for Billy's innocence.

Some readers may find the characterization of Jackson melodramatic and unreal. One danger in this type of story is that the symbolic character may not be credible. Human nature is so variable and contradictory that a person can scarcely serve as a consistent symbol unless his personality is simplified, and sometimes this simplification results in exaggeration or distortion. Because any symbol is somewhat ambiguous, the full significance of a character like Major Molineux or the tramp in "Blackberry Winter" is left to the reader's interpretation. The effect that the symbolic figure has on the young man is usually unspecified; it is clear that the narrator in "Blackberry Winter" did not realize the full import of his encounter with the tramp until long afterward. Yet the young man should not be totally separate from the symbolic figure; if he senses a kinship with the adult world of violence and guilt, his confrontation is truly "fearful."

NATHANIEL HAWTHORNE

My Kinsman, Major Molineux

AFTER THE KINGS of Great Britain had assumed the right of appointing the colonial governors, the measures of the latter seldom met with the ready and general approbation which had been paid to those of their predecessors, under the original charters. The people looked with most jealous scrutiny to the exercise of power which did not emanate from themselves, and they usually rewarded their rulers with slender gratitude for the compliances by which, in softening their instructions from beyond the sea, they had incurred the reprehension of those who gave them. The annals of Massachusetts Bay will inform us, that of six governors in the space of about forty years from the surrender of the old charter, under James II, two were imprisoned by a popular insurrection; a third, as Hutchinson inclines to believe, was driven from the province by the whizzing of a musketball; a fourth, in the opinion of the same historian, was hastened to his grave by continual bickerings with the House of Representatives; and the remaining two, as well as their successors, till the Revolution, were favored with few and brief intervals of peaceful sway. The inferior members of the court party, in times of high political excitement, led scarcely a more desirable life. These remarks may serve as a preface to the following adventures, which chanced upon a summer night, not far from a hundred years ago. The reader, in order to avoid a long and dry detail of colonial affairs, is requested to dispense with an account of the train of circumstances that had caused much temporary inflammation of the popular mind.

It was near nine o'clock of a moonlight evening, when a boat crossed the ferry with a single passenger, who had obtained his conveyance at that unusual hour by the promise of an extra fare. While he stood at the landing-place, searching in either pocket for the means

From *The Works of Nathaniel Hawthorne*. (Boston: The Jefferson Press, 1883), III, 616–641. First published as "My Uncle Molineux" in *The Token* (1832); included in *The Snow-Image and Other Twice-Told Tales* (1852).

of fulfilling his agreement, the ferryman lifted a lantern, by the aid of which, and the newly risen moon, he took a very accurate survey of the stranger's figure. He was a youth of barely eighteen years, evidently country-bred, and now, as it should seem, upon his first visit to town. He was clad in a coarse gray coat, well worn, but in excellent repair; his under garments were durably constructed of leather, and fitted tight to a pair of serviceable and well-shaped limbs; his stockings of blue yarn were the incontrovertible work of a mother or a sister; and on his head was a three-cornered hat, which in its better days had perhaps sheltered the graver brow of the lad's father. Under his left arm was a heavy cudgel formed of an oak sapling, and retaining a part of the hardened root; and his equipment was completed by a wallet, not so abundantly stocked as to incommode the vigorous shoulders on which it hung. Brown, curly hair, well-shaped features, and bright, cheerful eyes were nature's gifts, and worth all that art could have done for his adornment.

The youth, one of whose names was Robin, finally drew from his pocket the half of a little province bill of five shillings, which, in the depreciation in that sort of currency, did but satisfy the ferryman's demand, with the surplus of a sexangular piece of parchment, valued at three pence. He then walked forward into the town, with as light a step as if his day's journey had not already exceeded thirty miles, and with as eager an eye as if he were entering London city, instead of the little metropolis of a New England colony. Before Robin had proceeded far, however, it occurred to him that he knew not whither to direct his steps; so he paused, and looked up and down the narrow street, scrutinizing the small and mean wooden buildings that were scattered on either side.

"This low hovel cannot be my kinsman's dwelling," thought he, "nor yonder old house, where the moonlight enters at the broken casement; and truly I see none hereabouts that might be worthy of him. It would have been wise to inquire my way of the ferryman, and doubtless he would have gone with me, and earned a shilling from the Major for his pains. But the next man I meet will do as well."

He resumed his walk, and was glad to perceive that the street now became wider, and the houses more respectable in their appearance. He soon discerned a figure moving on moderately in advance, and hastened his steps to overtake it. As Robin drew nigh, he saw that the passenger was a man in years, with a full periwig of gray hair, a wide-skirted coat of dark cloth, and silk stockings rolled above his knees. He carried a long and polished cane, which he struck down perpendicularly before him at every step; and at regular intervals he uttered two successive hems, of a peculiarly solemn and sepulchral intonation. Having made these observations, Robin laid hold of the skirt of the old man's coat, just when the light from the open door and windows of a barber's shop fell upon both their figures.

"Good evening to you, honored sir," said he, making a low bow, and still retaining his hold of the skirt. "I pray you tell me whereabouts is the dwelling of my kinsman, Major Molineux."

The youth's question was uttered very loudly; and one of the barbers, whose razor was descending on a well-soaped chin, and another who was dressing a Ramillies wig, left their occupations, and came to the door. The citizen, in the meantime, turned a long-favored countenance upon Robin, and answered him in a tone of excessive anger and annoyance. His two sepulchral hems, however, broke into the very centre of his rebuke, with most singular effect, like a thought of the cold grave obtruding among wrathful passions.

"Let go my garment, fellow! I tell you, I know not the man you speak of. What! I have authority, I have—hem, hem—authority; and if this be the respect you show for your betters, your feet shall be brought acquainted with the stocks by daylight, tomorrow morning!"

Robin released the old man's skirt, and hastened away, pursued by an ill-mannered roar of laughter from the barber's shop. He was at first considerably surprised by the result of his question, but, being a shrewd youth, soon thought himself able to account for the mystery.

"This is some country representative," was his conclusion, "who has never seen the inside of my kinsman's door, and lacks the breeding to answer a stranger civilly. The man is old, or verily—I might be tempted to turn back and smite him on the nose. Ah, Robin, Robin! even the barber's boys laugh at you for choosing such a guide! You will be wiser in time, friend Robin."

He now became entangled in a succession of crooked and narrow streets, which crossed each other, and meandered at no great distance from the water-side. The smell of tar was obvious to his nostrils, the masts of vessels pierced the moonlight above the tops of the buildings, and the numerous signs, which Robin paused to read, informed him that he was near the centre of business. But the streets were empty, the shops were closed, and lights were visible only in the second stories of a few dwelling-houses. At length, on the corner of a narrow lane, through which he was passing, he beheld the broad countenance of a British hero swinging before the door of an inn, whence proceeded the voices of many guests. The casement of one of the lower windows was thrown back, and a very thin curtain permitted Robin to distinguish a party at supper, round a well-furnished table. The fragrance of the good cheer steamed forth into the

outer air, and the youth could not fail to recollect that the last remnant of his travelling stock of provision had yielded to his morning
appetite, and that noon had found and left him dinnerless.

"Oh, that a parchment three-penny might give me a right to sit
down at yonder table!" said Robin, with a sigh. "But the Major
will make me welcome to the best of his victuals; so I will even step
boldly in, and inquire my way to his dwelling."

He entered the tavern, and was guided by the murmur of voices
and the fumes of tobacco to the public-room. It was a long and low
apartment, with oaken walls, grown dark in the continual smoke,
and a floor which was thickly sanded, but of no immaculate purity.
A number of persons—the larger part of whom appeared to be mari-
ners, or in some way connected with the sea—occupied the wooden
benches, or leather-bottomed chairs, conversing on various matters,
and occasionally lending their attention to some topic of general interest. Three or four little groups were draining as many bowls of
punch, which the West India trade had long since made a familiar
drink in the colony. Others, who had the appearance of men who
lived by regular and laborious handicraft, preferred the insulated
bliss of an unshared potation, and became more taciturn under its
influence. Nearly all, in short, evinced a predilection for the Good
Creature in some of its various shapes, for this is a vice to which, as
Fast Day sermons of a hundred years ago will testify, we have a long
hereditary claim. The only guests to whom Robin's sympathies inclined him were two or three sheepish countrymen, who were using
the inn somewhat after the fashion of a Turkish caravansary; they
had gotten themselves into the darkest corner of the room, and
heedless of the Nicotian atmosphere, were supping on the bread of
their own ovens, and the bacon cured in their own chimney-smoke.
But though Robin felt a sort of brotherhood with these strangers,
his eyes were attracted from them to a person who stood near the
door, holding whispered conversation with a group of ill-dressed associates. His features were separately striking almost to grotesque-
ness, and the whole face left a deep impression on the memory. The
forehead bulged out into a double prominence, with a vale between; the nose came boldly forth in an irregular curve, and its
bridge was of more than a finger's breadth; the eyebrows were deep
and shaggy, and the eyes glowed beneath them like fire in a cave.

While Robin deliberated of whom to inquire respecting the kinsman's dwelling, he was accosted by the innkeeper, a little man in a
stained white apron, who had come to pay his professional welcome
to the stranger. Being in the second generation from a French Prot-
estant, he seemed to have inherited the courtesy of his parent na-

tion; but no variety of circumstances was ever known to change his voice from the one shrill note in which he now addressed Robin.

"From the country, I presume, sir?" said he, with a profound bow. "Beg leave to congratulate you on your arrival, and trust you intend a long stay with us. Fine town here, sir, beautiful buildings, and much that may interest a stranger. May I hope for the honor of your commands in respect to supper?"

"The man sees a family likeness! the rogue has guessed that I am related to the Major!" thought Robin, who had hitherto experienced little superfluous civility.

All eyes were now turned on the country lad, standing at the door, in his worn three-cornered hat, gray coat, leather breeches, and blue yarn stockings, leaning on an oaken cudgel, and bearing a wallet on his back.

Robin replied to the courteous innkeeper, with such an assumption of confidence as befitted the Major's relative. "My honest friend," he said, "I shall make it a point to patronize your house on some occasion, when"—here he could not help lowering his voice— "when I may have more than a parchment three-pence in my pocket. My present business," continued he, speaking with lofty confidence, "is merely to inquire my way to the dwelling of my kinsman, Major Molineux."

There was a sudden and general movement in the room, which Robin interpreted as expressing the eagerness of each individual to become his guide. But the innkeeper turned his eyes to a written paper on the wall, which he read, or seemed to read, with occasional recurrences to the young man's figure.

"What have we here?" said he, breaking his speech into little dry fragments. " 'Left the house of the subscriber, bounden servant, Hezekiah Mudge,—had on, when he went away, gray coat, leather breeches, master's third-best hat. One pound currency reward to whosoever shall lodge him in any jail of the province.' Better trudge, boy; better trudge!"

Robin had begun to draw his hand towards the lighter end of the oak cudgel, but a strange hostility in every countenance induced him to relinquish his purpose of breaking the courteous innkeeper's head. As he turned to leave the room, he encountered a sneering glance from the bold-featured personage whom he had before noticed; and no sooner was he beyond the door, than he heard a general laugh, in which the innkeeper's voice might be distinguished, like the dropping of small stones into a kettle.

"Now, is it not strange," thought Robin, with his usual shrewdness,—"is it not strange that the confession of an empty pocket

should outweigh the name of my kinsman, Major Molineux? Oh, if
I had one of those grinning rascals in the woods, where I and my
oak sapling grew up together, I would teach him that my arm is
heavy though my purse be light!"

On turning the corner of the narrow lane, Robin found himself
in a spacious street, with an unbroken line of lofty houses on each
side, and a steepled building at the upper end, whence the ringing
of a bell announced the hour of nine. The light of the moon, and
the lamps from the numerous shop-windows, discovered people pro-
menading on the pavement, and amongst them Robin hoped to recognize his hitherto inscrutable relative. The result of his former inquiries made him unwilling to hazard another, in a scene of such
publicity, and he determined to walk slowly and silently up the
street, thrusting his face close to that of every elderly gentleman, in
search of the Major's lineaments. In his progress, Robin encountered many gay and gallant figures. Embroidered garments of showy
colors, enormous periwigs, gold-laced hats, and silver-hilted swords
glided past him and dazzled his optics. Travelled youths, imitators
of the European fine gentlemen of the period, trod jauntily along,
half dancing to the fashionable tunes which they hummed, and
making poor Robin ashamed of his quiet and natural gait. At
length, after many pauses to examine the gorgeous display of goods
in the shop-windows, and after suffering some rebukes for the impertinence of his scrutiny into people's faces, the Major's kinsman
found himself near the steepled building, still unsuccessful in his
search. As yet, however, he had seen only one side of the thronged
street; so Robin crossed, and continued the same sort of inquisition
down the opposite pavement, with stronger hopes than the philosopher seeking an honest man, but with no better fortune. He had arrived about midway towards the lower end, from which his course
began, when he overheard the approach of some one who struck
down a cane on the flag-stones at every step, uttering, at regular intervals, two sepulchral hems.

"Mercy on us!" quoth Robin, recognizing the sound.

Turning a corner, which chanced to be close at his right hand, he
hastened to pursue his researches in some other part of the town.
His patience now was wearing low, and he seemed to feel more
fatigue from his rambles since he crossed the ferry, than from his
journey of several days on the other side. Hunger also pleaded
loudly within him, and Robin began to balance the propriety of demanding, violently, and with lifted cudgel, the necessary guidance
from the first solitary passenger whom he should meet. While a resolution to this effect was gaining strength, he entered a street of

mean appearance, on either side of which a row of ill-built houses was straggling towards the harbor. The moonlight fell upon no passenger along the whole extent, but in the third domicile which Robin passed there was a half-opened door, and his keen glance detected a woman's garment within.

"My luck may be better here," said he to himself.

Accordingly, he approached the door, and beheld it shut closer as he did so; yet an open space remained, sufficing for the fair occupant to observe the stranger, without a corresponding display on her part. All that Robin could discern was a strip of scarlet petticoat, and the occasional sparkle of an eye, as if the moonbeams were trembling on some bright thing.

"Pretty mistress," for I may call her so with a good conscience, thought the shrewd youth, since I know nothing to the contrary,— "my sweet pretty mistress, will you be kind enough to tell me whereabouts I must seek the dwelling of my kinsman, Major Molineux?"

Robin's voice was plaintive and winning, and the female, seeing nothing to be shunned in the handsome country youth, thrust open the door, and came forth into the moonlight. She was a dainty little figure, with a white neck, round arms, and a slender waist, at the extremity of which her scarlet petticoat jutted out over a hoop, as if she were standing in a balloon. Moreover, her face was oval and pretty, her hair dark beneath the little cap, and her bright eyes possessed a sly freedom, which triumphed over those of Robin.

"Major Molineux dwells here," said this fair woman.

Now, her voice was the sweetest Robin had heard that night, the airy counterpart of a stream of melted silver; yet he could not help doubting whether that sweet voice spoke Gospel truth. He looked up and down the mean street, and then surveyed the house before which they stood. It was a small, dark edifice of two stores, the second of which projected over the lower floor, and the front apartment had the aspect of a shop for petty commodities.

"Now, truly, I am in luck," replied Robin, cunningly, "and so indeed is my kinsman, the Major, in having so pretty a housekeeper. But I prithee trouble him to step to the door; I will deliver him a message from his friends in the country, and then go back to my lodgings at the inn."

"Nay, the Major has been abed this hour or more," said the lady of the scarlet petticoat; "and it would be to little purpose to disturb him to-night, seeing his evening draught was of the strongest. But he is a kind-hearted man, and it would be as much as my life's worth to let a kinsman of his turn away from the door. You are the good old gentleman's very picture, and I could swear that was his rainy-weather hat. Also he has garments very much resembling those leather small-clothes. But come in, I pray, for I bid you hearty welcome in his name.'

So saying, the fair and hospitable dame took our hero by the hand; and the touch was light, and the force was gentleness, and though Robin read in her eyes what he did not hear in her words, yet the slender-waisted woman in the scarlet petticoat proved stronger than the athletic country youth. She had drawn his half-willing footsteps nearly to the threshold, when the opening of a door in the neighborhood startled the Major's housekeeper, and, leaving the Major's kinsman, she vanished speedily into her own domicile. A heavy yawn preceded the appearance of a man, who, like the Moonshine of Pyramus and Thisbe, carried a lantern, needlessly aiding his sister luminary in the heavens. As he walked sleepily up the street, he turned his broad, dull face on Robin, and displayed a long staff, spiked at the end.

"Home, vagabond, home!" said the watchman, in accents that seemed to fall asleep as soon as they were uttered. "Home, or we'll set you in the stocks by peep of day!"

"This is the second hint of the kind," thought Robin. "I wish they would end my difficulties, by setting me there to-night."

Nevertheless, the youth felt an instinctive antipathy towards the guardian of midnight order, which at first prevented him from asking his usual question. But just when the man was about to vanish behind the corner, Robin resolved not to lose the opportunity, and shouted lustily after him,—

"I say, friend! will you guide me to the house of my kinsman, Major Molineux?"

The watchman made no reply, but turned the corner and was gone; yet Robin seemed to hear the sound of drowsy laughter stealing along the solitary street. At that moment, also, a pleasant titter saluted him from the open window above his head; he looked up, and caught the sparkle of a saucy eye; a round arm beckoned to him, and next he heard light footsteps descending the staircase within. But Robin, being of the household of a New England clergyman, was a good youth, as well as a shrewd one; so he resisted temptation, and fled away.

He now roamed desperately, and at random, through the town, almost ready to believe that a spell was on him, like that by which a wizard of his country had once kept three pursuers wandering, a whole winter night, within twenty paces of the cottage which they sought. The streets lay before him, strange and desolate, and the lights were extinguished in almost every house. Twice, however, little parties of men, among whom Robin distinguished individuals in outlandish attire, came hurrying along; but, though on both occasions they paused to address him, such intercourse did not at all enlighten his perplexity. They did but utter a few words in some language of which Robin knew nothing, and perceiving his inability to answer, bestowed a curse upon him in plain English and hastened away. Finally, the lad determined to knock at the door of every mansion that might appear worthy to be occupied by his kinsman, trusting that perseverance would overcome the fatality that had hitherto thwarted him. Firm in this resolve, he was passing beneath the walls of a church, which formed the corner of two streets, when, as he turned into the shade of its steeple, he encountered a bulky stranger, muffled in a cloak. The man was proceeding with the speed of earnest business, but Robin planted himself full before him, holding the oak cudgel with both hands across his body as a bar to further passage.

"Halt, honest man, and answer me a question," said he, very resolutely. "Tell me, this instant, whereabouts is the dwelling of my kinsman, Major Molineux!"

"Keep your tongue between your teeth, fool, and let me pass!" said a deep, gruff voice, which Robin partly remembered. "Let me pass, I say, or I'll strike you to the earth!"

"No, no, neighbor!" cried Robin, flourishing his cudgel, and then thrusting its larger end close to the man's muffled face. "No, no, I'm not the fool you take me for, nor do you pass till I have an answer to my question. Whereabouts is the dwelling of my kinsman, Major Molineux?"

The stranger, instead of attempting to force his passage, stepped back into the moonlight, unmuffled his face, and stared full into that of Robin.

"Watch here an hour, and Major Molineux will pass by," said he.

Robin gazed with dismay and astonishment on the unprecedented physiognomy of the speaker. The forehead with its double prominence, the broad hooked nose, the shaggy eyebrows, and fiery eyes were those which he had noticed at the inn, but the man's complexion had undergone a singular, or, more properly, a twofold change. One side of the face blazed an intense red, while the other was black as midnight, the division line being in the broad bridge of the nose; and a mouth which seemed to extend from ear to ear was black or red, in contrast to the color of the cheek. The effect was as if two individual devils, a fiend of fire and a fiend of darkness, had united themselves to form this infernal visage. The stranger grinned in Robin's face, muffled his party-colored features, and was out of sight in a moment.

"Strange things we travellers see!" ejaculated Robin.

He seated himself, however, upon the steps of the church-door, resolving to wait the appointed time for his kinsman. A few moments
were consumed in philosophical speculations upon the species of
man who had just left him; but having settled this point shrewdly,
rationally, and satisfactorily, he was compelled to look elsewhere for
his amusement. And first he threw his eyes along the street. It was of
more respectable appearance than most of those into which he had
wandered; and the moon, creating, like the imaginative power, a
beautiful strangeness in familiar objects, gave something of romance
to a scene that might not have possessed it in the light of day. The
irregular and often quaint architecture of the houses, some of whose
roofs were broken into numerous little peaks, while others ascended,
steep and narrow, into a single point, and others again were square;
the pure snow-white of some of their complexions, the aged darkness of others, and the thousand sparklings, reflected from bright
substances in the walls of many; these matters engaged Robin's attention for a while, and then began to grow wearisome. Next he endeavored to define the forms of distant objects, starting away, with
almost ghostly indistinctness, just as his eyes appeared to grasp them;
and finally he took a minute survey of an edifice which stood on the
opposite side of the street, directly in front of the church-door,
where he was stationed. It was a large, square mansion, distinguished from its neighbors by a balcony, which rested on tall pillars,
and by an elaborate Gothic window, communicating therewith.

"Perhaps this is the very house I have been seeking," thought
Robin.

Then he strove to speed away the time, by listening to a murmur
which swept continually along the street, yet was scarcely audible,
except to an unaccustomed ear like his; it was a low, dull, dreamy
sound, compounded of many noises, each of which was at too great
a distance to be separately heard. Robin marvelled at this snore of a
sleeping town, and marvelled more whenever its continuity was broken by now and then a distant shout apparently loud where it originated. But altogether it was a sleep-inspiring sound, and, to shake
off its drowsy influence, Robin arose, and climbed a window-frame,
that he might view the interior of the church. There the moonbeams
came trembling in, and fell down upon the deserted pews, and extended along the quiet aisles. A fainter yet more awful radiance was
hovering around the pulpit, and one solitary ray had dared to rest
upon the open page of the great Bible. Had nature, in that deep
hour, become a worshipper in the house which man had builded?
Or was that heavenly light the visible sanctity of the place,—visible
because no earthly and impure feet were within the walls? The
scene made Robin's heart shiver with a sensation of loneliness

stronger than he had ever felt in the remotest depths of his native woods; so he turned away and sat down again before the door. There were graves around the church, and now an uneasy thought obtruded into Robin's breast. What if the object of his search, which had been so often and so strangely thwarted, were all the time mouldering in his shroud? What if his kinsman should glide through yonder gate, and nod and smile to him in dimly passing by? "Oh that any breathing thing were here with me!" said Robin.

Recalling his thoughts from this uncomfortable track, he sent them over forest, hill, and stream, and attempted to imagine how that evening of ambiguity and weariness had been spent by his father's household. He pictured them assembled at the door, beneath the tree, the great old tree, which had been spared for its huge twisted trunk and venerable shade, when a thousand leafy brethren fell. There, at the going down of the summer sun, it was his father's custom to perform domestic worship, that the neighbors might come and join with him like brothers of the family, and that the wayfaring man might pause to drink at that fountain, and keep his heart pure by freshening the memory of home. Robin distinguished the seat of every individual of the little audience; he saw the good man in the midst, holding the Scriptures in the golden light that fell from the western clouds; he beheld him close the book and all rise up to pray. He heard the old thanksgivings for daily mercies, the old supplications for their continuance, to which he had so often listened in weariness, but which were now among his dear remembrances. He perceived the slight inequality of his father's voice when he came to speak of the absent one; he noted how his mother turned her face to the broad and knotted trunk; how his elder brother scorned, because the beard was rough upon his upper lip, to permit his features to be moved; how the younger sister drew down a low hanging branch before her eyes; and how the little one of all, whose sports had hitherto broken the decorum of the scene, understood the prayer for her playmate, and burst into clamorous grief. Then he saw them go in at the door; and when Robin would have entered also, the latch tinkled into its place, and he was excluded from his home.

"Am I here, or there?" cried Robin, starting; for all at once, when his thoughts had become visible and audible in a dream, the long, wide, solitary street shone out before him.

He aroused himself, and endeavored to fix his attention steadily upon the large edifice which he had surveyed before. But still his mind kept vibrating between fancy and reality; by turns, the pillars of the balcony lengthened into the tall, bare stems of pines, dwindled down to human figures, settled again into their true shape and size, and then commenced a new succession of changes. For a single moment, when he deemed himself awake, he could have sworn that a visage—one which he seemed to remember, yet could not absolutely name as his kinsman's—was looking towards him from the Gothic window. A deeper sleep wrestled him and nearly overcame him, but fled at the sound of footsteps along the opposite pavement. Robin rubbed his eyes, discerned a man passing at the foot of the balcony, and addressed him in a loud, peevish, and lamentable cry.

"Hallo, friend! must I wait here all night for my kinsman, Major Molineux?"

The sleeping echoes awoke, and answered the voice; and the passenger, barely able to discern a figure sitting in the oblique shade of the steeple, traversed the street to obtain a nearer view. He was himself a gentleman in his prime, of open, intelligent, cheerful, and altogether prepossessing countenance. Perceiving a country youth, apparently homeless and without friends, he accosted him in a tone of real kindness, which had become strange to Robin's ears.

"Well, my good lad, why are you sitting here?" inquired he. "Can I be of service to you in any way?"

"I am afraid not, sir," replied Robin, despondingly; "yet I shall take it kindly, if you'll answer me a single question. I've been searching, half the night, for one Major Molineux; now, sir, is there really such a person in these parts, or am I dreaming?"

"Major Molineux! The name is not altogether strange to me," said the gentleman, smiling. "Have you any objection to telling me the nature of your business with him?"

Then Robin briefly related that his father was a clergyman, settled on a small salary, at a long distance back in the country, and that he and Major Molineux were brothers' children. The Major, having inherited riches, and acquired civil and military rank, had visited his cousin, in great pomp, a year or two before; had manifested much interest in Robin and an elder brother, and, being childless himself, had thrown out hints respecting the future establishment of one of them in life. The elder brother was destined to succeed to the farm which his father cultivated in the interval of sacred duties; it was therefore determined that Robin should profit by his kinsman's generous intentions, especially as he seemed to be rather the favorite, and was thought to possess other necessary endowments.

"For I have the name of being a shrewd youth," observed Robin, in this part of his story.

"I doubt not you deserve it," replied his new friend, good-naturedly; "but pray proceed."

"Well, sir, being nearly eighteen years old, and well grown, as you see," continued Robin, drawing himself up to his full height, "I thought it high time to begin the world. So my mother and sister put me in handsome trim, and my father gave me half the remnant of his last year's salary, and five days ago I started for this place, to pay the Major a visit. But, would you believe it, sir! I crossed the ferry a little after dark, and have yet found nobody that would show me the way to his dwelling; only, an hour or two since, I was told to wait here, and Major Molineux would pass by."

"Can you describe the man who told you this?" inquired the gentleman.

'Oh, he was a very ill-favored fellow, sir," replied Robin, "with two great bumps on his forehead, a hook nose, fiery eyes; and what struck me as the strangest, his face was of two different colors. Do you happen to know such a man, sir?"

"Not intimately," answered the stranger, "but I chanced to meet him a little time previous to your stopping me. I believe you may trust his word, and that the Major will very shortly pass through this street. In the mean time, as I have a singular curiosity to witness your meeting, I will sit down here upon the steps and bear you company."

He seated himself accordingly, and soon engaged his companion in animated discourse. It was but of brief continuance, however, for a noise of shouting, which had long been remotely audible, drew so much nearer that Robin inquired its cause.

"What may be the meaning of this uproar?" asked he. "Truly, if your town be always as noisy, I shall find little sleep while I am an inhabitant."

"Why, indeed, friend Robin, there do appear to be three or four riotous fellows abroad to-night," replied the gentleman. "You must not expect all the stillness of your native woods here in our streets. But the watch will shortly be at the heels of these lads and"—

"Ay, and set them in the stocks by peep of day," interrupted Robin, recollecting his own encounter with the drowsy lantern-bearer. "But, dear sir, if I may trust my ears, an army of watchmen would never make head against such a multitude of rioters. There were at least a thousand voices went up to make that one shout."

"May not a man have several voices, Robin, as well as two complexions?" said his friend.

"Perhaps a man may; but Heaven forbid that a woman should!" responded the shrewd youth, thinking of the seductive tones of the Major's housekeeper.

The sounds of a trumpet in some neighboring street now became so evident and continual, that Robin's curiosity was strongly excited. In addition to the shouts, he heard frequent bursts from many

instruments of discord, and a wild and confused laughter filled up
the intervals. Robin rose from the steps, and looked wistfully towards a point whither people seemed to be hastening.

"Surely some prodigous merry-making is going on," exclaimed he.
"I have laughed very little since I left home, sire, and should be
sorry to lose an opportunity. Shall we step around the corner by that
darkish house, and take our share of the fun?"

"Sit down again, sit down, good Robin," replied the gentleman,
laying his hand on the skirt of the gray coat. "You forget that we
must wait here for your kinsman; and there is reason to believe that
he will pass by, in the course of a very few moments."

The near approach of the uproar had now disturbed the neighborhood; windows flew open on all sides; and many heads, in the
attire of the pillow, and confused by sleep suddenly broken, were
protruded to the gaze of whoever had leisure to observe them. Eager
voices hailed each other from house to house, all demanding the explanation, which not a soul could give. Half-dressed men hurried
towards the unknown commotion, stumbling as they went over the
stone steps that thrust themselves into the narrow foot-walk. The
shouts, the laughter, and the tuneless bray, the antipodes of music,
came onwards with increasing din, till scattered individuals, and
then denser bodies, began to appear round a corner at the distance
of a hundred yards.

"Will you recognize your kinsman, if he passes in this crowd?" inquired the gentleman.

"Indeed, I can't warrant it, sir; but I'll take my stand here, and
keep a bright lookout," answered Robin, descending to the outer
edge of the pavement.

A mighty stream of people now emptied into the street, and came
rolling slowly towards the church. A single horseman wheeled the
corner in the midst of them, and close behind him came a band of
fearful wind-instruments, sending forth a fresher discord now that
no intervening buildings kept it from the ear. Then a redder light
disturbed the moonbeams, and a dense multitude of torches shone
along the street, concealing, by their glare, whatever object they illu-
minated. The single horseman, clad in a military dress, and bearing
a drawn sword, rode onward as the leader, and, by his fierce and
variegated countenance, appeared like war personified; the red of
one cheek was an emblem of fire and sword; the blackness of the
other betokened the mourning that attends them. In his train were
wild figures in the Indian dress, and many fantastic shapes without
a model, giving the whole march a visionary air, as if a dream had
broken forth from some feverish brain, and were sweeping visibly
through the midnight streets. A mass of people, inactive, except as

applauding spectators, hemmed the procession in; and several women ran along the sidewalk, piercing the confusion of heavier sounds with their shrill voices of mirth or terror.

"The double-faced fellow has his eye upon me," muttered Robin, with an indefinite but an uncomfortable idea that he was himself to bear a part in the pageantry.

The leader turned himself in the saddle, and fixed his glance full upon the country youth, as the steed went slowly by. When Robin had freed his eyes from those fiery ones, the musicians were passing before him, and the torches were close at hand; but the unsteady brightness of the latter formed a veil which he could not penetrate. The rattling of wheels over the stones sometimes found its way to his ear, and confused traces of a human form appeared at intervals, and then melted into the vivid light. A moment more, and the leader thundered a command to halt: the trumpets vomited a horrid breath, and then held their peace; the shouts and laughter of the people died away, and there remained only a universal hum, allied to silence. Right before Robin's eyes was an uncovered cart. There the torches blazed the brightest, there the moon shone out like day, and there, in tar-and-feathery dignity, sat his kinsman, Major Molineux!

He was an elderly man, of large and majestic person, and strong, square features, betokening a steady soul; but steady as it was, his enemies had found means to shake it. His face was pale as death, and far more ghastly; the broad forehead was contracted in his agony, so that his eyebrows formed one grizzled line; his eyes were red and wild, and the foam hung white upon his quivering lip. His whole frame was agitated by a quick and continual tremor, which his pride strove to quell, even in those circumstances of overwhelming humiliation. But perhaps the bitterest pang of all was when his eyes met those of Robin; for he evidently knew him on the instant, as the youth stood witnessing the foul disgrace of a head grown gray in honor. They stared at each other in silence, and Robin's knees shook, and his hair bristled, with a mixture of pity and terror. Soon, however, a bewildering excitement began to seize upon his mind; the preceding adventures of the night, the unexpected appearance of the crowd, the torches, the confused din and the hush that followed, the spectre of his kinsman reviled by that great multitude,— all this, and, more than all, a perception of tremendous ridicule in the whole scene, affected him with a sort of mental inebriety. At that moment a voice of sluggish merriment saluted Robin's ears; he turned instinctively, and just behind the corner of the church stood the lantern-bearer, rubbing his eyes, and drowsily enjoying the lad's amazement. Then he heard a peal of laughter like the ringing of silvery bells; a woman twitched his arm, a saucy eye met his, and he saw the lady of the scarlet petticoat. A sharp, dry cachinnation appealed to his memory, and, standing on tiptoe in the crowd, with his white apron over his head, he beheld the courteous little innkeeper. And lastly, there sailed over the heads of the multitude a great, broad laugh, broken in the midst by two sepulchral hems; thus, "Haw, haw, haw,—hem, hem,—haw, haw, haw, haw!"

The sound proceeded from the balcony of the opposite edifice, and thither Robin turned his eyes. In front of the Gothic window stood the old citizen, wrapped in a wide gown, his gray periwig exchanged for a nightcap, which was thrust back from his forehead, and his silk stockings hanging about his legs. He supported himself on his polished cane in a fit of convulsive merriment, which manifested itself on his solemn old features like a funny inscription on a tombstone. Then Robin seemed to hear the voices of the barbers, of the guests of the inn, and of all who had made sport of him that night. The contagion was spreading among the multitude, when all at once, it seized upon Robin, and he sent forth a shout of laughter that echoed through the street,—every man shook his sides, every man emptied his lungs, but Robin's shout was the loudest there. The cloud-spirits peeped from their silvery islands, as the congregated mirth went roaring up the sky! The Man in the Moon heard the far bellow. "Oho," quoth he, "the old earth is frolicsome tonight!"

When there was a momentary calm in that tempestuous sea of sound, the leader gave the sign, the procession resumed its march. On they went, like fiends that throng in mockery around some dead potentate, mighty no more, but majestic still in his agony. On they went, in counterfeited pomp, in senseless uproar, in frenzied merriment, trampling all on an old man's heart. On swept the tumult, and left a silent street behind.

"Well, Robin, are you dreaming?" inquired the gentleman, laying his hand on the youth's shoulder.

Robin started, and withdrew his arm from the stone post to which he had instinctively clung, as the living stream rolled by him. His cheek was somewhat pale, and his eye not quite as lively as in the earlier part of the evening.

"Will you be kind enough to show me the way to the ferry?" said he, after a moment's pause.

"You have, then, adopted a new subject of inquiry?" observed his companion, with smile.

"Why, yes, sir," replied Robin, rather dryly. "Thanks to you, and to my other friends, I have at last met my kinsman, and he will scarce desire to see my face again. I begin to grow weary of town life, sir. Will you show me the way to the ferry?"

"No, my good friend Robin,—not to-night, at least," said the gentleman. "Some few days hence, if you wish it, I will speed you on your journey. Or, if you prefer to remain with us, perhaps, as you are a shrewd youth, you may rise in the world without the help of your kinsman, Major Molineux."

HERMAN MELVILLE

Redburn

While the scene last described was going on, we were all
startled by a horrid groaning noise down in the forecastle; and all
at once someone came rushing up the scuttle in his shirt, clutching
something in his hand, and trembling and shrieking in the most
frightful manner, so that I thought one of the sailors must be mur-
dered below.

But it all passed in a moment; and while we stood aghast at the
sight, and almost before we knew what it was, the shrieking man
jumped over the bows into the sea, and we saw him no more. Then
there was a great uproar; the sailors came running upon deck; and
the chief mate ran forward, and learning what had happened, began
to yell out his orders about the sails and yards; and we all went to
pulling and hauling the ropes, till at last the ship lay almost still on
the water. Then they loosed a boat, which kept pulling round the
ship for more than an hour, but they never caught sight of the man.
It seemed that he was one of the sailors who had been brought
aboard dead drunk, and tumbled into his bunk by his landlord; and
there he had lain till now. He must have suddenly waked up, I suppose, raging mad with the delirium tremens, as the chief mate called
it, and finding himself in a strange silent place, and knowing not
how he had got there, he had rushed on deck, and so, in a fit of
frenzy, put an end to himself.

This event, happening at the dead of night, had a wonderfully
solemn and almost awful effect upon me. I would have given the

From *The Works of Herman Melville* (1922–24 ed.), (New York: Russell & Russell,
1963), V, 63–66, 71–79, 315–318, 380–383. *Redburn* was first published in
1849. In the "scene last described," Redburn was ridiculed by the other sailors for
naively asking why the ship's bell was rung so frequently.

whole world, and the sun and moon, and all the stars in heaven, if they had been mine, had I been safe back at Mr. Jones', or still better, in my home on the Hudson River. I thought it an ill-omened voyage, and railed at the folly which had sent me to sea, sore against the advice of my best friends, that is to say, my mother and sisters.

Alas! poor Wellingborough, thought I, you will never see your home any more. And in this melancholy mood I went below, when the watch had expired, which happened soon after. But to my terror, I found that the suicide had been occupying the very bunk which I had appropriated to myself, and there was no other place for me to sleep in. The thought of lying down there now seemed too horrible to me, and what made it worse was the way in which the sailors spoke of my being frightened. And they took this opportunity to tell me what a hard and wicked life I had entered upon, and how that such things happened frequently at sea, and they were used to it. But I did not believe this; for when the suicide came rushing and shrieking up the scuttle, they looked as frightened as I did; and besides that, and what makes their being frightened still plainer, is the fact, that if they had had any presence of mind they could have prevented his plunging overboard, since he brushed right by them. However, they lay in their bunks smoking, and kept talking on some time in this strain, and advising me as soon as ever I got home to pin my ears back, so as not to hold the wind, and sail straight away into the interior of the country, and never stop until deep in the bush, far off from the least running brook, never mind how shallow, and out of sight of even the smallest puddle of rainwater.

This kind of talking brought the tears into my eyes, for it was so true and real, and the sailors who spoke it seemed so false-hearted and insincere; but for all that, in spite of the sickness at my heart, it made me mad, and stung me to the quick, that they should speak of me as a poor trembling coward, who could never be brought to endure the hardships of a sailor's life; for I felt myself trembling, and knew that I was but a coward then, well enough, without their telling me of it. And they did not say I was cowardly because they perceived it in me, but because they merely supposed I must be, judging, no doubt, from their own secret thoughts about themselves; for I felt sure that the suicide frightened them very badly. And at last, being provoked to desperation by their taunts, I told them so to their faces; but I might better have kept silent, for they now all united to abuse me. They asked me what business I, a boy like me, had to go to sea, and take the bread out of the mouth of honest sailors, and fill a good seaman's place; and asked me whether I ever dreamed of becoming a captain, since I was a gentleman with white hands; and

if I ever *should* be, they would like nothing better than to ship
aboard my vessel and stir up a mutiny. And one of them, whose
name was Jackson, of whom I shall have a good deal more to say by
and by, said, I had better steer clear of him ever after, for if ever I
crossed his path, or got into his way, he would be the death of me,
and if ever I stumbled about in the rigging near *him,* he would
make nothing of pitching me overboard; and that he swore too,
with an oath. At first, all this nearly stunned me, it was so unfore-
seen; and then I could not believe that they meant what they said,
or that they could be so cruel and black-hearted. But how could I
help seeing that the men who could thus talk to a poor, friendless
boy, on the very first night of his voyage to sea, must be capable of
almost any enormity. I loathed, detested, and hated them with all
that was left of my bursting heart and soul, and I thought myself
the most forlorn and miserable wretch that every breathed. May I
never be a man, thought I, if to be a boy is to be such a wretch. And
I wailed and wept, and my heart cracked within me, but all the
time I defied them through my teeth, and dared them to do their
worst.

At last they ceased talking and fell fast asleep, leaving me awake,
seated on a chest with my face bent over my knees between my
hands. And there I sat, till at length the dull beating against the
ship's bows, and the silence around, soothed me down, and I fell
asleep as I sat.

He Gives Some Account of One of His Shipmates Called Jackson

While we sat eating our beef and biscuit, two of the men got into a
dispute, about who had been seafaring the longest; when Jackson,
who had mixed the *burgoo,* called upon them in a loud voice to
cease their clamour, for he would decide the matter for them. Of
this sailor I shall have something more to say as I get on with my
narrative; so I will here try to describe him a little.

Did you ever see a man with his hair shaved off, and just recovered from the yellow fever? Well, just such a looking man was this
sailor. He was as yellow as gamboge, had no more whisker on his
cheek than I have on my elbows. His hair had fallen out, and left
him very bald, except in the nape of his neck, and just behind the
ears, where it was stuck over with short little tufts, and looked like a
worn-out shoebrush. His nose had broken down in the middle, and
he squinted with one eye, and did not look very straight out of the
other. He dressed a good deal like a Bowery boy; for he despised the
ordinary sailor-rig, wearing a pair of great over-all blue trowsers, fas-

tened with suspenders, and three red woollen shirts, one over the other; for he was subject to the rheumatism, and was not in good health, he said; and he had a large white wool hat, with a broad rolling brim. He was a native of New York city, and had a good deal to say about *highbinders* and *rowdies,* whom he denounced as only good for the gallows; but I thought he looked a good deal like a *highbinder* himself.

His name, as I have said, was Jackson; and he told us he was a near relation of General Jackson of New Orleans, and swore terribly if anyone ventured to question what he asserted on that head. In fact he was a great bully, and being the best seaman on board, and very overbearing every way, all the men were afraid of him, and durst not contradict him, or cross his path in anything. And what made this more wonderful was that he was the weakest man, bodily, of the whole crew; and I have no doubt that young and small as I was then, compared to what I am now, I could have thrown him down. But he had such an overawing way with him, such a deal of brass and impudence, such an unflinching face, and withal was such a hideous-looking mortal, that Satan himself would have run from him. And besides all this, it was quite plain that he was by nature a marvellously clever, cunning man, though without education; and understood human nature to a kink, and well knew whom he had to deal with; and then, one glance of his squinting eye was as good as a knock-down, for it was the most deep, subtle, infernal-looking eye that I ever saw lodged in a human head. I believe, that by good rights it must have belonged to a wolf, or starved tiger; at any rate, I would defy any oculist to turn out a glass eye half so cold, and snaky, and deadly. It was a horrible thing; and I would give much to forget that I have ever seen it; for it haunts me to this day.

It was impossible to tell how old this Jackson was; for he had no beard, and no wrinkles, except small crow's-feet about the eyes. He might have seen thirty, or perhaps fifty years. But according to his own account, he had been to sea ever since he was eight years old, when he first went as a cabin-boy in an Indiaman, and ran away at Calcutta. And according to his own account, too, he had passed through every kind of dissipation and abandonment in the worst parts of the world. He had served in Portuguese slavers on the coast of Africa; and with a diabolical relish used to tell of the *middle passage,* where the slaves were stewed, heel and point, like logs, and the suffocated and dead were unmanacled, and weeded out from the living every morning, before washing down the decks; how he had been in a slaving schooner which, being chased by an English cruiser off Cape Verde, received three shots in her hull, which raked through and through a whole file of slaves, that were chained.

He would tell of lying in Batavia during a fever, when his ship lost a man every few days, and how they went reeling ashore with the body, and got still more intoxicated by way of precaution against the plague. He would talk of finding a cobra-di-capello, or hooded snake, under his pillow in India, when he slept ashore there. He would talk of sailors being poisoned at Canton with drugged *shampoo*, for the sake of their money; and of the Malay ruffians, who stopped ships in the straits of Gaspar, and always saved the captain for the last, so as to make him point out where the most valuable goods were stored.

His whole talk was of this kind; full of piracies, plagues, and poisonings. And often he narrated many passages in his own individual career which were almost incredible, from the consideration that few men could have plunged into such infamous vices, and clung to them so long, without paying the death penalty.

But in truth, he carried about with him the traces of these things, and the mark of a fearful end nigh at hand; like that of King Antiochus of Syria, who died a worse death, history says, than if he had been stung out of the world by wasps and hornets.

Nothing was left of this Jackson but the foul lees and dregs of a man; he was thin as a shadow; nothing but skin and bones; and sometimes used to complain that it hurt him to sit on the hard chests. And I sometimes fancied it was the consciousness of his miserable, broken-down condition, and the prospect of soon dying like a dog, in consequence of his sins, that made this poor wretch always eye me with such malevolence as he did. For I was young and handsome, at least my mother so thought me, and as soon as I became a little used to the sea, and shook off my low spirits somewhat, I began to have my old colour in my cheeks, and, spite of misfortune, to appear well and hearty; whereas *he* was being consumed by an incurable malady, that was eating up his vitals, and was more fit for a hospital than a ship.

As I am sometimes by nature inclined to indulge in unauthorised surmisings about the thoughts going on with regard to me, in the people I meet; especially if I have reason to think they dislike me; I will not put it down for a certainty that what I suspected concerning this Jackson relative to his thoughts of me was really the truth. But only state my honest opinion, and how it struck me at the time; and even now, I think I was not wrong. And indeed, unless it was so, how could I account to myself for the shudder that would run through me when I caught this man gazing at me, as I often did; for he was apt to be dumb at times, and would sit with his eyes fixed, and his teeth set, like a man in the moody madness.

I well remember the first time I saw him, and how I was startled at his eye, which was even then fixed upon me. He was standing at the ship's helm, being the first man that got there when a steersman was called for by the pilot; for this Jackson was always on the alert for easy duties, and used to plead his delicate health as the reason for assuming them as he did; though I used to think, that for a man in poor health, he was very swift on the legs; at least when a good place was to be jumped to; though that might only have been a sort of spasmodic exertion under strong inducements, which everyone knows the greatest invalids will sometimes show.

And though the sailors were always very bitter against anything like *sogering,* as they called it; that is, anything that savoured of a desire to get rid of downright hard work; yet I observed that, though this Jackson was a notorious old *soger* the whole voyage (I mean, in all things not perilous to do, from which he was far from hanging back), and in truth was a great veteran that way, and one who must have passed unhurt through many campaigns; yet they never presumed to call him to account in any way; or to let him so much as think what they thought of his conduct. But I often heard them call him many hard names behind his back; and sometimes, too, when, perhaps, they had just been tenderly inquiring after his health before his face. They all stood in mortal fear of him; and cringed and fawned about him like so many spaniels; and used to rub his back after he was undressed and lying in his bunk; and used to run up on deck to the cook-house to warm some cold coffee for him; and used to fill his pipe, and give him chews of tobacco, and mend his jackets and trowsers; and used to watch, and tend, and nurse him every way. And all the time he would sit scowling on them, and found fault with what they did; and I noticed, that those who did the most for him, and cringed the most before him, were the very ones he most abused; while two or three who held more aloof, he treated with a little consideration.

It is not for me to say what it was that made a whole ship's company submit so to the whims of one poor miserable man like Jackson. I only know that so it was; but I have no doubt, that if he had had a blue eye in his head, or had had a different face from what he did have, they would not have stood in such awe of him. And it astonished me to see that one of the seamen, a remarkably robust and good-humoured young man from Belfast in Ireland, was a person of no mark or influence among the crew; but on the contrary was hooted at, and trampled upon, and made a butt and laughing-stock; and more than all, was continually being abused and snubbed by Jackson, who seemed to hate him cordially, because of his great strength and fine person, and particularly because of his red cheeks.

But then, this Belfast man, although he had shipped for an *able seaman,* was not much of a sailor; and that always lowers a man in the eyes of a ship's company; I mean, when he ships for an *able seaman,* but is not able to do the duty of one. For sailors are of three classes—*able seamen, ordinary seamen,* and *boys;* and they receive different wages according to their rank. Generally, a ship's company of twelve men will only have five or six able seamen, who if they prove to understand their duty every way (and that is no small matter either, as I shall hereafter show, perhaps) are looked up to, and thought much of by the ordinary seamen and boys, who reverence their very pea-jackets, and lay up their sayings in their hearts.

But you must not think from this that persons called *boys* aboard merchant ships are all youngsters, though to be sure, I myself was called a *boy,* and a boy I was. No. In merchant ships, a *boy* means a green-hand, a landsman on his first voyage. And never mind if he is old enough to be a grandfather, he is still called a *boy;* and boy's work is put upon him.

But I am straying off from what I was going to say about Jackson's putting an end to the dispute between the two sailors in the forecastle after breakfast. After they had been disputing some time about who had been to sea the longest, Jackson told them to stop talking; and then bade one of them open his mouth; for, said he, I can tell a sailor's age just like a horse's—by his teeth. So the man laughed, and opened his mouth; and Jackson made him step out under the scuttle, where the light came down from deck; and then made him throw his head back, while he looked into it, and probed a little with his jack-knife, like a baboon peering into a junk-bottle. I trembled for the poor fellow, just as if I had seen him under the hands of a crazy barber, making signs to cut his throat, and he all the while sitting stock-still, with the lather on, to be shaved. For I watched Jackson's eye and saw it snapping, and a sort of going in and out, very quick, as if it were something like a forked tongue; and somehow, I felt as if he were longing to kill the man; but at last he grew more composed, and after concluding his examination, said, that the first man was the oldest sailor, for the ends of his teeth were the evenest and most worn down; which, he said, arose from eating so much hard sea-biscuit; and this was the reason he could tell a sailor's age like a horse's.

At this, everybody made merry, and looked at each other, as much as to say—*Come, boys, let's laugh;* and they did laugh; and declared it was a rare joke.

This was always the way with them. They made a point of shouting out whenever Jackson said anything with a grin; that being the sign to them that he himself thought it funny; though I heard many good jokes from others pass off without a smile; and once Jackson himself (for, to tell the truth, he sometimes had a comical way with him, that is, when his back did not ache) told a truly funny story, but with a grave face when, not knowing how he meant it, whether for a laugh or otherwise, they all sat still, waiting what to do, and looking perplexed enough; till at last Jackson roared out upon them for a parcel of fools and idiots; and told them to their beards, how it was; that he had purposely put on his grave face, to see whether they would not look grave too; even when he was telling something that ought to split their sides. And with that he flouted and jeered at them, and laughed them all to scorn; and broke out in such a rage that his lips began to glue together at the corners with a fine white foam.

He seemed to be full of hatred and gall against everything and everybody in the world; as if all the world was one person, and had done him some dreadful harm, that was rankling and festering in his heart. Sometimes I thought he was really crazy; and often felt so frightened at him, that I thought of going to the captain about it, and telling him Jackson ought to be confined, lest he should do some terrible thing at last. But upon second thoughts, I always gave it up; for the captain would only have called me a fool, and sent me forward again.

But you must not think that all the sailors were alike in abasing themselves before this man. No: there were three or four who used to stand up sometimes against him; and when he was absent at the wheel, would plot against him among the other sailors, and tell them what a shame and ignominy it was that such a poor miserable wretch should be such a tyrant over much better men than himself. And they begged and conjured them as men to put up with it no longer, but the very next time that Jackson presumed to play the dictator, that they should all withstand him, and let him know his place. Two or three times nearly all hands agreed to it, with the exception of those who used to slink off during such discussions; and swore that they would not any more submit to be ruled by Jackson. But when the time came to make good their oaths, they were mum again, and let everything go on the old way; so that those who had put them up to it had to bear all the brunt of Jackson's wrath by themselves. And though these last would stick up a little at first, and even mutter something about a fight to Jackson; yet in the end, finding themselves unbefriended by the rest, they would gradually become silent, and leave the field to the tyrant, who would then fly out worse than ever, and dare them to do their worst, and jeer at them for white-livered poltroons, who did not have a mouthful of heart in them. At such times, there were no bounds to his contempt; and indeed, all the time he seemed to have even more contempt than hatred for everybody and everything.

As for me, I was but a boy; and at any time aboard ship a boy is expected to keep quiet, do what he is bid, never presume to interfere, and seldom to talk unless spoken to. For merchant sailors have a great idea of their dignity, and superiority to *greenhorns* and *landsmen,* who know nothing about a ship; and they seem to think that an *able seaman* is a great man; at least a much greater man than a little boy. And the able seamen in the *Highlander* had such grand notions about their seamanship that I almost thought that able seamen received diplomas, like those given at colleges; and were made a sort of *A.M.'s* or *Masters of Arts.*

But though I kept thus quiet, and had very little to say, and well knew that my best plan was to get along peaceably with everybody, and indeed endure a good deal before showing fight, yet I could not avoid Jackson's evil eye, nor escape his bitter enmity. And his being my foe set many of the rest against me; or at least they were afraid to speak out for me before Jackson; so that at last I found myself a sort of Ishmael in the ship, without a single friend or companion; and I began to feel a hatred growing up in me against the whole crew—so much so, that I prayed against it, that it might not master my heart completely, and so make a fiend of me, something like Jackson.

A LIVING CORPSE*

It was destined that our departure from the English strand should be marked by a tragical event, akin to the sudden end of the suicide which had so strongly impressed me on quitting the American shore.

Of the three newly shipped men, who in a state of intoxication had been brought on board at the dock gates, two were able to be engaged at their duties in four or five hours after quitting the pier. But the third man yet lay in his bunk, in the self-same posture in which his limbs had been adjusted by the crimp, who had deposited him there.

His name was down on the ship's papers as Miguel Saveda, and for Miguel Saveda the chief mate at last came forward, shouting down the forecastle scuttle, and commanding his instant presence on

---

* Stories of drunkards dying from spontaneous combustion were common in temperance literature. Melville may have read of such an incident in *Jacob Faithful* (1834) by Frederick Marryat. Dickens described such a death four years after *Redburn* in *Bleak House* (1853).

deck. But the sailors answered for their new comrade; giving the mate to understand that Miguel was still fast locked in his trance, and could not obey him; when, muttering his usual imprecation, the mate retired to the quarter-deck.

This was in the first dog-watch, from four to six in the evening. At about three bells, in the next watch, Max the Dutchman, who, like most old seamen, was something of a physician in cases of drunkenness, recommended that Miguel's clothing should be removed, in order that he should lie more comfortably. But Jackson, who would seldom let anything be done in the forecastle that was not proposed by himself, capriciously forbade this proceeding.

So the sailor still lay out of sight in his bunk, which was in the extreme angle of the forecastle, behind the *bowsprit bitts*—two stout timbers rooted in the ship's keel. An hour or two afterward, some of the men observed a strange odour in the forecastle, which was attributed to the presence of some dead rat among the hollow spaces in the side planks; for some days before, the forecastle had been smoked out, to extirpate the vermin overrunning her. At midnight, the larboard watch, to which I belonged turned out; and instantly as every man waked he exclaimed at the now intolerable smell, supposed to be heightened by the shaking up of the bilge-water from the ship's rolling.

'Blast that rat!' cried the Greenlander.

'He's blasted already,' said Jackson, who in his drawers had crossed over to the bunk of Miguel. 'It's a water-rat, shipmates, that's dead; and here he is,'—and with that he dragged forth the sailor's arm, exclaiming, 'Dead as a timber-head!'

Upon this the men rushed toward the bunk, Max with the light, which he held to the man's face.

'No, he's not dead,' he cried, as the yellow flame wavered for a moment at the seaman's motionless mouth. But hardly had the words escaped, when, to the silent horror of all, two threads of greenish fire, like a forked tongue, darted out between the lips: and in a moment the cadaverous face was crawled over by a swarm of worm-like flames.

The lamp dropped from the hand of Max, and went out; while covered all over with spires and sparkles of flame, that faintly crackled in the silence, the uncovered parts of the body burned before us, precisely like a phosphorescent shark in a midnight sea.

The eyes were open and fixed; the mouth was curled like a scroll, and every lean feature firm as in life; while the whole face, now wound in curls of soft blue flame, wore an aspect of grim defiance and eternal death. Prometheus, blasted by fire on the rock.

One arm, its red shirt-sleeve rolled up, exposed the man's name, tattooed in vermillion, near the hollow of the middle joint; and as if there was something peculiar in the painted flesh, every vibrating letter burned so white, that you might read the flaming name in the flickering ground of blue.

"Where's that d——d Miguel?' was now shouted down among us from the scuttle by the mate, who had just come on deck, and was determined to have every man up that belonged to his watch.

'He's gone to the harbour where they never weigh anchor,' coughed Jackson. 'Come you down, sir, and look.'

Thinking that Jackson intended to beard him, the mate sprang down in a rage; but recoiled at the burning body as if he had been shot by a bullet. 'My God!' he cried, and stood holding fast to the ladder.

'Take hold of it,' said Jackson at last, to the Greenlander; 'it must go overboard. Don't stand shaking there, like a dog; take hold of it, I say! But stop'—and smothering it all in the blankets, he pulled it partly out of the bunk.

A few minutes more, and it fell with a bubble among the phosphorescent sparkles of the damp night sea, leaving a coruscating wake as it sank.

This event thrilled me through and through with unspeakable horror; nor did the conversation of the watch during the next four hours on deck at all serve to soothe me.

But what most astonished me, and seemed most incredible, was the infernal opinion of Jackson, that the man had been actually dead when brought on board the ship; and that knowingly, and merely for the sake of the month's advance, paid into his hand upon the strength of the bill he presented, the body-snatching crimp had knowingly shipped a corpse on board of the *Highlander,* under the pretence of its being a live body in a drunken trance. And I heard Jackson say, that he had known of such things having been done before. But that a really dead body ever burned in that manner I cannot even yet believe. But the sailors seemed familiar with such things; or at least with the stories of such things having happened to others.

For me, who at that age had never so much as happened to hear of a case like this, of animal combustion, in the horrid mood that came over me, I almost thought the burning body was a premonition of the hell of the Calvinists, and that Miguel's earthly end was a foretaste of his eternal condemnation.

Immediately after the burial, an iron pot of red coals was placed in the bunk, and in it two handfuls of coffee were roasted. This done, the bunk was nailed up, and was never opened again during the voyage; and strict orders were given to the crew not to divulge what had taken place to the emigrants; but to this, they needed no commands.

After the event, no one sailor but Jackson would stay alone in the forecastle by night or by noon; and no more would they laugh or sing, or in any way make merry there, but kept all their pleasantries for the watches on deck. All but Jackson: who, while the rest would be sitting silently smoking on their chests, or in their bunks, would look toward the fatal spot, and cough, and laugh, and invoke the dead man with incredible scoffs and jeers. He froze my blood, and made my soul stand still.

The Last End of Jackson

'Off Cape Cod!' said the steward, coming forward from the quarter-deck, where the captain had just been taking his noon observation; sweeping the vast horizon with his quadrant, like a dandy circumnavigating the dress circle of an amphitheatre with his glass.

Off Cape Cod! and in the shore-bloom that came to us—even from that desert of sand-hillocks—methought I could almost distinguish the fragance of the rose-bush my sisters and I had planted, in our far inland garden at home. Delicious odours are those of our mother earth; which like a flower-pot set with a thousand shrubs, greets the eager voyager from afar.

The breeze was stiff, and so drove us along that we turned over two broad, blue furrows from our bows, as we ploughed the watery prairie. By night it was a reef-topsail breeze; but so impatient was the captain to make his port before a shift of wind overtook us, that even yet we carried a main-top-gallant-sail, though the light mast sprung like a switch.

In the second dog-watch, however, the breeze became such, that at last the order was given to douse the top-gallant-sail, and clap a reef into all three topsails.

While the men were settling away the halyards on deck, and before they had begun to haul out the reef-tackles, to the surprise of several, Jackson came up from the forecastle, and, for the first time in four weeks or more, took hold of a rope.

Like most seamen, who during the greater part of a voyage have been off duty from sickness, he was, perhaps, desirous, just previous to entering port, of reminding the captain of his existence, and also that he expected his wages; but, alas! his wages proved the wages of sin.

At no time could he better signalise his disposition to work than upon an occasion like the present; which generally attracts every soul on deck, from the captain to the child in the steerage.

His aspect was damp and death-like; the blue hollows of his eyes were like vaults full of snakes; and issuing so unexpectedly from his dark tomb in the forecastle, he looked like a man raised from the dead.

Before the sailors had made fast the reef-tackle, Jackson was tottering up the rigging; thus getting the start of them, and securing his place at the extreme weather-end of the topsail-yard—which in reefing is accounted the post of honour. For it was one of the characteristics of this man, that though when on duty he would shy away from mere dull work in a calm, yet in tempest-time he always claimed the van, and would yield it to none; and this, perhaps, was one cause of his unbounded dominion over the men.

Soon we were all strung along the main-topsail-yard; the ship rearing and plunging under us, like a runaway steed; each man gripping his reef-point, and sideways leaning, dragging the sail over toward Jackson, whose business it was to confine the reef corner to the yard.

His hat and shoes were off; and he rode the yard-arm end, leaning backward to the gale, and pulling at the earing-rope, like a bridle. At all times, this is a moment of frantic exertion with sailors, whose spirits seem then to partake of the commotion of the elements, as they hang in the gale, between heaven and earth; and *then* it is, too, that they are the most profane.

'Haul out to windward!' coughed Jackson, with a blasphemous cry, and he threw himself back with a violent strain upon the bridle in his hand. But the wild words were hardly out of his mouth when his hands dropped to his side, and the bellying sail was spattered with a torrent of blood from his lungs.

As the man next him stretched out his arm to save, Jackson fell headlong from the yard, and with a long seethe, plunged like a diver into the sea.

It was when the ship had rolled to windward, which with the long projection of the yard-arm over the side, made him strike far out upon the water. His fall was seen by the whole upward-gazing crowd on deck, some of whom were spotted with the blood that trickled from the sail, while they raised a spontaneous cry, so shrill and wild, that a blind man might have known something deadly had happened.

Clutching our reef-points, we hung over the stick and gazed down to the one white, bubbling spot, which had closed over the head of our shipmate; but the next minute it was brewed into the common yeast of the waves, and Jackson never arose. We waited a few minutes, expecting an order to descend, haul back the fore-yard, and man the boat; but instead of that, the next sound that greeted us was, 'Bear a hand, and reef away, men!' from the mate.

Indeed, upon reflection, it would have been idle to attempt to save Jackson; for besides that he must have been dead ere he struck the sea—and if he had not been dead then, the first immersion must have driven his soul from his lacerated lungs—our jolly-boat would have taken full fifteen minutes to launch into the waves.

And here it should be said that the thoughtless security in which too many sea-captains indulge would, in case of some sudden disaster befalling the *Highlander,* have let us drop into our graves.

Like most merchant ships, we had but two boats: the long-boat and the jolly-boat. The long-boat, by far the largest and stoutest of the two, was permanently bolted down to the deck, by iron bars attached to its sides. It was almost as much of a fixture as the vessel's keel. It was filled with pigs, fowls, firewood, and coals. Over this the jolly-boat was capsized without a *thole-pin* in the gunwales; its bottom bleaching and cracking in the sun.

Judge, then, what promise of salvation for us, had we shipwrecked; yet in this state one merchant ship out of three keeps its boats. To be sure, no vessel full of emigrants, by any possible precautions, could in case of a fatal disaster at sea hope to save the tenth part of the souls on board; yet provision should certainly be made for a handful of survivors, to carry home the tidings of her loss; for even in the worst of the calamities that befell patient Job, some *one* at least of his escaped to report it.

In a way that I never could fully account for, the sailors, in my hearing at least, and Harry's, never made the slightest allusion to the departed Jackson. One and all they seemed tacitly to unite in hushing up his memory among them. Whether it was that the severity of the bondage under which this man held every one of them did really corrode in their secret hearts, that they thought to repress the recollection of a thing so degrading, I cannot determine; but certain it was, that *his* death was *their* deliverance; which they celebrated by an elevation of spirits unknown before. Doubtless, this was to be in part imputed, however, to their now drawing near to their port.

STEPHEN CRANE

An Experiment in Misery

IT WAS LATE AT NIGHT, and a fine rain was swirling softly down, causing the pavements to glisten with hue of steel and blue and yellow in the rays of the innumerable lights. A youth was trudging slowly, without enthusiasm, with his hands buried deep in his trousers pockets, toward the downtown places where beds can be hired for coppers. He was clothed in an aged and tattered suit, and his derby was a marvel of dust-covered crown and torn rim. He was going forth to eat as the wanderer may eat, and sleep as the homeless sleep. By the time he had reached City Hall Park he was so completely plastered with yells of "bum" and "hobo," and with various unholy epithets that small boys had applied to him at intervals, that he was in a state of the most profound dejection. The sifting rain saturated the old velvet collar of his overcoat, and as the wet cloth pressed against his neck, he felt that there no longer could be pleasure in life. He looked about him searching for an outcast of highest degree that they two might share miseries, but the lights threw a quivering glare over rows and circles of deserted benches that glistened damply, showing patches of wet sod behind them. It seemed that their useful freights had fled on this night to better things. There were only squads of well-dressed Brooklyn people who swarmed toward the bridge.

The young man loitered about for a time and then went shuffling off down Park Row. In the sudden descent in style of the dress of the crowd he felt relief, and as if he were at last in his own country. He began to see tatters that matched his tatters. In Chatham Square there were aimless men strewn in front of saloons and lodging-houses, standing sadly, patiently, reminding one vaguely of the attitudes of chickens in a storm. He aligned himself with these men, and turned slowly to occupy himself with the flowing life of the great street.

From *The Work of Stephen Crane*, edited by Wilson Follett, XI, 21–34. (New York: Russell & Russell, 1963).

Through the mists of the cold and storming night, the cable cars went in silent procession, great affairs shining with red and brass, moving with formidable power, calm and irresistible, dangerful and gloomy, breaking silence only by the loud fierce cry of the gong. Two rivers of people swarmed along the sidewalks, spattered with black mud which made each shoe leave a scar-like impression. Overhead, elevated trains with a shrill grinding of the wheels stopped at the station, which upon its leg-like pillars seemed to resemble some monstrous kind of crab squatting over the street. The quick fat puffings of the engines could be heard. Down an alley there were sombre curtains of purple and black, on which street lamps dully glittered like embroidered flowers.

A saloon stood with a voracious air on a corner. A sign leaning against the front of the doorpost announced "Free hot soup to-night!" The swing doors, snapping to and fro like ravenous lips, made gratified smacks as the saloon gorged itself with plump men, eating with astounding and endless appetite, smiling in some indescribable manner as the men came from all directions like sacrifices to a heathenish superstition.

Caught by the delectable sign, the young man allowed himself to be swallowed. A bartender placed a schooner of dark and portentous beer on the bar. Its monumental form upreared until the froth atop was above the crown of the young man's brown derby.

"Soup over there, gents," said the bartender affably. A little yellow man in rags and the youth grasped their schooners and went with speed toward a lunch-counter, where a man with oily but imposing whiskers ladled genially from a kettle until he had furnished his two mendicants with a soup that was steaming hot, and in which there were little floating suggestions of chicken. The young man, sipping his broth, felt the cordiality expressed by the warmth of the mixture, and he beamed at the man with oily but imposing whiskers, who was presiding like a priest behind an altar. "Have some more, gents?" he inquired of the two sorry figures before him. The little yellow man accepted with a swift gesture, but the youth shook his head and went out, following a man whose wondrous seediness promised that he would have a knowledge of cheap lodging-houses.

On the sidewalk he accosted the seedy man. "Say, do you know a cheap place to sleep?"

The other hesitated for a time, gazing sideways. Finally he nodded in the direction of the street. "I sleep up there," he said, "when I've got the price."

"How much?"

"Ten cents."

The young man shook his head dolefully. "That's too rich for me."

At that moment there approached the two a reeling man in strange garments. His head was a fuddle of bushy hair and whiskers, from which his eyes peered with a guilty slant. In a close scrutiny it was possible to distinguish the cruel lines of a mouth which looked as if lips had just closed with satisfaction over some tender and piteous morsel. He appeared like an assassin steeped in crimes performed awkwardly.

But at this time his voice was tuned to the coaxing key of an affectionate puppy. He looked at the men with wheedling eyes, and began to sing a little melody for charity. "Say, gents, can't yeh give a poor feller a couple of cents t' get a bed? I got five, an' I gits anudder two I gits me a bed. Now, on th' square, gents, can't yeh jest gimme two cents t' git a bed? Now, yeh know how a respecterble gentlem'n feels when he's down on his luck, an' I——"

The seedy man, staring with imperturbable countenance at a train which clattered overhead, interrupted in an expressionless voice: "Ah, go t' hell!"

But the youth spoke to the prayerful assassin in tones of astonishment and inquiry. "Say, you must be crazy! Why don't yeh strike somebody that looks as if they had money?"

The assassin, tottering about on his uncertain legs, and at intervals brushing imaginary obstacles from before his nose, entered into a long explanation of the psychology of the situation. It was so profound that it was unintelligible.

When he had exhausted the subject, the young man said to him: "Let's see th' five cents."

The assassin wore an expression of drunken woe at this sentence, filled with suspicion of him. With a deeply pained air he began to fumble in his clothing, his red hands trembling. Presently he announced in a voice of bitter grief, as if he had been betrayed: "There's on'y four."

"Four," said the young man thoughtfully. "Well, look-a here, I'm a stranger here, an' if ye'll steer me to your cheap joint I'll find the other three."

The assassin's countenance became instantly radiant with joy. His whiskers quivered with the wealth of his alleged emotions. He seized the young man's hand in a transport of delight and friendliness.

"B' Gawd," he cried, "if ye'll do that, b'Gawd, I'd say yeh was a damned good fellow, I would, an' I'd remember yeh all m'life, I would, b' Gawd, an' if I ever got a chance I'd return the compliment"—he spoke with drunken dignity—"b'Gawd, I'd treat yeh white, I would, an' I'd allus remember yeh."

The young man drew back looking at the assassin coldly. "Oh, that's all right," he said. "You show me th' joint—that's all you've got t' do."

The assassin, gesticulating gratitude, led the young man along a dark street. Finally he stopped before a little dusty door. He raised his hand impressively. "Look-a here," he said, and there was a thrill of deep and ancient wisdom upon his face, "I've brought yeh here, an' that's my part, ain't it? If th' place don't suit yeh, yeh needn't git mad at me, need yeh? There won't be no bad feelin', will there?"

"No," said the young man.

The assassin waved his arm tragically, and led the march up the steep stairway. On the way the young man furnished the assassin with three pennies. At the top a man with benevolent spectacles looked at them through a hole in a board. He collected their money, wrote some names on a register, and speedily was leading the two men along a gloom-shrouded corridor.

Shortly after the beginning of this journey the young man felt his liver turn white, for from the dark and secret places of the building there suddenly came to his nostrils strange and unspeakable odours, that assailed him like malignant diseases with wings. They seemed to be from human bodies closely packed in dens; the exhalations from a hundred pairs of reeking lips; the fumes from a thousand bygone debauches; the expression of a thousand present miseries.

A man, naked save for a little snuff-coloured undershirt, was parading sleepily along the corridor. He rubbed his eyes and, giving vent to a prodigious yawn, demanded to be told the time.

"Half-past one."

The man yawned again. He opened a door, and for a moment his form was outlined against a black, opaque interior. To this door came the three men, and as it was again opened the unholy odours rushed out like fiends, so that the young man was obliged to struggle as against an overpowering wind.

It was some time before the youth's eyes were good in the intense gloom within, but the man with benevolent spectacles led him skilfully, pausing but a moment to deposit the limp assassin upon a cot. He took the youth to a cot that lay tranquilly by the window, and showing him a tall locker for clothes that stood near the head with the ominous air of a tombstone, left him.

The youth sat on his cot and peered about him. There was a gas-jet in a distant part of the room, that burned a small flickering orange-hued flame. It caused vast masses of tumbled shadows in all parts of the place, save where, immediately about it, there was a little grey haze. As the young man's eyes became used to the darkness, he could see upon the cots that thickly littered the floor the forms of men sprawled out, lying in death-like silence, or heaving and snoring with tremendous effort, like stabbed fish.

The youth locked his derby and his shoes in the mummy-case near him, and then lay down with an old and familiar coat around his shoulders. A blanket he handled gingerly, drawing it over part of the coat. The cot was covered with leather, and as cold as melting snow. The youth was obliged to shiver for some time on this affair, which was like a slab. Presently, however, his chill gave him peace, and during this period of leisure from it he turned his head to stare at his friend the assassin, whom he could dimly discern where he lay sprawled on a cot in the abandon of a man filled with drink. He was snoring with incredible vigour. His wet hair and beard dimly glistened, and his inflamed nose shone with subdued lustre like a red light in a fog.

Within reach of the youth's hand was one who lay with yellow breast and shoulders bare to the cold draughts. One arm hung over the side of the cot, and the fingers lay full length upon the wet cement floor of the room. Beneath the inky brows could be seen the eyes of the man, exposed by the partly opened lids. To the youth it seemed that he and this corpse-like being were exchanging a prolonged stare, and that the other threatened with his eyes. He drew back, watching his neighbour from the shadows of his blanket-edge. The man did not move once through the night, but lay in this stillness as of death like a body stretched out expectant of the surgeon's knife.

And all through the room could be seen the tawny hues of naked flesh, limbs thrust into the darkness, projecting beyond the cots; upreared knees, arms hanging long and thin over the cot-edges. For the most part they were statuesque, carven, dead. With the curious lockers standing all about like tombstones, there was a strange effect of a graveyard where bodies were merely flung.

Yet occasionally could be seen limbs wildly tossing in fantastic nightmare gestures, accompanied by guttural cries, grunts, oaths. And there was one fellow off in a gloomy corner, who in his dreams was oppressed by some frightful calamity, for of a sudden he began to utter long wails that went almost like yells from a hound, echoing wailfully and weird through this chill place of tombstones where men lay like the dead.

The sound, in its high piercing beginnings that dwindled to final melancholy moans, expressed a red and grim tragedy of the unfathomable possibilities of the man's dreams. But to the youth these were not merely the shrieks of a vision-pierced man: they were an utterance of the meaning of the room and its occupants. It was to him the protest of the wretch who feels the touch of the imperturbable granite wheels, and who then cries with an impersonal eloquence, with a strength not from him, giving voice to the wail of a whole section, a class, a people. This, weaving into the young man's brain, and mingling with his views of the vast and sombre shadows that, like mighty black fingers, curled around the naked bodies, made the young man so that he did not sleep, but lay carving the biographies for these men from his meagre experience. At times the fellow in the corner howled in a writhing agony of his imaginations.

Finally, a long lance-point of gray light shot through the dusty panes of the window. Without, the young man could see roofs drearily white in the dawning. The point of light yellowed and grew brighter, until the golden rays of the morning sun came in bravely and strong. They touched with radiant colour the form of a small fat man who snored in stuttering fashion. His round and shiny bald head glowed suddenly with the valour of a decoration. He sat up, blinked at the sun, swore fretfully, and pulled his blanket over the ornamental splendours of his head.

The youth contentedly watched this rout of the shadows before the bright spears of the sun, and presently he slumbered. When he awoke he heard the voice of the assassin raised in valiant curses. Putting up his head, he perceived his comrade seated on the side of the cot engaged in scratching his neck with long fingernails that rasped like files.

"Hully Jee, dis is a new breed. They've got can-openers on their feet." He continued in a violent tirade.

The young man hastily unlocked his closet and took out his shoes and hat. As he sat on the side of the cot lacing his shoes, he glanced about and saw that daylight had made the room comparatively commonplace and uninteresting. The men, whose faces seemed stolid, serene, or absent, were engaged in dressing, while a great crackle of bantering conversation arose.

A few were parading in unconcerned nakedness. Here and there were men of brawn, whose skins shone clear and ruddy. They took splendid poses, standing massively like chiefs. When they had dressed in their ungainly garments there was an extraordinary change. They then showed bumps and deficiencies of all kinds.

There were others who exhibited many deformities. Shoulders were slanting, humped, pulled this way and pulled that way. And notable among these latter men was the little fat man who had refused to allow his head to be glorified. His pudgy form, builded like a pear, bustled to and fro, while he swore in fishwife fashion. It appeared that some article of his apparel had vanished.

The young man attired himself speedily, and went to his friend the assassin. At first the latter looked dazed at the sight of the youth. This face seemed to be appealing to him through the cloud-wastes of his memory. He scratched his neck and reflected. At last he grinned, a broad smile gradually spreading until his countenance was a round illumination. "Hello, Willie," he cried cheerily.

"Hello," said the young man. "Are yeh ready t' fly?"

"Sure." The assassin tied his shoe carefully with some twine and came ambling.

When he reached the street the young man experienced no sudden relief from unholy atmospheres. He had forgotten all about them, and had been breathing naturally, and with no sensation of discomfort or distress.

He was thinking of these things as he walked along the street, when he was suddenly startled by feeling the assassin's hand, trembling with excitement, clutching his arm, and when the assassin spoke, his voice went into quavers from a supreme agitation.

"I'll be hully, bloomin' blowed if there wasn't a feller with a nightshirt on up there in that joint."

The youth was bewildered for a moment, but presently he turned to smile indulgently at the assassin's humour. "Oh, you're a damned liar," he merely said.

Whereupon the assassin began to gesture extravagantly and take oath by strange gods. He frantically placed himself at the mercy of remarkable fates if his tale were not true. "Yes, he did! I cross m'heart thousan' times!" he protested, and at the moment his eyes were large with amazement, his mouth wrinkled in unnatural glee. "Yessir! A nightshirt! A hully white nightshirt!"

"You lie!"

"No, sir!" I hope ter die b'fore I kin get anudder ball if there wasn't a jay wid a hully, bloomin' white nightshirt!"

His face was filled with the infinite wonder of it. "A hully white nightshirt," he continually repeated.

The young man saw the dark entrance to a basement restaurant. There was a sign which read "No mystery about our hash!" and there were other age-stained and world-battered legends which told him that the place was within his means. He stopped before it and spoke to the assassin. "I guess I'll get somethin' t' eat."

At this the assassin, for some reason, appeared to be quite embarrassed. He gazed at the seductive front of the eating-place for a moment. Then he started slowly up the street. "Well, good-bye, Willie," he said bravely.

For an instant the youth studied the departing figure. Then he called out, "Hol' on a minnet." As they came together he spoke in a certain fierce way, as if he feared that the other would think him to be charitable. "Look-a here, if yeh wanta git some breakfas' I'll lend yeh three cents t' do it with. But say, look-a here, you've gotta git out an' hustle. I ain't goin' t' support yeh, or I'll go broke b'fore night. I ain't no millionaire."

"I take me oath, Willie," said the assassin earnestly, "th' on'y thing I really needs is a ball. Me t'roat feels like a fryin'-pan. But as I can't get a ball, why, th' next bes' thing is breakfast, an' if yeh do that for me, b' Gawd, I say yeh was th' whitest lad I ever see."

They spent a few moments in dexterous exchanges of phrases, in which they each protested that the other was, as the assassin had originally said, "a respecterble gentlem'n." And they concluded with mutual assurances that they were the souls of intelligence and virtue. Then they went into the restaurant.

There was a long counter, dimly lighted from hidden sources. Two or three men in soiled white aprons rushed here and there.

The youth bought a bowl of coffee for two cents and a roll for one cent. The assassin purchased the same. The bowls were webbed with brown seams, and the tin spoons wore an air of having emerged from the first pyramid. Upon them were black moss-like encrustations of age, and they were bent and scarred from the attacks of long-forgotten teeth. But over their repast the wanderers waxed warm and mellow. The assassin grew affable as the hot mixture went soothingly down his parched throat, and the young man felt courage flow in his veins.

Memories began to throng in on the assassin, and he brought forth long tales, intricate, incoherent, delivered with a chattering swiftness as from an old woman. "—great job out'n Orange. Boss keep yeh hustlin', though, all time. I was there three days, and then I went an' ask 'im t' lend me a dollar. 'G-g-go ter the devil,' he says, an' I lose me job.

"South no good. Damn niggers work for twenty-five an' thirty cents a day. Run white man out. Good grub, though. Easy livin'.

"Yas; useter work little in Toledo, raftin' logs. Make two or three dollars er day in the spring. Lived high. Cold as ice, though, in the winter.

"I was raised in northern N'York. O-o-oh, yeh jest ought to live there. No beer ner whisky, though, 'way off in the woods. But all th' good hot grub yeh can eat. B' Gawd, I hung around there long as I could till th' ol' man fired me. "Git t' hell outa here, yeh wuthless skunk, git t' hell outa here, an' go die,' he says. "You're a hell of a father," I says, 'you are,' an' I quit 'im."

As they were passing from the dim eating place, they encountered an old man who was trying to steal forth with a tiny package of food, but a tall man with an indomitable moustache stood dragon-fashion, barring the way of escape. They heard the old man raise a plaintive protest. "Ah, you always want to know what I take out, and you never see that I usually bring a package in here from my place of business."

As the wanderers trudged slowly along Park Row, the assassin began to expand and grow blithe. "B' Gawd, we've been livin' like kings," he said, smacking appreciative lips.

"Look out, or we'll have t' pay fer it t'-night," said the youth with gloomy warning.

But the assassin refused to turn his gaze toward the future. He went with a limping step, into which he injected a suggestion of lamb-like gambols. His mouth was wreathed in a red grin.

In City Hall Park the two wanderers sat down in the little circle of benches sanctified by traditions of their class. They huddled in their old garments, slumbrously conscious of the march of the hours which for them had no meaning.

The people of the street hurrying hither and thither made a blend of black figures, changing, yet frieze-like. They walked in their good clothes as upon important missions, giving no gaze to the two wanderers seated upon the benches. They expressed to the young man his infinite distance from all that he valued. Social position, comfort, the pleasures of living were unconquerable kingdoms. He felt a sudden awe.

And in the background a multitude of buildings, of pitiless hues and sternly high, were to him emblematic of a nation forcing its regal head into the clouds, throwing no downward glances; in the sublimity of its aspirations ignoring the wretches who may flounder at its feet. The roar of the city in his ear was to him the confusion of strange tongues, babbling heedlessly; it was the click of coin, the voice of the city's hopes, which were to him no hopes.

He confessed himself an outcast, and his eyes from under the lowered rim of his hat began to glance guiltily, wearing the criminal expression that comes with certain convictions.

SHERWOOD ANDERSON

I Want to Know Why

WE GOT UP at four in the morning, that first day in the east.
On the evening before we had climbed off a freight train at the edge
of town, and with the true instinct of Kentucky boys had found our
way across town and to the race track and the stables at once. Then
we knew we were all right. Hanley Turner right away found a nigger
we knew. It was Bildad Johnson who in the winter works at Ed
Becker's livery barn in our home town, Beckersville. Bildad is a good
cook as almost all our niggers are and of course he, like everyone in
our part of Kentucky who is anyone at all, likes the horses. In the
spring Bildad begins to scratch around. A nigger from our country
can flatter and wheedle anyone into letting him do most anything
he wants. Bildad wheedles the stable men and the trainers from the
horse farms in our country around Lexington. The trainers come
into town in the evening to stand around and talk and maybe get
into a poker game. Bildad gets in with them. He is always doing
little favors and telling about things to eat, chicken browned in a
pan, and how is the best way to cook sweet potatoes and corn bread.
It makes your mouth water to hear him.

When the racing season comes on and the horses go to the races
and there is all the talk on the streets in the evenings about the new
colts, and everyone says when they are going over to Lexington or to
the spring meeting at Churchhill Downs or to Latonia, and the
horsemen that have been down to New Orleans or maybe at the
winter meeting at Havana in Cuba come home to spend a week before they start out again, at such a time when everything talked
about in Beckersville is just horses and nothing else and the outfits
start out and horse racing is in every breath of air you breathe, Bildad shows up with a job as cook for some outfit. Often when I think
about it, his always going all season to the races and working in the
livery barn in the winter where horses are and where men like to

From Sherwood Anderson, *The Triumph of the Egg.* (New York: B. W. Huebsch,
1921), pp. 5–20. First published in *Smart Set*, November, 1919.

come and talk about horses. I wish I was a nigger. It's a foolish thing to say, but that's the way I am about being around horses, just crazy. I can't help it.

Well, I must tell you about what we did and let you in on what I'm talking about. Four of us boys from Beckersville, all whites and sons of men who live in Beckersville regular, made up our minds we were going to the races, not just to Lexington or Louisville, I don't mean, but to the big eastern track we were always hearing our Beckersville men talk about, to Saratoga. We were all pretty young then. I was just turned fifteen and I was the oldest of the four. It was my scheme. I admit that and I talked the others into trying it. There was Hanley Turner and Henry Rieback and Tom Tumberton and myself. I had thirty-seven dollars I had earned during the winter working nights and Saturdays in Enoch Myer's grocery. Henry Rieback had eleven dollars and the others, Hanley and Tom had only a dollar or two each. We fixed it all up and laid low until the Kentucky spring meetings were over and some of our men, the sportiest ones, the ones we envied the most, had cut out—then we cut out too.

I won't tell you the trouble we had beating our way on freights and all. We went through Cleveland and Buffalo and other cities and saw Niagara Falls. We bought things there, souvenirs and spoons and cards and shells with pictures of the falls on them for our sisters and mothers, but thought we had better not send any of the things home. We didn't want to put the folks on our trail and maybe be nabbed.

We got into Saratoga as I said at night and went to the track. Bildad fed us up. He showed us a place to sleep in hay over a shed and promised to keep still. Niggers are all right about things like that. They won't squeal on you. Often a white man you might meet, when you had run away from home like that, might appear to be all right and give you a quarter or a half dollar or something, and then go right and give you away. White men will do that, but not a nigger. You can trust them. They are squarer with kids. I don't know why.

At the Saratoga meeting that year there were a lot of men from home. Dave Williams and Arthur Mulford and Jerry Myers and others. Then there was a lot from Louisville and Lexington Henry Rieback knew but I didn't. They were professional gamblers and Henry Rieback's father is one too. He is what is called a sheet writer and goes away most of the year to tracks. In the winter when he is home in Beckersville he don't stay there much but goes away to cities and deals faro. He is a nice man and generous, is always sending Henry presents, a bicycle and a gold watch and a boy scout suit of clothes and things like that.

My own father is a lawyer. He's all right, but don't make much money and can't buy me things and anyway I'm getting so old now I don't expect it. He never said nothing to me against Henry, but Hanley Turner and Tom Tumberton's fathers did. They said to their boys that money so come by is no good and they didn't want their boys brought up to hear gamblers' talk and be thinking about such things and maybe embrace them.

That's all right and I guess the men know what they are talking about, but I don't see what it's got to do with Henry or with horses either. That's what I'm writing this story about. I'm puzzled. I'm getting to be a man and want to think straight and be O.K., and there's something I saw at the race meeting at the eastern track I can't figure out.

I can't help it, I'm crazy about thoroughbred horses. I've always been that way. When I was ten years old and saw I was growing to be big and couldn't be a rider I was so sorry I nearly died. Harry Hellinfinger in Beckersville, whose father is Postmaster, is grown up and too lazy to work, but likes to stand around in the street and get up jokes on boys like sending them to a hardware store for a gimlet to bore square holes and other jokes like that. He played one on me. He told me that if I would eat a half a cigar I would be stunted and not grow any more and maybe could be a rider. I did it. When father wasn't looking I took a cigar out of his pocket and gagged it down some way. It made me awful sick and the doctor had to be sent for, and then it did no good. I kept right on growing. It was a joke. When I told what I had done and why most fathers would have whipped me but mine didn't.

Well I didn't get stunted and didn't die. It serves Harry Hellinfinger right. Then I made up my mind I would like to be a stable boy, but had to give that up too. Mostly niggers do that work and I knew father wouldn't let me go into it. No use to ask him.

If you've never been crazy about thoroughbreds it's because you've never been around where they are much and don't know any better. They're beautiful. There isn't anything so lovely and clean and full of spunk and honest and everything as some race horses. On the big horse farms that are all around our town Beckersville there are tracks and the horses run in the early morning. More than a thousand times I've got out of bed before daylight and walked two or three miles to the tracks. Mother wouldn't of let me go but father always says, "Let him alone." So I got some bread out of the bread box and some butter and jam, gobbled it and lit out.

At the tracks you sit on the fence with men, whites and niggers, and they chew tobacco and talk, and then the colts are brought out. It's early and the grass is covered with shiny dew and in another

field a man is plowing and they are frying things in a shed where
the track niggers sleep, and you know how a nigger can giggle and
laugh and say things that make you laugh. A white man can't do it
and some niggers can't but a track nigger can every time.

And so the colts are brought out and some are just galloped by
stable boys, but almost every morning on a big track owned by a
rich man who lives maybe in New York, there are always, nearly
every morning, a few colts and some of the old race horses and geldings and mares that are cut loose.

It brings a lump up into my throat when a horse runs. I don't
mean all horses but some. I can pick them nearly every time. It's in
my blood like in the blood of race track niggers and trainers. Even
when they just go slop-jogging along with a little nigger on their
backs I can tell a winner. If my throat hurts and it's hard for me to
swallow, that's him. He'll run like Sam Hill when you let him out.
If he don't win every time it'll be a wonder and because they've got
him in a pocket behind another or he was pulled or got off bad at
the post or something. If I wanted to be a gambler like Henry Rieback's father I could get rich. I know I could and Henry says so too.
All I would have to do is to wait 'til that hurt comes when I see a
horse and then bet every cent. That's what I would do if I wanted
to be a gambler, but I don't.

When you're at the tracks in the morning—not the race tracks but
the training tracks around Beckersville—you don't see a horse, the
kind I've been talking about, very often, but it's nice anyway. Any
thoroughbred, that is sired right and out of a good mare and
trained by a man that knows how, can run. If he couldn't what
would he be there for and not pulling a plow?

Well, out of the stables they come and the boys are on their backs
and it's lovely to be there. You hunch down on top of the fence and
itch inside you. Over in the sheds the niggers giggle and sing. Bacon
is being fried and coffee made. Everything smells lovely. Nothing
smells better than coffee and manure and horses and niggers and
bacon frying and pipes being smoked out of doors on a morning
like that. It just gets you, that's what it does.

But about Saratoga. We was there six days and not a soul from
home seen us and everything came off just as we wanted it to, fine
weather and horses and races and all. We beat our way home and
Bildad gave us a basket with fried chicken and bread and other
eatables in, and I had eighteen dollars when we got back to Beckersville. Mother jawed and cried but Pop didn't say much. I told everything we done except one thing. I did and saw that alone. That's
what I'm writing about. It got me upset. I think about it at night.
Here it is.

At Saratoga we laid up nights in the hay in the shed Bildad had showed us and ate with the niggers early and at night when the race people had all gone away. The men from home stayed mostly in the grandstand and betting field, and didn't come out around the places where the horses are kept except to the paddocks just before a race when the horses are saddled. At Saratoga they don't have paddocks under an open shed as at Lexington and Churchill Downs and other tracks down in our country, but saddle the horses right out in an open place under trees on a lawn as smooth and nice as Banker Bohon's front yard here in Beckersville. It's lovely. The horses are sweaty and nervous and shine and the men come out and smoke cigars and look at them and the trainers are there and the owners, and your heart thumps so you can hardly breathe.

Then the bugle blows for post and the boys that ride come running out with their silk clothes on and you run to get a place by the fence with the niggers.

I always am wanting to be a trainer or owner, and at the risk of being seen and caught and sent home I went to the paddocks before every race. The other boys didn't but I did.

We got to Saratoga on a Friday and on Wednesday the next week the big Mullford Handicap was to be run. Middlestride was in it and Sunstreak. The weather was fine and the track fast. I couldn't sleep the night before.

What had happened was that both these horses are the kind it makes my throat hurt to see. Middlestride is long and looks awkward and is a gelding. He belongs to Joe Thompson, a little owner from home who only has a half dozen horses. The Mullford Handicap is for a mile and Middlestride can't untrack fast. He goes away slow and is always way back at the half, then he begins to run and if the race is a mile and a quarter he'll just eat up everything and get there.

Sunstreak is different. He is a stallion and nervous and belongs on the biggest farm we've got in our country, the Van Riddle place that belongs to Mr. Van Riddle of New York. Sunstreak is like a girl you think about sometimes but never see. He is hard all over and lovely too. When you look at his head you want to kiss him. He is trained by Jerry Tillford who knows me and has been good to me lots of times, lets me walk into a horse's stall to look at him close and other things. There isn't anything as sweet as that horse. He stands at the post quiet and not letting on, but he is just burning up inside. Then when the barrier goes up he is off like his name, Sunstreak. It makes you ache to see him. It hurts you. He just lays down and runs like a bird dog. There can't anything I ever see run like him except Middlestride when he gets untracked and stretches himself.

Gee! I ached to see that race and those two horses run, ached and

dreaded it too. I didn't want to see either of our horses beaten. We
had never sent a pair like that to the races before. Old men in Beckersville said so and the niggers said so. It was a fact.

Before the race I went over to the paddocks to see. I looked a last
look at Middlestride, who isn't such a much standing in a paddock
that way, then I went to see Sunstreak.

It was his day. I knew when I see him. I forgot all about being
seen myself and walked right up. All the men from Beckersville
were there and no one noticed me except Jerry Tillford. He saw me
and something happened. I'll tell you about that.

I was standing looking at that horse and aching. In some way, I
can't tell how, I knew just how Sunstreak felt inside. He was quiet
and letting the niggers rub his legs and Mr. Van Riddle himself put
the saddle on, but he was just a raging torrent inside. He was like
the water in the river at Niagara Falls just before its goes plunk
down. That horse wasn't thinking about running. He don't have to
think about that. He was just thinking about holding himself back
'til the time for the running came. I knew that. I could just in a
way see right inside him. He was going to do some awful running
and I knew it. He wasn't bragging or letting on much or prancing
or making a fuss, but just waiting. I knew it and Jerry Tillford his
trainer knew. I looked up and then that man and I looked into each
other's eyes. Something happened to me. I guess I loved the man as
much as I did the horse because he knew what I knew. Seemed to
me there wasn't anything in the world but that man and the horse
and me. I cried and Jerry Tillford had a shine in his eyes. Then I
came away to the fence to wait for the race. The horse was better
than me, more steadier, and now I know better than Jerry. He was
the quietest and he had to do the running.

Sunstreak ran first of course and he busted the world's record for
a mile. I've seen that if I never see anything more. Everthing came
out just as I expected. Middlestride got left at the post and was way
back and closed up to be second, just as I knew he would. He'll get
a world's record too some day. They can't skin the Beckersville country on horses.

I watched the race calm because I knew what would happen. I
was sure. Hanley Turner and Henry Rieback and Tom Tumberton
were all more excited than me.

A funny thing had happened to me. I was thinking about Jerry
Tillford the trainer and how happy he was all through the race. I
liked him that afternoon even more than I ever liked my own father. I almost forgot the horses thinking that way about him. It was
because of what I had seen in his eyes as he stood in the paddocks
beside Sunstreak before the race started. I knew he had been watch-

ing and working with Sunstreak since the horse was a baby colt, had taught him to run and be patient and when to let himself out and not to quit, never. I knew that for him it was like a mother seeing her child do something brave or wonderful. It was the first time I ever felt for a man like that.

After the race that night I cut out from Tom and Hanley and Henry. I wanted to be by myself and I wanted to be near Jerry Tillford if I could work it. Here is what happened.

The track in Saratoga is near the edge of town. It is all polished up and trees around, the evergreen kind, and grass and everything painted and nice. If you go past the track you get to a hard road made of asphalt for automobiles, and if you go along this for a few miles there is a road turns off to a little rummy-looking farm house set in a yard.

That night after the race I went along that road because I had seen Jerry and some other men go that way in an automobile. I didn't expect to find them. I walked for a ways and then sat down by a fence to think. It was the direction they went in. I wanted to be as near Jerry as I could. I felt close to him. Pretty soon I went up the side road—I don't know why—and came to the rummy farm house. I was just lonesome to see Jerry, like wanting to see your father at night when you are a young kid. Just then an automobile came along and turned in. Jerry was in it and Henry Rieback's father, and Arthur Bedford from home, and Dave Williams and two other men I didn't know. They got out of the car and went into the house, all but Henry Rieback's father who quarreled with them and said he wouldn't go. It was only about nine o'clock, but they were all drunk and the rummy looking farm house was a place for bad women to stay in. That's what it was. I crept up along a fence and looked through a window and saw.

It's what give me the fantods. I can't make it out. The women in the house were all ugly mean-looking women, not nice to look at or be near. They were homely too, except one who was tall and looked a little like the gelding Middlestride, but not clean like him, but with a hard ugly mouth. She had red hair. I saw everything plain. I got up by an old rose bush by an open window and looked. The women had on loose dresses and sat around in chairs. The men came in and some sat on the women's laps. The place smelled rotten and there was rotten talk, the kind a kid hears around a livery stable in a town like Beckersville in the winter but don't ever expect to hear talked when there are women around. It was rotten. A nigger wouldn't go into such a place.

I looked at Jerry Tillford. I've told you how I had been feeling about him on account of his knowing what was going on inside of

Sunstreak in the minute before he went to the post for the race in which he made a world's record.

Jerry bragged in that bad woman house as I know Sunstreak wouldn't never have bragged. He said that he made that horse, that it was him that won the race and made the record. He lied and bragged like a fool. I never heard such silly talk.

And then, what do you suppose he did! He looked at the woman in there, the one that was lean and hardmouthed and looked a little like the gelding Middlestride, but not clean like him, and his eyes began to shine just as they did when he looked at me and at Sunstreak in the paddocks at the track in the afternoon. I stood there by the window—gee!—but I wished I hadn't gone away from the tracks, but had stayed with the boys and the niggers and the horses. The tall rotten looking woman was between us just as Sunstreak was in the paddocks in the afternoon.

Then, all of a sudden, I began to hate that man. I wanted to scream and rush in the room and kill him. I never had such a feeling before. I was so mad clean through that I cried and my fists were doubled up so my finger nails cut my hands.

And Jerry's eyes kept shining and he waved back and forth, and then he went and kissed that woman and I crept away and went back to the tracks and to bed and didn't sleep hardly any, and then next day I got the other kids to start home with me and never told them anything I seen.

I been thinking about it ever since. I can't make it out. Spring has come again and I'm nearly sixteen and go to the tracks mornings same as always, and I see Sunstreak and Middlestride and a new colt named Strident I'll bet will lay them all out, but no one thinks so but me and two or three niggers.

But things are different. At the tracks the air don't taste as good or smell as good. It's because a man like Jerry Tillford, who knows what he does, could see a horse like Sunstreak run, and kiss a woman like that the same day. I can't make it out. Darn him, what did he want to do like that for? I keep thinking about it and it spoils looking at horses and smelling things and hearing niggers laugh and everything. Sometimes I'm so mad about it I want to fight someone. It gives me the fantods. What did he do it for? I want to know why.

JO PAGANO

The Disinherited

IT WAS PRETTY DARK by the time I got to the jungle, a mile or so
outside of town. Walking along the tracks, I could see the flare of
the fire rising above the edge of the gully, and I could hear the mutter
of men's voices. I stepped to the edge of the gully and looked down.
Heads and eyes turned up to me. There were perhaps a dozen men
around the fire, including a couple of kids not over fifteen years old.
I felt the quick, sharp appraisal of scrutinizing eyes as I made my
way down to them. A five-gallon oil can was set on an oven of rocks
over the fire, and I could smell the pungent odor of cooking stew.
Bent over the can was a big red-headed man with a scar running
down his right cheek. I went up to him and held out the spuds and
the one onion I had lifted off the Jap's wagon back in town.

"Have you got enough spuds?" I said, with a mild attempt at joc-
ularity.

He looked at the spuds and then at me.

"Put 'em in," he said.

I pulled out my pocket-knife and peeled the spuds and the onion,
then cut them up and threw them into the can. Then I sat down on
the ground with my back against a big rock. The smell of the stew
made my stomach jump. I hadn't eaten since morning.

Pretty soon it was ready and we all crowded around. The two kids
hung in the background. They had white, hungry faces beneath
their grime, and I felt sorry for them. We heaped the stew on whatever we had to hold it with, tin cans, cups—some of the old-timers
had army plates that they put away very carefully in their bundles
after the meal—and sat down to eat. The stew had a sour taste but I
wolfed it down. What did I care how it tasted? This time tomorrow
I would be home.

After we had eaten—I could have eaten more, but there was nothing more to eat—we washed out the big can and cached it back of
some rocks. I rolled a cigarette and leaned back against the rock and

From *Scribner's Magazine*, XCIV (November, 1933), 293–298.

looked the other men over. They did not differ essentially from a thousand men I had looked at in jungles and on freights and in flop-houses during the past year. All men who are on the bum have a certain general similarity, regardless of their individual differences. They have all a lean, sullen look about them, and this lean sullenness stamps them like a label. In this group I was looking at now there were, besides the two kids and the scar-faced man, a gaunt old fellow with gray hair and the face of a grocer, a skinny, pimply-faced youth with a couple of teeth missing out of the front of his mouth, two or three Mexicans, a big Negro with his chin all broken out in sores, and a hatchet-faced man whom I immediately recognized to be what is known, among men on the bum, as a wolf. A wolf is a man who picks up young boys on the road, for various reasons it is not necessary to go into here. There are hundreds of wolves on the road, and there are thousands of boys who fall prey to them. I mention these things because I want to give a true picture of that group around the fire. It would be easy to make them sound colorful and picturesque. The truth of it is, there was nothing colorful or picturesque or poetic about them. They were just a gang of hungry and filthy men banded together like the remnants of some bedraggled, defeated army; and in their faces you could read the story of malnutrition and desperation, of viciousness and hardship and disease.

I turned my face from them and, lying on my back, folded my hands beneath my head and looked at the stars. And I thought of home. For a year I had been on the bum and now I was sick of it, and I was going home. In that year I had gone a long, long way from home—oh, not so much in actual distance, though I had covered plenty of miles at that. But home is a place that means something clean and decent and sweet, and I had gone a long way from those things in the year I had been away. And now I was going back. For months I had ached to return home, and I had fought against the desire, but now I could not hold out any longer. I lay there and looked at the stars and thought of home, and I said to myself: "What's the use? What's the use of going back there?" But something inside of me refused to listen to all the reasons why I could not go back. I kept saying to myself: "I am going home," and I saw my mother and sister before me, and a warm happy feeling poured through me.

A whistle floated out over the tracks.

"There she is."

We all got up except those who were heading north. The two kids, the big Negro, the wolf, and a couple of others stayed. As we went up the side of the gully I glanced back and saw the kids looking up at us, their faces red in the firelight. One of them waved. I waved back and ran down the tracks toward the water-tank, raising my coat-collar against the wind.

II

As luck would have it, we found an open box-car and piled inside. I curled up in a corner and went to sleep almost immediately. I woke up with the dawn slipping in through the crack in the door. The men were sprawled out all over the car, and I could smell the close, sour smell of their bodies, and I could hear snores and wheezes from chapped, open lips. I went to the door and looked outside. We were coming down through Glendale. Morning hung like a mist over houses, and once I saw a milk-wagon turning the corner of a street. It seemed strange to see these houses and streets and the milk-wagon, to know that life still went on in houses, that people still slept in beds and had fresh milk delivered to their doors.

The sun was well up by the time we pulled into Los Angeles, and you could hear roosters crowing and you could see people moving about in yards and houses. The freight was pulling in slowly and I dropped off it as we were going beneath a bridge in the north end of town. Up above the bridge was a park, wet and green beneath the sun, and at the base of a road that wound up through the park was a red and white service station. I went into the toilet and washed my hands and face good and clean and then shaved. After I had shaved I felt a lot better, and shivers of excitement were darting through me as I started for home.

But when I turned into our street my legs got suddenly weak and I ducked back of a tree and rolled a cigarette. There was still time to turn back. I could see the lawn and the front of the house and my heart started pounding. At last I threw the cigarette down and started for the house, walking quickly so that I would get there before I lost my nerve. The front door was open but the screen was latched. I rang the bell. In a couple of seconds footsteps came down the hall. It was my sister, Louise.

"Bill!" she cried, fumbling at the latch and throwing the door open.

"Hello, sis," I said, trying to act calm.

"Bill!" she repeated, her voice catching; then suddenly she threw her arms about me. My throat choked up and I blinked my eyes to hold back the tears.

"Where's mother?"

"In the kitchen. Mamma, mamma!"

"Yes dear; what is it?"

"It's Bill, mamma. Bill's come home!"

"Bill? Bill?"

She came running out into the hall wiping her hands on her apron, her hair bouncing over her ears.

"Oh, my boy, my darling boy!" she moaned, throwing her arms about me and holding me close. She was crying and Louise was sniffling and I felt hot tears flooding my own eyes.

"Where have you been? Why didn't you write? Have you been sick?"

"No, I'm all right," I said, wiping my eyes on my sleeve. "Please don't cry, mom. What's the use of me coming home if you're going to act like that?"

"Oh! You look so thin. Are you hungry?"

"No," I lied. "But I'm a little tired," I added. "Have you got any coffee?"

We went into the kitchen. My mother had got a lot older in the year I had been away. Her hair was almost completely gray, now, and her forehead was full of wrinkles. And there was something else, too, a kind of uncertainty about her that I had never seen before. Suddenly I realized that my mother had become an old woman, and there was something strange and unfamiliar about her.

And not only she had changed. The house itself seemed different. The furniture was the same, and the rooms were the same rooms I used to know, but yet some indefinable change had taken place in the house, and I could not understand exactly what it was, but it was like something that is dying. The furniture was getting old now —the kitchen table was badly scratched and the tile on the sink had a big crack running through its side; the window curtains looked a little shabby, and the plaster on the wall above the stove was peeling badly. My mother had on an old dress, and her apron looked as if it had been washed and re-washed until the very grain in the cloth was visible. And even Louise looked old and worn. She is only twenty-two, but she looked at least twenty-six or seven. She was considerably thinner than she used to be and her hair was not kept as pretty as she used to keep it. Louise had always been proud of her hair, I remembered; but now it was done up with a couple of pins in the back and the short hairs on her neck looked unkempt. She had no makeup on and her face looked dry and sallow, and her lips chapped. And her eyes were nervous and uncertain too: she kept looking away from me, as though ashamed that I should see her like this, and at the same time there was something defensive in her attitude, as if she were saying: "Well, I can't help it, can I?"

My mother sat beside me at the table while Louise heated the coffee, and all the time I felt this strange thing that was like death in the house. It was a horrible sensation and I kept trying to fight it off. I kept trying to feel happy that I was home, that I was seeing my mother and sister again, but I did not feel happy. I could hardly look at my mother. I looked everywhere but at her and I felt so awkward and self-conscious that I wanted to get up and run out. But I sat there at the table and tried to whip up some response. I tried again and again to feel "I'm home."

"How's dad?" I asked my mother.

"He's—all right."

"Is he still working for McClelland?"

"Yes."

"Well, that's good. It's better than nothing."

I had some bread and butter with the coffee and then went up-stairs to take a bath. I wanted to get out of their sight as quickly as possible, but my mother came upstairs with me. In my room she pulled open a drawer of the dresser and I saw my shirts, all washed and ironed. I glanced at her standing there beside the dresser look-ing up at me with that dazed, fumbling look in her eyes, and a sick feeling went over me. I wanted to say something—anything, to break this horrible strangeness I felt toward her; but I could not think of anything to say. I put my arm around her shoulder.

"Thanks, mom."

"Your suit is hanging in the closet," she said. "I fixed the lining, so it's all right to wear. If there's anything else you want, just call. I'll be waiting downstairs."

She kissed me—a little uncertainly, as if she were not quite sure whether I would welcome the caress—and went out.

The hot-water knob in the bathtub was broken off at one side and I wondered if things were so bad they couldn't even afford to buy a water-knob. Things couldn't be that bad. But still, the old man wasn't making much, and he owed everybody in town, and there was a mortgage on the house. I looked at the broken knob and felt ashamed of myself. I ought to be home helping. That's what other people would say about me, and that was what, standing looking at the knob, I said about myself; but out of twelve months before I left home I had worked exactly six weeks. I hadn't brought in enough to pay for my own board, let alone help the folks out. It was almost impossible to find work. And what little work I did find was all tem-porary; a day here, a day there. If I remember right, I made about forty dollars in something like eight months. I had looked every-where for work, and I would have done anything. It is hard, I know, for those who have not confronted such a situation to realize that it can be possible for a man to want work and still not be able to find it. I have heard people say: "If these men really wanted work they could find it." On the bum I have gone to houses and asked to work for a meal and people have looked at me as if I were a criminal because I didn't have a job. Jesus Christ, they must think we like to live like stinking hungry rats.

It looked funny to see myself in regular clothes again. The suit looked as if it didn't belong on me. My neck stuck up skinnily out of the shirt collar, and my hands seemed twice as big as they ought to be, and my knuckles looked like walnuts. Sun and wind had burned my face to a dark, rough brown, and my hair was bleached almost yellow in spots and the skin along the edge of my ears was rough and red. In my overalls these things weren't so noticeable, but in this regular suit and white shirt I looked like a monkey in store clothes. I started to laugh, but suddenly I did not feel like laughing.

I turned and was about to start out of the room when I noticed my books, stuck in the book-case beside the bed. The moment I saw them Janice bubbled to my mind, as if she had been waiting to be remembered. I stood stock-still and looked at the books. I wanted to go over and take out my old "Piersol's Anatomy" and run through it, but forced myself not to. There was no use, I thought, in rubbing it in. I looked at the books for a moment longer, then closed the door softly and went downstairs. There was one thing more I had to do, now that I was home.

III

It took me about a half-hour to get out to the U. I borrowed a quarter from my mother and rode there on the street-car. It was too far to walk. An empty feeling went through me as I approached the campus. It all looked the same, bright and green beneath the sun. They were kicking a football around on the athletic field. I watched them for a minute or two. It was like watching something from a long way off. I wondered what kids in school thought about now. How could they take the playing of games seriously? How could they take their studies seriously? Sitting in their rooms poring over text-books—how could they confine their eyes to the pages? Printed words, printed little dead words telling of dead things: Greece and Rome and the Italy of the Renaissance. George Washington and the British; Lincoln and the Civil War. Dates and names; words and words; and all the time a paralyzed world gasping for breath outside the door. Could they not feel this world, those kids poring over their books inside the classrooms? I wondered what they thought of the future. I wondered what they thought when they read in newspapers of the millions of unemployed, of farmers threatening to defend their homes with shotguns against foreclosures, of the miners' children barefoot in the snow; of the bread-lines in the great cities, and the disease and helplessness afflicting millions. What did they think about, reading the dead words in their books?

I stood watching them kicking the football beneath the sun, then turned and started across the campus. The buildings seemed abnormally quiet. It was as though I had been expecting some kind of movement, of vibration in the air, and instead I felt the lack of movement; there was an emptiness that I cannot exactly describe, but it was there nevertheless; it was in the great stone buildings, in the windows, in the grass and benches and trees. I went down a shady walk and came out facing the Arts and Science building. Where I stood was a big elm tree and the tree cut off some of my view of the building but I could see the wide stone steps leading up to the entrance. Something choking closed about my heart. It was on those steps that I had seen Janice for the first time. That was a long time ago that Janice stood on those steps with me looking up at her but right now it seemed as if it might have been only yesterday.

It seemed a million years since I had been a student here, but some of the things that happened to me were like yesterday. I thought of old classmates, of my profs, of the study rooms; I thought of crisp afternoons in the fall, and football rallies, and the whistle of the referee floating up over the stands at the opening of a big game. And I thought of other things. I thought of Janice with her blue eyes, coming in a yellow sweater to meet me; I thought of afternoons walking her home from school, the big front porch of her house and her kid brother Tommy with his fox-terrier and his bicycle with the taped handle-bars. And all the time it was like remembering something from a long, long way off, something out of another life, a life that was dead.

What was I looking for? I stared at the buildings and there was something I wanted out of them, but I could not get it. I didn't know what it was I wanted the buildings to give me, but I longed to feel as if I had come back to something that meant something to me, something that had reality and familiarity, something that would *recognize* me; but it was not there. The buildings were just a group of old stone buildings standing on a green campus with a lot of trees around it, and I was a stranger wandering about looking.

It was late in the afternoon when I got back to the house. I felt weak and tired, all drained out, and my temples were throbbing so hard I could barely see. As soon as I got in the house I said hello to my mother and went right on up to my room. I could not stand being with her. It was a horrible feeling to look at my mother and see that tired face, the tired wavering eyes. I lay down on the bed and tried to go to sleep but I could not sleep. If I could only get to sleep I could forget for awhile. You can't think when you're sleeping. I lay there and said to myself: "Sleep, sleep." I said it over and over again but the word got mixed up with other words and I thought of all kinds of crazy things. I thought of that Mexican whose legs got sheared off when he fell beneath the train that hot morning going into San Diego. I saw him as plainly as if he were right in front of me, with his hands sticking up in the air like pitchforks and the sickening scream he let out. I jumped involuntarily when I thought of him and something icy trickled through my stomach and I turned over on my side. "Sleep, sleep," I said to myself. And then I thought of Janice. All of a sudden—like that—I thought of her, and something calm and sweet flowed through me. I tried to fill myself with the thought of her. I tried to fill my head and my body and the room with her. I tried to close out everything but the memory of her, but even while I tried something else in me was saying: "What's the use?"

And suddenly I could not stand it any more. "God damn it, God damn it!" I yelled, beating the pillow: and then I stopped short, surprised at the sound of my voice. I looked at the pillow stupidly, and then I got up off the bed and went to the window. Outside children were playing on the street. The sun was going down and the sky was filled with a red glow. Shadows were spreading along the sidewalk. I stood and watched the shadows and the playing children. Janice had loved children. She had always talked about the children we would have when we got married. She had always talked about the children we would have when I finished school and had my degree in medicine and had got started. I looked at the shadows and thought of the children Janice and I would have had if my dad's business had not failed and I had been able to finish school. Looking out the window at the playing children my thoughts kept reaching back into this other world and something inside of me was squirming and squirming. Suddenly I wanted to run. I turned abruptly from the window and started across the room, but when I got to the door I paused. Where was I going? I stared at the knob, then turned and went slowly back to the bed. "Jesus Christ," I thought, burying my head in the pillow. "Oh, Jesus, Jesus Christ!"

IV

I must have dozed off a little because when I heard the door slamming downstairs it startled me wide-awake. The old man was home.

In a few moments I heard voices, and then silence. They were telling him now, I thought. I saw my father with his big shoulders and cold eyes, not saying much but looking and listening, and my stomach twitched nervously. I dreaded the thought of facing him. He is not an easy man to face, with those cold eyes that look straight at you and his bluff, belligerent manner. I rolled a cigarette and sucked at it, trying to get up nerve enough to go downstairs. The door opened. I turned my head and saw Louise, come to call me to dinner.

"Papa's home," she said, looking at me, then at the floor self-consciously.

"I know—I heard him come in."

"Dinner's about ready. Mamma said to come down if you're ready."

She looked up at me from beneath her lashes and I thought I saw her lips quiver a little, but I could not be sure. I wanted to put my arms around her, to tell her how pretty she looked, but the words stuck in my throat. She stood looking at me like that from beneath her lashes for a moment; then went out of the room.

After a few moments I got up and went downstairs. My mother came out of the kitchen. She too had changed her dress and powdered her face a little, but her eyes looked red and swollen.

"Your father's home," she said.

"I know. Louise told me."

"He's in there," nodding toward the living-room.

I turned from her and went in. The sooner this was over the better, I thought. He was seated in his deep chair beside the floor lamp with his back turned partly toward me. The evening paper was lifted up in front of his face but I could tell he was not reading. I saw his huge shoulders, and his big hands on the paper, and I felt smaller and smaller as I went toward him.

"Hello, dad."

The paper rustled and then his body shifted and he turned around. And what I saw was this: I saw an old man with sunken, furtive eyes.

"Hello, son," he said, half-rising wearily and putting his hand out. I shook his hand with my eyes on the floor and sat down on a chair opposite him. And what I felt in those few seconds I cannot put down. There are no words to express the numb, choking feeling it gave me to see what had become of my father.

"Well, how is everything, dad?" I said. I had to say something.

"So-so," he said. "Just so-so."

"Well, it'll pick up," I said. "It's bound to pick up."

"Yes," he said, looking at me out of those wavering eyes. "It's bound to pick up"; but in his voice was neither hope nor conviction.

My mother came to the door and called us to dinner, and we rose and followed her into the dining-room. My father's tread was slow and heavy.

My mother had fried a chicken and as she set it on the table my father looked at it and then at her, but she avoided his glance. And she had fried some sweet potatoes, too, and baked some summer squash. They were all my favorite dishes and she had prepared them all for me, but I found it difficult to eat. I thought of other meals I had eaten, the meals I had eaten on the bum, the watery soup and stale bread in relief agencies, the hand-outs, the stews in jungles: I thought of the jails I had slept in, and the flop-houses, of fast and slow freights, and the army of wandering men and boys running like homeless ghosts across the face of America.

"What's the matter, dear? Don't you like the chicken?"

"What? Oh; oh, sure, it's great."

V

After the meal was over and the last dish had been washed and dried I asked Louise to come out with me on the porch. Now the darkness had completely fallen and lights bloomed in houses and the air was filled with the indescribable, nostalgic scent of the summer night.

"Sit down," I said. "I want to ask you something."

She sat down on the old wicker porch-seat with its sagging back and looked up at me.

"I want you to tell me the truth," I said. "Just how bad are things?"

"Pretty bad," she said, and a kind of grim look came into her dark eyes.

"I gathered that," I said. "But just how bad? Aren't you working?"

"Working! I haven't worked a month since you left. They're hiring stenographers for ten dollars a week, and even then you can't find a job."

"What about the old man? Is he making enough for you all to get by?"

"He gets twenty dollars a week. Mr. McClelland had to cut him last month. He said he just couldn't help it, business is so bad. But he told papa not to worry; he said he'll always have a job with him, if it's only night watchman. He's been wonderful to us—I don't know what we would have done if it hadn't been for him."

"Yeah, I know," I said. "But suppose something should happen to the old man; what would mother do? Have they been able to save anything?"

"I don't think so, but there's his insurance. I heard them talking about it the other night. Papa said thank God his insurance is all paid for."

"Christ!" I said. "Do they talk about that?"

"Yes. Oh, Bill!" she said suddenly. "You have no idea how terrible it is to feel a burden on them. Sometimes I think I'll go crazy if I don't find a job. I've thought of leaving like you did, but where could I go? I'm not a man like you."

"I know," I said. "I know how you feel. Tell me, has mamma been crying? I mean, this afternoon? Her eyes looked red when I came downstairs."

She did not answer at once, and then she nodded.

"What about?"

"You," she said, looking at me. "She's so worried about you. She says she doesn't know what's going to become of you."

"Hasn't she got enough to worry about without worrying about me?"

"Well, you know how she is," she said.

"Yeah, I know how she is." I sucked at my cigarette and looked off down the street. A few yards away a dog was sniffing at something in the gutter. I watched him for a moment, when suddenly I heard a bird call. Once, twice; and a whole submerged world of sensations whirled into being. I thought of fields in the night, of the fields of strawberries in Oregon beneath the stars. It was a fleeting recollection and it vanished as swiftly as it had come.

"Do you think I'll be able to find a job?" I asked.

"I don't know where. It's worse than before you left. That's one of the things mamma was crying about this afternoon, she's so worried. There just isn't any work. Both the Jarvis boys have been out of work for months, and they go out every morning looking. I don't know what's going to become of people if something doesn't happen pretty soon."

"They'll get drunk on beer," I said.

"What?"

"Nothing." I took another drag of the cigarette, then looked at her. "It's pretty tough on you, isn't it, kid?"

"Me? Oh! I'm all right. Only I feel so helpless."

"Yeah," I said. "I know."

I finished my cigarette and we went inside. I went up to my room and took off my shoes and lay down in the dark and tried to keep from thinking. After awhile I heard the sounds of the family going to bed. Presently the sounds ceased, and a profound silence fell over the house. I rolled a cigarette and lay in the dark smoking. Twenty dollars a week, I thought. By the time they paid the grocery bill and the taxes and the interest on the mortgage and bought clothes and car-fare there would not be much left over. I thought of the year before I went away, that year when I had not been able to find more than a few weeks' work. If things were even that bad now, let alone worse like Louise had said, it might be months before I could find anything to do. A sick, tangled feeling went through me. "I can't sponge on them," I thought. "Jesus, they're having it tough enough as it is." And suddenly, I thought of Louise when she had come into my room to call me to dinner: I saw her standing before me in her worn dress looking shamefacedly at the floor.

I lay for a moment longer on the bed, watching the way the cigarette smoke curled upward; then I put the cigarette out and got up and went in my bare feet to the window. I held the curtain aside and looked out at the street, cold and gray beneath the street-lamp. The houses all around seemed dead as graves. Somewhere a man was coughing, a dry, rasping cough. That was the only sound. I stood looking out at the street for a few moments, then let the curtain fall and turned back into the room and pulled on my shoes.

At the corner I turned and looked back, but an intervening tree cut off my view of the house. I lifted my coat collar and went on down the street.

WALLACE STEGNER

Goin' to Town

AFTER THE NIGHT'S RAIN the yard was spongy and soft under the boy's bare feet. He stood at the edge of the packed dooryard in the flat thrust of sunrise looking at the ground washed clean and smooth and trackless, feeling the cool firm mud under his toes. Experimentally he lifted his right foot and put it down in a new place, pressed, picked it up again to look at the neat imprint of straight edge and curving instep and the five round dots of toes. The air was so fresh that he sniffed at it as he would have sniffed at the smell of cinnamon.

Lifting his head backward, he saw how the prairie beyond the fireguard looked darker than in dry times, healthier with green-brown tints, smaller and more intimate somehow than it did when the heat waves crawled over scorched grass and carried the horizons backward into dim and unseeable distances. And standing in the yard above his one clean sharp footprint, feeling his own verticality in all that spread of horizontal land, he sensed how the prairie shrank on this morning and how he himself grew. He was immense. A little jump would crack his head on the sky; a few strides would take him to any horizon.

His eyes turned south, into the low south sky, cloudless, almost colorless in the strong light. Just above the brown line of the horizon, faint as a watermark on pale blue paper, was the wavering tracery of the mountains, tenuous and far off, but today accessible for the first time. His mind had played among those ghostly summits for uncountable lost hours; today, in a few strides, they were his. And more: under the shadow of those peaks, under those Bearpaws that he and his mother privately called the Mountains of the Moon, was Chinook; and in Chinook, on this Fourth of July, were the band, the lemonade stands, the crowds, the parade, the ball game,

From Wallace Stegner, *The Women on the Wall.* (Boston: Houghton Mifflin Company), 1950, pp. 79–92. First published in *The Atlantic Monthly*, CLXV (June, 1940), 770–776.

the fireworks, that his mind had hungered toward in anticipation for three weeks.

His shepherd pup lay watching, belly down on the damp ground. In a gleeful spasm the boy stooped down to flap the pup's ears, then bent and spun like an Indian in a war dance while the wide-mouthed dog raced around him. And when his father came to the door in his undershirt, yawning, running a hand up the back of his head and through his hair, peering out from gummed eyes to see how the weather looked, the boy watched him, and his voice was one deep breathing relief from yesterday's rainy fear.

"It's clear as a bell," he said.

His father yawned again, clopped his jaws, rubbed his eyes, mumbled something from a mouth furry with sleep. He stood on the doorstep scratching himself comfortably, looking down at the boy and the dog.

"Gonna be hot," he said slyly. "Might be too hot to drive."

"Aw, Pa!"

"Gonna be a scorcher. Melt you right down to axle grease riding in that car."

The boy regarded him doubtfully, saw the lurking sly droop of his mouth. "Aw, we are too going!"

At his father's laugh he burst from his immobility like a sprinter starting, raced one complete circle of the house with the dog after him. When he flew around past his father again his voice trailed out behind him at the corner of the house. "Gonna feed the hens," he said. His father looked after him, scratched himself, laughed suddenly, and went back indoors.

Through chores and breakfast the boy moved with the dream of a day's rapture haunting his eyes, but that did not keep him from swift and agile helpfulness. He didn't even wait for commands. He scrubbed himself twice, slicked down his hair, hunted up clean clothes, wiped the mud from his shoes with a wet rag and put them on. While his mother packed the shoe box of lunch he stood at her elbows proffering aid. He flew to stow things in the topless old Ford. He got a cloth and polished the brass radiator. Once or twice, jumping around to help, he looked up to catch his parents watching him, or looking at each other with the knowing, smiling expression in the eyes that said they were calling each other's attention to him.

"Just like a race horse," his father said once, and the boy felt foolish, swaggered, twisted his mouth down in a leer, said "Awww!" But in a moment he was hustling them again. They ought to get going, with fifty miles to drive. And long before they were ready he was standing beside the Ford, licked and immaculate and so excited that his feet jumped him up and down without his volition or knowledge.

It was eight o'clock before his father came out, lifted off the front seat, poked the flat stick down into the gas tank, and pulled it out again dripping. "Pretty near full," he said. "If we're gonna drive up to the mountains we better take a can along, though. Fill that two-gallon one with the spout."

The boy ran, dug the can out of the shed, filled it from the spigot of the sixty-gallon drum that stood on a plank support to the north of the farmhouse. When he came back, his left arm stuck straight out and the can knocking against his legs, his mother was settling herself into the back seat among the parcels and waterbags.

"Goodness!" she said. "This is the first time I've been the first ready since I don't know when. I should think you'd have got all this done last night."

"Plenty time." The father stood looking down at the boy, grinning. "All right, race horse. You want to go to this shindig, you better hop in."

The boy was up into the front seat like a squirrel. His father walked around in front of the car. "Okay," he said. "You look sharp now. When she kicks over, switch her onto magneto and pull the spark down."

The boy said nothing. He looked upon the car, as his father did, with respect and a little awe. They didn't use it much, and starting it was a ritual like a fire drill. The father unscrewed the four-eared brass plug, looked down into the radiator, screwed the cap back on, and bent to take hold of the crank. "Watch it now," he said.

The boy felt the gentle heave of the springs, up and down, as his father wound the crank. He heard the gentle hiss in the bowels of the engine as the choke wire was pulled out, and his nostrils filled with the strong, volatile odor of gasoline. Over the slope of the radiator his father's brown strained face lifted up. "Is she turned on all right?"

"Yup. She's on battery."

"Must of flooded her. Have to let her rest a minute."

They waited—and then after a few minutes the wavelike heaving of the springs again, the rise and fall of the blue shirt and bent head over the radiator, the sighing swish of the choke, a stronger smell of gasoline. The motor had not even coughed.

The two voices came simultaneously from the car. "What's the matter with it?"

His brow puckered in an intent and serious scowl, the father stood blowing mighty breaths. "Son of a gun," he said. Coming around, he pulled at the switch to make sure it was clear over, adjusted the spark and gas levers. A fine mist of sweat made his face shine like oiled leather in the sun.

"There isn't anything really wrong with it, is there?" the mother said, and her voice wavered uncertainly on the edge of fear.

"I don't see how there could be," he said. "She's always started right off, and she was running all right when I drove her in here."

The boy looked at his mother where she sat erect among the things in the seat. She looked all dressed up, a flowered dress, a hat with hard red varnished cherries on it pinned to her red hair. For a moment she sat, stiff and nervous. "What'll you have to do?" she said.

"I don't know. Look into the motor."

"Well, I guess I'll get in out of the sun while you do it," she said, and, opening the door, she fumbled her way out of the clutter.

The boy felt her exodus like a surrender, a betrayal. If they didn't hurry up they'd miss the parade. In one motion he bounced out of the car. "Gee whiz!" he said. "Let's do something. We got to get started."

"Keep your shirt on," his father grunted. Lifting the hood, he bent his head inside, studying the engine. His hand went out to test wires, wiggle spark-plug connections, make tentative pulls at the choke. The weakly hinged hood slipped and came down across his wrist, and he swore, pushing it back. "Get me the pliers," he said.

For ten minutes he probed and monkeyed. "Might be the spark plugs," he said. "She don't seem to be getting any fire through her."

The mother, sitting on a box in the shade, smoothed her flowered voile dress nervously. "Will it take long?"

"Half-hour."

"Any day but this!" she said. "I don't see why you didn't make sure last night."

He breathed through his nose and bent over the engine again. "Don't go laying on any blame," he said. "It was raining last night."

One by one the plugs came out, were squinted at, scraped with a knife blade, the gap tested with a thin dime. The boy stood on one foot, then on the other, time pouring like a flood of uncatchable silver dollars through his hands. He kept looking at the sun, estimating how much time there was left. If they got it started right away they might still make it for the parade, but it would be close. Maybe they'd drive right up the street while the parade was on, and be part of it. . . .

"Is she ready?" he said.

"Pretty quick."

He wandered over by his mother, and she reached out and put an arm around his shoulders, hugging him quickly. "Well, anyway

we'll get there for the band and the ball game and the fireworks,"
he said. "If she doesn't start till noon we c'n make it for those."

"Sure," she said. "Pa'll get it going in a minute. We won't miss
anything, hardly."

"You ever seen skyrockets, Ma?"

"Once."

"Are they fun?"

"Wonderful," she said. "Just like a million stars, all colors, exploding all at once."

His feet took him back to his father, who straightened up with a
belligerent grunt. "Now!" he said. "If the sucker doesn't start
now . . ."

And once more the heaving of the springs, the groaning of the
turning engine, the hiss of choke. He tried short, sharp half-turns, as
if to catch the motor off guard. Then he went back to the stubborn
laboring spin. The back of his blue shirt was stained darkly, the
curving dikes of muscle along the spine's hollow showing cleanly
where the cloth stuck. Over and over, heaving, stubborn at first,
then furious, until he staggered back panting.

"God damn!" he said. "What you suppose is the matter with the
damn thing?"

"She didn't even cough once," the boy said, and, staring up at his
father's face full of angry bafflement, he felt the cold fear touch
him. What if it didn't start at all? What if they never get to any of
it? What if, all ready to go, they had to turn around and unload the
Ford and not even get out of the yard? His mother came over and
they stood close together, looking at the Ford and avoiding each
other's eyes.

"Maybe something got wet last night," she said.

"Well, it's had plenty time to dry out," said his father.

"Isn't there anything else you could try?"

"We can jack up the hind wheel, I guess. But there's no damn
reason we ought to have to."

"Well, if you have to, you'll have to," she said briskly. "After
planning it for three weeks we can't just get stuck like this. Can we,
son?"

His answer was mechanical, his eyes steady on his father. "Sure
not," he said.

The father opened his mouth to say something, saw the boy's lu-
gubrious face, and shut his lips again. Without a word he pulled off
the seat and got out the jack.

The sun climbed steadily while they jacked up one hind wheel
and blocked the car carefully so that it wouldn't run over anybody
when it started. The boy helped, and when they were ready again

he sat in the front seat so full of hope and fear that his whole body was one taut concentration. His father stooped, his cheek pressed against the radiator as a milker's cheek touches the flank of a cow. His shoulder dropped, jerked up. Nothing. Another jerk. Nothing. Then he was rolling in a furious spasm of energy, the wet dark back of his shirt rising and falling. And inside the motor only the futile swish of the choke and the half sound, half feel of cavernous motion as the crankshaft turned over. The Ford bounced on its springs as if the front wheels were coming off the ground on every upstroke. Then it stopped, and the boy's father was hanging on the radiator, breathless, dripping wet, swearing: "Son of a dirty, lousy, stinking, corrupted..."

The boy, his eyes dark, stared from his father's angry wet face to his mother's, pinched with worry. The pup lay down in the shade and put his head on his paws. "Gee whiz," the boy said. "Gee whiz!" He looked at the sky, and the morning was half gone.

His shoulders jerking with anger, the father threw the crank half-way across the yard and took a step or two toward the house. "The hell with the damn thing!"

"Harry, you can't!"

He stopped, glared at her, took an oblique look at the boy, bared his teeth in an irresolute, silent swearword. "Well, God, if it won't go!"

"Maybe if you hitched the horses to it," she said.

His laugh was short and choppy. "That'd be fine!" he said. "Why don't we just hitch up and let the team haul this damned old boat into Chinook?"

"But we've got to get it started! Why wouldn't it be all right to let them pull it around? You push it sometimes on a hill and it starts."

He looked at the boy again, jerked his eyes away with an exasperated gesture, as if he held the boy somehow accountable. The boy stared, mournful, defeated, ready to cry, and his father's head swung back unwillingly. Then abruptly he winked, mopped his head and neck, and grinned. "Think you want to go, uh?"

The boy nodded. "All right!" his father's voice snapped crisply. "Fly up in the pasture and get the team. Hustle!"

On the high lope the boy was off up the coulee bank. Just down under the lip of the swale, a quarter-mile west, the bay backs of the horses and the black dot of the colt showed. Usually he ran circumspectly across that pasture, because of the cactus, but now he flew. With shoes it was all right, and even without shoes he would have run—across burnouts, over stretches so undermined with gopher holes that sometimes he broke through to the ankle, staggering.

Skimming over patches of cactus, soaring over a badger hole, plunging down into the coulee and up the other side, he ran as if bears were after him. The black colt, spotting him, hoisted his tail and took off in a spectacular, stiff-legged sprint across the flats, but the bays merely lifted their heads to watch him. He slowed, came up walking, laid a hand on the mare's neck and untied the looped halter rope. She stood for him while he scrambled and wriggled and kicked his way to her back, and then they were off, the mare in an easy lope, the gelding trotting after, the colt stopping his wild show-off career and wobbling hastily and ignominiously after his departing mother.

They pulled up before the Ford, the boy sliding off to throw the halter rope to his father. "Shall I get the harness?" he said, and before anyone could answer he was off running, to come back lugging one heavy harness, tugs trailing little furrows in the damp bare earth. He dropped it, turned to run again, his breath laboring in his lungs. "I'll get the other'n," he said.

With a short, almost incredulous laugh his father looked at his mother and shook his head before he threw the harness on the mare. When the second one came he laid it over the gelding, pushed against the heavy shoulder to get the horse into place. The gelding resisted, pranced a little, got a curse and a crack with the rope across his nose, jerked back and trembled and lifted his feet nervously, and set one shod hoof on his owner's instep. The father, unstrung by the hurry and the heat and the labor and the exasperation of a morning when nothing went right, kicked the horse savagely in the belly. "Get in there, you damned big blundering ox! Back! Back, you bastard! Whoa! Whoa, now!"

With a heavy rope for a towline he hitched the now-skittish team to the axle. Without a word he stopped and lifted the boy to the mare's back. "All right," he said, and his face relaxed in a quick grin. "This is where we start her. Ride 'em around in a circle, not too fast."

Then he climbed into the Ford, turned on the switch to magneto, fussed with the levers. "Let her go!" he said.

The boy kicked the mare ahead, twisting as he rode to watch the Ford heave forward as a tired, heavy man heaves to his feet, begin rolling after him, lurching on the uneven ground, jerking and kicking and making growling noises when his father let the emergency brake off and put it in gear. The horses settled as the added pull came on them, flattened into their collars, swung in a circle, bumped each other, skittered. The mare reared, and the boy shut his eyes and clung. When he came down, her leg was entangled in the towline and his father was climbing cursing out of the Ford to straighten it out. His father was mad again, and yelled at him. "Keep 'em apart! There ain't any tongue. You got to keep Dick kicked over on his own side."

And again the start, the flattening into the collars, the snapping tight of the tugs under his legs. This time it went smoothly, the Ford galloped after the team in lumbering, plunging jerks. The mare's eyes rolled white, and she broke into a trot, pulling the gelding after her. Desperately the boy clung to the knotted and shortened reins, his ears alert for the grumble of the Ford starting behind him. The pup ran beside the team yapping in a high, falsetto idiot monotone, crazy with excitement.

They made three complete circles of the back yard between house and chicken coop before the boy looked back again. "Won't she start?" he shouted. He saw his father rigid begind the wheel, heard his ripping burst of swearwords, saw him bend and glare down into the mysterious inwards of the engine through the pulled-up floorboards. Guiding the car with one hand, he fumbled down below, one glaring eye just visible over the cowl.

"Shall I stop?" the boy shouted. Excitement and near-despair made his voice a tearful scream. But his father's wild arm waved him on. "Go on, go on! Gallop 'em! Pull the guts out of this thing. Run 'em, run 'em!"

And the galloping—the furious, mud-flinging, rolling-eyed galloping around the circle already rutted like a road, the Ford, now in savagely held low, growling and surging and plowing behind; the mad yapping of the dog, the erratic scared bursts of runaway from the colt, the mother in sight briefly for a quarter of each circle, her hands to her mouth and her eyes hurt, and behind him in the Ford his father in a strangling rage, yelling him on, his lips back over his teeth and his face purple.

Until finally they stopped, the horses blown, the boy white and tearful and still, the father dangerous with unexpended wrath. The boy slipped off, his lip bitten between his teeth, not crying now but ready to at any moment, the corners of his eyes prickling with it, and his teeth tight on his misery. His father climbed over the side of the car and stood looking as if he wanted to tear the thing apart with his bare hands.

Shoulders sagging, tears trembling to fall, his jaw aching with the need to cry, the boy started toward his mother. As he came near his father he looked up, their eyes met, and he saw his father's blank with impotent rage. Dull hopelessness swallowed him. Not any of it, his mind said. Not even any of it—no parade, no ball game, no band, no fireworks. No lemonade or ice cream or paper horns or fire-crackers. No close sight of the mountains that throughout every summer called like a legend from his horizons. No trip, no adventure—none of it, nothing.

Everything he was feeling was in that one still look. In spite of him his lip trembled, and he choked off a sob, his eyes on his father's face, on the brows pulling down and the eyes narrowing.

"Well, don't blubber!" his father shouted at him. "Don't stand there looking at me as if it was me that was keeping you from your picnic!"

"I can't—help it," the boy said, and with a kind of terror he felt the grief swelling up, overwhelming him, driving the voice out of him in a wail. Through the blur of his crying he saw the convulsive tightening of his father's face, and then all the fury of a maddening morning concentrated itself in a swift backhand blow that knocked the boy staggering.

He bawled aloud, from pain, from surprise, from outrage, from pure desolation, and ran to bury his face in his mother's skirts. From that muffled sanctuary he heard her angry voice. "No," she said. "It won't do any good to try to make up to him now. Go on away somewhere till he gets over it."

She rocked him against her, but the voice she had for his father was bitter with anger. "As if he wasn't hurt enough already!" she said.

He heard the heavy, quick footsteps going away, and for a long time he lay crying into the voile flowers. And when he had cried himself out, and had listened apathetically to his mother's soothing promises that they would go in the first chance they got, go to the mountains, have a picnic under some waterfall, maybe be able to find a ball game going on in town, some Saturday—when he had listened and became quiet, wanting to believe it but not believing it at all, he went inside to take off his good clothes and his shoes and put on his old overalls again.

It was almost noon when he came out to stand in the front yard looking southward toward the impossible land where the Mountains of the Moon lifted above the plains, and where, in the town at the foot of the peaks, crowds would now be eating picnic lunches, drinking pop, getting ready to go out to the ball field and watch heroes in real uniforms play ball. The band would be braying now from a bunting-wrapped stand, kids would be tossing firecrackers, playing in a cool grove. . . .

In the still heat his face went sorrowful and defeated, and his eyes searched the horizon for the telltale watermark. But there was nothing but waves of heat crawling and lifting like invisible flames; the horizon was a blurred and writhing flatness where earth and sky met in an indistinct band of haze. This morning two strides would have taken him there; now it was gone.

Looking down, he saw at his feet the clean footprint that he had made in the early morning. Aimlessly he put his right foot down and pressed. The mud was drying but in a low place he found a spot that would still take an imprint. Very carefully, as if he were performing some ritual for his life, he went around, stepping and leaning, stepping and leaning, until he had a circle six feet in diameter of delicately exact footprints, straight edge and curving instep and the five round dots of toes.

ROBERT PENN WARREN

Blackberry Winter

It was getting into June and past eight o'clock in the morning, but there was a fire—even if it wasn't a big fire, just a fire of chunks —on the hearth of the big stone fireplace in the living room. I was standing on the hearth, almost into the chimney, hunched over the fire, working my bare toes slowly on the warm stone. I relished the heat which made the skin of my bare legs warp and creep and tingle, even as I called to my mother, who was somewhere back in the dining room or kitchen, and said: "But it's June, I don't have to put them on!"

"You put them on if you are going out," she called.

I tried to assess the degree of authority and conviction in the tone, but at that distance it was hard to decide. I tried to analyze the tone, and then I thought what a fool I had been to start out the back door and let her see that I was barefoot. If I had gone out the front door or the side door she would never have known, not till dinner time anyway, and by then the day would have been half gone, and I would have been all over the farm to see what the storm had done and down to the creek to see the flood. But it had never crossed my mind that they would try to stop you from going barefoot in June, no matter if there had been a gully-washer and a cold spell.

Nobody had ever tried to stop me in June as long as I could remember, and when you are nine years old, what you remember seems forever; for you remember everything and everything is important and stands big and full and fills up Time and is so solid that you can walk around and around it like a tree and look at it. You are aware that time passes, that there is a movement in time, but that is not what Time is. Time is not a movement, a flowing, a wind then, but is, rather, a kind of climate in which things are, and when a thing happens it begins to live and keeps on living and

From Robert Penn Warren, *The Circus in the Attic and Other Stories*. (New York: Harcourt, Brace and Company), 1947, pp. 63–87.

stands solid in Time like the tree that you can walk around. And if there is a movement, the movement is not Time itself, any more than a breeze is climate, and all the breeze does is to shake a little the leaves on the tree which is alive and solid. When you are nine, you know that there are things that you don't know, but you know that when you know something you know it. You know how a thing has been and you know that you can go barefoot in June. You do not understand that voice from back in the kitchen which says that you cannot go barefoot outdoors and run to see what has happened and rub your feet over the wet shivery grass and make the perfect mark of your foot in the smooth, creamy, red mud and then muse upon it as though you had suddenly come upon that single mark on the glistening auroral beach of the world. You have never seen a beach, but you have read the book and how the footprint was there.

The voice had said what it had said, and I looked savagely at the black stockings and the strong, scuffed brown shoes which I had brought from my closet as far as the hearth rug. I called once more, "But it's June," and waited.

"It's June," the voice replied from far away, "but it's blackberry winter."

I had lifted my head to reply to that, to make one more test of what was in that tone, when I happened to see the man.

The fireplace in the living room was at the end; for the stone chimney was built, as in so many of the farmhouses in Tennessee, at the end of a gable, and there was a window on each side of the chimney. Out of the window on the north side of the fireplace I could see the man. When I saw the man I did not call out what I had intended, but, engrossed by the strangeness of the sight, watched him, still far off, come along the path by the edge of the woods.

What was strange was that there should be a man there at all. That path went along the yard fence, between the fence and the woods which came right down to the yard, and then on back past the chicken runs and on by the woods until it was lost to sight where the woods bulged out and cut off the back field. There the path disappeared into the woods. It led on back, I knew, through the woods and to the swamp, skirted the swamp where the big trees gave way to sycamores and water oaks and willows and tangled cane, and then led on to the river. Nobody ever went back there except people who wanted to gig frogs in the swamp or to fish in the river or to hunt in the woods, and those people, if they didn't have a standing permission from my father, always stopped to ask permission to cross the farm. But the man whom I now saw wasn't, I could tell even at that distance, a sportsman. And what would a sportsman have been doing down there after a storm? Besides, he was coming from the river, and nobody had gone down there that morning. I knew that for a fact, because if anybody had passed, certainly if a stranger had passed, the dogs would have made a racket and would have been out on him. But this man was coming up from the river and had come up through the woods. I suddenly had a vision of him moving up the grassy path in the woods, in the green twilight under the big trees, not making any sound on the path, while now and then, like drops off the eaves, a big drop of water would fall from a leaf or bough and strike a stiff oak leaf lower down with a small, hollow sound like a drop of water hitting tin. That sound, in the silence of the woods, would be very significant.

When you are a boy and stand in the stillness of woods, which can be so still that your heart almost stops beating and makes you want to stand there in the green twilight until you feel your very feet sinking into and clutching the earth like roots and your body breathing slow through its pores like the leaves—when you stand there and wait for the next drop to drop with its small, flat sound to a lower leaf, that sound seems to measure out something, to put an end to something, to begin something, and you cannot wait for it to happen and are afraid it will not happen, and then when it has happened, you are waiting again, almost afraid.

But the man whom I saw coming through the woods in my mind's eye did not pause and wait, growing into the ground and breathing with the enormous, soundless breathing of the leaves. Instead, I saw him moving in the green twilight inside my head as he was moving at that very moment along the path by the edge of the woods, coming toward the house. He was moving steadily, but not fast, with his shoulders hunched a little and his head thrust forward, like a man who has come a long way and has a long way to go. I shut my eyes for a couple of seconds, thinking that when I opened them he would not be there at all. There was no place for him to have come from, and there was no reason for him to come where he was coming, toward our house. But I opened my eyes, and there he was, and he was coming steadily along the side of the woods. He was not yet even with the back chicken yard.

"Mama," I called.

"You put them on," the voice said.

"There's a man coming," I called, "out back."

She did not reply to that, and I guessed that she had gone to the kitchen window to look. She would be looking at the man and wondering who he was and what he wanted, the way you always do in the country, and if I went back there now she would not notice right off whether or not I was barefoot. So I went back to the kitchen.

She was standing by the window. "I don't recognize him," she said, not looking around at me.

"Where could he be coming from?" I asked.

"I don't know," she said.

"What would he be doing down at the river? At night? In the storm?"

She studied the figure out the window, then said, "Oh, I reckon maybe he cut across from the Dunbar place."

That was, I realized, a perfectly rational explanation. He had not been down at the river in the storm, at night. He had come over this morning. You could cut across from the Dunbar place if you didn't mind breaking through a lot of elder and sassafras and blackberry bushes which had about taken over the old cross path, which nobody ever used any more. That satisfied me for a moment, but only for a moment. "Mama," I asked, "what would he be doing over at the Dunbar place last night?"

Then she looked at me, and I knew I had made a mistake, for she was looking at my bare feet. "You haven't got your shoes on," she said.

But I was saved by the dogs. That instant there was a bark which I recognized as Sam, the collie, and then a heavier, churning kind of bark which was Bully, and I saw a streak of white as Bully tore round the corner of the back porch and headed out for the man. Bully was a big, bone-white bull dog, the kind of dog that they used to call a farm bull dog but that you don't see any more, heavy chested and heavy headed, but with pretty long legs. He could take a fence as light as a hound. He had just cleared the white paling fence toward the woods when my mother ran out to the back porch and began calling, "Here you, Bully! Here you!"

Bully stopped in the path, waiting for the man, but he gave a few more of those deep, gargling, savage barks that reminded you of something down a stone-lined well. The red clay mud, I saw, was splashed up over his white chest and looked exciting, like blood.

The man, however, had not stopped walking even when Bully took the fence and started at him. He had kept right on coming. All he had done was to switch a little paper parcel which he carried from the right hand to the left, and then reach into his pants pocket to get something. Then I saw the glitter and knew that he had a knife in his hand, probably the kind of mean knife just made for devilment and nothing else, with a blade as long as the blade of a frog-sticker, which will snap out ready when you press a button in the handle. The knife must have had a button in the handle, or else how could he have had the blade out glittering so quick and with just one hand?

Pulling his knife against the dogs was a funny thing to do, for Bully was a big, powerful brute and fast, and Sam was all right. If those dogs had meant business, they might have knocked him down and ripped him before he got a stroke in. He ought to have picked up a heavy stick, something to take a swipe at them with and something which they could see and respect when they came at him. But he apparently did not know much about dogs. He just held the knife blade close against the right leg, low down, and kept on moving down the path.

Then my mother had called, and Bully had stopped. So the man let the blade of the knife snap back into the handle, and dropped it into his pocket, and kept on coming. Many women would have been afraid with the strange man who they knew had that knife in his pocket. That is, if they were alone in the house with nobody but a nine-year-old boy. And my mother was alone, for my father had gone off, and Dellie, the cook, was down at her cabin because she wasn't feeling well. But my mother wasn't afraid. She wasn't a big woman, but she was clear and brisk about everything she did and looked everybody and everything right in the eye from her own blue eyes in her tanned face. She had been the first woman in the county to ride a horse astride (that was back when she was a girl and long before I was born), and I have seen her snatch up a pump gun and go out and knock a chicken hawk out of the air like a busted skeet when he came over her chicken yard. She was a steady and self-reliant woman, and when I think of her now after all the years she has been dead, I think of her brown hands, not big, but somewhat square for a woman's hands, with square-cut nails. They looked, as a matter of fact, more like a young boy's hands than a grown woman's. But back then it never crossed my mind that she would ever be dead.

She stood on the back porch and watched the man enter the back gate, where the dogs (Bully had leaped back into the yard) were dancing and muttering and giving sidelong glances back to my mother to see if she meant what she had said. The man walked right by the dogs, almost brushing them, and didn't pay them any attention. I could see now that he wore old khaki pants, and a dark wool coat with stripes in it, and a gray felt hat. He had on a gray shirt with blue stripes in it, and no tie. But I could see a tie, blue and reddish, sticking in his side coat-pocket. Everything was wrong about what he wore. He ought to have been wearing blue jeans or overalls, and a straw hat or an old black felt hat, and the coat, granting that he might have been wearing a wool coat and not a jumper, ought not to have had those stripes. Those clothes, despite the fact that they were old enough and dirty enough for any tramp, didn't belong there in our back yard, coming down the path, in Middle Tennessee, miles away from any big town, and even a mile off the pike.

When he got almost to the steps, without having said anything, my mother, very matter-of-factly, said, "Good morning."

"Good morning," he said, and stopped and looked her over. He did not take off his hat, and under the brim you could see the perfectly unmemorable face, which wasn't old and wasn't young, or thick or thin. It was grayish and covered with about three days of stubble. The eyes were a kind of nondescript, muddy hazel, or something like that, rather bloodshot. His teeth, when he opened his mouth, showed yellow and uneven. A couple of them had been knocked out. You knew that they had been knocked out, because there was a scar, not very old, there on the lower lip just beneath the gap.

"Are you hunting work?" my mother asked him.

"Yes," he said—not "yes, mam"—and still did not take off his hat.

"I don't know about my husband, for he isn't here," she said, and didn't mind a bit telling the tramp, or whoever he was, with the mean knife in his pocket, that no man was around, "but I can give you a few things to do. The storm has drowned a lot of my chicks. Three coops of them. You can gather them up and bury them. Bury them deep so the dogs won't get at them. In the woods. And fix the coops the wind blew over. And down yonder beyond that pen by the edge of the woods are some drowned poults. They got out and I couldn't get them in. Even after it started to rain hard. Poults haven't got any sense."

"What are them things—poults?" he demanded, and spat on the brick walk. He rubbed his foot over the spot, and I saw that he wore a black, pointed-toe low shoe, all cracked and broken. It was a crazy kind of shoe to be wearing in the country.

"Oh, they're young turkeys," my mother was saying. "And they haven't got any sense. I oughtn't to try to raise them around here with so many chickens, anyway. They don't thrive near chickens, even in separate pens. And I won't give up my chickens." Then she stopped herself and resumed briskly on the note of business. "When you finish that, you can fix my flower beds. A lot of trash and mud and gravel has washed down. Maybe you can save some of my flowers if you are careful."

"Flowers," the man said, in a low impersonal voice which seemed to have a wealth of meaning, but a meaning which I could not fathom. As I think back on it, it probably was not pure contempt. Rather, it was a kind of impersonal and distant marveling that he should be on the verge of grubbing in a flower bed. He said the word, and then looked off across the yard.

"Yes, flowers," my mother replied with some asperity, as though she would have nothing said or implied against flowers. "And they were very fine this year." Then she stopped and looked at the man. "Are you hungry?" she demanded.

"Yeah," he said.

"I'll fix you something," she said, "before you get started." She turned to me. "Show him where he can wash up," she commanded, and went into the house.

I took the man to the end of the porch where a pump was and where a couple of wash pans sat on a low shelf for people to use before they went into the house. I stood there while he laid down his little parcel wrapped in newspaper and took off his hat and looked around for a nail to hang it on. He poured the water and plunged his hands into it. They were big hands, and strong looking, but they did not have the creases and the earth-color of the hands of men who work outdoors. But they were dirty, with black dirt ground into the skin and under the nails. After he had washed his hands, he poured another basin of water and washed his face. He dried his face, and with the towel still dangling in his grasp, stepped over to the mirror on the house wall. He rubbed one hand over the stubble on his face. Then he carefully inspected his face, turning first one side and then the other, and stepped back and settled his striped coat down on his shoulders. He had the movements of a man who has just dressed up to go to church or a party—the way he settled his coat and smoothed it and scanned himself in the mirror.

Then he caught my glance on him. He glared at me for an instant out of the bloodshot eyes, then demanded in a low, harsh voice, "What you looking at?"

"Nothing," I managed to say, and stepped back a step from him.

He flung the towel down, crumpled, on the shelf, and went toward the kitchen door and entered without knocking.

My mother said something to him which I could not catch. I started to go in again, then thought about my bare feet, and decided to go back of the chicken yard, where the man would have to come to pick up the dead chicks. I hung around behind the chicken house until he came out.

He moved across the chicken yard with a fastidious, not quite finicking motion, looking down at the curdled mud flecked with bits of chicken-droppings. The mud curled up over the soles of his black shoes. I stood back from him some six feet and watched him pick up the first of the drowned chicks. He held it up by one foot and inspected it.

There is nothing deader looking than a drowned chick. The feet curl in that feeble, empty way which back when I was a boy, even if I was a country boy who did not mind hog-killing or frog-gigging, made me feel hollow in the stomach. Instead of looking plump and fluffy, the body is stringy and limp with the fluff plastered to it, and the neck is long and loose like a little string of rag. And the eyes have that bluish membrane over them which makes you think of a very old man who is sick about to die.

The man stood there and inspected the chick. Then he looked all around as though he didn't know what to do with it.

"There's a great big old basket in the shed," I said, and pointed to the shed attached to the chicken house.

He inspected me as though he had just discovered my presence, and moved toward the shed.

"There's a spade there, too," I added.

He got the basket and began to pick up the other chicks, picking each one up slowly by a foot and then flinging it into the basket with a nasty, snapping motion. Now and then he would look at me out of the blood-shot eyes. Every time he seemed on the verge of saying something, but he did not. Perhaps he was building up to say something to me, but I did not wait that long. His way of looking at me made me so uncomfortable that I left the chicken yard.

Besides, I had just remembered that the creek was in flood, over the bridge, and that people were down there watching it. So I cut across the farm toward the creek. When I got to the big tobacco field I saw that it had not suffered much. The land lay right and not many tobacco plants had washed out of the ground. But I knew that a lot of tobacco round the country had been washed right out. My father had said so at breakfast.

My father was down at the bridge. When I came out of the gap in the osage hedge into the road, I saw him sitting on his mare over the heads of the other men who were standing around, admiring the flood. The creek was big here, even in low water; for only a couple of miles away it ran into the river, and when a real flood came, the red water got over the pike where it dipped down to the bridge, which was an iron bridge, and high over the floor and even the side railings of the bridge. Only the upper iron work would show, with the water boiling and frothing red and white around it. That creek rose so fast and so heavy because a few miles back it came down out of the hills, where the gorges filled up with water in no time when a rain came. The creek ran in a deep bed with limestone bluffs along both sides until it got within three quarters of a mile of the bridge, and when it came out from between those bluffs in flood it was boiling and hissing and steaming like water from a fire hose.

Whenever there was a flood, people from half the county would come down to see the sight. After a gully-washer there would not be any work to do anyway. If it didn't ruin your crop, you couldn't plow and you felt like taking a holiday to celebrate. If it did ruin your crop, there wasn't anything to do except to try to take your mind off the mortgage, if you were rich enough to have a mortgage, and if you couldn't afford a mortgage you needed something to take your mind off how hungry you would be by Christmas. So people would come down to the bridge and look at the flood. It made something different from the run of days.

There would not be much talking after the first few minutes of trying to guess how high the water was this time. The men and kids just stood around, or sat their horses or mules, as the case might be, or stood up in the wagon beds. They looked at the strangeness of the flood for an hour or two, and then somebody would say that he had better be getting on home to dinner and would start walking down the gray, puddled limestone pike, or would touch heel to his mount and start off. Everybody always knew what it would be like when he got down to the bridge, but people always came. It was like church or a funeral. They always came, that is, if it was summer and the flood unexpected. Nobody ever came down in winter to see high water.

When I came out of the gap in the bodock hedge, I saw the crowd, perhaps fifteen or twenty men and a lot of kids, and saw my father sitting his mare, Nellie Gray. He was a tall, limber man and carried himself well. I was always proud to see him sit a horse, he was so quiet and straight, and when I stepped through the gap of the hedge that morning, the first thing that happened was, I remember, the warm feeling I always had when I saw him up on a horse, just sitting. I did not go toward him, but skirted the crowd on the far side, to get a look at the creek. For one thing, I was not sure what he would say about the fact that I was barefoot. But the first thing I knew, I heard his voice calling, "Seth!"

I went toward him, moving apologetically past the men, who bent their large, red or thin, sallow faces above me. I knew some of the men, and knew their names, but because those I knew were there in a crowd, mixed with the strange faces, they seemed foreign to me, and not friendly. I did not look up at my father until I was almost within touching distance of his heel. Then I looked up and tried to read his face, to see if he was angry about my being barefoot. Before I could decide anything from that impassive, high-boned face, he had leaned over and reached a hand to me. "Grab on," he commanded.

I grabbed on and gave a little jump, and he said, "Up-see-daisy!" and whisked me, light as a feather, up to the pommel of his McClellan saddle.

"You can see better up here," he said, slid back on the cantle a little to make me more comfortable, and then, looking over my head at the swollen, tumbling water, seemed to forget all about me. But his right hand was laid on my side, just above my thigh, to steady me.

I was sitting there as quiet as I could, feeling the faint stir of my father's chest against my shoulders as it rose and fell with his breath, when I saw the cow. At first, looking up the creek, I thought it was just another big piece of driftwood steaming down the creek in the ruck of water, but all at once a pretty good-size boy who had climbed part way up a telephone pole by the pike so that he could see better yelled out, "Golly-damn, look at that-air cow!"

Everybody looked. It was a cow all right, but it might just as well have been driftwood; for it was dead as a chunk, rolling and roiling down the creek, appearing and disappearing, feet up or head up, it didn't matter which.

The cow started up the talk again. Somebody wondered whether it would hit one of the clear places under the top girder of the bridge and get through or whether it would get tangled in the drift and trash that had piled against the upright girders and braces. Somebody remembered how about ten years before so much driftwood had piled up on the bridge that it was knocked off its foundations. Then the cow hit. It hit the edge of the drift against one of the girders, and hung there. For a few seconds it seemed as though it might tear loose, but then we saw that it was really caught. It bobbed and heaved on its side there in a slow, grinding, uneasy fashion. It had a yoke around its neck, the kind made out of a forked limb to keep a jumper behind fence.

"She shore jumped one fence," one of the men said.

And another: "Well, she done jumped her last one, fer a fack."

Then they began to wonder about whose cow it might be. They decided it must belong to Milt Alley. They said that he had a cow that was a jumper, and kept her in a fenced-in piece of ground up the creek. I had never seen Milt Alley, but I knew who he was. He was a squatter and lived up the hills a way, on a shirt-tail patch of set-on-edge land, in a cabin. He was pore white trash. He had lots of children. I had seen the children at school, when they came. They were thin-faced, with straight, sticky-looking, dough-colored hair, and they smelled something like old sour buttermilk, not because they drank so much buttermilk but because that is the sort of smell which children out of those cabins tend to have. The big Alley boy drew dirty pictures and showed them to the little boys at school.

That was Milt Alley's cow. It looked like the kind of cow he would have, a scrawny, old, sway-backed cow, with a yoke around her neck. I wondered if Milt Alley had another cow.

"Poppa," I said, "do you think Milt Alley has got another cow?"

"You say 'Mr. Alley,' " my father said quietly.

"Do you think he has?"

"No telling," my father said.

Then a big gangly boy, about fifteen, who was sitting on a scraggly little old mule with a piece of croker sack thrown across the saw-tooth spine, and who had been staring at the cow, suddenly said to nobody in particular, "Reckin anybody ever et drownt cow?"

He was the kind of boy who might just as well as not have been the son of Milt Alley, with his faded and patched overalls ragged at the bottom of the pants and the mud-stiff brogans hanging off his skinny, bare ankles at the level of the mule's belly. He had said what he did, and then looked embarrassed and sullen when all the eyes swung at him. He hadn't meant to say it, I am pretty sure now. He would have been too proud to say it, just as Milt Alley would have been too proud. He had just been thinking out loud, and the words had popped out.

There was an old man standing there on the pike, an old man with a white beard. "Son," he said to the embarrassed and sullen boy on the mule, "you live long enough and you'll find a man will eat anything when the time comes."

"Time gonna come fer some folks this year," another man said.

"Son," the old man said, "in my time I et things a man don't like to think on. I was a sojer and I rode with Gin'l Forrest, and them things we et when the time come. I tell you. I et meat what got up and run when you taken out yore knife to cut a slice to put on the fire. You had to knock it down with a carbeen butt, it was so active. That-air meat would jump like a bullfrog, it was so full of skippers."

But nobody was listening to the old man. The boy on the mule turned his sullen sharp face from him, dug a heel into the side of the mule and went off up the pike with a motion which made you think that any second you would hear mule bones clashing inside that lank and scrofulous hide.

"Cy Dundee's boy," a man said, and nodded toward the figure going up the pike on the mule.

"Reckin Cy Dundee's young-uns seen times they'd settle fer drownt cow," another man said.

The old man with the beard peered at them both from his weak, slow eyes, first at one and then at the other. "Live long enough," he said, "and a man will settle fer what he kin git."

Then there was silence again, with the people looking at the red, foam-flecked water.

My father lifted the bridle rein in his left hand, and the mare turned and walked around the group and up the pike. We rode on up to our big gate, where my father dismounted to open it and let me myself ride Nellie Gray through. When he got to the lane that led off from the drive about two hundred yards from our house, my father said, "Grab on." I grabbed on, and he let me down to the ground. "I'm going to ride down and look at my corn," he said. "You go on." He took the lane, and I stood there on the drive and watched him ride off. He was wearing cowhide boots and an old hunting coat, and I thought that that made him look very military, like a picture. That and the way he rode.

I did not go to the house. Instead, I went by the vegetable garden and crossed behind the stables, and headed down for Dellie's cabin. I wanted to go down and play with Jebb, who was Dellie's little boy about two years older than I was. Besides, I was cold. I shivered as I walked, and I had gooseflesh. The mud which crawled up between my toes with every step I took was like ice. Dellie would have a fire, but she wouldn't make me put on shoes and stockings.

Dellie's cabin was of logs, with one side, because it was on a slope, set on limestone chunks, with a little porch attached to it, and had a little whitewashed fence around it and a gate with plow-points on a wire to clink when somebody came in, and had two big white oaks in the yard and some flowers and a nice privy in the back with some honeysuckle growing over it. Dellie and Old Jebb, who was Jebb's father and who lived with Dellie and had lived with her for twenty-five years even if they never had got married, were careful to keep everything nice around their cabin. They had the name all over the community for being clean and clever Negroes. Dellie and Jebb were what they used to call "white-folks' niggers." There was a big difference between their cabin and the other two cabins farther down where the other tenants lived. My father kept the other cabins weatherproof, but he couldn't undertake to go down and pick up after the litter they strewed. They didn't take the trouble to have a vegetable patch like Dellie and Jebb or to make preserves from wild plum, and jelly from crab apple the way Dellie did. They were shiftless, and my father was always threatening to get shed of them. But he never did. When they finally left, they just up and left on their own, for no reason, to go and be shiftless somewhere else. Then some more came. But meanwhile they lived down there, Matt Rawson and his family, and Sid Turner and his, and I played with their children all over the farm when they weren't working. But when I wasn't around they were mean sometimes to Little Jebb. That was because the other tenants down there were jealous of Dellie and Jebb.

I was so cold that I ran the last fifty yards to Dellie's gate. As soon as I had entered the yard, I saw that the storm had been hard on Dellie's flowers. The yard was, as I have said, on a slight slope, and the water running across had gutted the flower beds and washed out all the good black woods-earth which Dellie had brought in. What little grass there was in the yard was plastered sparsely down on the ground, the way the drainage water had left it. It reminded me of the way the fluff was plastered down on the skin of the drowned chicks that the strange man had been picking up, up in my mother's chicken yard.

I took a few steps up the path to the cabin, and then I saw that the drainage water had washed a lot of trash and filth out from under Dellie's house. Up toward the porch, the ground was not clean any more. Old pieces of rag, two or three rusted cans, pieces of rotten rope, some hunks of old dog dung, broken glass, old paper, and all sorts of things like that had washed out from under Dellie's house to foul her clean yard. It looked just as bad as the yards of the other cabins, or worse. It was worse, as a matter of fact, because it was a surprise. I had never thought of all that filth being under Dellie's house. It was not anything against Dellie that the stuff had been under the cabin. Trash will get under any house. But I did not think of that when I saw the foulness which had washed out on the ground which Dellie sometimes used to sweep with a twig broom to make nice and clean.

I picked my way past the filth, being careful not to get my bare feet on it, and mounted to Dellie's door. When I knocked, I heard her voice telling me to come in.

It was dark inside the cabin, after the daylight, but I could make out Dellie piled up in bed under a quilt, and Little Jebb crouched by the hearth, where a low fire simmered. "Howdy," I said to Dellie, "how you feeling?"

Her big eyes, the whites surprising and glaring in the black face, fixed on me as I stood there, but she did not reply. It did not look like Dellie, or act like Dellie, who would grumble and bustle around our kitchen, talking to herself, scolding me or Little Jebb, clanking pans, making all sorts of unnecessary noises and mutterings like an old-fashioned black steam thrasher engine when it has got up an extra head of steam and keeps popping the governor and rumbling and shaking on its wheels. But now Dellie just lay up there on the bed, under the patch-work quilt, and turned the black face, which I scarcely recognized, and the glaring white eyes to me.

"How you feeling?" I repeated.

"I'se sick," the voice said croakingly out of the strange black face

324   THE YOUNG MAN IN AMERICAN LITERATURE

which was not attached to Dellie's big, squat body, but stuck out from under a pile of tangled bedclothes. Then the voice added: "Mighty sick."

"I'm sorry," I managed to say.

The eyes remained fixed on me for a moment, then they left me and the head rolled back on the pillow. "Sorry," the voice said, in a flat way which wasn't question or statement of anything. It was just the empty word put into the air with no meaning or expression, to float off like a feather or a puff of smoke, while the big eyes, with the whites like the peeled white of hard-boiled eggs, stared at the ceiling.

"Dellie," I said after a minute, "there's a tramp up at the house. He's got a knife."

She was not listening. She closed her eyes.

I tiptoed over to the hearth where Jebb was and crouched beside him. We began to talk in low voices. I was asking him to get out his train and play train. Old Jebb had put spool wheels on three cigar boxes and put wire links between the boxes to make a train for Jebb. The box that was the locomotive had the top closed and a length of broom stick for a smoke stack. Jebb didn't want to get the train out, but I told him I would go home if he didn't. So he got out the train, and the colored rocks, and fossils of crinoid stems, and other junk he used for the load, and we began to push it around, talking the way we thought trainmen talked, making a chuck-chuck-ing sound under the breath for the noise of the locomotive and now and then uttering low, cautious toots for the whistle. We got so interested in playing train that the toots got louder. Then, before he thought, Jebb gave a good, loud *toot-toot,* blowing for a crossing.

"Come here," the voice said from the bed.

Jebb got up slow from his hands and knees, giving me a sudden, naked, inimical look.

"Come here!" the voice said.

Jebb went to the bed. Dellie propped herself weakly up on one arm, muttering, "Come closer."

Jebb stood closer.

"Last thing I do, I'm gonna do it," Dellie said. "Done tole you to be quiet."

Then she slapped him. It was an awful slap, more awful for the kind of weakness which it came from and brought to focus. I had seen her slap Jebb before, but the slapping had always been the kind of easy slap you would expect from a good-natured, grumbling Negro woman like Dellie. But this was different. It was awful. It was so awful that Jebb didn't make a sound. The tears just popped out and ran down his face, and his breath came sharp, like gasps.

Dellie fell back. "Cain't even be sick," she said to the ceiling. "Git sick and they won't even let you lay. They tromp all over you. Cain't even be sick." Then she closed her eyes.

I went out of the room. I almost ran getting to the door, and I did run across the porch and down the steps and across the yard, not caring whether or not I stepped on the filth which had washed out from under the cabin. I ran almost all the way home. Then I thought about my mother catching me with the bare feet. So I went down to the stables.

I heard a noise in the crib, and opened the door. There was Big Jebb, sitting on an old nail keg, shelling corn into a bushel basket. I went in, pulling the door shut behind me, and crouched on the floor near him. I crouched there for a couple of minutes before either of us spoke, and watched him shelling the corn.

He had very big hands, knotted and grayish at the joints, with calloused palms which seemed to be streaked with rust with the rust coming up between the fingers to show from the back. His hands were so strong and tough that he could take a big ear of corn and rip the grains right off the cob with the palm of his hand, all in one motion, like a machine. "Work long as me," he would say, "and the good Lawd'll give you a hand lak cass-ion won't nuthin' hurt." And his hands did look like cast iron, old cast iron streaked with rust.

He was an old man, up in his seventies, thirty years or more older than Dellie, but he was strong as a bull. He was a squat sort of man, heavy in the shoulders, with remarkably long arms, the kind of build they say the river natives have on the Congo from paddling so much in their boats. He had a round bullet-head, set on powerful shoulders. His skin was very black, and the thin hair on his head was now grizzled like tufts of old cotton batting. He had small eyes and a flat nose, not big, and the kindest and wisest old face in the world, the blunt, sad, wise face of an old animal peering tolerantly out on the goings-on of the merely human creatures before him. He was a good man, and I loved him next to my mother and father. I crouched there on the floor of the crib and watched him shell corn with the rusty cast-iron hands, while he looked down at me out of the little eyes set in the blunt face.

"Dellie says she's might sick," I said.

"Yeah," he said.

"What's she sick from?"

"Woman-mizry," he said.

"What's woman-mizry?"

"Hit comes on 'em," he said. "Hit just comes on 'em when the time comes."

"What is it?"

"Hit is the change," he said. "Hit is the change of life and time."

"What changes?"

"You too young to know."

"Tell me."

"Time come and you find out everthing."

I knew that there was no use in asking him any more. When I asked him things and he said that, I always knew that he would not tell me. So I continued to crouch there and watch him. Now that I had sat there a little while, I was cold again.

"What you shiver fer?" he asked me.

"I'm cold. I'm cold because it's blackberry winter," I said.

"Maybe 'tis and maybe 'tain't," he said.

"My mother says it is."

"Ain't sayen Miss Sallie doan know and ain't sayen she do. But folks doan know everthing."

"Why isn't it blackberry winter?"

"Too late fer blackberry winter. Blackberries done bloomed."

"She said it was."

"Blackberry winter just a leetle cold spell. Hit come and then hit go away, and hit is growed summer of a sudden lak a gunshot. Ain't no tellen hit will go way this time."

"It's June," I said.

"June," he replied with great contempt. "That what folks say. What June mean? Maybe hit is come cold to stay."

"Why?"

"Cause this-here old yearth is tahrd. Hit is tahrd and ain't gonna perduce. Lawd let hit come rain one time forty days and forty nights, 'cause He was tahrd of sinful folks. Maybe this-here old yearth say to the Lawd, Lawd, I done plum tahrd, Lawd, lemme rest. And Lawd say, Yearth, you done your best, you give 'em cawn and you give 'em taters, and all they think on is they gut, and, Yearth, you kin take a rest."

"What will happen?"

"Folks will eat up everthing. The yearth won't perduce no more. Folks cut down all the trees and burn 'em cause they cold, and the yearth won't grow no more. I been tellen 'em. I been tellen folks. Sayen, maybe this year, hit is the time. But they doan listen to me, how the yearth is tahrd. Maybe this year they find out."

"Will everything die?"

"Everthing and everbody, hit will be so."

"This year?"

"Ain't no tellen. Maybe this year."

"My mother said it is blackberry winter," I said confidently, and got up.

"Ain't sayen nuthin' agin Miss Sallie," he said.

I went to the door of the crib. I was really cold now. Running, I had got up a sweat and now I was worse.

I hung on the door, looking at Jebb, who was shelling corn again.

"There's a tramp came to the house," I said. I had almost forgotten the tramp.

"Yeah."

"He came by the back way. What was he doing down there in the storm?"

"They comes and they goes," he said, "and ain't no tellen."

"He had a mean knife."

"The good ones and the bad ones, they comes and they goes. Storm or sun, light or dark. They is folks and they comes and they goes lak folks."

I hung on the door, shivering.

He studied me a moment, then said, "You get on to the house. You ketch yore death. Then what yore mammy say?"

I hesitated.

"You git," he said.

When I came to the back yard, I saw that my father was standing by the back porch and the tramp was walking toward him. They began talking before I reached them, but I got there just as my father was saying, "I'm sorry, but I haven't got any work. I got all the hands on the place I need now. I won't need any extra until wheat thrashing."

The stranger made no reply, just looked at my father.

My father took out his leather coin purse, and got out a half-dollar. He held it toward the man. "This is for half a day," he said.

The man looked at the coin, and then at my father, making no motion to take the money. But that was the right amount. A dollar a day was what you paid them back in 1910. And the man hadn't even worked half a day.

Then the man reached out and took the coin. He dropped it into the right side pocket of his coat. Then he said, very slowly and without feeling: "I didn't want to work on your——farm."

He used the word which they would have frailed me to death for using.

I looked at my father's face and it was streaked white under the sunburn. Then he said, "Get off this place. Get off this place or I won't be responsible."

The man dropped his right hand into his pants pocket. It was the pocket where he kept the knife. I was just about to yell to my father about the knife when the hand came back out with nothing in it. The man gave a kind of twisted grin, showing where the teeth had been knocked out above the new scar. I thought that instant how maybe he had tried before to pull a knife on somebody else and had got his teeth knocked out.

So now he just gave that twisted, sickish grin out of the unmemorable, grayish face, and then spat on the brick path. The glob landed just about six inches from the toe of my father's right boot. My father looked down at it, and so did I. I thought that if the glob had hit my father's boot something would have happened. I looked down and saw the bright glob, and on one side of it my father's strong cowhide boots, with the brass eyelets and the leather thongs, heavy boots splashed with good red mud and set solid on the bricks, and on the other side the pointed-toe, broken, black shoes, on which the mud looked so sad and out of place. Then I saw one of the black shoes move a little, just a twitch first, then a real step backward.

The man moved in a quarter circle to the end of the porch, with my father's steady gaze upon him all the while. At the end of the porch, the man reached up to the shelf where the wash pans were to get his little newspaper-wrapped parcel. Then he disappeared around the corner of the house and my father mounted the porch and went into the kitchen without a word.

I followed around the house to see what the man would do. I wasn't afraid of him now, no matter if he did have the knife. When I got around in front, I saw him going out the yard gate and starting up the drive toward the pike. So I ran to catch up with him. He was sixty yards or so up the drive before I caught up.

I did not walk right up even with him at first, but trailed him, the way a kid will, about seven or eight feet behind, now and then running two or three steps in order to hold my place against his longer stride. When I first came up behind him, he turned to give me a look, just a meaningless look, and then fixed his eyes up the drive and kept on walking.

When we had got around the bend in the drive which cut the house from sight, and were going along by the edge of the woods, I decided to come up even with him. I ran a few steps, and was by his side, or almost, but some feet off to the right. I walked along in this position for a while, and he never noticed me. I walked along until we got within sight of the big gate that let on the pike.

Then I said: "Where did you come from?"

He looked at me then with a look which seemed almost surprised that I was there. Then he said, "It ain't none of yore business."

We went on another fifty feet.

Then I said, "Where are you going?"

He stopped, studied me dispassionately for a moment, then sud-

denly took a step toward me and leaned his face down at me. The
lips jerked back, but not in any grin, to show where the teeth were
knocked out and to make the scar on the lower lip come white with
the tension.

He said: "Stop following me. You don't stop following me and I
cut yore throat, you little son-of-a-bitch."

Then he went on to the gate, and up the pike.

That was thirty-five years ago. Since that time my father and
mother have died. I was still a boy, but a big boy, when my father
got cut on the blade of a mowing machine and died of lockjaw. My
mother sold the place and went to town to live with her sister. But
she never took hold after my father's death, and she died within
three years, right in middle life. My aunt always said, "Sallie just
died of a broken heart, she was so devoted." Dellie is dead, too, but
she died, I heard, quite a long time after we sold the farm.

As for Little Jebb, he grew up to be a mean and ficey Negro. He
killed another Negro in a fight and got sent to the penitentiary,
where he is yet, the last I heard tell. He probably grew up to be
mean and ficey from just being picked on so much by the children
of the other tenants, who were jealous of Jebb and Dellie for being
thrifty and clever and being white-folks' niggers.

Old Jebb lived forever. I saw him ten years ago and he was about
a hundred then, and not looking much different. He was living in
town then, on relief—that was back in the Depression—when I went
to see him. He said to me: "Too strong to die. When I was a young
feller just comen on and seen how things wuz, I prayed the Lawd. I
said, Oh, Lawd, gimme strength and meke me strong fer to do and
to in-dure. The Lawd hearkened to my prayer. He give me strength.
I was in-duren proud fer being strong and me much man. The
Lawd give me my prayer and my strength. But now He done gone
off and fergot me and left me alone with my strength. A man doan
know what to pray fer, and him mortal."

Jebb is probably living yet, as far as I know.

That is what has happened since the morning when the tramp
leaned his face down at me and showed his teeth and said: "Stop
following me. You don't stop following me and I cut yore throat,
you little son-of-a-bitch." That was what he said, for me not to follow him. But I did follow him, all the years.

Questions for Study, Discussion, and Writing

1. PERSPECTIVES

Horrocks: *The Nature of Adolescence.* In what ways does modern culture facilitate the transition to adulthood? In what ways does it fail to do so? Do you agree with this author's view that adolescence is less difficult in a "nonrestrictive environment"? What kind of novel or short story do you imagine might be based on the somewhat discredited idea of adolescence as a period of storm and stress that culminates in a rebirth or a sudden transformation of personality? What is meant by the statement that adolescence is "culturally determined"? Do the "five points of reference" suggest any reasons why adolescence has been such a popular subject for writers of fiction?

Freud: *On Schoolboy Psychology.* In the stories in this collection, find examples of "ambivalent" emotional attitudes. How does Freud's theory regarding the importance of a child's first six years in establishing emotional attitudes affect stories of initiation? Freud describes the process by which a teacher or another adult becomes a substitute (surrogate) father. Discuss instances of this phenomenon as it occurs in actual life or in one of the stories. Find a story in which a boy's "imago" of his father resembles Freud's description in the fourth paragraph from the close of this essay. Find a story in which a boy's disillusionment with his father resembles that described in the third paragraph from the close.

Lerner: *Growing up in America.* Do you agree that American culture disapproves of "the withdrawn and reflective personality"? Do any of the stories support this idea? Do you agree that young Americans are under an obligation to succeed? Are the demands made on young men too high? Is the phrase "social violence and cultural emptiness" an accurate description of American cities from the viewpoint of youth? Would growing up in America be easier if the culture were less "dynamic" and young men learned a "tolerance of deprivation"? How would this tolerance affect the life of a typical college student? Do you agree with the comparison between a working class gang and college? Which of the stories seems the best example of "the loss of social innocence"? Do you agree that the "Mark Twain tradition of boyhood" predominates in American homes? How would you define this tradition? Can you find any examples in the stories of conflict between a young man's "cultural image of self" and his "identity image of self"?

Whiting and others: *The Function of Male Initiation Ceremonies.* Can you find any example in American society of an observance of the transition from boyhood to manhood? Can you find any examples of initiation ordeals, though perhaps not as rigorous as those of the Thonga? Do you agree that our society suffers from a "decrease in the authority of the father"? How might a "change of residence" serve the same purpose as an initiation ceremony? The last paragraph of this article implies that some substitute for an initiation ceremony might reduce juvenile delinquency. Can you suggest any possibilities? Do you agree with the closing sentence?

Marcus: *What Is an Initiation Story?* This article contains brief critical judgments on three of the stories included in this volume (those by Steinbeck, Anderson, and Warren). Compare these judgments with your own reactions to the stories. Be prepared to discuss as an example of initiation one of the following stories: Ernest Hemingway's "Indian Camp," "The Battler," "My Old Man" (*In Our Time*, 1925), or "The Killers" (*Men Without Women*, 1927); William Faulkner's "The Old People" or "The Bear" (*Go Down, Moses*, 1942); John Steinbeck's "Flight" (*The Long Valley*, 1938); or F. Scott Fitzgerald's "The Freshest Boy" (*Taps at Reveille*, 1935). Compare the various definitions of initiation cited by Marcus. How do they differ? Which seem most satisfactory? Do you agree that an initiation story need not involve evil or guilt? Which stories in this volume contain an element of ritual? Which story in this volume seems the clearest example of "tentative" initiation? Which seems the clearest example of "uncompleted" initiation? Which seems the clearest example of "decisive" initiation?

2. BLOOD RITES

Cooper: *The Deerslayer.* Cooper's narratives often succeed in spite of his somewhat awkward style. Can you point out examples of trite or ponderous phrasing? What indications can you find that Deerslayer (Natty Bumppo) is young and inexperienced? How does the natural setting contrast with human actions? Natty Bumppo frequently refers to his "gifts." Can you suggest a synonym or two for this term as he uses it? Can you find instances of the expression of white racial superiority that a modern reader might find objectionable?

Steinbeck: *The Promise*. Are Jody's daydreams characteristic of a boy his age? How do they contribute to the total effect of the story? Contrast Jody's relationship with Billy and with his father. Are there any suggestions of rivalry or jealousy between the two men? How effective is the closing paragraph of the story? What does it suggest about the effect of this experience on Jody? Would you prefer that his emotions were described? Comment on Steinbeck's descriptions of nature. Do you find any indications that he studied biology and once worked as a professional biologist?

Davis: *Open Winter*. Like "The Promise," this story involves the mentor-pupil relationship of an older man and a young boy. Compare the two stories with respect to this theme. How does Pop Apling induce Beech to drive the horses to the railroad? Is Beech's reluctance assumed or genuine? Although Ream Gervais never appears in the story, he is characterized rather vividly. What kind of man is he? Contrast him with Apling. What does Beech learn from his accomplishment in delivering the horses? How do you interpret the last sentence of the story?

3. DISENCHANTMENT

Twain: *Old Times on the Mississippi*. Point out incidents that reveal the narrator as inexperienced, naive, or gullible. Compare the opening and closing paragraphs of this selection. How has the narrator been changed by his experience? Describe his attitude toward his youthful self. Can you relate the idea that familiarity diminishes or destroys "romance and beauty" to another activity? college? a job? a love affair? travel? Is Twain justified in applying it to the practice of medicine? Like many initiation narratives, this one involves a young man's education. Evaluate the effectiveness of the pilot's methods of teaching. Although this selection is not primarily funny, it contains many touches of Mark Twain's characteristic humor. Point out examples of language used for humorous effect.

James: *The Pupil*. Discuss the ironic implications of Pemberton's resolution in the opening paragraph that he will first improve Morgan's attitude toward his mother. Can you find other examples of irony derived from ignorance or inexperience? What the reader learns in this story comes to him through the consciousness of Pemberton. How would the effect of the story have been changed if James had entered the mind of Morgan? of Mrs. Moreen? Look up "moreen" in a dictionary. How does the meaning of the common noun relate to James's characters? In what sense is Pemberton himself a "pupil"? How is he changed by his association with the Moreens? Is Pemberton guilty of arousing false hopes in Morgan? The ending of the story would be grossly melodramatic if James had not carefully prepared for it. Point out instances of his foreshadowing the fact that Morgan is physically frail. In a preface written for the New York edition of his works, James described Morgan as an "urchin" who has "sensibility in abundance" and who sees the "prowling precarious life of his parents . . . measures and judges it, measures and judges them." Can you find examples of Morgan's sensitivity, of his ability to understand people and situations?

Frederic: *The Eve of the Fourth.* Approximately how old is Andrew, the narrator? What indications are there that Andrew has had a rather sheltered upbringing? How does this affect his reaction to the reported death of Lieutenant Hemingway and to Miss Stratford's grief? Does Andrew lose any other illusions besides his admiration for Billy Norris? What do you imagine will happen the next time Andrew meets his hero, Billy Norris? Would this story be more effective for a modern reader if the ending were different? How might a contemporary writer have concluded it? This story effectively recreates the atmosphere of a small town Fourth of July over a century ago. How has observance of this holiday changed?

Cozzens: *Total Stranger.* What do descriptive details in the opening paragraph suggest about the father? How typical is the gulf between father and son portrayed in this story?

How old would you estimate the boy to be? Explain the significance of the title. The automobile emphasizes the gulf between generations. What might be used similarly in a story written today? In approximately what year would you estimate that the story takes place? The narrator as an adult is looking back at his boyhood self. Describe his attitude. How has his attitude toward his father changed with the passing of time?

Ellison: *Battle Royal.* Explain the phrase in the second paragraph "separate like the fingers of one hand." What Negro leader originated it? How, generally, do contemporary Negroes regard this idea? Discuss ironic contrasts between the theme of the narrator's commencement oration and the atmosphere of the stag party where he delivers it. What are the implications of the emphasis on sex, violence, and money at the smoker? Does the narrator discover that his grandfather's deathbed advice was true or false?

Describe the narrator's attitude toward the other Negro youths. How does it change? Can you deduce the significance of the phrase "invisible man," which is the title of the novel in which this episode appears?

Malamud: *The Magic Barrel.* What aspects of his personality does Leo Finkle unintentionally reveal during his first conference with the matchmaker? Describe the self-knowledge that comes to Leo Finkle after his meeting with Lily Hirschorn. Why does Leo see Stella as his "redemption"? Discuss the implications of Salzman's bitter remark about his daughter: "If you can love her, then you can love anybody." How does Malamud suggest Jewish speech although he uses little actual dialect? Malamud's technique in most of his fiction combines naturalistic details, wry humor, and mysticism. Find examples of each in this story. One critic described Malamud's theme as the process of a *schlemiel* becoming a *mensch.* Find the meanings of these Yiddish words and comment on the adequacy of this statement.

Webb: *Homecoming.* If you have seen the movie version of *The Graduate,* compare its treatment of the opening episode with that of the novel. Ben's mood at his parent's party is not identified or analyzed, but is conveyed almost entirely by dialogue and action. Do you find this more or less effective than a description of his thoughts and emotions would have been? What seem to be some of the reasons for Ben's withdrawn attitude at the party? How typical is Ben's feeling that all his achievements in college are "nothing"? What readers do you imagine would most enjoy this novel: men or women? young or middle-aged? Do you sympathize with Ben's parents? Why or why not? Although these episodes are not funny to any of the participants, they are amusing to a reader. Analyze the reasons for this. What difficulties face a writer who tries to describe the seduction of a young man by an older woman?

4. FEARFUL CONFRONTATIONS

Hawthorne: *My Kinsman, Major Molineux.* One interpretation of this story sees Robin as a symbol of young, revolutionary America and his uncle as a symbol of entrenched British authority. Comment on the adequacy of this interpretation. Another interpretation sees the story in Freudian terms as an Oedipal search for a father and his ritual rejection or murder. Do you agree or disagree with this interpretation? Until rather recently, this story had been overlooked or slighted by many critics discussing Hawthorne. Can you suggest any reasons that it has been "rediscovered" recently? Why does it appeal to the contemporary imagination? Can you suggest any possible reasons for the fact that Hawthorne withheld this story for twenty years and did not include it in such collections as *Twice-Told Tales* (1837)? What historical event accounts for the fact that members of the mob are disguised? How do the disguises contribute to the effect of the story? Compare the responses to each of Robin's inquiries. What is the significance of the laughter, in which Robin finally joins? Is Hawthorne's description of Robin as "a shrewd youth" ironical? Interpret the close of the story. How has Robin been changed by his experience? Is his desire to leave Boston indicative of a new maturity or of a reversion to childhood? Hawthorne's imagination functioned allegorically, seeing people, places, and actions in symbolic terms. What is the symbolic significance of Robin himself, of the city he wanders through, and of each of his encounters?

Melville: *Redburn.* Describe the boy Redburn as he is characterized in these four episodes. Do Jackson's appearance and the stories he tells suggest that Melville intended him as a symbolic figure? If so, what does he symbolize? Is he credible as a human being? If you have read *Moby Dick,* can you point out any resemblances between that novel and *Redburn?* How do you account for the fact that Jackson, though physically weak, is able to tyrannize over the rest of the crew? Are there any hints that Redburn has been reared in a strict religious family?

Crane: *An Experiment in Misery.* An important feature of Crane's style is his use of startling comparisons. Analyze a few of his more unusual similes in this story and consider ways in which the connotation of each contributes to the general effect. Estimate the age of the young man. In the original version of this sketch, the youth chooses to live with the city's derelicts in order to learn about their lives. Does this help explain the title? Would it diminish the force of the sketch if it were made clear at the outset that the young man's stay in the slum is voluntary? Are there any suggestions in the first two paragraphs that the young man is a newcomer in the slum? What is the significance of the fact that the naked men in the flophouse stand "like chiefs" but appear ugly and deformed after they dress? How have the young man's attitudes been changed by his experience?

Anderson: *I Want to Know Why.* Does the style suit the characterization of the narrator? Do any expressions seem uncharacteristic of a fifteen-year-old boy? If you have read *Huckleberry Finn,* compare Twain's style with Anderson's. What is the chief source of suspense in this story? The story contains many references to Negroes— all of them favorable despite the use of the pejorative term "nigger." What qualities do the Negroes have that the boy admires? What kind of life does he associate with them? What is the significance of the boy's refusal to gamble and make money from his intuitive feelings about horses? Comment on the numerous comparisons between animals and human beings. Is the glorification of instinct as superior to human reason acceptable to you? The narrator recognizes prostitutes when he sees them and he has heard obscene language before. What is it, then, that disturbs him so deeply at the "rummy looking farmhouse"? Compare the scene at the paddock when the boy looks at Jerry Tillford with the scene at the farmhouse.

Pagano: *The Disinherited.* Compare the description of tramps in this story with the one in "An Experiment in Misery." Point out other indications besides unemployment that this story was first published in 1933. Would the effect of the story be different if it were told in the third person instead of the first? What sort of future is suggested for Bill, the narrator? How does Bill's first meeting with his father differ from what he expected?

Stegner: *Goin' to Town.* Describe the mood created in the first three paragraphs. Contrast it with the two closing paragraphs. Approximately how old is the boy? Can you suggest any reason for the fact that the three characters are not given proper names. Would you describe the father as cruel? Why or why not? The action in this story is presented from the immediacy of the boy's point of view. How might the effect change if it were told in retrospect, as is done in "Total Stranger"? Compare this story with "The Promise" by Steinbeck. Consider the use of description, the fantasies of anticipation, the characterization of the two boys, and their relationships with their parents.

Warren: *Blackberry Winter.* Describe the mood created by the opening paragraphs of the story. Compare Seth with Jody in "The Promise" or with the boy in "Goin' to Town." Analyze Seth's relationship with his father. Seth is nine. How might his reactions be different if he were seven years older? How deeply is Seth affected by his encounter with the tramp at the time it occurs? Did he realize the horror of the situation only after he became an adult? Do you agree with Mordecai Marcus that there is an element of "melodramatic cheating" in the close of the story? How do other incidents such as the scenes at the bridge and in Dellie's cabin correlate with the encounter with the tramp? How does Warren suggest that the tramp is totally alien in this rural area? Why do you think Warren told the story in the first person? Interpret the last sentence of the story.

Notes on the Authors

SHERWOOD ANDERSON: After giving up a prosperous business in 1912, Sherwood Anderson (1876–1941) devoted the rest of his life to writing. At his best in *Winesburg, Ohio* (1919) and a few short stories, he succeeded in suggesting the baffled yearnings and frustrations of simple, semi-articulate characters. Modern literature has in many respects passed him by, but he is one of the pioneers who made that literature possible.

SAMUEL L. CLEMENS: Probably the best loved American author, Samuel L. Clemens (1835–1910) made his pen name, Mark Twain, known throughout the world. As a boy in frontier Missouri, a journeyman printer, a Mississippi River pilot, and a miner and reporter in Nevada and California, he absorbed American experience to the fullest and afterward transmuted it into such works as *Life on the Mississippi* (1883) and *The Adventures of Huckleberry Finn* (1884).

JAMES FENIMORE COOPER: A prolific writer of fiction, social commentary, history, and biography, James Fenimore Cooper (1789–1851) developed in the five novels of the Leatherstocking saga a full-length, larger-than-life portrait of Natty Bumppo. His characterization, based in part on the life of Daniel Boone, established many of the stereotyped qualities of the frontier scout in fiction and drama.

JAMES GOULD COZZENS: Although he is a native of Chicago, James Gould Cozzens (b.1903) has spent most of his life in the vicinity of New York. Of his numerous novels, *Guard of Honor* (1948), a novel about the Air Force in World War II, was awarded the Pulitzer Prize, and *By Love Possessed* (1957) was a national best-seller.

STEPHEN CRANE: As a young freelance reporter, Stephen Crane (1871–1900) was fascinated by the New York Bowery, and "An Experiment in Misery" was a result of his explorations of that colorful district, as was his first novel, *Maggie, A Girl of the Streets* (1892). In *The Red Badge of Courage* (1895) and several short stories he achieved a vivid impressionistic style, psychological insight, and a conception of man's basic loneliness that prefigured the best of modern fiction.

H. L. DAVIS: Born in southwestern Oregon, H. L. Davis (1896–1960) worked as a sheepherder at the age of ten and became a ranch hand two years later, suggesting that "Open Winter" may be partially autobiographical. He was awarded the Pulitzer Prize in 1936 for his first novel, *Honey in the Horn.*

RALPH ELLISON: A native of Oklahoma, Ralph Ellison (b.1914) now lives in New York City. He frequently writes and lectures on contemporary literature. His novel *Invisible Man* (1952) pictures effectively the alienation of the Negro from American society.

HAROLD FREDERIC: A native of Utica, New York, Harold Frederic (1856–1898) drew on his memories of that town during the Civil War for a number of stories, which he once described as "the best things I have done or ever shall do." Neglected until recently, Frederic is now recognized as an important pioneer in the development of American realism, especially for *The Damnation of Theron Ware,* a psychological study of the spiritual and intellectual degeneration of a clergyman.

SIGMUND FREUD: The founder of psychoanalysis, Sigmund Freud (1856–1939) spent virtually his entire life in Vienna, Austria. After experimenting with hypnosis in the treatment of hysteria, he devised the technique of free-association. His attribution of psychoneuroses to unconscious sexual conflicts drew strong criticism; but his theories, including those revised by his successors, have been a major influence on twentieth century thought.

NATHANIEL HAWTHORNE: One of the first major American writers of fiction, Nathaniel Hawthorne (1804–1864) explored problems of evil and responsibility in novels like *The Scarlet Letter* (1850) and in a number of short stories. Descended from an old Salem, Massachusetts, family, he was fascinated by the history of colonial New England and frequently used it as a setting for his fiction.

JOHN E. HORROCKS: A member of the graduate psychology faculty of The Ohio State University, John E. Horrocks (b.1913) is the author of a widely used textbook on adolescent psychology that places special emphasis on guidance and counseling.

HENRY JAMES: Born in New York, Henry James (1843–1916) lived in England after 1876, and the confrontation of the Old World and the New is the subject of much, though by no means all, of his fiction. Described by a biographer as "the architect of the modern novel," he was one of the first writers to show a serious concern with craftsmanship, and his sensitivity to nuances of human motivation and his experiments with narrative methods expanded the scope of fiction.

MAX LERNER: Educator, columnist, and social analyst, Max Lerner (b.1902) is best known for *America as a Civilization* (1957), in which he analyzes interrelationships of American institutions and the contemporary scene.

BERNARD MALAMUD: A native of Brooklyn, Bernard Malamud (b.1914) has published several distinguished novels, including *The Assistant* (1957) and *The Fixer* (1966). He has taught English in the New York City evening high schools, at Oregon State University, and at Bennington College.

MORDECAI MARCUS: A member of the English faculty at the University of Nebraska, Mordecai Marcus (b.1925) has published a number of critical articles in the field of American literature.

HERMAN MELVILLE: Relatively neglected during his lifetime, Herman Melville (1819–1891) has been recognized in the twentieth century as one of America's greatest novelists. He served on a number of ships before he was twenty-five and afterward drew on this experience for the materials of his books, most notably for his masterpiece, *Moby Dick* (1851).

Jo PAGANO: "The Disinherited" was the first short story published in a national magazine by Jo Pagano (b.1906). He has published several books, including *Golden Wedding* (1943), a novel about an Italian-American family, and has written extensively for motion pictures and television.

WALLACE STEGNER: A native of Iowa, Wallace Stegner (b.1909) grew up in Salt Lake City. He has written novels and short stories on a wide range of themes, and since 1945 has been professor of English and director of the Writing Center at Stanford University.

JOHN STEINBECK: In the four (originally three) short stories entitled collectively *The Red Pony*, which are partly autobiographical, John Steinbeck (1902-1968) describes a young boy living on an isolated ranch near Salinas, California. His account of the migration of the Joads from the Dust Bowl and their struggle to survive in California, *The Grapes of Wrath*, was awarded the Pulitzer Prize in 1940.

MARK TWAIN: See Samuel L. Clemens.

ROBERT PENN WARREN: A native of Kentucky, Robert Penn Warren (b.1905) is highly respected as a poet, as a novelist, and as a literary critic. Like Faulkner, he has concerned himself with such themes as moral responsibility and the impingement of the past on the present. His novel *All the King's Men,* based in part on the career of Huey P. Long of Louisiana, was awarded the Pulitzer Prize in 1947, and the movie based on it was designated the best film of 1949 by the Academy of Motion Picture Arts and Sciences.

CHARLES WEBB: Born in San Francisco and   ambridge, Massachusetts, Charles Webb (b.1939) graduated from Williams College in 1961. He received a fellowship from his alma mater that enabled him to write his first novel, *The Graduate* (1963).

JOHN M. W. WHITING: A member of the faculty of the Harvard Graduate School of Education, John M. W. Whiting (b.1908) has published extensively on anthropological and educational subjects.